Praise for *The Age of Responsibility*

Wayne Visser's *The Age of Responsibility* elegantly and persuasively demonstrates the limits and failures of traditional CSR and also the kinds of reforms needed to create conditions for genuine corporate responsibility. Rich with insight, information and analyses, and highly readable for its excellent writing and poignant stories, the book is a crucial contribution to understanding where we are with CSR and what we need to do to move forward.

Joel Bakan, author of *The Corporation: The Pathological Pursuit
of Profit and Power* (book and documentary film)

Amongst the advocates of CSR as an innovative management approach, Wayne Visser is a well-known voice. This new book states more clearly than most why CSR should not be dismissed, but would benefit from some serious rethinking.

Michael Blowfied, Senior Research Fellow at the Smith School of Enterprise
and the Environment, Oxford University and author of *Corporate Responsibility*

The Age of Responsibility is an important book that should be studied carefully by all those seriously interested in the past, present and future of CSR. For me, the most noteworthy contribution is his "ages and stages" of CSR. Visser identifies five overlapping economic periods and classifies their stages of CSR, modus operandi, key enablers, and stakeholder targets. In forward-looking fashion, he crafts five insightful principles of CSR 2.0 and presents his DNA Model of CSR 2.0 which integrates knowledge and sets forth a more inclusive view of CSR. This book is a significant contribution to the theory and practice of CSR and it will be valued by academics and practitioners alike. I strongly recommend it.

Archie B. Carroll, Professor of Management Emeritus,
Terry College of Business and co-author of *Business and Society*

A challenging and thought provoking book. In an age when corporate responsibility is a must for most large businesses, Wayne Visser reminds us that global environmental and social pressures show little sign of receding. He asks: are we as practitioners complacent, or worse, part of the problem? There is hope and optimism but only if we are brave and bold enough to re-engineer corporate responsibility. Read on . . .

Yogesh Chauhan, Chairman of the Corporate Responsibility Group
and BBC Chief Adviser Corporate Responsibility.

An authoritative tome on the CSR movement. It provides a comprehensive framework to understand the various stages of (and motivations for) CSR in organizations and the economy to date, and a clear vision of what a truly sustainable and responsible tomorrow entails. This is an eminently well-researched and well-structured book that flows coherently with deep insights and valuable vignettes.

Willie Cheng, author of *Doing Good Well: What does
(and does not) make sense in the nonprofit world.*

The Age of Responsibility provides a much-needed wake up call for the corporate responsibility movement. This highly readable account of where CSR has gone wrong and where it needs to go next is essential reading for anyone interested in the role business can play in creating a just and sustainable society. This is the best CSR book you'll read all year.

Andrew Crane, George R. Gardiner Professor of Business Ethics
at Schulich School of Business, York University
and co-author of *Business Ethics*

The Age of Responsibility breathes new life into CSR, both by redefining it as Corporate Sustainability and Responsibility and by highlighting why CSR has so far failed to make much difference in the way companies respond to pressing global challenges. In his inimitable style, using clear frameworks and illustrative case studies, Wayne Visser brings real insight to a complex set of ideas at a time when they are needed most. Bring on CSR 2.0!

Polly Courtice, Director of the University of Cambridge
Programme for Sustainability Leadership

In this time of seemingly widespread corporate malfeasance Wayne Visser has put his finger on why CSR has failed to deliver on its promise and what can be done to right the ship. *The Age of Responsibility* is a must read for anyone concerned about the future of business.

Bob Doppelt, Executive Director of The Resource Innovation Group
and The Climate Leadership Initiative

CSR 1.0 did remarkably well through the latest Great Recession, despite having precariously little to say on the big issues of the day and no ready-to-go blueprint for economic transformation. As a result, we are seeing a massive reboot going on in the CSR industry – and Wayne Visser is a consistently reliable guide to (and champion of) the emerging CSR 2.0 mindsets and practices.

John Elkington, Co-Founder and Director of Volans Ventures
and co-author of *The Power of Unreasonable People*

It is difficult to run a sustainable business in an unsustainable world. So forget about the defensive, charitable, promotional and strategic versions of CSR. *The Age of Responsibility* is a call for companies to shift to CSR 2.0 – where success is judged by improvements in the overall socio-cultural, economic and ecological systems. If not, CSR will continue to fail, argues Wayne Visser. With an array of cases Visser guides you through the evolution of business responsibility – from the Ages of Greed, Philanthropy, Marketing and Management to the Age of Responsibility – and shares the five principles of sustainable business actions. Wayne Visser's insightful book is at the same time a compelling personal story about the existential questioning of whether or how it is possible to make a difference through CSR.

Tania Ellis, international speaker, business advisor
and author of *The New Pioneers*

Through a concise analysis of recent economic history and through the wisdom of parables, Visser's book offers an illuminating analysis of the heart of greed—and of the path our institutions can take to move from corporate responsibility as a form of occasional philanthropy to an ethic of responsibility that is radically transformative. Visser's new economic myth or meta-narrative creates a compelling vision of a possible sustainable world.

Betty Sue Flowers, Professor Emerita at the University
of Texas at Austin and co-author of *Presence: An Exploration
of Profound Change in People, Organizations, and Society*

Wayne Visser has rightly identified responsibility as one of the defining issues of our time. Executives, students and citizens should read this book, and make it an integral part of our conversation about business.

Ed Freeman, Director of the Business Roundtable Institute
for Corporate Ethics at the University of Virginia Darden School
of Business and author of *Strategic Management: A Stakeholder Approach*

High marks for Wayne Visser who brings us a book that both challenges the conventional state of CSR in very fresh and bold fashion, and offers a provocative new vision of CSR 2.0. What is most energizing about this book is that it provides a well documented historical and analytical framework on the progression of CSR over the past century. But in analyzing the current state of CSR, it recognizes that despite amazing achievements and progress, CSR has to leap frog into a new world, one that recognizes the new DNA of business, and one that calls for a CSR 2.0 that goes far beyond the models that currently exist. The new Principles of CSR 2.0 that Visser puts at the heart of this book provide the business community and the CSR world a new path for incorporating the complexity of the social and environmental issues that confront today's corporation, a CSR that can serve as a more transformative force for economic and social sustainability. What a refreshing and creative read! There are few books that can cut to the chase and provide a thoughtful analysis of the current state of CSR while at the same time opening up a vision for tomorrow. This is a contribution to the CSR world that is long overdue and most welcome.

> **Brad Googins**, Associate Professor in Organisation Studies
> at the Carroll School of Management, and former Director
> of the Boston College Center for Corporate Citizenship

Your new book deserves to become an instant classic. It brings together so many ideas, writings, and stages in the development of CSR. It is a liberal education on the relation of business to society. I hope that it is read not only by companies but becomes a required reading in business schools to prepare business students for a higher level of thinking about their future role and impact. I am happy to endorse the book: A most impressive book! I will recommend it to every company to figure out why they are practicing CSR and how to really practice it to make a difference to their profits, people, and the planet.

> **Philip Kotler**, S. C. Johnson and Son Distinguished Professor
> of International Marketing at Kellogg School of Management,
> Northwestern University and author of *Corporate Social Responsibility*

The Age of Responsibility will change the way you think about CSR, allowing you to discard myths and to work towards a systemic view of CSR. Wayne Visser holds up a mirror to the CSR community and to business and society itself, providing a brilliant lens with which to see our past and envision a new future. Visser projects a new type of CSR he terms "CSR 2.0". *The Age of Responsibility* is a call to arms: inspiring, engaging and visionary.

> **Deborah Leipziger**, author of *The Corporate Responsibility Code Book*
> and *SA8000: The Definitive Guide to the New Social Standard*

The Age of Responsibility and its proposed CSR 2.0 – perhaps better called Systemic or Radical Corporate Sustainability and Responsibility – shows, in the same way that Natural Capitalism does, that reinventing our industrial model is not only imperative – socially, environmentally, economically and morally – but also a great opportunity for those pioneers that blaze the trail.

> **L. Hunter Lovins**, President of Natural Capitalism Solutions
> and co-author of *Natural Capitalism*

Whether corporate social responsibility has failed, or whether it is still finding its feet pending further market pull, one thing is clear: without a life-giving understanding of responsibility as the ability to respond there's no point to anything. Wayne Visser does us all a service in exploring the opportunities and challenges that such responsibility entails.

> **Alastair McIntosh**, Professor at the Centre for Human Ecology,
> Strathclyde University and author of *Hell and High Water*

All individuals interested in the evolution of Corporate Sustainability and Responsibility should feel compelled to join Wayne Visser in his quest to better understand why efforts to implement CSR practices have not yet yielded the desired outcomes. In *The Age of Responsibility*, he draws on his gift for language and storytelling to lay out the case for a new kind of CSR – CSR 2.0. Using Web 2.0 as a metaphor, Visser identifies the interconnectedness of humans in their efforts to define what the world of business should look like. The journey is thought provoking, an education on where CSR has been and where it needs to go and a story imploring the reader to seek out "a unique and invaluable way to make a difference through CSR".

Josetta McLaughlin, Associate Professor of Management
at Walter E. Heller College of Business Administration,
Roosevelt University

The good news: Business is shifting from making money in the simplest way possible towards solving global problems and making money in the process. The bad news: Progress is slow. Wayne Visser paints the big picture using an astounding amount of detailed knowledge.

Jorgen Randers, Professor of Climate Strategy
at the Norwegian School of Management and co-author
of *Limits to Growth: The 30-Year Update*

A world based on rights without responsibility can only lead to destruction. And when the rights are unbridled rights of giant corporations they trample on the earth and people. Wayne Visser's *The Age of Responsibility* calls for a vital shift from rights to responsibility. It is a must read for all.

Vandana Shiva, author of *Earth Democracy* and *Soil Not Oil*

CSR 2.0 is a great concept. Good luck with it. And as Wayne Visser rightly adds: smart government regulation is absolutely essential.

Ernst von Weizsäcker, author of *Factor 5: Transforming the Global
Economy through 80% Improvements in Resource Productivity*

The book is a thought provoking and cutting edge addition to the CSR literature. It integrates strategic and stakeholder perspectives to provide a new model of implementing change and innovative thinking. In extending the paradigm of CSR it promotes the role of leaders in bringing about positive societal change through stakeholder engagement and it does so through an understanding of the practical issues facing business leaders of today. Moreover, it challenges every one of us to think and act differently, to bring about mass global change enacted at the local level, and to incorporate social enterprises and social networks in this transformation. The global financial crisis has further reinforced the timeliness of this book and its arguments of a new way of thinking and acting in the area of sustainability and responsibility to bring about systemic change.

Suzanne Young, Associate Professor and Director of Corporate
Responsibility and Global Citizenship at the Graduate
School of Management, La Trobe University

The Age of Responsibility

CSR 2.0 and the New DNA of Business

Wayne Visser, PhD

A John Wiley & Sons, Ltd, Publication

Registered office
John Wiley & Sons Ltd, The Atrium, Southern Gate, Chichester, West Sussex, PO19 8SQ,
United Kingdom

For details of our global editorial offices, for customer services and for information about
how to apply for permission to reuse the copyright material in this book please see our
website at www.wiley.com

Library of Congress Cataloging-in-Publication Data
Visser, Wayne.
  The Age of Responsibility : CSR 2.0 and the New DNA of Business / Wayne Visser.
    p. cm
   Includes bibliographical references and index.
  ISBN 978-0-470-68857-1 (hardback)
  1. Social responsibility of business—Case studies. I. Title.
  HD60.V56 2011
  658.4'08—dc22

                                                       2010050390

A catalogue record for this book is available from the British Library.
ISBN 978-0-470-68857-1 (hardback), ISBN 978-1-119-97099-6 (ebk),
ISBN 978-1-119-97338-6 (ebk), ISBN 978-1-119-97339-3 (ebk)

Typeset in 9.5/15pt Bitstream by Thomson Digital, Noida, India

Contents

CONTENTS

List of boxes, cases, figures and tables

Boxes

Cases

Figures

Tables

Seeing farther, going further

In the beginning, responsible businesses were going to save the world. I remember because I was there. It was the late 1980s, and a new brand of socially and environmentally benevolent companies were emerging on the corporate landscape. The Body Shop, Ben & Jerry's, Patagonia, and my own company, Seventh Generation, to name just a few, were out not only to make money but to fundamentally change the way things worked doing it.

Driven by equal parts societal need and personal desire, and an ethos carried on patchouli smoke from the late 1960s, these companies were founded by entrepreneurs who confronted the regressive bent of the Reagan era with a determination to create a different operating model for the business community. This new paradigm would reconcile the historic conflict between corporate profits and cultural progress by selling products and services whose creation took every possible precaution to safeguard the environment and respect the rights and dignity of the people responsible for bringing them to market.

Those were heady days. We thought we could save the world and earn a living doing it. The idea seemed obvious and its execution relatively straightforward. And though the things we were doing had largely never been tried, every time one of them worked, the possibilities appeared even more endless than before. By the time of the big 20th anniversary of Earth Day in 1990, it was clear that corporate responsibility was a concept whose time had come. People the world over were eager for an evolutionary change from business-as-usual and the harm it was causing, and we were sure that it was only matter of time before the rest of the corporate world beat a path to our doorstep

Indeed, the business community did come knocking. Flash forward two decades, and it's rare to find a company of any appreciable size that doesn't offer a corporate responsibility (CR) report or tout some kind of progressive initiative. There are CR officers sitting in executive suites around the world and conferences on the subject well attended by Fortune 500 companies. Touchy-feely ad campaigns and self congratulatory press conferences abound. And some days it seems like nearly every product label has something to say about the change the goods within are helping to create.

Yet by virtually every measure, the world is in worse shape than it's ever been. Our atmosphere is overburdened with dangerous levels of greenhouse gases. Our planet's biodiversity and its ecosystems are under siege. Growing numbers of people are living in increasing poverty. Deadly toxins pollute our land and our bodies, yet health care remains a distant dream for far too many. We're running out of water. We're running out of natural resources. And we're running out of time.

So what happened?

The short answer is not enough. As the CR movement spread to the corporate mainstream, it lost its focus. What started as a relatively simple set of goals to protect the environment and human rights degenerated into a philanthropic free-for-all in which causes proliferated and an ever-expanding array of do-good choices and options presented itself to business management teams who were already on confusing ground. Corporate executives who saw the need for CR failed to adequately help their staffs translate their vision into action, and public expectations about what was truly important were misunderstood or not understood at all. The resulting disconnect between what was needed and what actually got done neutered too many promising efforts.

At the same time, countless companies did what companies do: they created an office or a department to deal with CR and told it to grow CR initiatives. But this compartmentalized approach had the effect of decoupling innumerable CR agendas from their company's actually daily workings and left programs trapped "inside the box" where nothing meaningful could happen.

In other cases, companies simply co-opted CR for their own purposes. This "greenwashing" was all about hype and appearance rather than honesty and action, and too many firms simply sought CR window dressing to help them look better in an increasingly informed world. They released fancy reports with pretty pictures. They had their CEOs photographed at CR conferences and summits. They purchased smaller more legitimately responsible companies for their halo effect and little more. But very rarely did they walk their talk.

Ironically, forces like these resulted in the one thing that CR supporters and naysayers can agree on: corporate responsibility in its present incarnation has been an enormous disappointment at best. It has not lifted people out of poverty. It has not protected the environment. It has not boosted community wellbeing. It has been too little, too late and at most has succeeded in getting some companies to aspire to simply do less damage than they did before. Instead of changing the world, CR merely evolved into a baseline requirement in every company's license to operate. Where it succeeded, it only managed to slow the rate of decay, which is hardly enough to do much more than maintain the status quo.

This, say CR's detractors, is proof that the movement's fundamental ideal—that a business can remake itself so as to create an overwhelming net benefit for society and the environment in addition to its own bottom line—is not a valid model for moving forward and tackling the extremely big issues we now need to address.

But that's wrong, and in this book, Wayne Visser shows us not only why but where we go from here. CR remains a valid approach ripe with promise and possibility. Yet as Visser quite importantly notes, this reaffirmation is dependent on the emergence of a new form of CR that takes a far more holistic view of its work and seeks not to affect piecemeal change but to engineer a series of systemic corrections that wisely recognize that since all our problems are connected our solutions must be, too. The job of CR advocates is to pull these new values into every last corner of the world's companies in order to impact each process and decision, and deliver a return on *purpose* as well as a return on investment.

Because though much has changed in the last 25 years, one thing hasn't: business is still the only force with the reach and resources to do what needs to be done as quickly and efficiently as possible.

After watching America's political process devolve in recent years into what is essentially an oversized argument punctuated by self-serving bursts of alarming obstructionism, it's clear that government is not the answer. Real leadership in Washington and other political capitals has long since been replaced by fearful strategic triangulation that replaces big ideas and bold action with anemic incremental change.

Nor are NGOs an effective alternative. There are too many of them too narrowly focused and too often at odds with each other. Even when added up, the non-profit world simply hasn't the authority, influence, or financial base to engineer change on a mass scale.

That leaves business as the only force in today's world that's got it all: a universal presence, an ability to get things done quickly and on as little as a CEO's say-so, and the economic clout required to engineer widespread systemic change with remarkable speed. Business is our best and indeed last hope, and it's time to put that hope to the test.

As this book wisely notes, change is no longer a matter of choice. Our present trajectory tells us it's coming whether we want it to or not. The only question is what form this change is going to take. If the corporate community fails to adopt and embrace meaningful CR, those changes will be grim indeed, and the world that will emerge may very possibly be too environmentally degraded and socially unstable for business to survive at all.

Business needs CR as much as the world itself does. This book is how we get to that better future. The journey starts with Visser's critical dissection of the role that business has played in the development of the many challenges we face and the first-generation failures of the CR movement to prevent them. It's as key an instructive moment as the movement has ever had, and we will do well to heed the important lessons this analysis brings to the table.

Yet it's when Visser looks at where we go from here that the book you are holding offers its biggest payoff. Upon seeing that the first iteration of CR was not enough, we could easily be left wondering what to do next. Having once given it our all, what's left to give? In Visser's view, the answer is plenty, and I agree. Rather than be frustrated by our previous lack of meaningful success, this roadmap to a more sane and just future offers ideas to get excited about. Visser's vision of what a new brand of CR could and should look like and his exploration of the kind of businesses it would breed is the medicine the movement has been seeking. It's at once a way out and way forward. We would be foolish in the extreme not to take it to heart and put it to work.

Over twenty years ago, a handful of individuals at a ragged assortment of companies tried to start a revolution. You're holding the book that can finish it. Take what it knows and use this wisdom to set your own business on the path to a better and more profitable place. Whether you're a CEO in a corner office or a worker on the line, read it, learn it, and spread its gospel as far and wide as you can. The hour may be late and the clock loudly ticking, but the story of responsible business is not over yet. There's still room for a happy ending. And the time has come for us to write it for ourselves.

Jeffrey Hollender
Co-Founder, Seventh Generation
Charlotte, VT
October 2010

Acknowledgements

As this book is the fruit of my efforts in corporate sustainability and responsibility (CSR) – through studies and work – over the past 20 years, there are too many people to thank individually.

However, I would like mention colleagues at Cap Gemini (*Stephen Asbury*) and KPMG (*Petrus Marais, Shireen Naidoo, George Molenkamp* and *Michael Kelly*), as well as fellow scholars at the Universities of Cape Town (*Vic Razis* and *Bruce Phillips*), Nottingham (*Jeremy Moon* and *Wendy Chapple*), York (*Andrew Crane* and *Dirk Matten*), La Trobe (*Suzanne Young*) and Cambridge (*Polly Courtice* and *Mike Peirce*).

Some of the quotations from thought leaders in the book are taken from interviews I conducted as part of the University of Cambridge Programme for Sustainability Leadership 'Top 50 Sustainability Books' project in 2008, an opportunity for which I am most grateful.

I would like to thank *Josetta McLaughlin* from Roosevelt University for her detailed review of the manuscript and helpful suggestions for improvement.

As ever, I am grateful to my family, who are a wellspring of encouragement, and my beloved *Indira*, who inspires me daily and is unfailing in her support.

About the author

Dr Wayne Visser is Founder and Director of the think-tank CSR International and the author/editor of twelve books, including nine on the role of business in society, such as *The A to Z of Corporate Social Responsibility* and *The World Guide to CSR*.

In addition, Dr Visser is Senior Associate at the University of Cambridge Programme for Sustainability Leadership, Visiting Professor of Sustainability at Magna Carta College, Oxford, and Adjunct Professor of CSR at La Trobe Graduate School of Management, Australia. Before getting his PhD in Corporate Social Responsibility (Nottingham University, UK), Dr Visser was Director of Sustainability Services for KPMG and Strategy Analyst for Cap Gemini in South Africa.

His other qualifications include an MSc in Human Ecology (Edinburgh University, UK) and a Bachelor of Business Science with Honours in Marketing (Cape Town University, South Africa). Dr Visser lives in London, UK, and enjoys art, writing poetry, spending time outdoors and travelling in his home continent of Africa.

In 2010, Dr Visser completed a 20 country 'CSR Quest' World Tour, to share best practices in corporate sustainability and responsibility. A full biography and much of his writing and art is on www.waynevisser.com. He will continue to upload new content on CSR 2.0 at http://ageofresponsibility. blogspot.com and www.csrinternational.org. If you wish to contact Dr Visser and share your own experience of CSR 2.0, or book him for a presentation, you can email him at wayne@waynevisser.com.

You can also follow him on Twitter (WayneVisser).

The call to responsibility

Our ability to respond

We have the Bill of Rights. What we need is a Bill of Responsibilities.
—Bill Maher

It is easy to dodge our responsibilities, but we cannot dodge the consequences of dodging our responsibilities.
—Josiah Charles Stamp

Let everyone sweep in front of his own door, and the whole world will be clean.
—Johann Wolfgang von Goethe

In times like these men should utter nothing for which they would not be willingly responsible through time and in eternity.
—Abraham Lincoln

The meaning of responsibility

Do you sigh when you hear the word *responsibility*? Perhaps responsibility is even a dirty word in your vocabulary. Perhaps you associate it with burdens and restrictions; the opposite of being carefree and without obligations. But responsibility doesn't have to be a chore, or a cage. It all depends how you think about it.

Responsibility is literally what it says – our ability to respond. It is a choice we make – whether to be attentive to our children's needs, whether to be mindful of the plight of those less fortunate, whether to be considerate of the impact we have on the earth and others. To be responsible is to be proactive in the world, to be sensitive to the interconnections, and to be willing to do something constructive, as a way of giving back.

Responsibility is the counterbalance to rights. If we enjoy the right to freedom, it is because we accept our responsibility not to harm or harass others. If we expect the right to fair treatment, we have a responsibility to respect the rule of law and honour the principle of reciprocity. If we believe in the right to have our basic needs met, we have the responsibility to respond when poverty denies those rights to others.

Taking responsibility, at home or in the workplace, is an expression of confidence in our own abilities, a chance to test our own limits, to challenge ourselves and to see how far we can go. Responsibility is the gateway to achievement. And achievement is the path to growth. Being responsible for something means that we are entrusted with realizing its potential, turning its promise into reality. We are the magicians of manifestation, ready to prove to ourselves and to others what can happen when we put our minds to it, if we focus our energies and concentrate our efforts.

Being responsible for someone – another person – is an even greater privilege, for it means that we are embracing our role as caregivers, helping others to develop and flourish. This is an awesome responsibility, in the truest sense, one which should be embraced with gratitude, not accepted reluctantly with trepidation. Responsibility asks no more of us than that we try our best, that we act in the highest and truest way we know. Responsibility is not a guarantee of success, but a commitment to trying.

So why is responsibility seen by many as such an onerous burden? Responsibility becomes onerous when choice is removed from the equation, when we do not realize our freedom to act differently, when we forget that we are allowed to say 'no'. Responsibility becomes pernicious when we take on too much, when we mistakenly think that more is always better, when we take on the guilt and expectations of others. Accepting too many responsibilities is, in fact, irresponsible – for it compromises our ability to respond. *Do few things but do them well* is the maxim of responsibility.

Being responsible also does not mean doing it all ourselves. Responsibility is a form of sharing, a way of recognizing that we're all in this together. 'Sole responsibility' is an oxymoron.

Taking responsibility is a way of taking ownership in our lives, of acknowledging our own hand in the shaping of destiny. Responsibility is the antidote for victimhood.

When we walk with awareness, we realize the enmeshed nature of reality, we see the subtle strands that make up the web of life, we accept that everything is linked to everything else. Responsibility is being conscious of the oneness of existence.

Responsibility, if we manage it well, should never be like the curse of Sisyphus, eternally rolling a rock uphill, but rather a blessing gratefully received. For what can be more joyous than making a positive contribution in the world, or making a difference in someone else's life?

Responsibility is the set of prints we leave in the sand, the mark of our passage. What tracks will you leave? Where is the place where you can most freely and effectively respond? The choice, as always, is yours.

I wrote these opening words on responsibility in 2005, and I believe they are more relevant today than they were back then. Responsibility is the choice we make to respond with care. This book, then, is a way of taking stock. What choices have we made – in the way we live our lives, in the way we do our work and in the way we run our businesses? How have we responded to the needs of our day – especially the social, environmental and ethical crises we face? And have our actions been taken with care – have we cared about our impacts on others?

I must admit to being slightly surprised (and a little dismayed) to find myself, 10 years after my first book, *Beyond Reasonable Greed*, still singing a similar refrain. I am once again arguing that business needs to 'shapeshift', to fundamentally rethink the purpose of business and to put into practice a genuinely sustainable and responsible ethos. There are fundamental differences though. Today, many of the problems are worse, more urgent and backed by more solid scientific evidence. In the interim, there has been a geopolitical shift away from the West, with the potential for more questioning of neoliberal economics and shareholder-driven capitalism. There are also more corporate corpses on the slab, allowing us to examine the nature of our greed disease. At the same time, awareness about our public social and environmental crises is much higher, and there are more genuine corporate sustainability and responsibility pioneers that provide living proof of what health and wellbeing *could* mean for business and society.

The fact is that now we know better what bad corporate magic looks like and the devastating consequences of practicing it. But we also know that magic spells can be broken by revealing the sleight of hand at work. It is my hope that by sharing some of the insights gained from the past 20 years of CSR wonder and trickery, we can move beyond magic to real responsibility –

responsibility of the kind that makes a tangible, positive, sustained impact on the lives of the world's poor and excluded and that visibly turns the tide on our wholesale destruction of ecosystems and species.

The failure of CSR

But I am getting ahead of myself. First let me say what I understand by CSR. I take CSR to stand for Corporate Sustainability and Responsibility, rather than Corporate Social Responsibility, but feel free use whichever proxy label you are most comfortable with. My definition is as follows: *CSR is the way in which business consistently creates shared value in society through economic development, good governance, stakeholder responsiveness and environmental improvement.* Put another way, *CSR is an integrated, systemic approach by business that builds, rather than erodes or destroys, economic, social, human and natural capital.* Given this understanding, my usual starting point for any discussion on CSR is to argue that it has failed. I will provide the data and arguments to back up this audacious claim in the paragraphs, pages and chapters that follow. But the logic is simple and compelling. A doctor judges his/her success by whether the patient is getting better (healthier) or worse (sicker). Similarly, we should judge the success of CSR by whether our communities and ecosystems are getting better or worse. And while at the micro level – in terms of specific CSR projects and practices – we can show many improvements, at the macro level almost every indicator of our social, environmental and ethical health is in decline.

I am not alone in my assessment. Indeed, Paul Hawken stated in *The Ecology of Commerce* in 1993 that 'If every company on the planet were to adopt the best environmental practice of the "leading" companies, the world would still be moving toward sure degradation and collapse.' Unfortunately, this is still true nearly 20 years later. Jeffrey Hollender, co-founder and former CEO of Seventh Generation, agrees, saying: 'I believe that the vast majority of companies fail to be "good" corporate citizens, Seventh Generation included. Most sustainability and corporate responsibility programs are about being less bad rather than good. They are about selective and compartmentalized "programs" rather than holistic and systemic change.'

In fact, there is no shortage of critics of CSR. For example, in 2004, Christian Aid issued a report called 'Behind the Mask: The Real Face of CSR', in which they argue that 'CSR is a completely inadequate response to the sometimes devastating impact that multinational companies can have in an ever-more globalized world – and it is actually used to mask that impact.' A more recent example is an article in the *Wall Street Journal* (23 August 2010) called 'The Case Against Corporate Social Responsibility', which claims that 'the idea that companies have a responsibility to act in the public interest and will profit from doing so is fundamentally flawed.' This is not the place to deconstruct these polemics. Suffice to say that they raise some of the same concerns I have – especially about the limits of voluntary action and the 'misdirection' that CSR sometimes represents. But I also disagree with many of their propositions – such as the notion that CSR is always a deliberate strategy to mislead, or that government regulation is the only solution to social and environmental problems.

Be that as it may, there are a number of ways to respond to my assertion that CSR has failed. One is to disagree with the facts and to suggest that things are getting better, not worse, as do the likes of Bjørn Lomborg in his *Skeptical Environmentalist* (2001). That is his and your prerogative. However, I find the evidence – some of which is presented below and which is widely available from credible sources like the United Nations – both compelling and convincing. Second, you might argue that solving these complex social, environmental and ethical problems is not the mandate of CSR, nor within its capacity to achieve. My response is that while business certainly cannot tackle our global challenges alone, unless CSR is actually about *solving* the problems and *reversing* the negative trends, what is the point? CSR then becomes little more than an altruistic conscience-easer at best; a manipulative image-management tool at worst.

My approach – and the essence of this book – is to say that while CSR *as it has been practised in the past* has failed, that doesn't mean that a different kind of CSR – one which addresses its limitations and reforms its nature – is destined to fail in the future. Hence, the first part of the book is about where we have gotten to with CSR to date – through the Ages of Greed, Philanthropy, Marketing and Management, using defensive, charitable, promotional and strategic CSR approaches respectively. The second part of the book then goes on to explore what CSR could (and in my view *should*) be in the Age of Responsibility – namely systemic or radical CSR, which I also call CSR 2.0. Along the way, I cite many best practice case studies, none of which are fully practising systemic CSR, but all of which have pieces of the puzzle that can instruct and inspire.

Our global footprint

Before we get into all that, however, let's start by putting some facts on the table that back up my claim that many of our global challenges are getting worse, not better – beginning with environmental impacts. According to the Global Footprint Network, humanity's ecological footprint, driven by the spread of capitalism and Western lifestyles globally, has more than tripled since 1961. Since the late 1980s, we have been in 'overshoot' – meaning that the world's ecological footprint has exceeded the earth's biocapacity. An ecological footprint analysis shows that while global biocapacity – the area available to produce our resources and capture our emissions – is 2.1 global hectares (ha) per person, the per person footprint is already 2.7 global ha.

The USA and China have the largest national footprints, each in total about 21% of global biocapacity, but US citizens each require an average of 9.4 global ha (or nearly 4.5 Planet Earths if the global population had US consumption patterns), while Chinese citizens use on average 2.1 global ha per person (one Planet Earth). Biocapacity is also unevenly distributed, with eight nations – the United States, Brazil, Russia, China, India, Canada, Argentina and Australia – containing more than half the world total. Population and consumption patterns make three of these countries ecological debtors, with footprints greater than their national biocapacity – the United States (with a footprint 1.8 times national biocapacity), China (2.3 times) and India (2.2 times).

A second environmental indicator is the Living Planet Index, compiled by the Zoological Society of London, which shows a nearly 30% decline since 1970 in nearly 5,000 measured populations of 1,686 species around the world. These dramatic losses in our natural wealth are being driven by deforestation and land conversion in the tropics (where species have declined by 50%) and the impact of dams, diversions and climate change on freshwater species (35% decline). Pollution, over-fishing and destructive fishing in marine and coastal environments are also taking a considerable toll.

Another indicator of the state of the planet is the UN Millennium Ecosystem Assessment, issued in 2005, which reaches similar conclusions: 60% of world ecosystem services have been degraded; of 24 evaluated ecosystems, 15 are being damaged; water withdrawals have doubled over the past 40 years; and over a quarter of all fish stocks are over-harvested. Since 1980, about 35% of mangroves have been lost; around 20% of corals have been lost in just 20 years and 20% more have been degraded; and species extinction rates are now 100–1,000 times above the background ('natural') rate. So, by all accounts, capitalism is failing spectacularly to control the environmental impacts of the economic activities that it is so successful at stimulating.

What many people fail to appreciate is how uneconomic this environmental destruction really is. For example, a 2010 study conducted for the UN by Trucost found the estimated combined damage of the world's 3,000 biggest companies was worth $2.2 trillion in 2008 – a figure bigger than the national economies of all but seven countries in the world that year, and equal to one-third of the average profits of those companies. In 2010, The Economics of Ecosystems and Biodiversity (TEEB) study also found that degradation of the Earth's ecosystems and biodiversity due to deforestation alone costs us natural capital worth somewhere between $1.9 and $4.5 trillion every year.

Our global weather

Our environmental impacts and associated economic costs are no more dramatically evident than on the issue of climate change. The 4th Assessment Report of the Intergovernmental Panel on Climate Change (IPPC) concluded that global atmospheric concentrations of greenhouse gases (GHGs) have increased markedly since 1750 as a result of human activities. Ice-core records spanning thousands of years show that GHG concentrations today far exceed recent historical levels, with carbon dioxide (CO_2, the most important GHG) growing from 280 parts-per-million (ppm) in pre-industrial times, to 379 ppm in 2005. This exceeds the natural range over the last 650,000 years. Moreover, the rate of increase in CO_2 concentration has been faster in the last decade than at any point since measurement began.

The spike in carbon emissions is mainly due to fossil fuel use, although changes in land use are also a big factor. Other GHG concentrations like methane have also been increasing. Despite occasional theatrics by climate sceptics, there is overwhelming scientific consensus that the climate system is definitely warming and that human activity is the primary cause eleven of the 12 years to 2006 were among the warmest since records began. Trends over 1900 to 2005 indicate significantly increased precipitation in areas such as northern Europe and drying in areas like the Mediterranean. Longer, more intense droughts have been seen since the 1970s and there have been widespread changes in extreme temperatures over the last 50 years. It is highly likely (more than 90% probable) that these changes in the climate system are human-caused and are a result of the increase in GHG concentrations.

The most recent 100-year linear trend shows a 0.74°C increase in temperature in the century to 2005 (which is larger than the 100-year trend of 0.6°C reported in 2001). Overall, the sea level is estimated to have risen by 0.17 metres during the 20th century. A warming of 0.2°C per decade over the next 20 years is predicted and there is a greater than 90% chance that climate changes during the 21st century will exceed the previous century. The current best estimate for the average temperature rise is 1.8°C to 4.0°C by 2100, with a possible range of 1.1°C to 6.4°C.

Specific predictions are also possible. For example, snow cover is expected to decrease and permafrost regions (which store vast amounts of methane) will likely see increases in thaw depth. Temperature extremes, heat waves and heavy precipitation events will continue to become more frequent and tropical cyclones are also likely to become more intense. The higher latitudes will probably see more precipitation and most sub-tropical regions less. Models show that the meridional overturning circulation (ocean conveyor belt) will slow during this century, though it is unlikely to undergo a large, abrupt transition. In addition, there is a greater than 50% chance that human activities have increased the risk of heat waves.

The 2006 Stern Review on *The Economics of Climate Change* concludes that climate change is 'the greatest market failure the world has ever seen' and estimates that the cost of action to reduce GHGs and avoid the worst impacts of climate change can be limited to about 1% of global GDP per year if action is immediate and decisive. By contrast, failure to act swiftly will damage economic growth. Specifically, inaction will result in a persistent annual loss of 5% of global GDP. If a wider range of impacts and risks is considered, this could be as high as 20% of GDP, or more.

It is important to emphasize that climate change is not just an environmental issue. A 2009 UNDP report estimates significant impacts of global warming on the world's 2.6 billion people surviving on less than $2 a day, including up to 600 million more people facing malnutrition due to the breakdown of agricultural systems resulting from increased exposure to drought, rising temperatures and more erratic rainfall. The report estimates potential productivity losses of 26% by 2060 in semi-arid areas of sub-Saharan Africa, home to some of the highest concentrations of poverty in the world. An additional 1.8 billion people are expected to experience water stress by 2080, with large areas of South Asia and northern China facing a grave ecological crisis as a result of glacial retreat and changing rainfall patterns. In addition, up to 332 million people in coastal and low-lying areas may be displaced by flooding and tropical storm activity, including more than 70 million Bangladeshis, 22 million Vietnamese, and six million Egyptians. Finally, related health effects suggest that as many as 400 million people are likely to face the risk of malaria as a result of climate change. *National Geographic* have also identified dengue fever as a major risk.

Our global village

The social impacts of our globalization activities are more ambiguous. On the one hand, critics like Naomi Klein, author of *No Logo* and *The Shock Doctrine*, argue that 'Gucci capitalism' results in labour exploitation and a 'race to the bottom'. In other words, capital flows to wherever the social or environmental standards are lowest. Not only this, but capitalism is designed to create the instability that we have seen in the markets, and those that suffer the most from this volatility are always the most vulnerable, namely the poor of the world. On the other hand, there has been undoubted progress in reducing global poverty. The 2010 UN Millennium Development Goals (MDGs) report shows that the number of people in developing regions living on less than $1.25 a day reduced from 1.8 billion in 1990 to 1.4 billion in 2005, while the overall poverty rate dropped from 46% to 27%.

Looking at specific countries, poverty rates in China are expected to fall to around 5% by 2015. India, too, has contributed to the large reduction in global poverty. Measured at the $1.25 a day poverty line, poverty rates there are expected to fall from 51% in 1990 to 24% in 2015, and the number of people living in extreme poverty will likely decrease by 188 million. It is in no small part due to these achievements by China and India that the developing world as a whole remains on track to achieve the MDG poverty reduction target by 2015. The overall poverty rate is expected to fall to 15% by 2015, which translates into around 920 million people living under the international poverty line – half the number in 1990.

Other areas of progress have been major advances in getting children into school in many of the poorest countries, especially in sub-Saharan Africa. There have also been remarkable improvements in key interventions. For example, for malaria and HIV control and measles immunization, the number of child deaths has been cut from 12.5 million in 1990 to 8.8 million in 2008. Between 2003 and 2008, the number of people receiving antiretroviral therapy increased tenfold – from 400,000 to 4 million – corresponding to 42% of the 8.8 million people who needed treatment for HIV infection.

Despite this remarkable progress, however, huge challenges remain. In 2009, 42 million people had been displaced by conflict or persecution, 80% of them in developing countries. The number of people who are undernourished has continued to grow, while slow progress in reducing the prevalence of hunger stalled – or even reversed itself – in the first decade of the century. Furthermore, about one in four children under the age of five are still underweight, mainly due to inadequate access to food, water, sanitation and health services, as well as poor care and feeding practices.

The situation with sanitation provides a window into the challenges that remain. Only about half of the developing world's population has adequate sanitation facilities. Disparities between rural and urban areas are daunting, with only 40% of rural populations covered. The gaps between rich and poor are equally stark: while 77% of the population in the richest 20% of households have acquired improved sanitation facilities, only 16% of those in the poorest households have had similar improvements. Disparities in access to care during pregnancy are also striking, with women in the richest households 1.7 times more likely than the poorest women to visit a skilled health worker at least once before birth. Similarly, in Southern Asia, 60% of children in the poorest areas are underweight, compared to 25% of children in the richest households.

Underscoring the inequality that we still face in the world, Gallup's 2010 global snapshot of wellbeing revealed that the percentage of people who are 'thriving' ranges from a high of 82% in Denmark to a low of 1% in Togo. Africa has the lowest wellbeing, with no country in this region showing a thriving indicator higher than 25%. In fact, of the 41 countries where thriving is 10% or lower, more than half are in Africa. Elsewhere in the world, however, disparities also exist. Thriving in the Americas is highest in Costa Rica (63%) and Canada (62%) and lowest in Cuba (24%) and Haiti (4%). In Europe, self-reported wellbeing is lowest in Bulgaria (6%) and highest in Denmark (82%) and Finland (75%). Similar disparities are evident in Asia. 'Thriving' is 60% or higher in New Zealand (63%), Israel (62%), and Australia (62%) and 10% or lower in 11 nations, with Cambodia at the bottom with 3%.

Our global dishonesty

One of the socio-economic cancers that aids and abets the poverty and inequality just described is corruption. According to Transparency International's 2009 Corruption Perceptions Index (CPI) – which is a measure of domestic, public sector corruption – the vast majority of the 180 countries included score below five on a scale from 0 (perceived to be highly corrupt) to 10 (perceived to have low levels of corruption). Fragile, unstable states that are scarred by war and ongoing conflict linger at the bottom of the index. These are Somalia, with a score of 1.1, Afghanistan at 1.3, Myanmar at 1.4 and Sudan tied with Iraq at 1.5. Highest scorers are New Zealand at 9.4, Denmark at 9.3, Singapore and Sweden tied at 9.2 and Switzerland at 9.0.

Looking at business, Transparency International's 2009 Global Corruption Barometer found that over half of those polled – with more than 73,000 respondents drawn from 69 countries and territories around the world – believe that the private sector uses bribes to influence public policy, laws and regulations. At the same time, half of the respondents expressed a willingness to pay a premium to buy from corruption-free companies. The Barometer also found that the poorest families continue to be punished by petty bribe demands. Across the board, low-income respondents were more likely to be met with bribe demands than high-income respondents. Furthermore, only three in ten respondents believed their government's efforts to fight corruption were effective, although opinion in sub-Saharan Africa was notably more positive than in other regions.

According to another of Transparency International's indexes – the 2008 Bribe Payers Index (BPI) – companies based in the emerging economic giants are perceived to routinely engage in bribery when doing business abroad. For example, Russia ranked last with a score of 5.9 (where 10 represents no corruption), just below China (6.5), Mexico (6.6) and India (6.8). At the other end of the spectrum, Belgium and Canada shared first place with a score of 8.8, while the Netherlands and Switzerland shared third place on the index with 8.7. Transparency International estimates that bribery, cartels and other corrupt practices undermine competition and contribute to a massive loss of resources for development in all countries, especially the poorest ones. For example, between 1990 and 2005, more than 283 private international cartels that cost consumers around the world an estimated $300 billion in overcharges were exposed.

Awkward questions

These bewildering facts and figures leave us with many troubling questions, or at least they should do. In this book, I am mainly concerned with those that involve business. For instance, I wrestle with the central question: are companies more a part of the problem or the solution? Is the net impact of business positive or negative? There are other questions too; awkward questions that cut even closer to the bone. For better or for worse, I chose corporate sustainability and responsibility as my way to make a positive difference in the world – the mark of my footprints in the sands of time. But given that CSR initiatives have increased dramatically over the same 50 years that many of the global problems described above have been getting worse, does that mean that CSR is ineffective?

It gets worse. Could the whole CSR bonanza be an unwitting accomplice to the spate of corporate crimes of recent decades? Am I quietly and unintentionally aiding and abetting our collective demise? After all, Enron was stuffed to the gills with CSR initiatives – from codes of conduct and ethics officers to corporate volunteering and community development programmes. And yet, when I attended a presentation years after the Enron debacle, an insider accountant, said that all the CSR programmes in the world could do nothing to change the internal culture of greed that had been nurtured and rewarded over decades by the organization.

Even Lehman Brothers, which I discuss in depth in the next chapter, had gotten savvy to the CSR trend. They issued annual Corporate Philanthropy reports and declared to their shareholders in 2007 that: 'Strong corporate citizenship is a key element of our culture. We actively leverage our intellectual capital, network of global relationships, and financial strength to help address today's critical social issues.' In 2007 they had an expert in socially responsible business practices join the firm as global head of Sustainability and president of the Council on Climate Change. Bizarrely, in 2008, the firm 'posthumously' received a CSR award for a 10-year mentoring project at a local secondary school in the East End of London.

I am sure all of these CSR programmes had their merits. And yet, if they did nothing to prevent the company from acting like a pirate on the high seas of finance, what good were they? If CSR cannot form the bedrock of ethical corporate behaviour, does it deserve to have 'responsibility' in its title? More worryingly still, if CSR is used to legitimize businesses or practices that are, at heart, irresponsible, surely CSR is partly to blame for the various corporate 'sins' that go undetected and unpunished? I am led to a very uncomfortable conclusion.

At worst, CSR in its most primitive form may be a smokescreen covering up systemically irresponsible behaviour. At best, even the most evolved CSR practices might just be a band-aid applied to a gaping wound that is haemorrhaging the lifeblood of the economy, society and the planet.

The ages and stages of CSR

This book is an attempt at answering some of these awkward questions, taking a critical look at the role of business in the global crises we face, and being honest with myself and all those working in corporate sustainability and responsibility about the limits of our impacts. At the same time, it is an opportunity to glimpse into the future; to start to sketch out what a different kind of CSR – indeed a different kind of business – might look like, one that will have a greater chance of succeeding where its predecessor has failed.

As intimated at the start of the chapter, I have found it useful to view the evolution of business responsibility in terms of five overlapping periods – the Ages of Greed, Philanthropy, Marketing, Management and Responsibility – each of which typically manifests a different stage of CSR, namely: Defensive,

Table 1 The ages and stages of CSR

Business age	Stage of CSR	Modus operandi	Key enabler	Stakeholder target
Greed	Defensive	Ad hoc interventions	Investments	Shareholders, government & employees
Philanthropy	Charitable	Donations	Projects	Communities
Marketing	Promotional	Public relations	Media	General public
Management	Strategic	Management systems	Codes	Shareholders & NGOs/CSOs
Responsibility	Systemic	Business models	Products	Regulators & customers

Charitable, Promotional, Strategic and Systemic CSR. My contention is that companies tend to move through these ages and stages (although they may have activities in several ages and stages at once), and that we should be encouraging business to make the transition to Systemic CSR in the dawning Age of Responsibility. If companies remain stuck in any of the first four stages, I don't believe we will turn the tide on the environmental, social and ethical crises that we face. Simply put, CSR will continue to fail.

The first part of the book explores each of these Ages in turn. However, let me introduce them here briefly. The Age of Greed is characterized by *Defensive CSR* in which all corporate sustainability and responsibility practices – which are typically limited – are undertaken only if and when it can be shown that shareholder value will be protected as a result. Hence, employee volunteer programmes (which show evidence of improved staff motivation, commitment and productivity) are not uncommon, nor are targeted expenditures (for example, on pollution controls) which are seen to fend off regulation or avoid fines and penalties.

Charitable CSR in the Age of Philanthropy is where a company supports various social and environmental causes through donations and sponsorships, typically administered through a Foundation, Trust or Chairman's Fund and aimed at empowering community groups or civil society organizations (CSOs).

Promotional CSR in the Age of Marketing is what happens when corporate sustainability and responsibility is seen mainly as a public relations opportunity to enhance the brand, image and reputation of the company. Promotional CSR may draw on the practices of Charitable and Strategic CSR and turn them into PR spin, which is often characterized as 'greenwash'.

Strategic CSR, emerging from the Age of Management, means relating CSR activities to the company's core business (like Coca-Cola's focus on water management), often through adherence to CSR codes and implementation of social and environmental management systems, which typically involve cycles of CSR policy development, goal and target setting, programme implementation, auditing and reporting.

Systemic CSR in the Age of Responsibility focuses its activities on identifying and tackling the root causes of our present unsustainability and irresponsibility, typically through innovating business models, revolutionizing their processes, products and services and lobbying for progressive national and international policies.

Hence, while Strategic CSR is focused at the micro level – supporting social or environmental issues that happen to align with its strategy (but without necessarily changing that strategy) – Systemic CSR focuses on understanding the interconnections of the macro level system – society and ecosystems – and changing its strategy to optimize the outcomes for this larger human and ecological system. The second part of the book focuses on how we might do that, exploring Systemic CSR – which I also refer to as CSR 2.0 – and delving into each of the five principles that characterize this new approach, namely: Creativity, Scalability, Responsiveness, Glocality and Circularity. The final section of the book looks at how we can make change happen, at a societal, organizational and individual level, ending with how we can all make a difference in our own unique way.

We begin our examination, in the wake of the global financial crisis, by looking at the Age of Greed that precipitated the near-meltdown of the world's economic system.

PART II

The ages and stages of CSR

The age of greed

The point is, ladies and gentleman, that greed, for lack of a better word, is good. Greed is right, greed works. Greed clarifies, cuts through, and captures the essence of the evolutionary spirit. Greed, in all of its forms – greed for life, for money, for love, knowledge – has marked the upward surge of mankind.

—Gordon Gekko

Earth provides enough to satisfy every man's need, but not every man's greed.

—Mahatma Gandhi

Two friends were at a party held at the mansion of a billionaire. One said, 'Wow! Look at this place! This guy has everything!' The other said, 'Yes, but I have something he'll never have: enough.'

—Unknown

A Native American grandfather talking to his young grandson tells the boy he has two wolves inside of him struggling with each other. The first is the wolf of peace, love and kindness. The other wolf is fear, greed and hatred. 'Which wolf will win, grandfather?' asks the young boy. 'Whichever one I feed,' is the reply.

—Native American proverb

Box 1: The age of greed – in a nutshell

Iconic leaders	Barings Bank
	Dutch East India Company
	Enron
	Lehman Brothers
	WorldCom
Period	Rising from 1972, when the first derivatives were traded to a peak in 2008, when the sub-prime crisis caused a global economic meltdown
Key ideas	Bigger is better
	Greed is good
	Privatize gains and socialize costs
	Primacy of shareholder interests
	Trust the `invisible hand' of the market
Commentators	Joel Bakan (academic, author & filmmaker)
	David Korten (author)
	Michael Moore (activist & filmmaker)
	George Soros (investor & author)
	Oliver Stone (filmmaker)
References	*When Corporations Rule the World* (David Korten, 1995)
	The Crisis of Global Capitalism: Open Society Endangered (George Soros, 1998)
	The Corporation: The Pathological Pursuit of Profit and Power (Joel Bakan, book & film, 2004)
	The Smartest Guys in the Room: The Amazing Rise and Scandalous Fall of Enron (Bethany McLean & Peter Elkind, book & film, 2004)
	Capitalism: A Love Story (Michael Moore, film, 2009)

Case 1: Larry McDonald and Lehman Brothers[1]

Larry McDonald was a child of the 'greed is good' 80s. But, unlike me, he actually lived the dream – and is still haunted by the nightmare that ensued. Looking back, there are several obvious pieces to the puzzle; factors that explain McDonald's unrelenting drive to become a high stakes player on Wall Street. His father was obsessed with business, and plastics made him a stack of money, enough to start his own brokerage firm. That obsession took its toll on family life, and McDonald soon found himself in a broken home, living with his mother and four siblings on a housing estate – at the wrong end of an 'urban version of Death Valley'.

Despite this, or more likely because of it, McDonald set his sights on escaping the mire of poverty. He now knew where he *did not* want to spend his life. And, thanks to his father's high-flying business career, he knew where wanted to get to. 'By the time I graduated from college in 1989', McDonald recalled, 'I had learned enough about Wall Street to understand that was the place I wanted to be, right out there in New York with the big dogs, playing in the major leagues of finance. The trouble was, my chances of getting in were zilch.'

Wall Street became McDonald's personal Holy Grail. He was smart enough to realize that he was still light years away, but he set himself a secret five-year target to make it there. First, he tried to get into one of the brokerage houses in New England. Hundreds of rejection letters later, he changed his strategy – he became a self-confessed 'new specialist in low cunning, deviousness and subterfuge'. He began lying his way past office security guards and executive personal

---

[1]This vignette is a true story, précised and adapted from Larry McDonald's book *A Colossal Failure of Common Sense: The Incredible Inside Story of the Collapse of Lehman Brothers.*

assistants, dressing up as a pizza delivery man, trying just about any-thing to get an audience with one of the branch managers.

One day, McDonald's *chutzpah* (if that's what you'd call it) paid off. But it wasn't the break he'd hoped for. 'Kid', the manager told him, 'I don't care what you sell for your first experience, but for Christ's sake get out there and sell 'em something, rather than wasting my time!' That was the clue, the key to breaking into the fortress of high finance. McDonald sprung into action and got a sales job, selling pork around the Cape and south-eastern Massachusetts. Midway through his second year, he was one of the top salesmen in the entire American Frozen Foods northeast region. Soon, there was an offer for a manage-ment job at their headquarters in Connecticut. He nearly accepted, but stopped himself just in time. Becoming the world's number one meat salesman was not his objective. Getting to Wall Street was. But how?

A friend from school convinced him that he needed to enrol at Phila-delphia business school and sit for the Series 7 Exam, because with-out it 'a future bond trader would be like a butcher without a meat cleaver'. But he needed a sponsor and a 'sleazy bucket shop' – an underworld operation, selling stock in fake shells of corporations to raise cash – was the way in. The deal was that they would sponsor McDonald and when he passed his exam, he would work for them, joining their 'fat chain-smoking salesmen that would say anything to their victims'.

McDonald made the Faustian bargain and passed the exam, but man-aged to get a job with Merrill Lynch in Philadelphia instead, thereby avoiding the bucket shop, which he regarded distastefully as the 'totally unacceptable face of capitalism'. McDonald worked hard, began specializing in convertible bonds, made good money and plotted his next move. While he was still scheming, he ran into an acquain-tance in a bar who worked for IBM and was about to start up one of the Cape's first Internet service providers. He convinced McDonald that, pretty soon, the dotcom boom would revolutionize everything – financial trading would go online.

Sensing a blockbuster opportunity, McDonald hatched a plot with an old friend to start up ConvertBond.com, which they launched in 1997. Pretty soon, *The Wall Street Journal* and CNBC television were featuring stories about them and the business took off. Despite running a seat-of-the-pants operation out of a small office above a strip mall, with 250,000 hits a day, their opinions on newly issued bonds started to hold considerable sway in the market. McDonald had caught the wave of the future, and it hadn't gone unnoticed by the 'big boys'. In the autumn of 1999, Morgan Stanley made an offer to take over Convert-Bond.com. Suddenly, McDonald was a 33-year old millionaire and working in Morgan Stanley's Stamford office – another step closer to Wall Street.

The dotcom bubble burst soon afterward, so McDonald had got out just in time. And more drama was to come. In 2001, McDonald was in the thick of convertible bonds action as first Pacific Gas and Electric filed for bankruptcy, then 9/11 happened, and finally the Enron debacle broke. He watched mesmerized as Enron, saddled with $65 billion in unpayable debt, spiralled to their death at the hands of the financial markets, with their share price plummeting from $90 to just a few cents. In the months that followed, a spate of bankruptcies rocked the world, all of companies that issued convertible bonds: Global Crossing, Qwest, NTL, Adelphia Communications and WorldCom. McDonald had a front-seat view of the whole financial operatic tragedy.

Alan Greenspan's response was to cut interest rates from 6% in December 2000 to 1% by July 2003. 'Thus began one of the greatest consumer borrowing bonanzas since the 1920s', reflected McDonald. 'This was the starting point of America living in a false economy, because all this free money was in defiance of the natural laws of the universe.' His father agreed: 'Here we go again' he warned. 'Straight back to the edge of the cliff.' But one person's poison is another's potion. Wall Street had just invented securitization – turning mortgage debts into tangible, tradable entities. 'What a pure stroke of genius', said McDonald. 'Hardly anyone noticed the minor flaws that would, in time, bankrupt half the world.'

As 2004 arrived, the flame of McDonald's ambitions burned strong as ever. 'I still wanted a seat at Wall Street's top table, right up there in the major leagues'. Fortunately, he knew someone who worked for Lehman's, that pinnacle of his ambition that had survived and thrived for over 150 years. The friend encouraged McDonald to apply for a position, and, after a series of gruelling interviews, he stepped into the lion's den. Admittedly, it had taken 16 years, rather than the five he had hoped for, but here he was, 'into the hierarchy, alongside some of Wall Street's smartest guys'.

For the next few years, McDonald's dream became an intoxicating, head-spinning reality. He would wake at 4 am and be at his desk before 6, working in a chilled, oxygen-fed trading office, taking no lunch, and leaving more than 12 hours later. It was tiring, but he found it exhilarating. 'We were in the presence of gods, the new Masters of the Universe, a breed of financial daredevils who conjured Lehman's billion-dollar profits out of one of the most complex markets ever to show its head above Wall Street's ramparts. This was the Age of the Derivative – the Wall Street neutron that provided atomic power to one of the most reckless housing booms in all of history.'

McDonald had his doubts about the sub-prime bonanza, but, he knew his limits: 'I didn't dare mention even a semblance of doubt, not to anyone. That would have been tantamount to high treason, as if the president of the United States had invited Osama Bin Laden to Camp David for the weekend'. Besides, McDonald was benefiting big time. Wall Street bonuses were 250% bigger than the average salary for all nonfinancial jobs in the city, and since 2003, thanks to derivatives, their total compensation had increased by nearly 50%. That was, in retrospect, 'on the high side', recalled McDonald. 'But that's what it was all about – record leverage, record bonuses.'

It later turned out that McDonald was not alone in his suspicions about the market's greed-fuelled behaviour. On 6 June 2006, all the staff in his unit in Lehman's were called into a meeting and addressed by one of the newly promoted managing directors. He said the US real estate market was 'pumped up like an athlete on steroids, rippling with a set of muscles that did not naturally belong there'. It was based on 'money that was not real money, home prices that were not real prices, and mortgages that were not grounded in any definition of reality'. The presentation went down like a lead balloon among the traders. 'Have you missed the fact that this bull market is exploding?' retorted one.

The prevailing opinion of eternal sunshine was hardly surprising. True, US consumer and corporate debt was stacking up – $1 trillion in 2000 and $2.7 trillion by 2005 – but Wall Street was still making shiploads of money, and everyone was bullish. Even *Time* magazine declared that 'the world economy is on track to enjoy another bumper year in 2006 as this twin American-Chinese engine continues to power ahead'. 'The outlook is basically for another Goldilocks kind of year', agreed Lara D. Tyson, then dean of London Business School. But some, including McDonald and a few bears[2] at Lehman, had spotted the cracks in the shining edifice of global financial markets.

Despite these early warning signals, the tide of optimism and greed continued to sweep through Lehman's, America and the world, and McDonald was riding high, making more than a tidy golden nest egg in the process. By the time the spring tide had turned into an incontestable financial tsunami, it was too late – too late for Lehman's and too late for McDonald. When 158-year old Lehman Brothers filed for Chapter 11 bankruptcy on 15 September 2008, owing $660 billion, it

---

[2]Traders who bet on a fall in prices for securities.

took a good portion of Wall Street, Main Street and the world economy down with it.

McDonald still lives just a few city blocks from the old Lehman Brothers
headquarters at 745 Seventh Avenue. Each time he walks past, he is
overcome with mixed emotions – mainly nostalgia, edged by a lingering
anger and still plagued by unanswerable questions. 'I stand and stare
upward, sorrowful beyond reason', McDonald confesses, 'and trapped
by the twin words of those possessed of flawless hindsight: *if only*.'

An unhealthy appetite

If only indeed. I began this chapter with Larry McDonald's true story, because I think it tells us something about the Age of Greed. This was
an age that began when the first financial derivatives were traded on
the Chicago Mercantile Exchange in 1972 and peaked (we hope) with
Lehman's collapse in 2008. It was a time when 'greed is good' and 'bigger
is better' were the dual-mottos that seemed to underpin the American
Dream. The invisible hand of the market went largely unquestioned.
Incentives – like Wall Street profits and traders' bonuses – were perverse,
leading not only to unbelievable wealth in the hands of a few speculators,
but ultimately to global financial catastrophe.

McDonald's story, I believe, gets to the heart of the nature of greed. The word
'greed' – from the old English *grædig* – has etymological roots that relate to
'hunger' and 'eagerness'. This is similar to the older word, *avarice*, coming
from Old French and Latin (*avere*), meaning 'to crave or long for'. Those are
characteristics that McDonald had in spades. The Greek word for greed – *phi-
largyros*, literally 'money-loving' – also has a familiar ring in McDonald's story.
The trouble is that capitalism in general, and the American Dream in particular, has tended to interpret this as a healthy trait. McDonald didn't believe he
was being unethical, or doing anything wrong. He was playing the game –
extremely well until it all collapsed like a house of cards – and being rewarded
handsomely for his aptitude, no questions asked.

No doubt McDonald would have been unfamiliar – or at least uncomfortable – with the German root of the word for greed (*habsüchtig*), which
means 'to have a sickness or disease'. And yet I believe this comes closer
to the real essence of greed, for it acts like a cancer in society, like a cell in
the body which becomes so selfish that it ultimately destroys its host.
As with cancer, however, the enabling environment is as important as the
greedy cell itself. As implied by the title of my book *Beyond Reasonable Greed*,
a certain measure of selfishness is natural, but it needs to be moderated
by norms, rules and cultural taboos that keep its destructive tendencies
in check.

It is worth reminding ourselves what the consequences of those destructive
tendencies can mean in the lives of millions of ordinary people. The financial cost of cleaning up after the global financial crisis – which ultimately
gets translated into a tax burden on the public – was estimated by the IMF
in August 2009 at £7.1 trillion ($11 trillion), enough to finance a £1,779
($2,748) handout for every man, woman and child on the planet. This
gargantuan sum includes capital injections pumped into banks in order to
prevent them from collapse, the cost of soaking up so-called toxic assets,
guarantees over debt and liquidity support from central banks.

And then there is the human cost of unemployment. In January 2010, the
International Labour Organization released figures showing that the global
unemployment rate for 2009 was 6.6%, or 212 million people, an increase
of almost 34 million over 2007. In the US alone, over 100,000 businesses
filed for bankruptcy in 2008 and 2009. At the same time, the World Bank
estimated that the financial crisis left an additional 50 million people
around the world in extreme poverty in 2009 and some 64 million in 2010
relative to a no-crisis scenario, principally in sub-Saharan Africa and
Eastern and South-Eastern Asia.

We should all be outraged by the dire human and economic fallout from
banking greed – and indeed many are. But it is important to remember that
the Age of Greed was not something 'out there'. It was not the preserve of a
few rogue traders, or even thoughtful and somewhat-concerned traders like

McDonald. We were all caught up in its web. Our global financial implosion was (and is) a multi-level phenomenon, incorporating executive greed, banking greed, financial market greed, corporate greed and, ultimately, greed embedded in the capitalist system.

Executive greed

The most convenient explanation for the financial crisis is to point a finger at the greed and irresponsibility of a few individual executives, like Lehman's Richard (Dick) Fuld. It is an argument with significant weight and popular appeal, as we always want a scapegoat to assuage our pain. We saw it all before with Enron. In 2000, Enron was the 7th largest company in America, with revenues of $111 billion and over 20,000 staff. When the company collapsed in 2001, due to various fraudulent accounting activities, the average severance payment was $45,000, while executives received bonuses of $55 million in the company's last year. Employees lost $1.2 billion in pensions and retirees lost $2 billion, but executives cashed in $116 million in stocks. The dissolution of the accounting firm, Andersen, also resulted in the loss of 85,000 jobs.

It is no surprise that Enron's executives took the fall and that not a single public tear was shed as a result. Jeffrey K. Skilling, the former CEO, pleaded not guilty but was found culpable on 19 counts of fraud, conspiracy, insider trading and lying to auditors. He was sentenced to more than 24 years in prison and a fine of $45 million. Kenneth L. Lay, Enron's former chairman, was found guilty on 10 counts, but died of heart failure before sentence was passed. And Andrew S. Fastow, the former chief financial officer, was sentenced to six years in prison for his part in the cover-up. So we had our scapegoats. They got what they deserved, and as far as Wall Street was concerned, they could go back to business greed as usual.

By the end of 2007, a similar pattern was already emerging, in large part due to the greed-hyped activities of Lehman Brothers and other financial institutions. With the financial crisis writing already writ large on the wall (including on Wall Street), Fuld and Lehman's president Joseph Gregory paid themselves stock bonuses of $35 million and $29 million respectively. Fuld continued to live in his enormous Greenwich mansion of over 9,000 square feet, valued at $10 million. And he certainly had no intention of giving up his four other homes and his art collection valued at $200 million.

Taken on their own, these examples of executive excess are outrageous enough. But the extent of creeping executive greed comes into even sharper focus when we look at trends in relative pay. In 1965, US CEOs in major companies earned 24 times more than a typical worker, but that ratio steadily grew to 35 in 1978 and 71 in 1989. By 2000, it had hit 298, and despite falling to 143 in 2002 (after the post-Enron stock market slump), it bounced back again and continued rising through the naughty 'noughties' (as the years 2000–2009 have become affectionately known).

According to *Fair Economy*, in 2007, despite the looming economic recession, CEO pay of the largest 500 companies in America (S&P 500) averaged $10.5 million, 344 times the pay of typical American workers and 866 times as much as minimum wage employees. The same year, the top 50 hedge and private equity fund managers earned an average of $588 million, according to *Alpha* magazine – more than 19,000 times as much as average worker pay. And in 2008, while the financial crisis was beginning to bite for ordinary citizens, average CEO pay went up to $10.9 million, while CEO perks averaged $365,000 – nearly 10 times the median salary of a full-time worker.

It is easy to go cross-eyed or brain-fried when confronted by a barrage of numbers like that. But there is one particular number that shocked me so much the first time I read it (in 1997) that I have never forgotten it. I believe I read it in Anita Roddick's book *Body and Soul* where she claimed that it would take one Haitian worker producing Disney clothes and dolls *166 years* to earn as much as Disney's then president, Michael Eisner, earned in *one day*. As I later wrote, 'Rather than spreading around wealth for the common good, it seems to me that Adam Smith's invisible hand has a compulsive habit of feeding itself.'

Banking greed

Horrific as these trends in executive greed are – and they certainly represent a responsibility train-wreck – I do not believe that the global financial crisis can be adequately explained by 'bad apples' (as the media liked to characterize these now-disgraced captains of industry). In addition to those leaders who were driven by personal greed, the sub-prime loans crisis was also a story of institutional greed, sparked and fuelled by deregulation of the financial sector since the 1980s. In particular, we can point to a number of poor US policy decisions that were to have disastrous consequences.

The first was President Bill Clinton's campaign promise to increase home ownership in poor and minority communities – a noble cause, to be sure, but one which put pressure on the banks to make riskier loans: two million of them between 1993 and 1999. The folly of this policy, while obvious in retrospect, did not pose any immediate concerns, as the housing market was strong and prices continued to rise. Over the same period, Clinton was coming under increasing pressure by the banking lobby to repeal the Glass-Steagall Act of 1933, a piece of post-Wall Street crash legislation that prevented commercial banks from merging with investment banks. The law was specifically put in place to prevent another global financial crisis and ensuing depression. At first, Clinton resisted, but the banks were relentless.

In 1998, one of the banks, Citicorp, decided to flout the law, announcing a $70 billion merger with Travelers Insurance. Clinton tried to block it but failed in the Senate, despite the fact that the merger was technically illegal. A year later, Clinton bowed to rising pressure and repealed the Glass-Steagall Act. This single action proved to be the 'butterfly effect' that would bring the world financial system to its knees. With the stroke of a pen, and bullied by the greed of the banks, Clinton had given permission for speculative financial traders to start gambling with the hard-earned deposits of ordinary Americans (and others). Soon, all manner of financial instruments exploded onto the market – from CDOs (collateralized debt obligations) and CLOs (collaterized loan obligations) to CMBSs (commercial mortgage-backed securities) and CDSs (credit default swaps).

For a year or two, it seemed like the party may have ended before it had begun, as Wall Street contemplated the bankruptcy of Enron and others which had issued convertible bonds. The 9/11 tragedy and dotcom crash was happening around the same time, and some measure of caution did return to the markets, but not for long. Alan Greenspan's slashing of interest rates to 1% was, like Clinton's repeal of Glass-Steagall, a butterfly effect that would cause a financial typhoon. Suddenly, not only was the housing market growing, but money was almost free. And with the help of all those newly invented financial voodoo instruments, the sub-prime party really got going.

It all seems surreal in retrospect, looking back as we now do from our economic hospital beds in 2010. How was it that preposterous loans like the NINJA mortgage – so called because No Income, No Job and no Assets were required to qualify – were ever allowed to exist? It didn't matter that you were poor and had no collateral. Not only would you get a mortgage, the broker would pay you 10% more than you needed to buy the house. The initial interest rate (what the brokers called the 'teaser rate') would be next to nothing, then increase five or tenfold in the years to come. The infallible logic behind this – if that isn't an oxymoron – was that house market prices would continue to rise steadily, and everyone would be a winner. If you couldn't pay your monthly instalments, no problem – just sell the house, pay off the mortgage and you would still have some money left over in your pocket.

The result was that, according to the Mortgage Bankers' Association, the number of sub-prime loans offered to borrowers with below average credit increased nearly 15 times between 1998 and 2007, from 421,330 to 6.2 million. Meanwhile, the banks were in a feeding frenzy, leveraging themselves to the hilt, so that they could make obscene profits from the market boom. To give you some idea, historically, a leverage of ten times

EBITDA[3] (where the company has debts of ten times its actual value) was considered very high. But by the time Lehman Brothers hit the iceberg, it was well on the way to being leveraged to 44 times its value, owing more than $700 billion. The face of banking greed was finally unmasked.

Financial market greed

Many global financial crisis analysts would stop there, satisfied that the combination of executive greed and banking greed provides sufficient explanation for the global responsibility crisis. And they certainly do represent the most obvious failures that caused the mother-of-all meltdowns. However, I do not believe that these two factors alone tell the whole story. To understand banking greed, we need to look at the nature of the financial markets as a whole – how they are designed, how they operate and the behaviours that they incentivize.

In order to understand what 'greed is good' really means – in terms of hard numbers – we must wrap our heads around the concept of financial derivatives. McDonald referred to derivatives as 'the Wall Street neutron'. But what are they? Put simply, they are speculative bets on changes in various market indicators (like currencies and interest rates), with the supposed effect of reducing overall risk. By the turn of the century, some three decades after their introduction, these esoteric financial instruments were growing at around 25% per year. Today, according to the Bank for International Settlements (BIS), the derivatives market is worth over $1,000 trillion (that's a quadrillion, with 15 zeros).

Why this is so significant is that most of this trade is not happening in the 'real economy', but rather in a parallel casino economy. Take trade in currencies, for example. In 1998, when 'new economists' like Hazel Henderson were starting to take note of these trends, around $1.5 trillion (that's 12 zeros) in currency was traded daily on the global markets, up 46% from

---

[3]Earnings before Interest, Taxes, Depreciation, and Amortization.

1994. But only 2.5% was linked to 'real economy' transactions such as trade, tourism, loans or genuine investments on stock markets. The other 97.5% (up from 20% in the 1970s) was pure speculation – a gambling economy in which financial traders were making eye-popping sums of money, without actually contributing anything tangible to the products and services that give us quality of life.

This unflattering characterization of financial markets is not one that is only applied by outside critics of Wall Street. Referring to one of the more modern varieties of derivatives, the credit default swap (CDS), McDonald recalled that 'in the merry month of May 2006, Wall Street took hold of this gambling concept and decided to transform itself into something between a Las Vegas casino and an off-track betting parlour'. Early in 2006, there were $26 trillion of CDS bets outstanding in the market. By the beginning of 2008, it was $70 trillion, with just 17 banks carrying that risk. And that was besides the $15 to $18 trillion in other derivatives and fancy instruments – an alphabet soup of CDOs, RMBSs, CMBSs, CLOs and ABSs.

This was all well and good when it was just a high-stakes game for rich kids to play. But as we have seen, with the repeal of the Glass-Steagall Act and the introduction of the Financial Services Modernization Act in 1999, the greed-infused, short-term obsessed gambling habits of Wall Street traders can have (and have had) very real and devastating effects on very real economies and very real people. Even today, in the aftermath of the financial crisis, very few of these financial market agents have taken responsibility, or been made accountable, nor have the financial market rules been significantly changed.

Perhaps we should belatedly listen to the warning of that great post-Depression economist John Maynard Keynes: 'Speculators may do no harm as bubbles on a steady stream of enterprise', he said. 'But the position is serious when enterprise becomes the bubble on a whirlpool of speculation. When the capital development of a country becomes a by-product of the activities of a casino, the job is likely to be ill-done.' Well, ill-done it has been – woefully ill-done. No wonder billionaire investor Warren Buffet first described derivatives as 'weeds priced as flowers', and later as 'financial weapons of mass destruction'. If Keynes were here today, standing with us on financial 'ground zero' and gazing at the post-apocalyptic debris of our once gleaming citadels of commerce, he might quite justifiably shake his head and mutter 'I told you so!'

Corporate greed

Even financial market greed may not be the ultimate cause of our woes. I am not quite so uncharitable as Howard Scott, who says the definition of a 'criminal' is 'a person with predatory instincts who has not sufficient capital to form a corporation'. But could it be that unbridled greed is, by design, the unavoidable outcome of corporate institutional design? We often forget that when corporations were originally introduced in America in the mid-1800s, it was with the explicit purpose of serving the public good (enshrined in a charter), with liable shareholders. Only later did the nature of the corporation change when the US Supreme Court ruled that a corporation should have the same rights as individuals, thus making it a legal person. The problem today, according to critics, is that the corporation is a 'person' with no moral conscience and an exclusive focus on the benefits of shareholders. This results in a pattern of social costs imposed by business in exchange for private gains for its executives and owners.

In his controversial, yet hugely influential book and documentary *The Corporation*, Canadian legal academic Joel Bakan suggests that corporations are, by their legal constitution, pathological in nature: 'The corporation has a legally defined mandate to relentlessly pursue – without exception – its own self-interest', he writes, 'regardless of the often harmful consequences it might cause to others. Lying, stealing and killing are not rare aberrations but the duty of the corporation when it serves the interests of its shareholders to do so.' This, according to Bakan, means that corporations have all the characteristics of a psychopath, as defined by the World Health Organization.

Not everyone – even among those concerned about business responsibility – would go quite this far in their diagnosis. But there is certainly little doubt about the in-built greed of the modern corporation. David Korten, author of *When Corporations Rule the World*, is among the many critics that remind us of the dangerous power of business – a world in which more than half of the top 100 'economies' are in fact multinational corporations. With such awesome power comes huge responsibility. Yet left their own devices, says Korten, many corporations are cost externalization machines – they will naturally and obsessively try to avoid paying for any negative human, community or environmental costs that they impose on society.

Korten believes the problem is even more fundamental than the corporations themselves. Talking to me in 2008, he reflected:

> If I were to rewrite the book now, I would probably put the title *When Corporations Rule the World* with a slash through 'Corporations' and a little carrot pointing to 'Money'. It's actually *When Money Rules the World*. This has become so much more obvious, so much stronger and so much more disruptive as we've seen the rampant speculation in the financial markets. That very structure drives a predatory dynamic in the corporate system that you really can't do very much about at the level of the individual corporation. You can do a little tinkering around the edges, but those are pretty limited relative to the depth of the changes that we need to navigate.

A personal odyssey into greed

Having shared these different perspectives on the greed-related causes of the financial crisis, I should admit that my views on business and greed are strongly shaped by my own particular intellectual journey over the past 20 years. Like McDonald, I grew up in the 'greed is good' 80s. That was even what we called it, when I was studying for my honours degree in business science. Admittedly, at the time I didn't really understand what it meant – or at least not in technical financial terms. I knew that junk bonds, derivatives and mergers and acquisitions were all the rage, and of course I had seen Oliver Stone's iconic masterpiece *Wall Street*. I had even heard of 'Black Monday', the infamous stock market crash of 19 October 1987, when the Dow Jones Industrial Average lost 22% in a single day. But I didn't really know the scale of greed that was in full swing by the time I graduated in 1991.

I suppose I felt it more indirectly, as the inevitable backdrop to my personal mission at the time, which was to bring about a 'new paradigm' in business – one which questioned three fundamental beliefs: that profit is the primary purpose of companies; that competition is the most effective mode of operation; and that management is a rational undertaking. It didn't take long – 18 months to be exact – for that personal mission to become deeply frustrated, as I entered the 'chew-em-up-and-spit-em-out' burnout track of international management consulting, working for Cap Gemini as a strategy analyst. To be fair, it was a remarkably steep learning curve and Gemini had some incredibly progressive ideas about business transformation. But in the end, we were in the business of making money – for ourselves and our clients. And therein lay the rub. I just couldn't shake the nagging belief that life and work are *not* just about the money. Sure we were transforming companies (or 're-engineering' them, to use the parlance of the day), but to what end? Yes, they came out the other side lean and mean, but at what cost?

The truth was that I just couldn't get excited about the money. *So what* if I helped to make a company more profitable – or, more to the point, helped to make their directors or shareholders richer? What about all the 'collateral damage' – the unfortunate people who were often 'let go', thanks to our quest for efficiency and shareholder returns? And who were these shareholders anyway? As far as I could tell, many were what are increasingly known as 'shareflippers' – traders who are in for a quick buck; who buy and sell shares without the least concern for the long-term prospects of the company, let alone its people or its environmental impacts.

Discovering institutionalized greed

In 1995, I quit the rat-race to do a Masters in Human Ecology at Edinburgh University in Scotland. That proved to be a pivotal decision, because it led me deeper into understanding the nature and extent of greed in business. The course director, Alastair McIntosh, was (and is) a fiery, red-bearded Scot with an MBA in Finance who taught us to question the colossus edifices of power, especially multinational companies. McIntosh was just the catalyst I needed to question 'business as usual', drawing as he did from his own experience as an activist. For instance, he was a key figure in the campaign to oust the English landlord of the island of Eigg and to indefinitely stall LaFarge's plans to build a 'super-quarry' on the island. Both inspiring stories are written up in McIntosh's book *Soil and Soul*.

Partly as a result of McIntosh's influence, when I had to choose a topic for an essay assignment on human ecology, I decided to look at the practice of usury (the charging of interest on loans), which has been condemned by philosophical and religious traditions for more than 4,000 years. My research on usury confirmed that issues of ethics in business go way back in history and, likewise, that greed is as ancient as the hominid caves of Sterkfontein in South Africa. But it also unveiled a surprising symptom of the greed sickness, namely the bizarre way that the modern banking system is constructed, in particular the method of fractional reserve banking.

Fractional reserve banking allows private banks to create loans equivalent to about seven times the amount of actual money (or assets, like gold) held in reserve. It seemed crazy to me then (and still does now) that private, profit-making organizations (and banks are, or were, clearly among the most private and the most profitable) are able to create money 'out of thin air' and then make more money by charging interest on these loans that they conjured into existence from the financial ether.

By contrast, I was mightily intrigued by radical alternatives, such as the creation of local currencies – especially the LETS or Local Exchange Trading

System, which has now been taken up by the emerging 'transition towns' movement – and the Islamic equity-based banking system. These have in-built checks and balances against greed. LETS was first established by Michael Linton in 1983 when his rural community in British Columbia, Canada, was devastated by an economic recession. The system allows members to trade both goods and services, using a combination of conventional dollars and community-created credits called 'Green Dollars', while members' balances are stored in a central computer program. There is no interest and no speculation in the LETS system.

Islamic banking is quite different, but tackles greed in its own way. It is centred around financial equity-based approaches, most notably *Mudarabah* – a joint venture between the bank and a 'partner', with both contributing to the capital of the project and sharing the profit or loss – and *Musharakah*, in which all the capital for an investment is provided by the bank in return for a predetermined share of the profit or loss of the business undertaking. The claimed advantages of the Islamic banking approach to finance are that it results in more just and equitable distribution of resources, less volatile business cycles, and more responsible and profitable lending due to closer bank–client relationships (remember, the banker shares losses and well as profits).

With my interest piqued, I chose 'a human and ecological critique of the UK financial system' as my Masters Dissertation topic. This was when I finally got to grips with what 'greed is good' really meant – in terms of hard numbers. In particular, I discovered the explosive financial derivatives trend that I have already discussed.

An inSANE economy?

This 'brave new world' of global finance made a big impression on me, and, after finishing my Masters, I co-founded the South African New Economics (SANE) Foundation with the lofty aim of 'promoting a socially just and environmentally sustainable economy'. If we can't change the rules of the game, I reasoned, how on earth can we expect the players (be they companies, managers or citizens) to behave differently? I still think that. This wasn't so much trailblazing as hanging onto the comet tail of others ahead of me, most notably those involved in setting up The Other Economic Summit (TOES) in 1984, which later became the hugely influential London-based think tank, The New Economics Foundation.

As I searched in vain for a more SANE agenda, the more I looked, the more it seemed that the so-called triumph of capitalism was in reality a disaster waiting to happen. The systemic risk of the casino economy was like a creaking San Andreas fault line through the heart of Western (and increasingly global) capitalism. My concern about these issues was in no way due to my prophetic powers. I was only reflecting already widely held beliefs among those in the 'new economics' movement. In retrospect, I'm not sure how many of us really believed that the global financial meltdown would ever happen. It was one of those 'taken to its logical conclusion' apocryphal warnings that we whispered smugly under our breaths, rather than shouting it from the rooftops. After all, no one wants to be known as a perpetual party-pooping doomsayer. How strange, therefore, that history has come so close to vindicating our timid 'cries in the desert'.

Through my work with the SANE Foundation, I also came across the trends in executive compensation that I have already quoted. Now I'm not one of those people that buy into the 'evil empire' and Darth Vader stereotypes of business and CEOs. But surely there is something fundamentally flawed in a system that allows corporate and individual greed to spiral out of control to the extent that it has? Surely there is a moral limit to inequity that will, sooner or later, cause the patience of billions of 'have-nots' to run out, thereby starting a bloody revolution against the small number of who 'have' so much. Little did I know then, in 1997, that the greed-treadmill would, in just a few short years, produce a cast of pantomime villains that even Oliver Stone would find incredible.

The belly of the beast

From 1997 to 2001, I had been getting up close and personal with many of the world's big brand multinationals, after establishing and heading up KPMG's Sustainability Services division in South Africa. The irony of working for one of the world's largest accounting firms, given what I knew about world finance, was not lost on me. Admittedly, I was not quite in the belly of the beast, but I was connected to the hand that fed (and sometimes stroked or prodded) the beast. And so, when the Enron bombshell exploded, I was an unwitting accessory (and agog spectator) to the crime – not directly, of course, but by virtue (or vice?) of working for one of the Big 5 (and soon to be Big 4) accounting firms. I was not financially affected and yet somehow I felt like I was straddling a fissure that led right to the epicentre of the quake.

Just how connected I was soon became clear. A series of hush-hush emergency meetings were held in the seminar rooms of KPMG, during which we were reassured by our leaders that we were safe; that this crisis had more to do with lacklustre US accounting practices than with the accounting profession *per se*; that our firm would never cover up for our clients in such a clandestine manner; and that although we could expect significantly more internal risk procedures from now on, other than that, it was full steam ahead, business as usual. Oh, and also that we would be merging with the firm in South Africa formerly known as Arthur Andersen, and we should be sensitive to the trauma they had endured.

As it happened, when the Enron story broke, I was just putting the finishing touches to the manuscript of my first book, which was to be called *Shapeshifting*. Between its covers, and with the coaching of co-author and former South African mining magnate Clem Sunter, I had tried to capture what I had learned over the past five years about implementing sustainability in business. My argument was that companies needed to 'shapeshift' from aggressive, lion-like predators into more caring, elephant-like creatures. It was a simplistic metaphor, but it worked. And now, just a few weeks before going to press, we had seen the death-roar of one of the biggest cats of all, an uber-lion.

To his credit, Sunter convinced me (kicking and screaming) to change my beloved title to *Beyond Reasonable Greed*, and we revised and beefed up the content to drive home the message. Now, as I re-read some of the observations we made, they seem to be more relevant today than they were in 2001. In the opening chapter, we said:

> If the unfolding Enron saga is disclosing anything, it is that corporate governance is sometimes not worth the (shredded) paper it is written on. . . . Bad magic has moved many companies into a state that is beyond reasonable greed. And the public have a good idea of the boundary between 'reasonable' and 'obscene'. . . . Their boards probably comprise the normal spectrum of saints and sinners; but somehow they have allowed themselves to be collectively swept along by the prevailing paradigm of success which is purely financial, and that in turn has led to unreasonable behaviour. In light of Enron's failure, this judgement may be overly kind and more cases of dodgy accounting, inflated profits and insider trading by the board may pop up in Corporate America and Corporate Europe. So we want to break the spell.

Reforming the citadels of greed

As it turned out, many more cases did raise their ugly heads, and shudder in the throes of death. In *Beyond Reasonable Greed*, we went on to say that we need a Reformation in business along the same lines as the one precipitated by Martin Luther in 1517. On 31 October of that year, he wrote an attack on the sale of indulgences (remissions of punishment for sin) in 95 theses which he nailed to a church door. His basic point was that the Church had become too interested in enriching itself at the expense of its true mission of providing spiritual leadership. It had lost the support of the population at large with its mercenary practices and obsession with grandeur and wealth.

In exactly the same way, the modern corporate world has lost the confidence of the citizen in the street. The high priests of business – the board of directors – are perceived as just another example of a group of privileged people driven by unreasonable greed and feathering their own nests. The customers and shareholders come a poor second and other stakeholders trail even further behind. The modern equivalent of indulgences is an astronomical salary, a large wad of share options and a corporate jet. And the modern equivalent of the flowery and unintelligible prayers which the Church used to recite in order to extract its indulgences from the peasantry is the purple prose and lofty sentiments expressed by companies in their mission statements, combined with a set of accounts that only the initiated can understand.

I left KPMG shortly after the book was published to pursue a PhD in Corporate Social Responsibility. It was time to question my own assumptions again. If anything, my interest in the question of greed had inflated, rather than diminished. In the years that followed, first at Nottingham University and then at Cambridge University, I watched as America cobbled together the knee-jerk legislation of Sarbanes Oxley. I listened as Judge Mervyn King, chairman of the extraordinarily progressive King Code on Corporate Governance, said: 'Moses tried it, and he failed. Sarbanes and Oxley tried it, and they will fail. We cannot legislate against dishonesty.' And all the while, I clung to my career in corporate sustainability and responsibility, believing that CSR's time had finally, really and truly, come.

Accomplice to the crime?

Today, in 2010, while the world is still reeling from the global recession, I find myself compelled to ask many of the difficult questions that were raised earlier, and more besides: Was this, as McDonald suggests in his book of the same name, 'a colossal failure of common sense'? Was it the greed of 'bad apples' like CEO Fuld, or the banks, insatiable bonus-driven traders? Or was it the pervasive culture of greed in Wall Street as a whole? What about the greed of politicians and governments who were happy to benefit from growth-on-steroids? And what about Main Street? Wasn't the public – we, the people – more than happy to greedily lap up those sub-prime loans?

All this begs the larger question: Is capitalism itself fundamentally flawed? Are we talking about endemic greed, built into the free-market system – a system which not only allowed, but encouraged the fantasy of double-digit profit growth and an endless bull market? Will capitalism, with its short-term, cost-externalization, shareholder-value focus always tend towards greed, at the expense of people and the planet? Will the scenario of 'over-shoot and collapse' that was computer modelled in the 1972 *Limits to Growth* report (and reaffirmed in revisions 20 and 30 years later) still come to pass? Has Karl Marx been vindicated in his critique though that, by de-sign, capitalism causes wealth and power to accumulate in fewer and fewer hands?

Perhaps the trillion-dollar question for me is not whether capitalism *per se* acts like a cancer gene of greed in society, but whether there are different types of capitalism, some of which are more benign than others? To date, the world has by and large been following the American model of share-holder-driven capitalism, and perhaps this is the version that is morally bankrupt and systemically flawed. Interestingly, a 2010 Pew poll of the American 'millennial generation' (currently aged between 18 and 30) showed that just 43% still describe capitalism as positive, while the same percentage now describe socialism as positive. Management guru Charles Handy seems to agree. Speaking to me in 2008, he confessed:

> I've always had my doubts about shareholder capitalism, because we keep talking about the shareholders as being owners of the business, but most of them haven't a clue what business they're in. They are basically punt-ers with no particular interest in the horse that they're backing, as long as it wins.

If we can learn one thing from the Age of Greed, it is that we have immense power to make change happen on a monumental scale, and with lightning speed. Greed has proved to be a high octane fuel in the rocket engine of globalization. But ultimately, it was an economic missile without a moral guidance system. I am under no illusions that the Age of Responsibility will vanquish greed. No doubt, the selfish gene will continue to spark our evolution. And yet, if we are successful, the Age of Responsibility will provide capitalism with that much-needed moral compass and Systemic CSR will provide business with a mission-critical social purpose. First, however, we must consider what has been going on in parallel to the greed-fest, because not everyone has been out to enrich only themselves.

3

The age of philanthropy

I resolved to stop accumulating and begin the infinitely more serious and diffi-cult task of wise distribution.

—Andrew Carnegie

As I started getting rich, I started thinking, 'What the hell am I going to do with all this money?' You have to learn to give. Over a three year period, I gave away half of what I had. To be honest, my hands shook as I signed it away. I knew I was taking myself out of the race to be the richest man in the world.

—Ted Turner

Is the rich world aware of how four billion of the six billion live? If we were aware, we would want to help out, we'd want to get involved.

—Bill Gates

I believe it is my duty to make money and still more money and to use the money I make for the good of my fellow man, according to the dictates of my conscience.

—John D. Rockefeller Sr.

Box 2: The age of philanthropy – in a nutshell

Iconic leaders	Andrew Carnegie
	John D. Rockefeller (Standard Oil)
	Ted Turner (CNN)
	Bill Gates (Microsoft)
	Warren Buffet
Period	Rising from 1889, with the publication of Andrew Carnegie's *Gospel of Wealth*, to a peak in 2006, when Warren Buffet gave $31 billion to the Bill and Melinda Gates Foundation (which already had $29 billion in assets)
Key ideas	Business should give back to society
	Economic benefits trickle down
	First get rich, then get generous
	The rich can save the poor
	With great wealth comes great responsibility
Commentators	Matthew Bishop and Michael Green (authors)
	Willie Cheng (author & consultant)
	Bill Clinton (former US president)
	Steven H. Goldberg (author)
	Peter Frumkin (author)
References	*Strategic Giving: The Art and Science of Philanthropy* (Peter Frumkin, 2006)
	Giving: How Each of Us Can Change the World (Bill Clinton, 2007)
	Philanthrocapitalism: How the Rich Can Save the World (Matthew Bishop & Michael Green, 2008)
	Doing Good Well: What Does (and Does Not) Make Sense in the Nonprofit World (Willie Cheng, 2009)
	Billions of Drops in Millions of Buckets: Why Philanthropy Doesn't Advance Social Progress (Steven H. Goldberg, 2009)

Case 2: John D. Rockefeller and Standard Oil

The name Rockefeller conjures up images of wealth, success, monopoly, the American Dream . . . and philanthropy. This is largely thanks to John D. Rockefeller, born in 1839 in New York and regarded by many as a business icon, a hero of industrialization, an ambassador for capitalism, the wealthiest man in history[4] and the original, great grandfather of philanthropy. But that is not the whole story. 'What makes him problematic – and why he continues to inspire ambivalent reactions', according to biographer Ron Chernow, 'is that his good side was every bit as good as his bad side was bad. Seldom has history produced such a contradictory figure.'

As with so many mythical figures, Rockefeller's story has humble beginnings. Chernow describes him as the son of 'a flamboyant, bigamous snake-oil salesman and a pious, straitlaced mother'. Perhaps more kindly, his father described himself as a 'botanic physician', so we can infer that he made his living selling herbal elixirs of one sort or another. The family settled in Cleveland, Ohio, just around the time that the great railroads were being built and the industrial revolution was making its way across the Atlantic.

John Davison was a bright kid, especially good with numbers, but like so many children of that era, his energies were channelled into work, rather than study, from a young age. As a result, he quickly learned some fundamental lessons of business. There is a story of him, at age 12, taking $50 that he had earned selling turkeys and loaning it to a

---

[4]By the time of his death in 1937, his net worth had grown to US$1.4 billion. Estimates place his inflation-adjusted net worth in the range of US$392–663 billion in today's money, and it is estimated that his personal fortune was equal to 1.53% of the total US economy in his day, far exceeding the likes of today's tycoons like Bill Gates.

neighbouring farmer at 7% interest. 'The impression was gaining ground with me', he later reflected, 'that it was a good thing to let the money be my servant and not make myself a slave to the money.'

Rockefeller's first proper job was as an assistant accountant, aged 16, working for a small produce commission firm, where he relished 'all the methods and systems of the office'. After working for three months, and no doubt influenced by his Baptist upbringing, he showed his first philanthropic tendencies, donating 6% of his salary to charity. By the time he was 20, he had upped this tithe to 10%, setting the pattern for a lifetime of generosity.

It is often said that those who wish to reap rewards first have to be brave enough to take risks. In Rockefeller's case, this meant striking out on his own in 1859, aged 20. Together with a young English partner, Maurice Clark, he set up a company, Clark & Rockefeller Produce and Commission, selling farm implements, fertilizers and household goods. Having established himself independently, his real breakthrough came when he took an even bigger leap into the emerging oil business.

When Rockefeller established Standard Oil in 1870, the industry was like the untamed frontiers of the Wild West – there were very few rules, the market was hugely volatile and there was no shortage of unscrupulous characters and shady wheeling and dealing afoot. By all accounts, Rockefeller resolved to both 'join 'em *and* beat 'em'. One of his first clandestine acts was to support a railroad cartel to control freight rates.

Quick success set a pattern for growing his oil empire, which biographer Segal describes as a 'self-reinforcing cycle of buying competing refiners, improving the efficiency of operations, pressing for discounts on oil shipments, undercutting the competition, making secret deals and raising investment pools'. His hard-ball tactics earned him notoriety in the industry. Over a four-month period in 1872, in what was later known as the 'Cleveland Conquest' or

'Cleveland Massacre', Standard Oil had absorbed 22 of its 26 Cleveland competitors.

Rockefeller's expansionist agenda followed a predictable pattern. He would make what he considered a fair offer for a rival business, with the threat that if they refused, he would drive them into bankruptcy through predatory pricing, and then buy up their assets for a song at auction. It was not an entirely greed-driven obsession. Rather, he saw himself as the industry's saviour, 'an angel of mercy', weeding out the weak and growing a strong, efficient and competitive industry.

The strategy worked. Through horizontal integration, bold efficiency drives and ruthless supply chain bargaining, Standard Oil brought order to a chaotic industry and drove down the price of oil. It developed over 300 oil-based products, from tar and paint to Vaseline and chewing gum. By the end of the 1870s, the company was refining over 90% of the oil in the US, and Rockefeller had become a millionaire. But his success was not without its critics.

In 1879, the Commonwealth of Pennsylvania indicted Rockefeller on monopoly charges and soon other courts in other states followed suit. In 1880, *New York World* characterized Standard Oil as 'the most cruel, impudent, pitiless, and grasping monopoly that ever fastened upon a country'. Apparently unphased, Rockefeller replied that 'in a business so large as ours . . . some things are likely to be done which we cannot approve. We correct them as soon as they come to our knowledge.'

Perhaps the ongoing controversy did take its toll, however. From the early 1890s, his health began to suffer and he had a partial nervous breakdown, losing all his hair, including his eyebrows. By the mid 1890s, Rockefeller retired from business and began devoting himself to distributing the estimated $1.5 billion he had accumulated through a lifetime of commercial ventures. His approach to philanthropy set the benchmark for generations to come.

First, he appointed a professional, Frederick T. Gates (over a hundred years before his unrelated namesake would take over the mantle of Master Philanthropist), to help manage and distribute his wealth, a task that later fell to his son, John D. Rockefeller Jr. As with his commercial ventures, John D. Sr. was obsessed with the effectiveness of his donations and the efficiency with which they were administered. His first priority was education, and he made his approach clear: 'To help an inefficient, ill-located, unnecessary school is a waste. . . . It is highly probable that enough money has been squandered on unwise educational projects to have built up a national system of higher education adequate to our needs, if the money had been properly directed to that end.'

Despite his conservative upbringing, Rockefeller was progressive in the causes that he supported. Among his many major donations to educational institutions (including, among others, the Universities of Chicago, Yale, Harvard and Columbia), in 1884 he funded Spelman College in Atlanta for African-American women. Realizing that social problems cannot be tackled piecemeal, he also established the General Education Board to promote education at all levels right across the country. Through the Board, Rockefeller established the collaborative principle of philanthropy, whereby his funding of free professional advice for improving instruction and education was supplemented by local money to build the high schools.

Rockefeller's involvement in education demonstrated keen insight into philanthropy that addresses root causes, rather than symptoms. Not only did he anticipate that education would have beneficial multiplier effects on people's general quality of life and the economy, but he realized that, as in business, in education you get what you pay for. Hence, in 1919, he donated $50 million to the Board to raise academic salaries, which were very low in the wake of the First World War.

Rockefeller was also able to put aside his personal biases in support of larger causes. For example, he reached beyond his paternally inspired preference for homeopathy and became a benefactor of medical science, founding the Rockefeller Institute for Medical Research in New York[5] in 1901 and the Rockefeller Sanitary Commission in 1909, an organization that eventually brought the hookworm infection that had long plagued the American South under control.

Another principle that Rockefeller built into his charitable activities was the importance of beneficiary support, or what we might today call stakeholder engagement. In particular, he introduced the 'conditional grant', which required the recipient to 'root the institution in the affections of as many people as possible who, as contributors, become personally concerned, and thereafter may be counted on to give to the institution their watchful interest and cooperation'. At the same time, he was conscious of the dangers of donor dependency, stating that 'charity is injurious unless it helps the recipient become independent of it'.

Much of Rockefeller's philanthropic legacy came together in The Rockefeller Foundation, established in 1913 to continue and expand the scope of the work of the Sanitary Commission in the areas of health, education and the arts. He is said to have given away $540 million over his lifetime and died in 1937, aged 98, with a residual estate worth 'only' $26 million. More important even than his individual contribution, he instilled the philanthropic tradition in his family, with his son, 'Junior', giving away over $537 million over his lifetime, and one of his grandsons, David Rockefeller, donating about $900 million to date. A Rockefeller Archive Center study in 2004 documents an incomplete list of 72 major institutions that the family has created or endowed up to the present day.

---

[5] In 1965, this became Rockefeller University after expanding its mission to include graduate education. It claims a connection to 23 Nobel laureates.

Apart from their established contribution in education and health, over the generations the Rockefeller family has also created more than 20 national parks and open spaces, leading the National Audubon Society, one of America's largest and oldest conservation organizations, to claim in 2005 that 'cumulatively, no other family in America has made the contribution to conservation that the Rockefeller family has made'.

So how should we remember Rockefeller? Some lump him in the category of America's great 'robber barons'; others regard him as the original great philanthropist. The enduring image that I most like is of him, in his later life, giving away dimes to adults and nickels to children wherever he went. He even gave a dime as a playful gesture to men like tyre mogul Harvey Firestone. It's almost as if he was saying, 'It's the principle of giving that matters most. It does not matter how much you give, but it does matter that you give with a generous heart.'

The wheels of wealth

The Rockefeller story is a good one to introduce the Age of Philanthropy, not only because of John D.'s iconic status as a tycoon and philanthropist, but also because his life and views on charity embody much of the philanthropic attitudes that still prevail today in business. At the heart of the Age – and its chief agent, Charitable CSR – is the notion of giving back to society. Rather interestingly, this presupposes that you have taken something away in the first place. Charitable CSR embodies the principle of sharing the fruits of success, irrespective of the path taken to achieve that success. It is the idea of post-wealth generosity, of making lots of money first and then dedicating oneself to the task of how best to distribute those riches, by way of leaving a legacy.

Of course, the ideals of charity and philanthropy pre-date Rockefeller. Like greed, charity is probably as old as humanity itself. And right from the beginning, there is an element of enlightened self-interest. For example, in the Hindu religious text, the *Rig Veda* (1,500–900 BC), we are told: 'If it is expected of every rich man to satisfy the poor implorer, let the rich person have a distant vision (for a rich man of today may not remain rich tomorrow). Remember that riches revolve from one man to another, as revolve the wheels of a chariot.' Similarly, in the *Upanishads*, another of the Hindu scriptures, it states: 'Like in a well, the more you fetch, the more water oozes. The more you give the more you get. This generosity is mandatory to every individual. Hurry to promise or pledge to help.'

Turning to the Far East, Confucius (551–479 BC) said: 'When wealth is centralized, the people are dispersed. When wealth is distributed, the people are brought together.' Hence, 'a man of humanity is one who, in seeking to establish himself, finds a foothold for others and who, desiring attainment for himself, helps others to attain'. When asked, 'Is there one word which may serve as a rule of practice for all one's life?' he replied, 'Is not *reciprocity* such a word? What you do not want done to yourself, do not do to others.'

This so-called Golden Rule, which we find in all the world's major religions, has come to represent the very essence of charity. In fact, the word charity derives from the Latin *caritas*, which means preciousness, dearness, or high price. In Christian theology, *caritas* became the standard Latin translation for the Greek word *agapē*, meaning an unlimited loving kindness to all others. Hence, in St Paul's Letter to the Corinthians, we read, in the King James Version of the Bible, of 'faith, hope and charity'. Of course, it is not only giving that is important, but also the nature of giving. There is a Jewish proverb that says: 'What you give for the cause of charity in health is gold; what you give in sickness is silver; what you give after death is lead.'

Islam also has a strong tradition of charity. *Zakāt*, or alms-giving for the purposes of alleviating poverty and helping those less fortunate, is one of the Five Pillars of Islam. The practice is generally in the form of an annual tithe or tax of 2.5% of an individual's wealth (although the percentage can vary by country and tradition), including money made through business, savings and income. The *zakāt* must also be above an agreed minimum (called *nisab*), which is said to be around $2,640 or the equivalent in any other currency. As important as the collection of *zakāt* is in a community, its fair distribution among the needy is even more important. Another form of charitable action by Muslims is *sadaqah*, which literally means 'righteousness' and refers to the voluntary giving of alms or charity. These ancient traditions are considered to be a personal responsibility for all Muslims, practised out of love for humanity, to ease the economic hardship of others and eliminate inequality.

There are numerous other religious and cultural variations on the theme. Philanthropy in Latin America typically revolves around *asistencialismo*, which is charitable giving for poverty alleviation. In Eastern Europe, Bulgarian communities have, over the years, raised donations to build churches, schools and cultural centres called *chitalishta*. In India, Gandhi's trusteeship concept has been adapted and applied to welfare acts. In Mexico, the Raramori, who still live in the mountains of the state of Chihuahua, use the expression *korima*, which means 'to share' resources in times of stress. In Southern Africa, *ubuntu* is the practice of humanism based on the collectivist notion that 'I am a person through other people'. And so on, all around the world.

For the love of humanity

This association between charity and love for humanity is echoed in the etymology of the word 'philanthropy', coined in 2,500 BC by playwright Aeschylus in *Prometheus Bound*. In the story, when the tyrannical god Zeus threatens to destroy humans, the god Prometheus (whose name means 'forethought') gives them – out of his 'philanthropos tropos' or 'humanity-loving character' – two empowering, life-enhancing, gifts: fire and hope. As a result, *philanthropia* came to be regarded by the Greeks as one of the keys to civilization.

Aristotle also had something to say on the matter: 'To give away money is an easy matter and in any man's power. But to decide to whom to give it and how large and when, and for what purpose and how, is neither in every man power nor an easy matter.' Seneca likewise philosophized on the subject, saying that 'a benefit consists not in what is done or given, but in the intention of the giver or doer'.

Although this classical view of philanthropy all but disappeared in the Middle Ages, it re-emerged in the early 17th century. Francis Bacon referred to the Greek concept in his essay on 'Goodness' and Henry Cockeram cited 'philanthropie' as a synonym for 'humanitie' in his English dictionary of 1623. Bacon went on to say: 'The desire for power in excess caused angels to fall; the desire for knowledge in excess caused man to fall; but in charity is no excess, neither can man or angels come into danger by it.'

Philanthropy set down American roots when, in 1837, Ralph Waldo Emerson celebrated the philanthropic spirit of the Revolution in his 'Concord Hymn'. In his 1844 essay, 'The Young American', he wrote:

> It seems so easy for America to inspire and express the most expansive and humane spirit; new-born, free, healthful, strong, the land of the laborer, of the democrat, of the philanthropist, of the believer, of the saint, she should speak for the human race. It is the country of the future.

Philanthropic traditions

There are records of early philanthropists throughout the world, as many of the 58 country contributors to *The World Guide to CSR* attest. One of the oldest traditions dates from the Ottoman era, which peaked in the 16th and 17th centuries, where successful merchants or nobles would often establish a *vakif*, which would act as a fund that could be used to maintain a mosque, pay for education, establish public works such as plumbing or water fountains, build health care facilities, or support the fine arts. Even today, powerful business dynasties in Turkey like the Sabancis and Kocs use this ancient vehicle for philanthropy.

In Sierra Leone, at the close of the 18th century, British philanthropists concerned about the welfare of the unemployed black poor established the St George's Bay Company to stimulate economic development. In another initiative, the Sierra Leone Company facilitated the return of several groups of formerly enslaved Africans, who went on to found Freetown in 1792.

Similarly, many of the wealthiest Azerbaijanis in Baku during the oil boom of the late 1800s and early 1900s belonged to a charitable organization – the Muslim Philanthropic Society – which collected money to support vulnerable groups. Other examples include the Caspian–Black Sea Oil Industrial and Trading Society, created by the Rothschilds in 1883, and the Council of the Baku Petro-Industrialists, which was involved in the construction of hospitals and schools.

In Pakistan, they have the tradition of the *Waqf* Islamic model, a kind of trust fund, which is an inalienable religious endowment for charitable or educational purposes, often in the form of property. For instance, in 1906 the Said brothers founded the Hamdard Dawa Khana (House of Medicine Herbal Pharmacy) and the family leadership of the next generation declared it a *Waqf* in 1953 as it prospered. Other examples include Hamdard University and the Forqan orphanage.

American icons

Without discounting these and many other international examples, it is true to say that many of the most iconic philanthropists emerged from the United States. Apart from the Rockefellers, there was the steel and railroads magnate Cornelius Vanderbilt (1794–1877), who was not only, like Rockefeller, one of the richest Americans who ever lived,[6] but also one of

---

[6]Vanderbilt's net worth in 1877 was estimated to be $105 million, accounting for 1.15% of the US economy at the time. He would have been worth between $143 billion and $178.4 billion in today's money, adjusted for inflation.

the most generous. Among his philanthropic activities, he gave $1 million – the largest charitable gift in American history at the time – to endow what would become Vanderbilt University, named in his honour.

Even more interesting, perhaps, was Andrew Carnegie (1835–1919), a Scottish-American industrialist who also made his fortune from steel and who developed an entire philosophy of business and philanthropy. Starting as a worker in a bobbin factory and ending as one of the richest men in America,[7] his rags-to-riches story turned him into a poster boy for the American Dream. Carnegie wrote in his diary, at age 33, that 'the amassing of wealth is one of the worst species of idolatry [and] no idol is more debasing than the worship of money'. Nevertheless, by the 1890s, Carnegie Steel was the largest and most profitable industrial enterprise in the world. What was different, however, was Carnegie's attitude to money, which he saw as a profane means to a more enlightened end:

> Man does not live by bread alone. I have known millionaires starving for lack of the nutriment which alone can sustain all that is human in man, and I know workmen, and many so-called poor men, who revel in luxuries beyond the power of those millionaires to reach. It is the mind that makes the body rich. There is no class so pitiably wretched as that which possesses money and nothing else. Money can only be the useful drudge of things immeasurably higher than itself. Exalted beyond this, as it sometimes is, it remains Caliban[8] still and still plays the beast. My aspirations take a higher flight. Mine be it to have contributed to the enlightenment and the joys of the mind, to the things of the spirit, to all that tends to bring into the lives of the toilers of Pittsburgh sweetness and light. I hold this the noblest possible use of wealth.

Carnegie later distilled his approach into a three-part dictum: (1) To spend the first third of one's life getting all the education one can; (2) to spend the

---

[7]Carnegie's net worth was estimated to be US$475 million, accounting for about 0.6% of the US economy at the time. He would have been worth between $75 billion and $298 billion in today's money, adjusted for inflation.

[8]Caliban is one of the protagonists in Shakespeare's play *The Tempest* and is described variously as a freckled monster, a wild man, a deformed man, or a beast man.

next third making all the money one can; and (3) to spend the last third giving it all away to worthwhile causes. He elaborates on his philosophy of wealth and philanthropy in his book *The Gospel of Wealth* (1889), saying:

> This, then, is held to be the duty of the man of wealth: first, to set an example of modest unostentatious living, shunning display; to provide moderately for the legitimate wants of those dependent upon him; and, after doing so, to consider all surplus revenues which come to him simply as trust funds which he is strictly bound as a matter of duty to administer in the manner which, in his judgment, is best calculated to produce the most beneficial results for the community.

Carnegie lived his philosophy to the end. Much of his charitable activity was directed towards education, peace and the arts, with the founding of the Carnegie Corporation of New York ('to promote the advancement and diffusion of knowledge and understanding'), the Carnegie Endowment for International Peace, Carnegie Mellon University and the Carnegie Museums of Pittsburgh. He is estimated to have donated most of his wealth – over $350 million – to various causes over the course of his life, leaving behind 'only' $30 million to his estate, obviously conscious of his own prophetic words that 'the man who dies thus rich dies disgraced'.

Modern philanthropists

It would be misleading to suggest that philanthropy emerged purely as a Western tradition. Many non-Western regions and countries have long and proud traditions of philanthropy. The difference, however, is that they tended historically to practise 'implicit philanthropy', by which I mean that it was considered culturally inappropriate and inconsistent with prevailing religious beliefs to make charitable acts public.[9] By contrast, individual

---

[9]There are, of course, exceptions like the Tata and Birla families in India and H.Z. Taghiyev (1823–1924) and Agha Musa Naghiyev (1849–1919) in Azerbaijan.

philanthropists in America and Britain have tended to be highly visible. Charity, in the Western tradition, evolved to become a public act, or for the more cynical, a public relations exercise.

Ask anyone to name the great philanthropists of the modern era and two names crop up repeatedly, branded into the public consciousness as much by their stratospheric business success as their mind-boggling donations. I am referring, of course, to Bill Gates and Warren Buffet. Microsoft mogul Gates, ranked by *Forbes* magazine as the richest person in the world between 1995 and 2007 and with net worth of around $58 billion in 2008, stunned fans and critics alike when he set up the Bill and Melinda Gates Foundation in 2000 and rapidly grew its assets to a staggering $30 billion by 2007. Equally jaw-dropping was the promise by the 'Oracle of Omaha', investment tycoon Buffett, to double the Gates Foundation assets by gifting over 80% of his personal wealth. In the spirit of Rockefeller and Carnegie, Gates plans to give away 95% of his wealth in his lifetime and Buffett plans to leave his children with just 'enough to do anything, but not enough to do nothing'.

Other individual philanthropists that have captured the public imagination include CNN founder Ted Turner, who in 1997 publicly gifted $1 billion of his then $3 billion fortune to the United Nations. George Soros, the outspoken Hungarian born Wall Street icon and author, is said to have given away around $4 billion through his Soros Foundation and Open Society Institute, while the flamboyant British serial entrepreneur and founder of Virgin, Richard Branson, pledged all of the future profits from his airline and train businesses – estimated at the time to be around $3 billion over ten years – as investments into clean energy.

Less known by the Western public perhaps, but no less successful or generous, are Sheikh Mohammed bin Rashid al-Maktoum, the ruler of Dubai, who established his namesake foundation with an endowment of $10 billion, and Li Ka-Shing, the Asian tycoon who, among many other business ventures, is the world's largest operator of container terminals and who has committed over $1 billion since 1980 through his foundation. In 2006,

Li also pledged to donate at least one-third of his personal wealth (then estimated at \$18.8 billion) in due course to his foundation, which he calls his 'third son'.

All of these individuals – and I could name many more – are prototypical philanthropists in the Rockefeller tradition: their charitable activities are funded out of their personal wealth, usually through a foundation bearing their name; their donations are highly public acts, communicated as a legacy statement; and the emphasis is on post-wealth generosity, rather than the ethics (or otherwise) of how they made their money in the first place.

Philanthrocapitalism

As a result of the generosity of these high profile philanthropists and, more to the point, the vast sums of money they are channelling towards any number of social, environmental and ethical causes, it is not surprising that the concept of 'philanthrocapitalism' has emerged in recent years. Authors of the highly acclaimed book of the same title, Matthew Bishop and Michael Green, describe this 'new movement' as follows:

> Who is going to lead the fight against poverty, build a sustainable future for our economies free from the threat of climate change, and take on the social problems that divide even the richest societies? For the past century, we have looked to governments to tackle these problems. But their track record has been, at best, mixed. . . . A group of wealthy entrepreneurs and business leaders is increasingly taking the initiative in creating these innovative new solutions. Rejecting the idea that business is about short-term profits, damn the consequences to society and the environment, these philanthrocapitalists think the winners from our economic system should give back and that business can 'do well by doing good'.

I must confess that I have a rather allergic reaction to the concept of philanthrocapitalism, not least the notion that was conveyed in the subtitle of the first edition of Bishop and Green's book, namely that 'the rich can save the world'. To me, this is not only an arrogant idea and an insult to the hundreds of millions of people who are achieving self-reliance without the need for a begging bowl, but it is also misinformed – it misjudges the nature of the problem, who or what needs saving, and the root causes of many of the world's most serious challenges. It also masks the potential complicity of 'some of the most powerful people on the planet', namely the philanthropists themselves, in creating the very problems they are trying to alleviate. They may be the 'winners from our economic system', but at what and whose cost? We should not forget that whenever there are winners, there are almost inevitably losers in greater measure.

My point is not that we should start a tycoon witch-hunt, but rather that we have to question the appropriateness and effectiveness of philanthropy in addressing those root causes, which have more to do with the Achilles heel of Western capitalism itself, namely the environmentally unsustainable and socially inequitable growth and lifestyles that it spawns. How, for example, does philanthrocapitalism address the Western consumption, production and trade practices that are wreaking havoc with the world's ecosystems and many of the world's poorest communities? By and large, it doesn't. Giving back after the fact is just a smokescreen, notwithstanding the generosity that it shows and the benefits that result.

I should add a caveat here, before I get branded as some kind of 'heartless bastard'. I am not opposed to philanthropy *per se*. And to the extent that philanthrocapitalism can make the charitable acts of the super-rich capitalist demigods more effective in helping society's most vulnerable, it should be supported. But for goodness sake, let us not propose it as some kind of superior model of capitalism. At heart, philanthrocapitalism bears all the hallmarks of where we have gone wrong with CSR in the first place. As dual approaches, both have completely failed to turn around the worst of our global environmental, social and ethical trends, and are in all likelihood distracting us from the true cause of systemic sustainability and responsibility.

Institutional philanthropy

Up to this point, we have been talking about individual philanthropists. But that is only one chapter in the story of the Age of Philanthropy. A natural consequence of the individual philanthropy movement was the emergence in the late 1800s in the West of institutional philanthropy, whereby charitable donations are funded directly from business profits, rather than from business leaders' personal wealth.

As CSR academic Archie Carroll observes in his chapter on 'The History of CSR' in *The Oxford Handbook of Corporate Social Responsibility*, among the first recorded instances we have of this approach is by Macy's of New York, which in 1875 contributed funds to an orphan asylum, and in 1887 listed 'gifts to charities' under 'miscellaneous expenses' in the company books. Charitable practices like these evolved in the early 20th century into giving corporate donations to charitable institutions, like the YMCA (Young Men's Christian Association), which was founded in London in 1844 and ran various community-related and social programmes, especially linked to railroad companies in the USA. Other popular charities around that time were the United Way Campaign, the Boy Scouts and the Community Chest.

It was not uncommon then (nor is it today) for religious institutions to play a brokering role in institutional philanthropy. For example, in Colombia, the business community supported charitable activities through Fundación Social, founded in 1911 by Father Jose María Campoamor, a Spanish Jesuit priest. Similarly, the Baku Jewish Charitable Society in Azerbaijan was largely funded by the lucrative oil companies, while in the United States, the Salvation Army and the Young Women's Christian Association (YWCA) also became the conduits for philanthropic donations.

The rise of foundations

After World War II, with the increasing proliferation of charities and the professionalization of corporate philanthropy, it became increasingly common for companies to institutionalize their giving by setting up a corporate foundation, sometimes also called a Chairman's Fund.

Today, the top 50 corporate foundations in the US all have assets of over $75 million, with the largest (Alcoa, Merck and Wells Fargo) topping $300 million. As impressive as this seems, I find it bizarre and rather disturbing (bearing in mind the corporate wealth that they represent) that even the largest of these is only roughly one-hundredth the size of the world's largest private (personal) foundation, namely the Bill and Melinda Gates Foundation, at $30 billion. Collectively, America's approximately 2,600 corporate foundations gave around $4.4 billion in 2007, according to the Foundation Centre – the same amount as the collective donations of only the top 4 private foundations. In fact, in 2006, corporate foundation giving accounted for just 11% of all foundation giving.

To me, this speaks volumes about the cult of the individual in Anglo Saxon culture. Without detracting from these individuals' staggering generosity, what does it say about their excessive personal wealth in the first place, and the social inequity that implies? And what does it say about relative levels of corporate giving? Why should these individuals be expected (or at least encouraged) to give away most of their fortunes (95% in the case of Gates), while corporations – with much more wealth in their collective hands – can only manage minimal levels by way of 'giving back' (less than 2% of pre-tax profits in most cases)?

Be that as it may, corporate foundations have become an important vehicle in the Age of Philanthropy. Many have joined together in grantmakers' associations, to share experiences, receive professional training, pool resources and connect grantmakers to those seeking funding. Examples include the Foundation Center, the Council on Foundations, the European Association for Philanthropy and Giving (EAPG), the Asia Pacific Philanthropy Consortium and the Africa Grantmakers' Affinity Group. Let us take a look then at what institutional philanthropy has accomplished.

The state of corporate giving

According to a 2005 international study by the National Volunteer and Philanthropy Center in Singapore, average rates of corporate giving around the world are about 1% of pre-tax profits. In the US, this has even been institutionalized by the One Percent Club, a voluntary association of companies which commit to this target. However, levels of corporate philanthropy do vary considerably country by country. American business appears to be the most generous, with average contributions of 1.6% of pre-tax profits, as compared with Canada (1.03%), the UK (0.95%) and Singapore (0.22%).

Unsurprisingly, these levels of giving has been affected by the financial crisis. The Conference Board Annual Survey on Corporate Contributions indicates that US charitable giving declined in 2008, while international giving increased. Among the 166 companies that participated in the survey, total contributions of $9.47 billion were distributed to recipients in the US and overseas in 2008, as compared to $10.97 billion in 2007. According to the report, pharmaceutical companies remain the top donor industry in the US and health and human services organizations received the largest share of corporate support, both in America and internationally.

Of course, there are huge variations within each country as well. Willie Cheng, in his book *Doing Good Well*, establishes a Charity Quotient for companies, which he depicts as a matrix with Internal Motivation on the one axis (from Self-Interest to Altruism) and External Manifestation on the other axis (from Low to High). Using this typology, corporate philanthropists are characterized as one of four types: 'Business is Business' (self-interested, low giving); 'CSR' (self-interested, high giving); 'Distracted' (altruistic, low giving) and 'Mission Accomplished' (altruistic, high giving). The fact that CSR is identified as a type of philanthropy in this model only serves to reinforce my view that many still regard CSR through a very narrow lens.

Strategic philanthropy

In 1970, the respected US economist Milton Friedman published an article in the *New York Times Magazine* (13 September) entitled 'The Social

Responsibility of Business is to Increase Profits'. In it, he called the 'doctrine of social responsibility' a 'fundamentally subversive doctrine in a free society' and argued that 'there is one and only one social responsibility of business – to use its resources and engage in activities designed to increase its profits, so long as it stays within the rules of the game, which is to say, engages in open and free competition without deception or fraud'. As such, he came to define one end of the spectrum of opinion on CSR: the purist, stockholder (or shareholder) view, a view which was once again given an airing in the *Wall Street Journals'* 'The Case Against Corporate Social Responsibility' article (23 August 2010) that I mentioned in the last chapter.

Despite his hard-line view, Friedman does allow some concessions:

> It may well be in the long run interest of a corporation that is a major employer in a small community to devote resources to providing amenities to that community or to improving its government. That may make it easier to attract desirable employees, it may reduce the wage bill or lessen losses from pilferage and sabotage or have other worthwhile effects. Or it may be that, given the laws about the deductibility of corporate charitable contributions, the stockholders can contribute more to charities they favour by having the corporation make the gift than by doing it themselves, since they can in that way contribute an amount that would otherwise have been paid as corporate taxes.

Although Friedman calls this 'hypocritical window-dressing' when done under 'the cloak of social responsibility', he concedes that these practices may be justified if they contribute to shareholders' interests. Hence, he is setting out an early version of what today is more popularly called 'strategic philanthropy' – the practice of social responsibility only when it is aligned with corporate profitability. Three decades later, academics Michael Porter and Michael Kramer have given this concept more structure and credibility – and with considerably less malice directed towards CSR.

In their 2002 *Harvard Business Review* article, 'The Competitive Advantage of Corporate Philanthropy', Porter and Kramer argue that:

Increasingly, philanthropy is used as a form of public relations or advertising, promoting a company's image through high-profile sponsorships. But there is a more truly strategic way to think about philanthropy. Corporations can use their charitable efforts to improve their competitive context – the quality of the business environment in the locations where they operate. Using philanthropy to enhance competitive context aligns social and economic goals and improves a company's long-term business prospects. Addressing context enables a company not only to give money but also leverage its capabilities and relationships in support of charitable causes.

Four years later in another *HBR* article, 'Strategy and Society: The Link Between Competitive Advantage and Corporate Social Responsibility', Porter and Kramer continued to build on the strategic philanthropy concept, expanding it to the broader CSR debate. I will return to this in the chapter on 'The Age of Management'. For now, it is worth noting that strategic philanthropy represents an evolution in corporate philanthropy that has generated considerable ferment and challenged many businesses to refocus their charitable activities.

Venture philanthropy

Another concept that has generated a lot of excitement is 'venture philanthropy'. Seemingly, it has origins in yet another *HBR* article, 'Virtuous Capital: What Foundations Can Learn from Venture Capitalists', by Christine W. Letts, William Ryan and Allen Grossman in 1997. Their basic message was that corporate foundations can be more effective if they 'develop hands-on partnering skills', for which venture capital firms offer a helpful benchmark: 'In addition to putting up capital, they closely monitor the companies in which they have invested, provide management support, and stay involved long enough to see the company become strong.'

Since then, a debate has raged about what exactly venture philanthropy is and whether it is plausible, ethical and desirable. After all, if the venture capitalists are treating their donations as an investment with expectations of a financial return, then is it philanthropy, or just business? And is it feasible to expect charities like community development organizations to generate a financial return in the first place? And what about the distinction between venture philanthropy and social enterprise, or Muhammad Yunus's concept of social business?

Distilling the debate in the way that only Wikipedia can, the online oracle suggests that there are three models of venture philanthropy. The first is traditional foundations practising high-engagement grantmaking. The second is organizations which are funded by individuals, but all engagement is done by professional staff. Examples cited include the Robin Hood Foundation in New York City and Tipping Point Community in the San Francisco Bay Area. The third is the partnership model, in which partner investors both donate the financial capital and engage with the grantees. An example is the Silicon Valley Social Venture Fund in San Jose, California.

Without getting heavily into the venture philanthropy debate, I do believe that – as with strategic philanthropy – it is symptomatic of the shift in our approach to tackling society's most intractable problems. What we have seen is that traditional charity has been, for the most part, invaluable in bringing about alleviation of social and environmental distress, but rather ineffective in achieving resolution of the problems themselves. The need for pure philanthropy, irrespective of its strategic alignment to donors, will always be there. There will always be emergencies, crises and urgent problems that don't link conveniently to business interests.

Venture philanthropy, on the other hand, recognizes that we need ways to scale up solutions, and one way is to link business with a social cause, and provide the capital it needs to be effective. Hence, I regard venture philanthropy as one of the transition tools that we need as we move to the Age of Responsibility, not least because it brings creativity and scalability to the table. It is one of the critical enablers that are facilitating the social enterprise revolution, which is discussed in more detail in later chapters.

While it is true that many companies, especially in developing countries, are still stuck in the Age of Philanthropy, there are also many, especially in the industrialized world, that have moved beyond it and into the Age of Marketing. It is in the Age of Marketing that we see companies taking philanthropy and other CSR practices and turning them to their commercial reputational benefit. And so this is what we shall explore next.

CHAPTER 4

The age of marketing

The value meals, two-for-one deals, and free refills of soda give a distorted sense of how much fast food actually costs. The real price never appears on the menu.

—Eric Schlosser

Industrialism created a limitless appetite for resource exploitation, and modern science provided the ethical and cognitive license to make such exploitation possible, acceptable, and desirable.

—Vandana Shiva

The lavish spending in the 1990s on marketing, mergers and brand extensions has been matched by a never-before-seen resistance to investing in production facilities and labour.

—Naomi Klein

You can't get there from here by any mechanism that depends on support from institutions that benefit from the status quo.

—Paul Hawken

Box 3: The age of marketing – in a nutshell

Iconic leaders	Chemicals industry
	Finance industry
	(Fast) Food industry
	Tobacco industry
	Oil and Gas industry
Period	Rising from 1965, with the publication of Ralph Nader's *Unsafe at any Speed*, to a peak in 2007, with the resignation of John Browne as CEO of BP
Key ideas	CSR is a gift to PR
	Greenwashing
	Lobbying against the public interest
	Perception is reality
	Reputation and brand matter most
Commentators	Ralph Nader (author & activist)
	Michael Blowfield and Alan Murray (authors & academics)
	Noreena Hertz (author & activist)
	Naomi Klein (author & activist)
	Vandana Shiva (scientist, author & activist)
References	*No Logo: Taking Aim at the Brand Bullies* (Naomi Klein, 1999)
	The Silent Takeover (Noreena Hertz, 2001)
	Fast Food Nation: The Dark Side of the All American Meal (Eric Schlosser, 2005)
	Soil Not Oil (Vandana Shiva, 2008)
	Corporate Responsibility: A Critical Introduction (Michael Blowfield & Alan Murray, 2008)

Case 3: John Browne and BP

On 1 May 2007, John Browne resigned as CEO of BP after 41 years with the company and 12 years at its helm. According to BBC Business Editor Robert Peston, it was a 'sad end to what was, until recently, a distinguished career'. The reason for his resignation, a year ahead of plan, was the imminent publication by a British tabloid of details about his homosexuality, and the fact that he lied to the courts about his relationship. That something so private – which should have been a mere footnote in Browne's biography – prematurely ended his career is a sad indictment of the bigoted times we still live in.

Be that as it may, John Browne's story is interesting not because of his personal life but rather his very public life during a time of great change and challenge at BP. How Browne came to be at BP in the first place was really thanks to his father, who worked for Anglo-Persian Oil, which later became British Petroleum. While Browne was studying Physics at Cambridge University and at the suggestion of his father, he began as an apprentice with BP in 1966. Needless to say, he never left, working his way up the ranks and holding various posts such as Group Treasurer of BP Finance International, Chief Financial Officer of BP America, CEO of Standard Oil Production Company and finally Group CEO in 1995.

His takeover date is important, because it was the same year that Shell was being heavily criticized for its proposed sinking of the Brent Spar oil platform in the north Atlantic, as well as its alleged complicity with the Nigerian government in the execution of human rights activist Ken Saro Wiwa. Browne would have taken special note of former Shell UK Chairman Malcolm Brinded's warning that 'the days when companies were judged solely in terms of economic performance and wealth creation have disappeared. For us, Brent Spar was the key turning point. It was a wakeup call, not only to Shell, but to the entire oil and gas industry, and to industry in general.'

Indeed, Browne would have been all too aware of a few skeletons in BP's own closet at that time. Most notably, the fact that between 1993 and 1995, BP's contractor Doyon Drilling was engaged in illegally dumping hazardous wastes on Endicott Island, Alaska, injecting it down the outer rim of the oil wells. When BP learned of the practice and failed to report it to the authorities, it contravened the so-called US Superfund legislation.[10] After a few years of legal wrangling, in 1999, BP agreed to a settlement of $22 million, which included a criminal fine of $500,000 (the maximum), $6.5 million in civil penalties, and BP's establishment of a $15 million environmental management system at all BP facilities in the US and Gulf of Mexico engaged in oil exploration, drilling or production.

Another skeleton was the allegations in 1996 of complicity of human rights abuses in Colombia. It was a seminal lesson for Browne, as he later recalled:[11] BP entered that country . . . seeking a tantalising prize of rich resources amidst violent insurrection, a polarized society and dark undercurrents in politics. . . . Clearly, security was a challenge but we assumed we had the answer – a thick barbed wire fence with security personnel and, if necessary, the help of the Colombian Army. What we hadn't realized was that a fence keeps you in as well as others out. . . . BP's presence – in particular, the payment of an unfortunately named dollar-per-barrel 'war tax' – was viewed as giving tacit support to a brutal military regime in which human rights were being trampled underfoot. . . . For the first time I realized that the company's brand, its reputation, and ultimately its value, had been laid on the line because of our failure to fully appreciate our human rights responsibilities.

---

[10]Comprehensive Environmental Response, Compensation and Liability Act.

[11]EIB Seminar on Business and Human Rights, London, Friday 4 June 2010.

Browne also inherited BP's membership of the Global Climate Coalition (GCC), a powerful lobby group created in 1989 shortly after the UN created the Intergovernmental Panel on Climate Change (IPCC). The GCC actively attempted to undermine emerging climate science and to derail international policy development. To his credit, Browne withdrew BP's membership in 1997. In a groundbreaking speech at Stanford University, he stated that 'the time to consider the policy dimensions of climate change is not when the link between greenhouse gases and climate change is conclusively proven, but when the possibility cannot be discounted and is taken seriously by the society of which we are part. We in BP have reached that point.' As *Petroleum Economist* put it, 'BP had left the church.'

Within the space of a few years, step by step, Browne began to transform the image of BP. One of the great watershed moments was in 1998 when Browne threw down the gauntlet to BP and the oil industry, promising to cut emissions from its own operations by 10% from 1990 levels by 2010, which was more than the average Kyoto Protocol country targets and certainly more than any other major oil company had committed to up until that time. In fact, they achieved the target four years later, eight years ahead of the target and at no net cost to the company.

Browne seemed to be doing and saying everything right and was slowly but surely becoming the darling of environmentalists that were desperate for signs of reform among the big brands. One crucial tool was public reporting. BP, having merged with Amoco at the end of 1998, issued their first Environmental and Social Report in 1999. In his CEO statement, Browne made encouraging statements like 'the environment is the primary challenge facing the industry' and 'there is no trade-off between our commercial and financial perform-ance and our standards of care'.

To reassure the market analysts, he promised 'to apply to our per-formance in these areas with the same rigour we apply to the delivery and reporting of our financial performance – measuring, setting targets as part of an overall performance contract and reporting openly on how we have done, using independent, external auditing and verification processes wherever possible'. I can, to a certain extent, attest that these were not just flowery words, as KPMG had been working with BP in helping to design an internal carbon emissions trading scheme – a progressive step for *any* company, let alone an oil major.

By 2000, Browne felt the company had earned enough public kudos to risk a major rebranding of BP. The company reportedly spent $7 million in researching the new 'Beyond Petroleum' Helios brand and $25 million on a campaign to support the brand change. When Browne justified the exercise by saying 'it's all about increasing sales, increasing margins and reducing costs at the retail sites', perhaps more people should have tempered their expectations. Certainly Greenpeace wasn't duped, concluding at the time that 'this is a triumph of style over substance. BP spent more on their logo this year than they did on renewable energy last year.' To make their point explicit, Greenpeace ran a counter campaign, using the same design as the BP advertisements, but adding the following text:

> We also harness Greenwash. Seen our ads on TV and in the Press? Impressed that we've finally got the message on climate change? Think again. We are also running a big advertising campaign in the US. Both versions have the same graphics, the same nifty tune, the same style. But whereas the Brits are told to 'work out your carbon footprint – it's a start', the American consumer is told: 'We're investing $15 bn in finding new oil and gas in the Gulf of Mexico – it's a start.

Antonia Juhasz, author of *The Tyranny of Oil* (2008), is similarly sceptical, claiming that at its peak, BP was spending 4% of its total capital and exploratory budget on renewable energy and that this has since declined, despite Browne's announcement in 2005 of BP's plans to double its investment in alternative and renewable energies 'to create a new low-carbon power business with the growth potential to deliver revenues of around $6 billion a year within the next decade'.

Sceptics notwithstanding, Browne had earned his new title as the 'Sun King', and his reputation was not only being earned with green stripes. BP was also one of the first companies to declare their support for the Publish-What-You-Pay campaign. However, after BP decided unilaterally to publish the value of taxes paid to the Angolan government, the state-owned oil partner, Sonangol, accused the company of breaking confidentiality clauses in its agreements and threatened to terminate its contracts. As a result, under advice from Browne, the UK's Blair government launched the Extractive Industries Transparency Initiative (EITI) in 2002 at the World Summit for Sustainable Development in Johannesburg to tackle the so-called 'resource curse' and ensure 'the verification and full publication of company payments and government revenues from oil, gas and mining'.

Success or failure is all about timing. If Browne had been a politician and had retired in 2003 after two four-year terms of office, he may still have been covered in glory, with his Sun King crown firmly in place. After all, he had turned BP into an oil major – perhaps even a competitor for Exxon Mobil – by creating a lean, mean, green machine. Instead, he hung onto power long enough to face the consequences of his own legacy of cost-cutting and rhetoric. As a result, between 2004 and 2007, the proverbial chickens came home to roost. Browne was left tarred and feathered.

While Browne had clearly prioritized environmental issues from the start, he had reason to be less nervous about health and safety risks. The last really serious BP incident had been in 1965, when Britain's first offshore oil rig, the Sea Gem, had capsized, killing 13 crew members. But that complacency, if indeed it existed, all changed on 23 March 2005, when an explosion and fire at BP's Texas City refinery killed 15 workers and injured more than 170 others. An investigation into the accident by the Occupational Safety and Health Administration (OSHA) ultimately found over 300 safety violations and fined BP $21 million – the largest fine in OSHA history at the time.

The story did not end there. In 2007, in a separate settlement related to the explosion, BP pleaded guilty to a violation of the federal Clean Air Act and agreed to pay a $50 million fine and to make safety upgrades to the plant. Complying with the terms of the OSHA settlement was also a condition of the Justice Department agreement. Blast victims challenged the plea deal, arguing that the fine was 'trivial' in light of BP's $22 billion profits in 2006. Two years later, in 2009, OSHA imposed an additional $87 million in fines, claiming that the company had not completed all the safety upgrades required under the agreement and alleging 439 new 'wilful' safety violations. Predictably, BP announced its contestation of the fine.

A few months after the Texas City explosion, BP's Thunder Horse[12] semi-submersible oil platform in the Gulf of Mexico almost became fully submersible after Hurricane Dennis hit. The rig had been evacuated before the storm, so no one was injured, and when the platform was re-stabilized, no serious damage had been incurred. However, during repairs, it was discovered by chance that the underwater manifold was severely cracked due to poorly welded pipes. While this was not the cause of the platform's instability, the rig's design engineer admitted that it could have caused a catastrophic oil spill.

In March 2006, BP was not so 'lucky', when it was found to be criminally liable for a corroded pipe on Alaska's North Slope that leaked 200,000 gallons of oil. In August of the same year, another leak appeared and the entire Prudhoe Bay operation had to be shut down. During the investigation, a federal grand jury subpoenaed records from a Seattle engineering firm that had been hired by Alaska to

---

[12]A joint-venture with Exxon-Mobil.

evaluate BP's pipeline-maintenance record and uncovered a draft report that was highly critical of BP, but somehow turned into a final report that was largely complimentary. Member of Congress, Rep. Jay Inslee, concluded that BP had made a 'wilful, conscious decision' to 'quash that information from the public'.

By the time of Browne's undignified exit into the wings of BP history in 2007, he was widely criticized for the dual crimes of greenwashing and instilling a cost-cutting culture that was the root cause of BP's spate of safety and environmental incidents. Even the new CEO, Tony Hayward, a year before taking over, admitted that BP had 'a management style that has made a virtue of doing more for less'. In an ironic twist of fate, in June 2010 Browne was appointed efficiency czar by the new British coalition government and tasked with finding £6.2 billion ($9.9 billion) in spending cuts. Less than a month later, one of the first casualties was the government's Sustainable Development Commission (SDC), shut down on the same day that the agency released its annual report showing tens of millions of pounds worth of savings from cutting fuel, water, waste and other resources as a result of its actions in government.

After taking over, Hayward quickly showed that he was not one for green rhetoric. Less than six months into the job, he announced BP's plans to invest nearly £1.5 billion ($2.3) to extract oil from the Canadian wilderness – the so-called Alberta tar sands[13] – an action which earned it a *Guardian* newspaper headline as 'the biggest environmental crime in history'.[14] Greenpeace claims that it takes about 29 kg of CO_2 to produce a barrel of oil conventionally, but as much as 125 kg for tar sands oil. It also believes the production threatens a

---

[13]In fact, Browne had sold BP's interests in the tar sands in 1999. But claims that the tar sands represent the biggest stock of oil outside Saudi Arabia obviously proved irresistible to Hayward.

[14]In hindsight, they might have reserved that headline for the Deepwater Horizon spill a few years later.

vast forest wilderness, greater than the size of England and Wales, which forms part of one of the world's biggest carbon sinks.

Two years later, Hayward's apparent 'back to the petroleum' strategy gained momentum when BP announced that it had shut down its alternative energy headquarters in London, accepted the resignation of its clean energy boss and imposed cuts in the alternative energy budget – from $1.4 billion (£850 million) in 2008 to between $500 million and $1 billion in 2009. Bizarrely, Hayward used this occasion to stress that BP remained as committed as ever to exploring new energy sources. No wonder *Grist* journalist Joseph Romm responded with an incredulous rant: 'Seriously, they gut the program and claim it is "reinforcement" of their commitment. Perhaps BP stands for "Beyond Prevarication" or "Beyond Pinocchio".'

Today, all of this history – the story of Browne, of Hayward and of BP – seems like a dress rehearsal for the main event. I am referring of course to the catastrophic 2010 Gulf of Mexico oil spill. On 20 April, an explosion and fire on the Deepwater Horizon drilling rig killed 11 workers and injured 17 others. The rig sank and the incident caused the wellhead on the ocean floor to start gushing oil. After numerous failed attempts, the oil flow was stopped for the first time with a temporary cap 87 days, 184 million gallons and one CEO later[15]. Time will tell whether this temporary fix – and the proposed permanent 'solution' in the form of relief wells – will prove conclusive.

Understandably, at the time of writing, estimates of the scale and conse-quences of the disaster still vary considerably, and will continue to change over time. However, on 17 July, the *Guardian* newspaper gath-ered the following numbers from the Associated Press and Friends of the Earth: $30 billion cost to BP (including a $20 billion damages fund); 444 sea turtles and 1,387 birds found dead; 572 miles of shoreline oiled;

---

[15]Hayward was forced to resign on 27 July 2010.

2,700 square miles of visible slick; 83,927 square miles closed to fishing; 1.82 million gallons of dispersant chemicals applied; and a $336 million market value of the spilled oil. One number that is hard to forget is that BP's share price lost 50% of its value in 50 days. Not surprisingly, speculation was rife about whether the company would survive intact, or whether it would be taken over, merged or disaggregated.

The lawsuits also started coming thick and fast. By 16 June, it faced more than 225 lawsuits in 11 US states. According to *Bloomberg*, investors in three states, including Louisiana and Alaska, have sued BP's board of directors for allegedly causing more than $50 billion in shareholder losses by failing to implement safety policies that would have prevented the spill. In a separate class-action lawsuit in Florida, the company is accused of 'a pattern' of criminal acts including fraud. On 16 July, BP announced that it had already paid $201 million to more than 32,000 claimants, including fishermen, who have received $32 million, and shrimpers, who have received $18 million. In addition, about $77 million has been paid for loss of income to a variety of occupations including deckhands and employees of seafood processing plants and other businesses.

The 'breaking news' as I write this chapter is that BP has admitted using Photoshop to exaggerate oil spill command centre activity. The oil spill has become a story that will run and run, like a snowball changing shape, gathering weight and increasing destruction as it goes. Many questions for now remain unanswered: Will BP recover its reputation? Will the sacrifice of Hayward be enough to quench the blood-lust of critics? Will this be chalked up as the worst environmental disaster in history? Will we look back on the Macondo blowout as the inadvertent tipping point that ushers in a new low-carbon future? Students, professors and CSR wonks will study this case for years to come. But for the purposes of this book and this chapter, it is simply the latest drama in the BP saga – the story of a corporate leader in the Age of Management that managed to become a poster for the Age of Marketing.

Magic tricks and military tactics

Why is BP such a good example of the Age of Marketing, which is charac-terised by misdirection? We must begin by asking what is meant by misdi-rection. Most commonly, it refers to a technique used when performing magic tricks – one hand distracts (often using a shiny object like a coin), while the other performs the deception. That is why we say 'the hand is quicker than the eye' and we are victims of a 'sleight of hand'. In the movie *Swordfish* the main character, Gabriel, reminds us that 'what the eyes see and the ears hear, the mind believes'. A typical distraction method is to use a large gesture (like dramatic sweeping arm movements) to conceal a small gesture (like using a hand to quickly hide an object).

One of the greatest modern maestros of misdirection is British TV celebrity illusionist Derren Brown. In his *Trick of the Mind* programmes, he tells us that he achieves his results using a combination of 'magic, suggestion, psy-chology, misdirection and showmanship'. One of my favourite set-ups is where Brown simultaneously plays nine of Britain's top chess players, including two Grand Masters. He seats them in a circle and makes a move against each player, one at a time, achieving a remarkable four wins, three losses and two draws. Unbeknown to them, what he was really doing was remembering and mimicking the moves of players opposite each other; hence, they were not playing him, but each other.

In sports, we have misdirection in the form of the feint in fencing and box-ing, which involves attacking into one line with the intention of switching to another line before the attack is completed. Similarly, in American foot-ball, there is the counter trey, where the offensive team feigns rushing one way, then attacks the defence in the opposite direction. Also in rugby we have the time-honoured 'dummy pass' or 'dummy runner'.

Apart from sport, history is also full of military examples of feint attacks and feint retreats, used to deceive enemies. For example, during the Battle of Hastings the Norman cavalry feigned retreat. As a result, the pursuing Saxons forfeited the advantage of height and the line was broken, providing the opportunity to fight in single handed combat on a neutral vantage point. Another famous feint retreat is the Parthian shot, whereby the Parthian (ancient Iranian) mounted archers would feign retreat; then, at full gallop, turn their bodies to face and shoot the chasing enemy.

Not surprisingly, misdirection is also a favourite tool of government intelligence agencies. One popular tactic is called the 'limited hangout'. Victor Marchetti, a former special assistant to the Deputy Director of the CIA and author of *Propaganda and Disinformation: How the CIA Manufactures History*, explains:

> A limited hangout is spy jargon for a favourite and frequently used gimmick of the clandestine professionals. When their veil of secrecy is shredded and they can no longer rely on a phony cover story to misinform the public, they resort to admitting – sometimes even volunteering – some of the truth while still managing to withhold the key and damaging facts in the case. The public, however, is usually so intrigued by the new information that it never thinks to pursue the matter further.

Criminals, of course, know misdirection well, especially pickpockets. Often working in teams, the pickpocket or their partners in crime will typically ask a question or bump into their victim to distract them from the thievery in progress. Dickens' timeless pickpocket Fagin, in the musical version of Oliver Twist, sings: 'Dear old gent passing by/Something nice takes his eye/Everything's clear, attack the rear/Get in and pick-a-pocket or two.'

In misdirection, what is said is as important as what is done. Beyond simple lying (which is an all-too-common technique in and of itself), the use of psychobabble and technobabble has become especially rife. 'Psychobabble' was coined by author and journalist Richard Dean Rosen in a 1975 *New York Times* cover story of the same title. Although it initially referred to the misuse of psychological terms, today it is generalized to mean the use of jargon, buzzwords and highly esoteric language to give an impression of plausibility through mystification, misdirection, and obfuscation. Technobabble is used in a similar way in an attempt to create a pseudoscientific impression that will enhance credibility.

Using smoke and mirrors

So much for the concept of misdirection. What about its application in business? The tobacco industry is a past master in the art of marketing-led deception. For decades, as research on the negative health impacts of smoking piled up, the industry sponsored a campaign of disinformation and deception. Let's start with what we know about tobacco. According to the World Health Organization (WHO), 'no other consumer product is as dangerous, or kills as many people. Tobacco kills more than AIDS, legal drugs, illegal drugs, road accidents, murder and suicide combined.' Of everyone alive today, 500 million will eventually be killed by smoking, and while 0.1 billion people died from tobacco use in the 20th century, ten times as many will die from the same cause in the 21st century.

This is not simply a health issue, but also an economic crisis. In America alone, smoking costs the economy $76 billion in health costs and lost productivity. Smoking-related diseases account for 6% of all health costs in the USA and, on average, a smoker takes 6.16 days of sick leave, as compared with 3.86 for non-smokers. Of all the trash collected in the USA in 1996, cigarette butts accounted for 20%. There are indirect costs as well. Every year 1 million fires are started by children using cigarette lighters. In 1997, China's worst forest fire was caused by cigarettes and killed 300 people, as well as making 5,000 homeless and destroying 1.3 million hectares of land. In 2000, fires caused by smoking reportedly cost $27 billion and killed 300,000 people.

The debate about the ethics of industry-sponsored research and the practice of misdirection by Big Tobacco reached its zenith when, in 1994, the CEOs of seven of America's largest tobacco companies[16] testified before the House Subcommittee on Health and the Environment of Congress, all denying that cigarettes are addictive. They all lied under oath.

---

[16]Philip Morris USA, RJ Reynolds Tobacco Company, US Tobacco, American Tobacco Company, Lorillard Tobacco Company, Liggett Group, Brown and Williamson Tobacco Company.

Two years later, an investigative article in *Vanity Fair* entitled 'The Man Who Knew Too Much' told the true story of Jeffrey Wigand, a research chemist working for the tobacco company, who planned to go on the *60 Minutes* TV show to expose the lies and deception of the industry, including the CEOs that he labelled 'The Seven Dwarves'. The story was later turned into the 1996 movie *The Insider* starring Russell Crowe as Wigand, which was nominated for seven Academy Awards (including Best Picture, Actor and Director) and five Golden Globes. Asked in an interview to separate fact from fiction in the movie, Wigand replied:

> Was I followed by an ex-FBI agent in the employ of Brown & Williamson? Yes. Was there a bullet found in my mailbox in January 1996? Yes. Did someone threaten to harm my family if I told the truth about the inner workings of the tobacco company I worked for? Yes. Did the tobacco industry attempt to undermine my integrity with a 500 page smear campaign? Yes.

The industry took another public relations hit in 2005, with the release of the movie, *Thank You for Smoking*. It is a satirical comedy that follows the machinations of Big Tobacco's chief spokesman Nick Naylor, who engages in PR-spin on behalf of cigarettes while trying to remain a role model for his 12-year-old son. Among the more amusing black humour scenes is one where Naylor and his friends – a firearm lobbyist and an alcohol lobbyist – meet every week and jokingly call themselves the 'Merchants of Death' or 'The MOD Squad'.

Of course, Hollywood represents the lighter end of a far more serious and significant anti-tobacco lobby that has built momentum over the past two decades. We have simultaneously seen a United Nations WHO campaign and numerous governments passing legislation restricting smoking in public places and banning nearly all forms of tobacco advertising. The tobacco companies themselves have been scrambling to regain their lost credibility and to present a more responsible face, seemingly with some success.

For example, companies like British American Tobacco (BAT) have engaged in extensive stakeholder consultation exercises and, since 2001, their businesses in more than 40 markets have produced Social Reports, many of which have won awards from organizations as diverse as the United Nations Environment Programme, PricewaterhouseCoopers and the Association of Certified Chartered Accountants. BAT has also been ranked in the Dow Jones Sustainability Index, the FTSE Ethical Bonus Index and Business in the Community (BITC) Corporate Responsibility Index, and they funded Nottingham University's International Centre for CSR.[17] If these accolades and associations are to be believed, 'responsible tobacco' is not an oxymoron after all.

Sowing the seeds of doubt

You might be forgiven for thinking that tobacco is an outlier. After all, no other industry (with the possible exception of armaments) kills people so systematically and publicly. Yet the tactics of misdirection are pervasive in businesses across all sectors. If anything, Big Tobacco simply served as inspiration for others to follow. For example, speaking about the climate change denial lobby, former US senator Tim Wirth, who spearheaded environmental issues as an undersecretary of State in the Clinton administration, concluded that 'they patterned what they did after the tobacco industry. Both figured, sow enough doubt, call the science uncertain and in dispute. That's had a huge impact on both the public and Congress.'

In a 2007 article for *Newsweek* called 'The Truth About Denial', Sharon Begley warned that:

> Outside Hollywood, Manhattan and other habitats of the chattering classes, the denial machine is running at full throttle – and continuing to

---

[17]I was a beneficiary, since I did my PhD in CSR at Nottingham University. Several of the university's medical academics reportedly resigned as a result of the sponsorship.

shape both government policy and public opinion. Since the late 1980s, this well-coordinated, well-funded campaign by contrarian scientists, free-market think tanks and industry has created a paralyzing fog of doubt around climate change. Through advertisements, op-eds, lobbying and media attention, greenhouse doubters (they hate being called deniers) argued first that the world is not warming; measurements indicating otherwise are flawed, they said. Then they claimed that any warming is natural, not caused by human activities. Now they contend that the looming warming will be minuscule and harmless.

This 'denial machine' found a temporary home in the previously mentioned Global Climate Coalition (GCC). The GCC, comprising mainly US companies with vested interests in the status quo (including virtually all of the large chemical, oil and motor companies[18]), was set up in 1989 after the first Intergovernmental Panel on Climate Change (IPCC) report, ostensibly 'to coordinate business participation in the international policy debate on the issue of global climate change and global warming'. Translation: To lobby against the emerging consensus of climate science (i.e. the IPCC, comprising around 2,500 of the world's most respected scientists) and policy development (i.e. the Kyoto Protocol, signed and ratified by 187 states, excluding the USA).

Apart from funding and highlighting any studies that sowed doubt in the public and political mind, the GCC distributed documents and videos raising concerns about the economic impacts of climate action and the potential benefits of global warming for agricultural yields. They also sponsored the Global Climate Information Project (GCIP), which ran anti-Kyoto Protocol advertisements stating 'It's Not Global and It Won't Work' and 'Americans will pay the price . . . 50 cents more for every gallon of gasoline'. It is perhaps not surprising that among the GCC's PR spin-doctors was Steven Milloy – who, according to investigative journalist

---

[18]Their website claimed that 'GCC members collectively represent more than 6 million businesses, companies and corporations in virtually every sector of U.S. business, agriculture and forestry'.

George Monbiot, was first funded by tobacco company Philip Morris – and Bruce Harrison, ironically considered 'the founder of green PR' because of his work for the pesticide industry in the 1960s, when he helped lead the attack on author Rachel Carson and her critical treatise *Silent Spring*.

Although the GCC became defunct in 2002, once its members realized that public and political opinion was turning against them, climate denial is far from over. A 2007 report by the Union of Concerned Scientists, entitled *Smoke, Mirrors & Hot Air*, documents how ExxonMobil adopted the tobacco industry's disinformation tactics, as well as some of the same organizations and personnel, to cloud the scientific understanding of climate change and delay action on the issue. According to the report, ExxonMobil funnelled nearly $16 million between 1998 and 2005 to a network of 43 advocacy organizations that seek to confuse the public on global warming science.

Hanging greenwashing out to dry

While many of these examples – and I could cite countless more, from the automotive, agricultural, chemicals and other industries – represent little more than the familiar toxic mix of old-fashioned dirty lobby tactics, many companies today in engage in far more subtle and seemingly plausible campaigns of misdirection – investing in environmental management systems, producing sustainability reports, and performing supply chain audits. Each of these actions is, on its own merits, laudable and to be encouraged; applauded even. But all too often, they are used as a smokescreen to mask the more damaging impacts and irresponsible practices of business.

Behind these actions lies a pervasive driver. According to the UN Global Compact and Accenture's 2010 CEO survey, three corporate attributes – brand, trust and reputation – were consistently cited by CEOs as their primary reason for acting on sustainability. Other drivers that were unrelated to PR were cited only half as much, namely the potential for revenue growth and cost reduction (cited by 44%), personal motivation (42%), consumer and customer demand (39%) and employee engagement and retention (31%). What's more, 48% of CEOs cited competing strategic priorities as a barrier to their sustainability efforts.

As we saw in the BP case, 'greenwash' has become one of the popular labels applied to PR-driven misdirection by companies on environmental issues. The word was coined by environmentalist David Bellamy in the 1980s and plays off of the concept of 'whitewashing' – literally painting over the cracks to cover up inherent faults. In 1999, the *Oxford English Dictionary* added the term, defining it as: 'Disinformation disseminated by an organization, so as to present an environmentally responsible public image; a public image of environmental responsibility promulgated by or for an organization, but perceived as being unfounded or intentionally misleading'. Jose Lopez, EVP of Operations at Nestlé admits that 'there is probably out there an environment for pretenders, for the greenwashers. It's going to get harder and harder to tell apart the greenwasher from the real guy. The reason is, we have a lot of information on what constitutes good sustainability practice', i.e. it's easier to copy apparently credible behaviour.

One classic example was an advertisement run by Shell which has a picture of a factory with flowers coming out of the smoke-stacks and claiming: 'We use our waste CO_2 to grow flowers'. There was a grain of truth in the claim - in the Netherlands the company did capture CO_2 and use it in floral hothouses. However, since Shell only used 0.325% of its CO_2 output in this way, the Advertising Standards Authority banned the advertisement, following complaints. As a result of this kind of greenwash, the UK's Committee of Advertising Practice (CAP) Code, enforced by the Advertising Standards Authority, created a clause for environmental claims in 1995. Since 1998, it has also published a non-binding 'Green Claims Code', advising advertisers on how best to make good claims. Despite this, greenwashing complaints, the majority of which are upheld, continue to rise year-on-year.

One rather fun, yet informative, publication is 'The Greenwash Guide' by Futerra. It lists 10 Signs of Greenwash, which include: (1) fluffy language (words or terms with no clear meaning, e.g. 'eco-friendly'); (2) green products versus a dirty company (such as efficient light bulbs made in a factory which pollutes rivers); (3) suggestive pictures (green images that indicate an un-justified green impact, e.g. flowers blooming from exhaust pipes); (4) irrelevant claims (emphasizing one tiny green attribute when everything else is un-green); (5) best in class (declaring you are slightly greener than the rest, even if the rest are pretty terrible); (6) just not credible ('eco friendly' cigarettes anyone? 'Greening' a dangerous product doesn't make it safe); (7) gobbledygook (jargon and information that only a scientist could check or understand); (8) imaginary friends (a 'label' that looks like third party endorsement . . . except it's made up); (9) no proof (it could be right, but where's the evidence?); and (10) out-right lying (totally fabricated claims or data).

Of course, this kind of misdirection does not only apply to environmental issues. After the launch of the UN Global Compact, companies started to be accused of 'bluewash' – a reference to the blue UN logo and businesses using association with the United Nations to appear more responsible than they really are. Likewise, although I haven't heard the term, I can imagine the 'redwash' brush being applied to companies claiming social, community or labour responsibility that masks their real negative impacts on society.

The invisible hand of marketing

It is not hard to see why a lot of the blame for misdirection gets laid on the marketing function in companies, especially corporate communications, advertising and public relations departments. A survey by the Institute of Business Ethics of 60 codes of ethics from a range of sectors and countries showed that 48% do not mention marketing or give any guidance to staff on what responsible, values-led marketing might be. The Marketing Society talks about the 'creation of customer-led demand' in their definition of marketing, which is another way of saying: artificially stimulating 'needs' – or more often, 'wants' or 'greeds'.[19]

Examples of manipulation are not hard to come by. In 1990, Volvo ran a television advertisement that showed a monster truck driving over a line of cars. Only the Volvo escaped unscathed, and for good reason – all of the other cars had been sabotaged and the Volvo had been reinforced. When the misrepresentation came to light, Volvo earned itself a $300,000 fine from the state of Texas and had to publish a 'corrective statement' in the *Wall Street Journal*.

In 2002, Sony Ericsson paid 60 actors to pose as 'fake tourists' in New York and ask passersby to help them to operate the new camera phone, while they extolled its virtues and never disclosed their commercial relationship with the company. In another version, actresses were hired to generate interest in their phones by playing an interactive version of the game of Battleships at either end of a bar. The scam was eventually exposed by the *Wall Street Journal* and the *60 Minutes* television programme. Actors were also hired by McDonald's in Japan – one thousand of them – to pose as customers queuing outside a store for a newly launched burger. The idea was to create a contagion of interest and excitement, but once again their link to the company was not revealed.

This is now known as 'stealth marketing' and is widely condemned as unethical and manipulative. Of course, it becomes more difficult to police in the age of YouTube, as a stealth advertisement by Australian brand Witchery showed. An actress posted a video claiming to be on a romantic quest to find a mystery man she met in a restaurant who left his jacket behind. Needless to say, the video generated a real buzz, with over 200,000 hits, before it was revealed as a viral marketing campaign to highlight the company's expansion of its clothing line – previously only for women – to men. It was all about the jacket and nothing to do with the fictitious romance. Clever? Sure. Misdirection? Absolutely.

---

[19]As someone with an Honours degree in Marketing, I feel like I am not speaking from a position of total ignorance when I say that.

From misdirection to redirection

The Age of Marketing is summed up by a 2006 statement by Ben Verwaayen, who was CEO of the telecommunications giant BT at the time: 'Until now, corporate social responsibility has been seen in many companies as something which has to be done, a box which needs to be ticked, in all too many cases, without much enthusiasm.'

This is a view echoed by editor Daniel Franklin in *The Economist's World in 2009 Yearbook*:

> Many companies pretend that their sustainability strategy runs deeper than it really does. It has become almost obligatory for executives to claim that CSR is 'connected to the core' of corporate strategy, or that it has become 'part of the DNA.' In truth, even ardent advocates of sustainability struggle to identify more than a handful of examples. More often the activities that go under the sustainability banner are a hodgepodge of pet projects at best tenuously related to the core business.

What we need, therefore, is less misdirection and more redirection – towards genuine corporate sustainability and responsibility. A step in the right direction is the adoption of Strategic CSR (although, as we have seen from BP's example, this can also be manipulated as a form of Promotional CSR). It is therefore to the Age of Management that we now turn our attention.

CHAPTER 5

The age of management

Nearly all my money is invested in businesses in which I believe I can truly say the first thought is of the welfare of the work people employed.

—George Cadbury

Sustainable development is dependent on responsible economic growth, with business as the engine of such growth. Hence, it is critical for the planet and its people that there be a business case for sustainable development.

—Bjorn Stigson

Increasingly, we think in terms of a 'triple bottom line,' focusing on economic prosperity, environmental quality, and – the element which business has tended to overlook – social justice.

—John Elkington

If the aim for those in the vanguard over the last decade was to embed social and environmental issues into codified practices for the mainstream business community, they should be quite satisfied that this task has been well advanced.

—Simon Zadek

Box 4: The age of management – in a nutshell

Iconic leaders	Anglo American
	Cadbury
	Nike
	Shell
	Starbucks
Period	Rising from 1977, with the launch of Global Sullivan Principles, to a peak in 2010, when the ISO 26000 social responsibility standard was launched
Key ideas	Aligning CSR priorities to strategy
	Embedding CSR through management systems
	Letting voluntary codes set the bar
	Making a business case for CSR
	Trusting business to self-regulate
Commentators	Archie Carroll (author & academic)
	Daniel C. Esty and Andrew S. Winston (authors & consultants)
	David Grayson and Adrian Hobbs (authors & academics)
	Deborah Leipziger (author & consultant)
	Stephan Schmidheiny (entrepreneur & author)
References	*Business and Society: Ethics and Stakeholder Management* (Archie Carroll, 1988, 2008)
	Walking the Talk: The Business Case for Sustainable Development (Charles O. Holliday, Stephan Schmidheiny, Philip Watts & WBCSD, 2002)
	The Corporate Responsibility Codebook (Deborah Leipziger, 2003, 2010)
	Corporate Social Opportunity (David Grayson & Adrian Hobbs, 2004)
	Green to Gold: How Smart Companies Use Environmental Strategy to Innovate (Daniel C. Esty & Andrew S. Winston, 2006, 2009)

Case 4: Cadbury Brothers and Cadbury

For many, the early hours of 19 January 2010 marked the end of an era – the end of Cadbury's 186 years of independence, as it accepted the $21.8 billion takeover offer from American food giant Kraft. A few days later, Todd Stitzer resigned as chief executive and made a telling statement:

> I spent 27 years of my life at this company. I absolutely love what it stands for and what it has done . . . the whole idea that 'doing good is good for business.' The intersection of principled capitalism and commercial and financial performance is what drives people at this company. They actually believe that not only are they great confectionery marketers or sellers or manufacturers but that it means something because the Cadbury Cocoa Partnership is investing in underdeveloped farming areas or because the chocolates have been certified by Fairtrade.

Stitzer's statement speaks volumes about the legacy built up by Cadbury over nearly 200 years, and hints at more widely expressed fears that the takeover may sound the death knell for the very family values that came to define the company. The business that Cadbury became – with annual sales in excess of $8 billion from operations in 60 countries, with 45,000 employees and with some of the world's most recognized brands, from Dairy Milk Chocolate, Flake and Creme Eggs to Clorets, Stimorol and Halls – is a far cry from where it all started.

The story begins in Victorian England when John Cadbury – one of Richard Tapper Cadbury's ten children – opened his first shop in 1824 in Birmingham, alongside his father's drapery and silk business. Cadbury's store sold tea, coffee, hops, mustard and the luxury commodities of cocoa and drinking chocolate, which he prepared by grinding cocoa beans from South and Central America and the West

Indies using a mortar and pestle. Although cocoa and drinking chocolate had been available in England since the 1650s, the price tag ensured that they remained the preserve of Britain's élite.

Within this niche market, John Cadbury's product experimentation and flair for promotion ensured that his business flourished. His first advertisement placed in the *Birmingham Gazette*, stated that 'John Cadbury is desirous of introducing to particular notice "Cocoa Nibs", prepared by himself, an article affording a most nutritious beverage for breakfast'. In 1831, he opened his first factory and by 1842 was selling 16 lines of drinking chocolate and cocoa in cake and powder forms.

Not that we would have recognized those products by today's standards. For a start, they were sold in blocks, a little of which had to be scraped into a cup or saucepan and mixed with hot milk or water. More significantly, however, cocoa and drinking chocolate were balanced with potato starch and sago flour to counter the high cocoa butter content, with any number of other 'healthy ingredients' added for good measure. John Cadbury's son, George, later described the drinking chocolate as a 'comforting gruel'.

Nevertheless, business continued to prosper, not least due to the reduction in taxes on imported cocoa beans in the mid 1850s, introduced by Prime Minister William Gladstone. Cocoa and drinking chocolate was now within reach of the mass public. At the same time, Cadbury received a Royal Warrant as 'manufacturers of cocoa and chocolate to Queen Victoria'.

Despite his early commercial success, Cadbury was not all about business. He grew up in the tradition of the Society of Friends, or Quakers, a nonconformist religious group formed in the 17th century. The Quakers became known in rapidly industrializing Britain for using business to achieve social aims, such as reducing poverty, tackling injustice, improving working conditions and encouraging temperance (abstinence or reduced dependence on alcohol). Cadbury was one of these conscience-driven business pioneers, alongside fellow Quakers like Joseph Rowntree, Samuel Tuke and Joseph Fry. In fact, many well-known organizations reportedly owe a seminal influence to the Quakers, including Amnesty International, Barclays Bank, Carr's, Cornell University, Friends Provident, Greenpeace, Oxfam and Sony.

As a member of the Temperance Society, one of Cadbury's primary motivations for selling tea, coffee and hot chocolate was to provide a mass-market alternative to alcohol, which was widely regarded as an exacerbating factor in poverty and deprivation among the working classes. Cadbury also led a campaign to ban the use of child labour for sweeping chimneys and set up the Animals' Friend Society, a forerunner of the Royal Society for the Prevention of Cruelty to Animals (RSPCA).

After retiring in 1861 due to ill health, Cadbury spent much of the remaining third of his life dedicated to civic and social work in Birmingham. However, his legacy did not end there. Many of his social reform ideas were taken up and extended by his sons, Richard and George, when they took over the business, aged 25 and 21.

In their first few years, the business nearly went under. In the end, however, a combination of technological changes and product innovation saved them. After visiting a competitor's factory (the Van Houten's) in the Netherlands, they introduced a new cocoa press that removed cocoa butter from the beans, leaving a more palatable essence that became the drinking chocolate we know today. The excess cocoa butter after pressing was made into 'eating chocolate', which soon became Cadbury's flagship product: Dairy Milk chocolate.

The Cadbury brothers are credited with introducing many of England's most progressive workplace practices. One of their most significant actions was to move their factory in 1879 from the grimy city of Birmingham to Bourneville in the English countryside – to create a 'factory in a garden'. There, they provided workers with numerous facilities that exceeded Victorian standards of the day, including heated dressing rooms, kitchens, gardens, sports fields and swimming pools. The company even organized leisure outings and summer camps for employees.

Working conditions were also progressive. Cadbury was the first company in England to introduce the five-and-a-half day working week. They were also pioneers in providing medical and dental facilities, offering a pension scheme and shutting the factory on bank holidays. Initially, they provided houses for senior staff only, but George Cadbury's vision soon grew more ambitious. 'If each man could have his own house, a large garden to cultivate and healthy surroundings', he reflected, 'then there will be for them a better opportunity of a happy family life.'

And so the Bourneville Village project was conceived: 120 acres of land near the factory was acquired in 1895 and houses built for Cadbury's workers and others in the area. The motivation was not only to provide affordable, convenient accommodation for employees, but also to prevent any less sensitive developers from acquiring the land and creating an urban sprawl. In 1900, Cadbury handed over the land and houses to a Trust, which still administers the real estate, separate from the company, but with Cadbury's managers as trustees.

Reforms continued throughout the 20th century, under the leadership of the Cadbury brothers and successive generations of the family. In 1905, 'works committees' were set up to deal with matters affecting employees, which became democratically elected 'works councils' in 1918. These councils had equal representation from management and workers and focused on working conditions, health, safety, education, training and social activities for employees. In 1969, the councils were unionized and the tradition of employee participation in labour relations continues to this day.

Not surprisingly, given their progressive track record on workplace issues, Cadbury also played a key role in addressing issues of fair trade and supply chain ethics. As far back as 1905, the Cadbury brothers stopped buying cocoa from São Tomé because of poor labour conditions. As a result, they helped found the cocoa industry in Ghana. A hundred years later, Cadbury launched its first Fairtrade labelled chocolate, which was the culmination of a whole raft of responsible supply chain management initiatives, including the Cadbury Cocoa Partnership (addressing child labour in Ghana and Cote d'Ivoire), the Roundtable on Sustainable Palm Oil (RSPO), the International Cocoa Initiative (ICI) and the Better Sugar Cane Initiative (BSCI).

Through these and various internal programmes, Cadbury set itself a 2010 target of 'sustainably sourcing' at least 50% of their key agricultural raw materials (cocoa, sugar, mint, palm oil, gum arabic, liquorice, hazelnuts, almonds and raisins). They also required all 3,000 key suppliers to acknowledge the Cadbury's Human Rights and Ethical Trading (HRET) policy and to register on the Supplier Ethical Data Exchange network (SEDEX), a not-for-profit organization that uses the latest technology to enable companies to maintain and share data on labour practices in the supply chain.

Prior to their takeover by Kraft, Cadbury's HRET policy was just one of 19 corporate policies covering various aspects of responsible business practice, from environment, health and safety to marketing, ethics and stakeholder engagement. Beyond these internal commitments, Cadbury also made very public commitments to responsibility, for example as a signatory to the Courtauld Agreement, WRAP (Waste & Resources Action Programme), the UN Millennium Development Goals (via the Business Call to Action) and the UN Global Compact.

Cadbury's regularly assessed their performance across all these numerous programmes by allowing themselves to be rated on Business in the Community's (BITC) Corporate Responsibility Index, the Dow Jones Sustainability Index, the FTSE4 Good Index and the Carbon Disclosure Project's Climate Change Leadership Index. They also used the Global Reporting Initiative's (GRI) G3 Sustainability

Reporting Guidelines to produce annual Corporate Responsibility & Sustainability reports.

In the last of these reports (2007/08), after consulting with over 400 different stakeholders, they concluded that the issues of most concern – with high potential impact on the company and high societal and investor interest – included food safety, health (including nutrition and obesity), financial performance, environment impacts and sustainable sourcing (plus ten other issues rated lower).

Responding to the health issue, Cadbury introduced a 12 Point Nutrition Action Plan in 2004, and a No Genetically Modified Organisms (GMOs) policy in Europe (elsewhere they were 'guided by the customer' and clearly labelled whether products contained GMOs). In response to environmental concerns, Cadbury bought Green & Blacks (an organic chocolate company) in 2005 and launched a 'Purple Goes Green' initiative in 2007, with 'delivery tracks' across six dimensions: energy, packaging, water, transport, waste and effluent and hazardous materials.

All these are just a sample of the social, environmental and ethical governance initiatives that are described in their 100+ page Corporate Responsibility & Sustainability report. I expect that John Cadbury, and all the generations of Cadbury that succeeded him, would have been justifiably proud of how the company turned out; and especially how its successive leaders and employees took a legacy of Quaker inspired values and built a multinational company with one of the most recognized and trusted brands in the world.

No wonder there was more than a hint of pride and sadness in CEO Todd Stitzer's parting words. He might have quoted W.B. Yeats[20] as he handed over the keys to Kraft: 'I have spread my dreams under your feet. Tread softly because you tread on my dreams.'

---

[20]He didn't. This is from 'He Wishes for the Cloths of Heaven'.

Business ethics through the ages

By all accounts, Cadbury is an outstanding example of a company that made a successful journey from an early pioneer in industrial welfare – where, as George Cadbury put it, 'the first thought is of the welfare of the work people employed' – to a modern, global, responsible company of the 21st century in which 'sustainable business practices are the bedrock of our strategy, represented through our Sustainability Commitments, namely to: promote responsible consumption; ensure ethical & sustainable sourcing; prioritize quality & safety; reduce carbon, water use & packaging; nurture & reward colleagues; and invest in communities'.

Cadbury are, in short, a prototypical company of the Age of Management and I will return to some of the features they encapsulate later in the chapter. To begin with, however, I want to explore how we got here – looking at a brief history of the corporate sustainability and responsibility movements.

Much like the origins of philanthropy, we can go back many thousands of years to discover the wellspring of responsible business practices. One of the clearest threads of ethical debate relating to business has been the practice of usury – or charging excessive interest on loans.

Usury can be traced back approximately four thousand years and during its subsequent history it has been repeatedly condemned, prohibited, scorned and restricted, mainly on moral, ethical, religious and legal grounds. Among its most visible and vocal critics have been the religious institutions of Hinduism, Buddhism, Judaism, Islam and Christianity, as well as ancient Western philosophers, politicians and various modern socio-economic reformers.

The earliest references to usury are in the Hindu *Vedic* (2,000–1,400 BC) and *Sutra* (700–100 BC) texts, as well as the Buddhist *Jatakas* (600–400 BC). Among the Ancient Western philosophers who condemned usury can be named Plato, Aristotle, the two Catos, Cicero, Seneca and Plutarch. The criticism of usury in Islam was well established during the Prophet Mohammed's life and reinforced by his teachings in the Holy Quran, dating back to around 600 AD. The original word used for usury in this text was *riba* which literally means 'excess or addition'. In Judaism, the Hebrew word for interest is *neshekh*, literally meaning 'a bite'.

In Christianity, the anti-usury movement reached its zenith in 1311 when Pope Clement V made the ban on usury absolute. This stance gradually weakened over the centuries, especially with the rise of pro-capitalist Protestantism, but even Luther and Calvin expressed reservations. Calvin, for instance, set out seven crucial instances in which interest remained sinful. Furthermore, the architects of capitalism and modern economic theory, Adam Smith and John Maynard Keynes, both felt that interest should be strictly controlled, to prevent its negative effects.

And what where these negative effects? There are six principal arguments against the practice of usury, namely that: it represents unearned income; it is a form of double-billing; it exploits the needy; it is a mechanism for the inequitable redistribution of wealth; it is an agent of economic instability; and it results in discounting the future. These critiques are explored in more detail in a paper I co-authored with Alastair McIntosh and published in *Accounting, Business & Financial History* in 1998. For the purposes of this chapter, I simply use them to illustrate that there has been a raging debate about the ethics of business for millennia.

The industrial welfare movement

The responsible business movement has more recent, direct and concrete roots through the emergence of the Industrial Welfare Movement in Victorian times, of which Cadbury was a part. As Archie Carroll describes in *The Oxford Handbook of Corporate Social Responsibility*, one of the pioneers was John H. Patterson, founder of National Cash Register in 1884. Much like Cadbury, he ensured the provision of hospital clinics, bath-houses, lunchrooms, recreational facilities and even profit sharing for his employees. He became especially known for constructing the first 'daylight factory' buildings in 1893, with floor-to-ceiling glass windows that let in light and could be opened to let in fresh air.

Around that time, the limits of industrial welfare were being challenged and tested in the courts. In a landmark case of 1883, West Cork Railroad tried to compensate employees for job losses when the company was closing down. However, the court forbade any payments, ruling that it could only spend money for the purposes of carrying on the business. Around the same time, the piano manufacturer Steinway was also taken to court, because it had bought a tract of land to be used for a church, library and school for employees. In this case, however, the court condoned the expenditure, since it could be regarded as a strategy for improving employee relations.

Hence, right back in the 1880s, the fault line between business interests and stakeholder interests was drawn, and the need to make a 'business case' for responsibility was firmly established. Bear in mind that this was still the era during which a Charter of Incorporation was only bestowed on those businesses that were socially useful – for example, water utilities or railroads. As legal academic and author of *The Corporation*, Joel Bakan, put it to me in 2008:

> The original notion of the corporation was that the sovereign would grant the status of corporation to a group of business people in order to acquit themselves of some responsibility to create something that was in the public good. . . . The notion that this was simply about creating wealth for the owners of the company was alien.

How different the world might have been if this principle remained in force. However, by the end of the Civil War, charters were available under any business pretext and were nearly impossible to revoke.

Another American pioneer in the Industrial Welfare Movement was Pullman Palace Car Company, which created a model industrial community in 1893 in the south of Chicago (much like Cadbury's Bourneville Village), including higher standards of housing, lighting, playgrounds, a church, an arcade, a theatre, a hotel and (somewhat more dubiously) a casino. The crucial lesson from these 19th century trailblazers was that they clearly understood that treating employees well was not only a noble thing to do, but was also good for business.[21]

Despite these early signs of enlightenment, the Industrial Welfare Movement was stopped in its tracks in the early 20th century by the combined forces of Frederick Taylor's doctrine of scientific management – based on his time-and-motion productivity studies – and the commercial success of Henry Ford's production line model. Glimmers of hope re-emerged with Elton Mayo's Hawthorne Works experiments of the 1920s, showing that a better working environment (lighting, heating, etc.) resulted in improved productivity. In fact, many concepts, like 'group dynamics', 'teamwork' and organizational 'social systems', all stem from Mayo's pioneering efforts. Even here, however, as with the court cases 50 years earlier, the insidious business case principle was being reinforced: better treatment of employees was only justified if it improved profitability.

Cracks in the industrial edifice

By the late 1930s, we see the seeds of an intellectual movement being sown, with the first books exploring social responsibility emerging, including Chester Barnard's *The Functions of the Executive* (1938), J.M. Clark's *Social Control of Business* (1939) and Theodore Krep's *Measurement of the Social Performance of Business* (1940). These were not simply academic ramblings, but rather reflected the growing sentiments in the populace at large.

Asked in a 1946 *Fortune Magazine* survey, 'Do you think that businessmen should recognize responsibility for the consequences of their actions in a sphere wider than that covered by their profit-and-loss statements?', 93.5% of the American public said 'yes'. And asked, 'What proportion of the businessmen you know would you rate as having a social consciousness of this sort?', most responded either 'about half' or 'about three quarters'.

---

[21] It must be noted that not everyone was a fan these industrial towns. For many, they represented a paternal system of control, censorship and manipulation by the company.

Just a few years later, we see the first cracks in the great edifice of industrial growth starting to appear, with Aldo Leopold, self-appointed spokesperson for the decades-old conservation movement, saying in his *Sand County Almanac* that 'our bigger-and-better society is like a hypochondriac, so obsessed with its own economic health as to have lost the capacity to remain healthy'. American economist Howard Bowen reflected on this seminal movement in his 1953 book *Social Responsibilities of Business*, using the term 'social responsibility' for the first time in a book title and earning him the accolade in some people's eyes as 'the father of corporate social responsibility'.

However, it wasn't until 1962 that business received its first serious critique for a failure of social responsibility, in the form of Rachel Carson's *Silent Spring*. In this scientific treatise, Carson lambasts the chemical industry for the accumulation of toxins like DDT in the environment, and their deadly bio-accumulative consequences up through the food chain. Indeed, many today regard *Silent Spring* as the birth sign of the modern environmental movement. Her poetic words still haunt and echo down the ages:

> It was a spring without voices. On the mornings that had once throbbed with the dawn chorus of robins, catbirds, doves, jays, wrens and scores of other bird voices, there was now no sound; only silence lay over the fields and woods and marsh. Even the streams were now lifeless. No witchcraft, no enemy action had silenced the rebirth of new life in this stricken world. The people had done it themselves.

In 1965, big business received its second shock attack, this time from legal activist Ralph Nader, regarded by many as the 'Father of the Modern US Consumer Movement' (apart from being a serial minority candidate for the US Presidency). In his book *Unsafe at Any Speed: The Designed-In Dangers of the American Automobile*, he went to war with the auto industry in general and General Motors in particular. 'A major contemporary problem', he said, 'is how to control the power of economic interests which ignore the harmful effects of their applied science and technology.'

Spaceship earth on a collision course

Around the same time, Kenneth Boulding, Barbara Ward and Buckminster Fuller gave the public a metaphor to visualize society's growing predicament: 'Spaceship Earth' – the planet as a closed system (apart from solar input).[22] 'One of the reasons we are struggling inadequately today', said Fuller, 'is that we reckon our costs on too shortsighted a basis and are later overwhelmed with the unexpected costs brought about by our shortsightedness.'

It was precisely those 'unexpected costs' that the Club of Rome decided to make explicit when they commissioned their *Limits to Growth* study, published in 1972. The findings were based on the world's first global computer simulation of five major trends: accelerating industrialization, rapid population growth, widespread malnutrition, depletion of non-renewable resources, and a deteriorating environment. Their overall conclusion, based on a range of scenarios, was that 'the behaviour mode of the system is clearly that of overshoot and collapse'.

Today, over 35 years later, co-author of the report Jorgen Randers sees no deviation from the path. In 2008, he told me:

> The real message of the *Limits to Growth* is that on a finite earth with rapid physical expansion, one must be very careful in not postponing action when problems start to emerge. You need to act very quickly. . . . And of course now, with climate change, we are seeing exactly the phenomenon that we were describing. So most likely this will be the overshoot and collapse, or an example of this, that we spoke about.

Another intellectual that added his voice of warning in 1973 was E.F. Schumacher, author of *Small is Beautiful*. 'Economic growth', he said, has become 'the abiding interest, if not the obsession, of all modern societies.'

---

[22]Kenneth Boulding's paper 'The Economics of the Coming Spaceship Earth'; Barbara Ward's *Spaceship Earth* (1966); and Buckminster Fuller's *Operating Manual for Spaceship Earth* (1969).

As a result, we have 'ever bigger machines, entailing ever bigger concentrations of economic power and exerting ever greater violence against the environment'. These 'big is beautiful' trends do not represent progress. On the contrary, he said, 'they are a denial of wisdom. Wisdom demands a new orientation of science and technology towards the organic, the gentle, the non-violent, the elegant and beautiful.'

So by the end of the 1970s, it was clear that 'Spaceship Earth' was on a collision course. Moreover, it was clear that it was our industrial model of growth that was propelling humanity towards self-destruction. Right around that time, British scientist James Lovelock gave us a theory of how Earth might react, given the threat. I am referring, of course, to the Gaia Hypothesis – the idea that the Earth acts like a living, self-regulating organism. When I interviewed him in 2008, Lovelock reflected on our current state of affairs:

> Living things, when threatened or stressed, at first resist – and the [Earth] system has been doing that for quite a while now . . . But somewhere around about 1900 we began to go beyond the limit. So now the system is doing the other thing that living things do and fleeing to a safe place that it knows. And the safe place which it's been at many times before is the hot regime where the global temperature is 5 or 6 degrees planet-wide hotter than now.

Towards a theory of responsibility

Business was not deaf to these criticisms and warnings, nor completely unresponsive. In the West, labour conditions were steadily improving, the discipline of Human Resources was emerging and in 1977, Reverend Leon Sullivan launched what might be regarded as the first CSR code – the Sullivan Principles, which set out the minimum acceptable labour practices for companies to remain in South Africa, which was still under the discriminatory system of apartheid. Several companies had also begun tackling the issues of waste. For example, 3M's Pollution Prevention Pays programme began in 1975, avoiding more than 2.6 billion pounds of pollutants and

Figure 1 Archie Carroll's CSR Pyramid[23]

saving more than $1 billion over the next 30 years. Germany was also a forerunner, launching its Blue Angel eco-label in 1978. What was still missing, however, was widespread agreement of what exactly were business's obligations to society.

This void was filled by American academic Archie Carroll who, in 1979, provided the first popular definition of corporate social responsibility (CSR), namely that it is the economic, legal, ethical and discretionary or philanthropic expectations that society has of business.[24] Based on subsequent empirical work, the definition was later presented as a pyramid of weighted importance (Figure 1 above), with economic responsibility at the base (i.e. most important), followed by legal and ethical dimensions and philanthropy at the apex (i.e. least emphasized). Despite considerable evolution in theory and practice since the 'CSR Pyramid' was first published in 1991, it has – together with Carroll's four-part definition – endured remarkably well.

---

[23]Carroll, A.B., 1991. The Pyramid of Corporate Social Responsibility: Toward the Moral Management of Organizational Stakeholders, *Business Horizons*, July-August.

[24]Carroll, A.B. (1979) 'A Three-Dimensional Model of Corporate Performance' *Academy of Management Review* 4(4): 497–505.

One of the reasons for the CSR Pyramid's longevity – besides its intuitive logic and business-friendly conceptualization – is that it can be applied in practice. For example, Unilever did two studies to investigate its economic impacts in Indonesia and South Africa. What they found was that in Indonesia, while they employed around 7,000 directly, they also created over 293,000 jobs indirectly through the supply chain. In South Africa, the ratio of direct to indirect jobs was 1:22. That in itself is a remarkable economic contribution, but it represents only one of numerous 'economic multipliers' identified by the International Business Leaders Forum (IBLF).

According the IBLF, in addition to creating jobs, companies generate investment, produce safe products and services, pay taxes, invest in human capital, establish local business linkages, spread international business standards, support technology transfer, and build physical and institutional infrastructure. Recognizing this greater set of economic impacts and contributions, beyond simply generating returns for shareholders, many companies are now including Economic Value Added statements in their annual reports.

The legal dimension of Carroll's CSR Pyramid is more controversial, since many regard social responsibility as a purely voluntary activity. Pragmatically speaking, however, many governments are weak, failing or corrupt and without the capacity to effectively police or enforce implementation of their legislation. Hence, voluntary legal compliance becomes genuine social responsibility. Legal responsibility also raises issues like tax avoidance, negative political lobbying and bribery and corruption, all of which should be acknowledged and addressed by responsible companies.

The voluntary versus mandatory debate

Of course, legal issues vary by region and by country. I can still remember a safety, health and environmental governance audit on a chemical company that I did when I was Director of Sustainability Services at KPMG. We visited facilities in five countries – South Africa, Germany, Netherlands, Italy and the US – and one of the things we asked was for their records of legal non-compliance, including fines and penalties. This was a relatively trivial matter in all countries but one, the United States. First, they had not just a few but thousands of non-compliances, which probably said more about the country's onerous legal requirements than the company's negligence. For instance, when we asked to see their air pollution permit documentation, they pointed to an entire bookshelf of lever arch files. Second, they didn't know what liability these non-compliances represented, because they were in constant negotiation with the government (applying the Federal Sentencing Guidelines principles) over the exact settlement amount of these.

On the question of legal responsibilities, I am often asked at talks I give whether CSR should be legislated. My answer is always the same: That depends what you mean. If you mean, should the government require companies to spend a certain percentage of their profits on CSR-related activities, as is being proposed in India, the answer is *no*. After all, that's just another kind of tax. What we need is for governments to have *effective* regulation (and enforcement) of the issues that CSR is trying to tackle – pollution, labour conditions, environmental degradation, human rights, corruption, etc. Take transparency for example. According to 2010 research across 30 countries by UNEP, KPMG, GRI and the Stellenbosch Business School, there are already 142 country standards or laws with some sustainability reporting requirement or guidance, of which 65% are mandatory.

Moving up a level on Carroll's CSR Pyramid, the issue of ethical responsibility could be the subject of an entire book itself.[25] With ancient roots in philosophy, business ethics has exploded as an area of study and practice, especially since it became strongly linked to the corporate governance movement of the 1990s. The financial scandals of Enron and WorldCom in 2001 (and many others since, like Parmalat and Lehman Brothers) have only served to concentrate the spotlight on business ethics, especially in America. We have seen the recruitment of armies of Ethics Officers, the drafting of endless Codes of Conduct and the widespread introduction of management tools like whistle-blowing. Many seem to forget the fact that many similar ethics policies and procedures already existed in the companies that so

---

[25] And indeed it already is. See *Business Ethics*, by Andrew Crane and Dirk Matten (2010).

spectacularly imploded. This should serve as a warning about the limitations of the cult of management when it comes to responsibility.

The final element of Carroll's CSR Pyramid, philanthropic responsibilities, has already been dealt with at length in the 'Age of Philanthropy' chapter. I will just add here that it is to his credit that Carroll represents philanthropy as the least significant part of CSR. This serves as a useful reminder to many, especially in developing countries, who still equate CSR with philanthropy. Not that Carroll's Pyramid is inscrutable. In fact, I have written and published several critiques of the model, to which I shall return in later chapters.[26] For now, however, we must give it its due place in the evolution of the Age of Management.

Challenging shareholder supremacy

In 1984, another American academic, Ed Freeman, introduced a conceptual framework which has become central to all discussions of responsibility, namely Stakeholder Theory.[27] According to the theory 'business can be understood as a set of relationships among groups which have a stake in the activities of that business, i.e. stakeholders. Stakeholders are those individuals or groups that can affect or can be affected by the achievement of the firm's core purpose.'[28] Implicitly, the stakeholder concept was (and remains) a challenge to the increasing domination of shareholder interests as the primary measure of effective management.

Stakeholder theory had an immensely hubristic effect, not only generating lively academic debate, but also achieving widespread application in business, as stakeholder management. Much of the early work was done around creating 'stakeholder maps', which plotted a company's relationship to all

---

[26]For example, my chapter 'Revisiting Carroll's CSR Pyramid: An African Perspective' in Pedersen & Huniche *Corporate Citizenship in Developing Countries* (2006), pp. 29–56.

[27]R.E. Freeman (1984) *Strategic Management: A Stakeholder Approach.*

[28]R.E. Freeman & E. Parmar 'Stakeholder Theory'. In Visser et al., *The A to Z of Corporate Social Responsibility* (2007) .

its 'interested and affected parties'. However, it quickly became evident that such a broad scoping exercise inevitably results in everybody being included as a stakeholder, which is not very useful. Hence, the practice of distinguishing between primary and secondary stakeholders emerged, or producing stakeholder webs in which not all stakeholders are equidistant from the centre. One of the most useful academic contributions to this evolving practice was Mitchell, Agle and Wood's (1997) proposition that stakeholders be ranked in three dimensions: power, legitimacy and urgency.[29]

Of course, relations with stakeholders are not always consensual. I remember asking one CEO in America to tell me about his stakeholder relationships. He asked what I meant, so I said, 'You know, NGOs, civil society organizations and the like.' 'They are not stakeholders,' he growled, 'they are the enemy!' Hard to believe, but I'm not kidding. One useful matrix that I came across classifies stakeholders on two axes: supportive or non-supportive, and active or inactive. Hence, supportive, active stakeholders are 'advocates'; non-supportive, inactive stakeholders are 'apathetic'; supportive, non-active are 'dormant'; and non-supportive, active are 'adversarial'. By implication, engagement approaches should vary depending on the type of stakeholder.

Ten years after its introduction by Freeman, the concept of stakeholder engagement was enshrined for the first time as a fundamental element of good management when it was included in the King Code on Corporate Governance in South Africa. First adopted in 1994, and following the UK's Cadbury Code in 1992, the King Code led the way by incorporating CSR into the heart of corporate governance. Today, stakeholder theory continues to be refined and expanded, with countries like Malaysia even considering changing their corporate law to give more prominence to stakeholders. Indeed, I often think that until we get this right – until stakeholders are given their legal, rightful and equal place at the

---

[29]R. Mitchell, B. Agle & D. Wood (2007) 'Towards a Theory of Stakeholder Identification: Defining the Principle of Who and What Really Counts' *Academy of Management Review* **22**(4), pp. 853–86.

negotiating table of business – all efforts at responsible business amount to little more than window dressing.

The quest to civilize cannibals

While this largely socially-dominated agenda was evolving, the environmental movement in the wake of Rachel Carson's *Silent Spring* continued to develop in parallel. 1970 saw the formation of Greenpeace and the celebration of the first Earth Day. Soon after, in 1972, the United Nations convened its seminal conference on the Human Environment in Stockholm. Then a series of industrial disasters shook the world – a chemical explosion near Seveso in Italy in 1976, the Union Carbide gas leak in Bhopal in India in 1984, the Chernobyl nuclear accident in Ukraine in 1986 and the Sandoz chemical spill into the Rhine River in Basel, Switzerland, in the same year – all with devastating human and ecological impacts.

Partly as a result of these disasters, as well as the increasingly worrying data on the state of the world being published by organizations like the Worldwatch Institute and the World Resources Institute, the UN formed the World Commission on Environment and Development, chaired by former Norwegian Prime Minister Gro Harlem Brundtland. In 1987, the Commission released its report, *Our Common Future*, which included the now famous definition of 'sustainable development' – 'development that meets the needs of the current generation without compromising the ability of future generations to meet their needs'. The landmark 'Earth Summit' in Rio de Janeiro followed in 1992, attracting 172 governments, 108 heads of state and around 47,000 people.

At last, business had a concept that they could wrap their emergent responsibility practices around. In preparation for the Earth Summit, Stephan Schmidheiny, together with the newly formed Business Council for Sustainable Development (BCSD), produced a set of 50 case studies and published them in a book called *Changing Course*. The BCSD through the International Chamber of Commerce, also launched the Business Charter for Sustainable Development. This opened the floodgates for a new era of codes, standards and guidelines.

One of the first to emerge was EMAS (the Eco-Management and Auditing Scheme) in 1993, and then a few years later, in 1996, the ISO 14001 standard on Environmental Management. ISO 14001 followed in the footsteps of the immensely successful ISO 9001 quality standard. According to the last ISO survey, by the end of 2008, at least 188,815 ISO 14001 certificates had been issued in 155 countries, up 22% from the previous year. Companies from the services sector accounted for 34% of certificates, compared to 29% in 2007. Recent growth has mainly come from China and other developing countries.

Much of the emphasis in the 1990s was still on eco-efficiency (coined and promoted by the World Business Council for Sustainable Development) and cleaner production (promoted by UNEP), since this produced the win-win outcome of environmental improvements and financial returns, thereby making a 'business case' for sustainable development.

At the time, John Elkington recalls feeling 'uneasy' with eco-efficiency agenda, both because it focused narrowly on financial aspects, rather than wider economic impacts, and also because it ignored the social dimension of human rights, labour issues, community impacts and the like. To correct this, he introduced the idea of the 'triple bottom line' of sustainability: integrated, balanced economic, social and environmental performance. Reflecting on the concept's success, Elkington said to me in 2008, 'It was, for corporate leaders, like popping a pill where you suddenly saw the world slightly differently.'

In 1997, Elkington pulled together his ideas on sustainability in *Cannibals with Forks*. The title came from a quote by the Polish poet Stanislaw Lec, who said, 'Would it be progress if cannibals learned to eat with forks?' For Elkington, the cannibals were companies – displaying aggressive, acquisitive behaviour in the marketplace – and the fork was the three prongs of the triple bottom line. The concept has been widely adopted and institutionalized through the Dow Jones Sustainability Index and the Global Reporting Initiative's Sustainability Reporting Guidelines, launched in 1999 and 2000 respectively.

If the (sweatshop) shoe fits

Elkington was right to shine a spotlight on business's attention deficit on social issues. This failing was illustrated spectacularly when, in November 1997, Nike was exposed for using sweatshops in Asia. This bombshell came just five months after Nike had, together with its peers, launched the World Federation of Sporting Goods Industry Code of Conduct. The scandal erupted when a report on labour conditions in one of their contract supplier factories in Vietnam, prepared by Nike's own auditors, Ernst & Young, was leaked to an activist NGO (TRAC/Corporate Watch) by a disgruntled employee. The firestorm of bad publicity that rained down on Nike resulted in, among other things, Nike being sued for violating California's Business and Professionals Code.

Partly in response, in 1998, Social Accountability International (SAI) launched SA 8000, a labour standard focused especially on labour conditions in the supply chain. SAI is now one of the world's leading social compliance training organizations, having provided training to over 20,000 people, including factory and farm managers, workers, brand compliance officers, auditors, labour inspectors, trade union representatives and other worker rights advocates. Today, SA 8000 certification covers over 2,000 facilities in 64 countries, across 66 industries, and over 1.1 million employees.

Perhaps it is not surprising that Nike's supply chain is now one of the most scrutinized in the world. The three main product lines of Nike's brand – footwear, apparel and equipment – are made by approximately 600 contract factories that employ more than 800,000 workers in 46 countries around the world. In 2005, Nike was the first company in its industry to disclose its factory list. They now claim to visit each factory, on average, 1.77 times per year, while the exact number of visits per individual factory depends on a factory's rating, its strategic importance and its performance history. In 2009, they also conducted 33 deeper studies, called Management Audit Verifications (MAV), and 267 environment, health and safety reviews.

Another standard that emerged as a result of these social engagement trends in the 1990s was Accountability's AA 1000 Framework, launched in 1999 as 'an accountability guideline on social and ethical accounting, auditing and reporting, including stakeholder engagement'. Under this umbrella, a number of related standards were spawned, including an Assurance Standard (AA 1000AS), Stakeholder Engagement Standard (AA 1000SES), Purpose and Principles (AA1000PP) and Framework for Integration (AA 1000FI).

Former CEO of Accountability Simon Zadek told me in 2008 that the standards were a response to the tension between *intensive* and *extensive* accountability 'with the modern corporation being the quintessential example of extreme forms of *intensive* accountability, to very narrowly defined sets of stakeholders . . . What's happened in the last decade and a half in the corporate responsibility space, conceptually, is that the pressure on companies has been to play out an increasingly *extensive* accountability model', i.e. being forced to take into account a wider set of stakeholder interests.

The rise and fall of corporate governance

In many ways, the 1990s were a decade of increasing convergence in responsibility, with not only the social and environmental agendas on the rise, but also the corporate governance movement taking hold. The UK took the lead, establishing a Committee on the Financial Aspects of Corporate Governance in 1991 under the chairmanship of Sir Adrian Cadbury, then Director of the Bank of England and retired Chairman of Cadbury Schweppes. The Committee's report in 1992 – the so-called Cadbury Report, including its code of best practice – set the standard for other similar initiatives around the world.

One of the first to follow was South Africa's King Committee on Corporate Governance in 1993, which issued its King Report and Code in 1994 under the chairmanship of former High Court judge and director of several companies, Mervyn King. King went further than Cadbury, going beyond the purely financial aspects of corporate governance and incorporating the concept of wider stakeholder accountability. Without a doubt, the different emphases were shaped by the operating context. At the time, London was still one of the great financial capitals of the world and South Africa was having its first democratic elections.

This divergence which began as a fissure was to become a canyon when subsequent updates were issued. The Cadbury Report was followed by the Greenbury Report (1995), Combined Code (1998, updated in 2003 and 2006), Turnbull Report (1999), Higgs Review (2003), Smith Report (2003) and Walker Review (2009), all of which continued to focus mostly on financial and organizational aspects of corporate governance (structure of the board, audit committees, remuneration committees, etc.). Hence, issues like sustainability and responsibility have to be inferred through generic clauses on risk and reputation, or passing references to environment, health and safety.

By contrast, updates to the King Report in 2002 and 2009 increasingly placed sustainability and responsibility at the heart of corporate governance. King II, for instance, included a substantial section on business ethics and an entire chapter on 'integrated sustainability reporting'. King III goes even further. As Mervyn King puts it, 'the philosophy of King III revolves around leadership, sustainability and corporate citizenship'. Speaking to me in 2010, King emphasized that directors are accountable to the company first, not shareholders, and a broader set of stakeholders provide a better perspective on what is good for the company in the long term. According to King, and speaking as a former South African High Court Judge, this is not inconsistent with corporate law in the US and elsewhere.

These contrasting views of corporate governance are all the more insightful considering the accounting scandals that came to characterize the first decade of the 21st century, from the collapse of Enron and WorldCom in the US in 2001, to Parmalat in Europe in 2003 and of course the devastating fallout from the 2008 financial meltdown, including Lehman Brothers and numerous others. America's post-Enron response was the Sarbanes-Oxley Act, over which Mervyn King remains deeply sceptical.

The rise of shareholder activism

A related trend to corporate governance in the Age of Management was the rise of socially responsible investment (SRI). As Steve Lydenberg, author of *Corporations and the Public Interest* (2005), explains in *The A to Z of Corporate Social Responsibility*, the history of SRI can be divided into two general periods, the first running from 1970 to the mid-1990s, and the second from the mid-1990s to the present.

In the first period, SRI was largely a North American phenomenon. Starting in the early 1970s, a limited number of SRI unit trusts (mutual funds) and money managers began serving retail investors and small institutions. Large institutional investors then became involved in SRI through the anti-apartheid South Africa divestment movement, which began in the 1970s and culminated in the early 1990s. Ultimately scores of US state and local pension funds, among others, screened billions of dollars in assets according to companies' labour records and levels of involvement in South Africa.

Throughout this period and continuing to today, US religious organizations played a leading role in shareholder activism through the annual filing of hundreds of shareholder resolutions on social and environmental issues. Simultaneously, a number of community development banks, credit unions and revolving loan funds were founded and attracted support from SRI investors.

During the second period, SRI developed into a worldwide phenomenon, starting in the United Kingdom, where it took root in the 1980s, and extending rapidly to Europe, and then to Asia, Africa, and Latin America. Starting in the late 1990s, Australia and Japan also developed active markets for SRI unit trusts (mutual funds) and the stock exchanges of South Africa, Israel, and Brazil launched 'SRI indexes' to encourage CSR among companies listed in those countries. Since 2000, a number of the public and private pension funds in Norway, Sweden, Denmark, the Netherlands and France have also imposed a variety of social and environmental standards in the management of a part, or all, of their assets.

Reflecting the global nature of this expansion, the United Nations became increasingly active in promoting SRI through the UN Environmental Programme's Financial Initiative and the launch in 2006 of the Principles for Responsible Investment. As of 2007, global SRI assets under management were $5 trillion, with $2.7 trillion of that total invested in the US, according to the Social Investment Forum. A 2009 report by Robeco and Booz & Company predicts that these will reach $26.5 trillion by 2015 – over 15% of the global total.

A cornucopia of codes

Looking back, we can see that the 1990s were the decade of CSR codes – not only EMAS, ISO 14001 and SA 8000, but also the Forest Steward Council (FSC) and Marine Stewardship Council (MSC) certification schemes, Green Globe standard (tourism sector), Corruption Perceptions Index, Fairtrade standard, Ethical Trading Initiative, Dow Jones Sustainability Index and OHSAS 18001 (health and safety), to mention just a few. But all that was just a warm-up act when we look at the last ten years, during which we have seen codes proliferate in virtually every area of sustainability and responsibility and all major industry sectors. So much so that in the *A to Z of Corporate Social Responsibility*, we included over 100 such codes, guidelines and standards – and that was just a selection of what is out there. To illustrate the point, here is a sample of what has been thrust onto corporate agendas since the year 2000:

The Carbon Disclosure Project; Global Alliance for Vaccines and Immunization; GRI Sustainability Reporting Guidelines; Kimberley Process (to stop trade in conflict diamonds); Mining and Minerals for Sustainable Development (MMSD) Project; UN Global Compact; UN Millennium Development Goals; Voluntary Principles on Human Rights; FTSE4Good Index; Global Business Coalition on HIV/AIDS; Global Fund to Fight AIDS, Tuberculosis and Malaria; Business Principles for Countering Bribery; Publish What Pay Campaign; Johannesburg Declaration on Sustainable Development;

London Principles (finance sector); AA 1000 Assurance Standard; Equator Principles (finance sector); Extractive Industries Transparency Initiative (EITI); Roundtable on Sustainable Palm Oil; Global Corruption Barometer; UN Convention Against Corruption; UNEP Finance Initiative; UN Norms on Business and Human Rights; World Bank Extractive Industries Review; AA 1000 Standard for Stakeholder Engagement; EU Greenhouse Gas Emissions Trading Scheme; Millennium Ecosystem Assessment; ISO 14064 Standard on Greenhouse Gas Accounting and Verification; Stern Review on the Economics of Climate Change; Bribe Payers' Index; UN Principles for Responsible Investment; ClimateWise Principles (insurance sector); UNEP Declaration on Climate Change; UN Principles for Responsible Management Education (PRME); Bali, Poznan and Copenhagen Communiqués (climate change) . . . and many, many more.

No wonder companies are suffering from code fatigue and audit exhaustion. It is the supreme paradox of the Age of Management – companies are pressured to standardize their efforts on sustainability and responsibility, while stakeholders and critics (myself included) remain unconvinced that this approach identifies or addresses the root causes of the problems we face. Many of the institutional failures over the past 20 years have, I would argue, been systemic failures of culture, rather than bureaucratic failures of management; they have more to do with a prevailing set of values than a particular set of procedures.

These examples of misdirection – some serious and malicious, some amusing and trivial – all point to a more fundamental malaise, namely that CSR, as it has been taught and practised over the past 50 years, is in deep crisis. If you're a cynic, you might say that CSR has proved itself to be a highly effective tool in the Age of Marketing. If you're a little more sympathetic, like me, you might simply conclude that CSR has failed. At worst, it has been a distraction; at best, an inadequate catalyst for the positive changes it claims to want to bring about in the world. Underlying the crisis in CSR is what I call the 'Three Curses of CSR 1.0'.

Table 2 The curses of CSR 1.0

Curses	Nature of the failing
Peripheral CSR	CSR has remained largely restricted to the biggest companies, and mostly confined to PR, or other departments, rather than being integrated across the business
Incremental CSR	CSR has adopted the quality management model, which results in incremental improvements that do not match the scale and urgency of the problems
Uneconomic CSR	CSR does not always make economic sense, as the short-term markets still reward companies that externalize their costs to society

The curse of peripheral CSR

The first of these curses is the *Curse of Peripheral CSR*. Returning to our BP example, here is a company with a long and mostly proud history, contributing highly useful products to society and practising extensive CSR management. Leaving the safety and environmental disasters aside for a moment, BP has made serious commitments to sustainability and responsibility and achieved a great deal in terms of measurable improvements in its safety, health, environmental, labour and human rights performance. And yet for all their flagship leadership in the Age of Management, we see that CSR has remained on the periphery. BP has not gone 'beyond petroleum'; quite the opposite in fact.

It is the same for many companies practising CSR. At worst – and I see this especially in developing countries that are stuck in the Philanthropic or Promotional CSR mode – CSR sits in a public relations, marketing, corporate affairs or human resources department. It is an 'add-on', used explicitly to improve brand equity or the company's reputation. At best – and more common in developed countries and among subsidiaries of multinationals – we see companies practising Strategic CSR by trying to align CSR activities with their industry impacts, or embedding CSR through management systems. Even so, they completely fail to change the strategic direction or core business of the company, or the harmful effects of its processes, products and services.

What BP and Enron and virtually every other leader in the Age of Marketing have in common is not the deliberate intention to mislead (although there are clear examples of this too), but rather a corporate culture – supported by a system of narrow institutional performance incentives, short-term market pressures and perverse economic measures of progress – that remains essentially in conflict with the objectives of sustainability and responsibility. When a trade-off has to be made between financial profitability and ethical standards, the choice is clear, irrespective of carefully crafted codes of practice on the boardroom wall. If there is a tug-of-war between economic growth and environmental impacts, the winner is clear, despite any number of ISO 14001 certificates. If customer demand for cheap products is at odds with fair labour conditions, consumerism triumphs over the needs of powerless workers in the supply chain from some far-flung land.

Once again, examples are not hard to find. As I am writing this (in July 2010), the headlines make the point. Marlboro cigarette manufacturer Philip Morris International has acknowledged 'serious concerns' after Human Rights Watch found 72 cases of child labour in a remote region of Kazakhstan – with children as young as ten in dismal conditions picking tobacco destined for the global company. The UK retailer Poundland has just been exposed for sweatshop activities. A boy of seven was found to be working 100 hours a week in an Indian factory, earning just 7p an hour to make napkin rings for the cut-price chain.

CSR has remained peripheral in another way. It hardly ever extends beyond the large, high-visibility branded companies in any country. All the CSR indexes and rankings, the CSR codes and standards, the CSR reports and audits are focused on a few thousand companies. The Global Reporting Initiative celebrated 1,000 reports in 2008 that are using their guidelines. SA 8000 certification still only covers 2,000 'facilities'. The UN Global

Compact has 5,300 business participants. These numbers are peripheral by any measure you care to choose. Even ISO 14001, with almost 190,000 certifications worldwide, pales into insignificance when you consider that the US Chamber of Commerce alone has more than 3 million members. If we are honest, CSR is the preserve of a tiny corporate élite, a miniscule business minority.

The curse of incremental CSR

Closely linked with the Peripheral curse – and driven especially by the Age of Management – is the *Curse of Incremental CSR*. To fully appreciate this issue, we have to go back to business guru Peter Drucker's 1954 book *The Practice of Management*, in which he introduced the concept of 'management by objectives', or MBOs. The concept is so endemic now as to seem like common sense, but it was quite a revolutionary concept at the time. The basic idea is to translate corporate strategy into a series of measurable objectives, which can be cascaded down through the organization. This allows managers to track and incentivize performance, while employees know what is expected of them and can reap the rewards if they meet their targets. Furthermore, if they participate in setting those objectives, they are likely to feel more motivated and empowered.

The MBO approach – together with subsequent tools like the Balanced Scorecard – unwittingly aids and abets the Age of Marketing, in the sense that it draws attention to voluntary incremental improvements, which distracts attention from the larger problems and deeper impacts of the business. In one of those bizarre ironies of history, the 'system' that would do more to embed the MBO approach than anything else was conceived by one of MBO's great detractors. I am referring to W. Edwards Deming and his total quality management (TQM) approach. Deming credits the inspiration for his theory of management to a 1927 meeting with Walter A. Shewhart of the Bell Telephone Laboratories, the originator of the concepts of statistical control of processes. Years later, during Allied occupation of Japan, Deming was asked by the US military to assist with the 1951 Japanese Census.

This led to an invitation by the Japanese Union of Scientists and Engineers (JUSE) for Deming to teach statistical control and quality management to its members. Japan's CEOs were impressed with Deming's idea that improving quality would reduce expenses, while increasing productivity and market share, and began to test and implement TQM in their factories, notably in their nascent motor industry. Not only did this assist Japan's economic rise in the second half of the 20th century, but it also spawned the international quality movement.

The TQM approach was later standardized through ISO 9001, first launched in 1987. By the end of 2008, nearly a million certifications had been issued. The key to total quality management, according to ISO 9001, is continuous improvement, which is predicated on setting objectives and reviewing performance against them. The designers of the standard seem to have overlooked (or ignored) Deming's objection to MBOs. Deming argued that a lack of understanding of systems commonly results in the misapplication of objectives. By contrast, a leader with an understanding of systems was more likely than a set of objectives to guide workers to an appropriate solution.

This point is important for the responsibility debate because the most widely practised CSR standard, ISO 14001, is designed explicitly to apply the ISO 9001 approach to management systems, including MBOs, to environmental management. That is not a bad thing in and of itself, and it has resulted in many welcome incremental improvements in the environmental performance of companies' *processes*. But the Achilles heel of ISO 14001 and all the other voluntary CSR standards that use MBOs is this: companies set their own objectives and make progress at their own pace and discretion. Furthermore, as with the Peripheral Curse, the MBOs approach has failed to challenge or significantly change companies' largest negative impacts, which are associated with either the nature of their business, the consumption-driven lifestyle they promote, or the impacts of their resource- and energy-intensive processes, products and services.

The net effect is that, despite more CSR than ever before, and despite laudable incremental improvements in CSR performance at the micro level, virtually every macro-level indicator we have of social, environmental or ethical quality – be it the gap between rich and poor, deforestation, biodiversity loss, carbon emissions or corruption – shows that things are still getting worse, not better. The incremental approach to CSR simply does not produce the scale and urgency of response that is required, nor does it get to the root of business's systemic unsustainability and irresponsibility in the shareholder-driven, growth-obsessed capitalist global economy.

The curse of uneconomic CSR

The third and final curse of CSR 1.0 is that the much touted 'business case' for CSR is not nearly as obvious, certain or practised as many assume. Let's start with the rhetoric. The World Business Council for Sustainable Development (WBCSD), which is the strongest proponent of the business case, suggests that it is predicated on five 'returns': operational efficiency, risk reduction, recruitment and retention of talent, protecting the resource base of raw materials, and creation of new markets, products and services. And it is certainly not hard to find ad-hoc examples of each of these 'win-wins'. But is there always a business case?

To answer this, we must look beyond the rhetoric and turn to academic research. The findings vary. For example, Griffen and Mahon (1997) reviewed 25 years of studies and found that a majority showed a positive link between CSR and financial performance, while Margolis and Walsh (2001) reviewed 80 studies, of which 42 show a positive relationship, 19 demonstrate no relationship and four find a negative one. Orlitzky, Schmidt and Rynes (2003) reviewed 52 studies and in most cases the studies suggest a positive association between CSR and profitability. Two reports by SustainAbility – *Buried Treasure* and *Developing Value* – also suggest mixed results. Some relationships between sustainability factors and business success factors are stronger than others, and in many cases no relationship exists. Laffer (2004), on the other hand, in a review of *Business Ethics* magazine's 100 Best Corporate Citizens found 'no significant positive correlation between CSR and business profitability as determined by standard measures'.

Academic and author of *The Market for Virtue*, David Vogel, similarly concludes that 'there is no definitive answer to the question of a financial link. It depends on an individual company's circumstances. Academics searching for a definitive corporate responsibility-financial performance link are barking up the wrong tree'. I tend to agree. There are far too many variables to isolate the impact of CSR on financial performance, except through very specific examples like eco-efficiency. What's more, are typical measures of CSR a reliable proxy for sustainability and responsibility? After all, if we had correlated Enron's CSR and financial performance prior to its demise, it would have pointed to a strong positive relationship, which makes a nonsense of the whole business case argument.

I have a more fundamental problem with the misdirection of CSR business case rhetoric' however. The real question we should be asking is: Does the market consistently reward sustainable and responsible performance by companies? Even without checking the data, we know intuitively from what we see going on in the world that the answer is an unequivocal *no*. With very few exceptions, the global markets today reward the externalization of social, environmental and ethical costs over the short term. *New York Times* journalist and author Thomas Friedman calls this the privatization of benefits and the socialization of costs, while activist writers like Naomi Klein call it 'the race to the bottom', referring to the tendency for companies to locate their production in places with the lowest labour or environmental standards, and hence the lowest costs.

To underscore the point, the Vice Fund (VICEX) in the US, which only invests in the so-called 'sin' industries like tobacco, alcohol, gambling and armaments, consistently outperforms the market over the long term, including socially responsible funds like the Domini Social Equity Mutual Fund (DSEFX). However, we don't need to go to extremes to prove the uneconomic nature of responsibility. Why are fairtrade and organic products, or renewable energy, more expensive than more generic products? Why does Exxon remain one of the largest and most profitable companies in the world? The fact of the matter is that, beyond basic legal compliance, the markets are designed to serve the financial and economic interests of the powerful, not the idealistic dreams of CSR advocates or the angry demands of civil society activists.

What's more, business leaders agree. The 2010 survey of 766 CEOs by the UN Global Compact and Accenture found that 34% cited lack of recognition from the financial markets as a barrier to achieving their sustainability goals. Nestlé's Jose Lopez is candid:

> At the same time that we are coming out with a lot of discussions regarding the importance of sustainability, the market continues. I had hoped that after the world lost 5 trillion dollars in market capitalization out of this nonsense financial crisis that companies would start to be measured by something else other than market capitalization. But the world doesn't seem to be going anywhere other than to measure companies by their market capitalization.[30]

So where does this leave us? I have argued that the Ages of Greed, Philanthropy, Marketing and Management have brought us to a point of crisis in CSR. Specifically, CSR is failing to turn around our most serious global problems – the very issues it purports to be concerned with – and may even be distracting us from the real issue, which is business's causal role in the social and environmental crises we face. The way I see it, that leaves us with three options for taking CSR forward, which I like to think of as Parrot, Ostrich and Phoenix scenarios.

---

[30]Interview with Polly Courtice, Director of the Cambridge Programme for Sustainability Leadership, 17 June 2010.

The *Way of the Parrot* is to tell it like it is: recognize the limitations of CSR and admit to its primary role as a business tactic for reputation management. The *Way of the Ostrich* is the status quo: pretend that CSR is working and that more of the same will be enough. The *Way of the Phoenix* is the transformative agenda: reconceptualize CSR as a radical or revolutionary concept that challenges the intransigent business and economic model and offers genuine solutions to our global challenges. The *Way of the Phoenix* is what I call Systemic CSR, or CSR 2.0, and is what we are just starting to see rising from the ashes of the previous ages, as we enter a new Age of Responsibility. The rest of the book starts to sketch what this alternative future may look like.

The age of responsibility

In dreams begin responsibility.

—William Butler Yeats

'It's a question of discipline,' the Little Prince told me later on. 'When you've finished washing and dressing each morning, you must tend your planet.'

—Antoine de Saint-Exupéry

Most of us can read the writing on the wall; we just assume it's addressed to someone else.

—Ivern Ball

The first industrial revolution is flawed. It is not working. It is unsustainable. It is a mistake and we must move on to another and better industrial revolution and get it right this time.

—Ray Anderson

Box 5: The age of responsibility – in a nutshell

Iconic leaders	Grameen Bank
	Interface
	Patagonia
	Seventh Generation
	The Body Shop
Period	Rising from 1994, with the publication of Paul Hawken's *The Ecology of Commerce* and Ray Anderson's 'spear in the chest' revelation
Key ideas	CSR has failed because it is incremental, peripheral and uneconomic
	More old-style CSR, or CSR 1.0, will not solve our global challenges
	The Internet revolution provides a metaphor for transforming CSR
	CSR 2.0, or Systemic CSR, is based on a new set of principles
	We need to unleash the 'long tail' of CSR
Commentators	John Elkington (author & consultant)
	Jeffrey Hollender and Bill Breen (business leaders & authors)
	William McDonough and Michael Braungart (authors & consultants)
	Peter Senge (author & academic)
	Muhammad Yunus (author & social entrepreneur)
References	*Cradle to Cradle: Remaking the Way We Make Things* (William McDonough & Michael Braungart, 2003)
	The Responsibility Revolution: How the Next Generation of Businesses Will Win (Jeffrey Hollender & Bill Breen, 2010)
	The Necessary Revolution: How Individuals and Organizations are Working Together to Create a Sustainable World (Peter Senge, Bryan Smith, Sarah Schley, Joe Laur & Nina Kruschwitz, 2008)
	Creating a World Without Poverty: Social Business and the Future of Capitalism (Muhammad Yunus, 2008)
	The Power of Unreasonable People: How Social Entrepreneurs Create Markets that Change the World (John Elkington & Pamela Hartigan, 2008)

Case 5: Ray Anderson and Interface

'I stand convicted by me, myself alone, not by anyone else, as a plunderer of the earth, but not by our civilization's definition. By our civilization's definition, I'm a captain of industry. In the eyes of many, a kind of modern day hero.' This is how Ray Anderson – founder of Interface, one of the world's largest manufacturers of carpet tiles – usually starts his speeches these days. It is a far cry from where Anderson, now in his 70s, started out: an honours graduate of Georgia Institute of Technology who, after 14 years at various positions at Deering-Milliken and Callaway Mills, set about founding a company to produce the first free-lay carpet tiles in 1973.

The company was formed out of a joint venture, led by Anderson, between the British company Carpets International and a group of American investors. Modular carpet tiles grew in popularity and by 1978 Interface sales had reached $11 million. The company went public in 1983 and in 1987 changed its name to Interface, Inc. All of this growth and success – to sales of around $600 million by 1993 – took place pursuing a conventional industrial strategy. Green issues were simply not a big thing in the first 20 years of the company's history. But that was starting to change, especially with the 1992 Earth Summit in Rio shining a spotlight on sustainable development.

Interface, like many companies at the time, got caught up in the ferment. By the summer of 1994 Interface customers were starting to ask difficult questions, like: What is your company doing for the environment? Anderson realized that 'the real answer was: not very much', so they set up a taskforce to assess the company's worldwide environmental position. The group, naturally enough, asked Anderson to kick off their first meeting with an environmental vision. Anderson panicked. He didn't have an environmental clue, much less a vision.

Synchronistically, Paul Hawken's book *The Ecology of Commerce* had just landed on Anderson's desk. He devoured it and was shocked to find himself moved to tears. He still recalls the moment vividly – he had reached page 19, a chapter on the 'Death of Birth', which was E.O. Wilson's expression for species extinction. 'It was a point of a spear into my chest, and I read on, and the spear went deeper, and it became an epiphany experience, a total change of mindset for myself and a change of paradigm.' What was his great revelation? 'It dawned on me that the way I'd been running Interface is the way of the plunderer; plundering something that's not mine, something that belongs to every creature on earth. And I said to myself: "The day must come when this is illegal, when plundering is not allowed. It must come." So, I said to myself, "My goodness, some day people like me will end up in jail".'

In this moment of profound clarity, Anderson saw that carpet manufacturing 'is a pretty abusive industry'. The process uses lots of petroleum and petroleum derivatives, both as components of synthetic carpet and to power its production. Dyeing carpet is also water- and energy-intensive. And when people are finished with the carpet, it goes into landfills where it lasts probably 20,000 years. Anderson concluded that his company – and business more generally – is part of the problem, not the solution. Paraphrasing Hawken, he realized that 'there is not an industrial company on earth, not an institution of any kind, not mine, not yours, not anyone's, that is sustainable'.

And so Anderson had his vision: Interface would become the world's first truly sustainable company. In fact, not only sustainable, but restorative. They would put back more than they take, and actively do good, not just avoid doing harm. After the speech, Anderson recalls, 'I heard the whispers: Has he gone round the bend?' To which he replied at once that he *had*. 'That's my job, to see what's around the bend.' Today, Anderson confesses, 'I didn't know what the hell I was talking about', but it galvanized the task group, which after some preliminary research, concluded that they could meet his goal by 2000.

Filled with enthusiasm, Anderson's first move was to send a strong signal to the market. He held a Green the Supply Chain meeting, with a simple message: those who come with us will get the business, those who don't, won't. The following year, 1995, he pulled together an Eco-Dream Team, and introduced a system of EcoMetrics[TM], designed to quantify the 'metabolism' of Interface, i.e. the mass and energy flow through the company's operations. Simply put, EcoMetrics assesses how much Interface takes in, in terms of materials and energy, and what comes out, in the forms of products and waste. Later, Interface also implemented a system of SocioMetrics[TM], to measure impacts on their people – the associates and communities they serve.

Inspired by their new vision and metrics, in 1995 Interface started innovating their products, first by launching an Evergreen Lease, which they described as 'selling carpet without selling carpet'. This was based on the idea of selling a service, rather than a product. Hence, Interface produces, installs, cleans, maintains and replaces the carpet for customers. Customers lease the service of keeping a space carpeted, rather than buying carpet. They get the services of a carpet's warmth, beauty, colour, texture and acoustics. Interface saw it – rightly I believe – as 'a whole new sustainable business model'.

By 1996, Interface had learned enough to conceptualize what they were doing in a Model of a Sustainable Company. The next year, their definition of 'sustainable' received added scientific rigour when they became the first company to adopt the Natural Step principles, which are four 'system conditions', developed by Swedish cancer researcher Karl-Henrik Robèrt. In 1998, Interface issued its first Sustainability Report and formed a Global Sustainability Council, while Anderson published his business biography of the journey so far, called *Mid Course Correction*. The company's product innovation also continued, with the introduction in 1999 of their Déjà vu™ collection, a carpet tile product using recycled nylon and 100% recycled vinyl secondary backing.

Despite all this great progress – which many described as revolutionary – as the millennium approached, it became blatantly obvious that their 'restorative company' goal was far more ambitious and difficult than Anderson or the environmental task team had ever imagined. It was time for a reality-check. The journey to a fully sustainable Interface would be like – as Anderson began to describe it – summiting 'a mountain higher than Everest' – difficult, yes, but with a careful and attentive plan, not impossible. So rather than change the goal, they changed the timeframe. The new deadline for 'Mission Sustainability' became 2020.

Carrying through the analogy, Interface identified Seven Fronts™ on Mount Sustainability through which they planned to ascend: (1) eliminating waste; (2) generating benign emissions; (3) using renewable energy; (4) closing the loop on production; (5) using resource-efficient transportation; (6) sensitizing stakeholders; and finally (7) redesigning commerce. Among the tools that have become central to the climb are life cycle assessment and biomimicry – Janine Benyus's idea of nature-inspired design.

These techniques have not only allowed Interface to choose the lowest impact options among existing processes, but also to innovate new products that are less resource- and energy-intensive and produce less waste. One of the first, in 2000, was called Entropy® tiles that install non-directionally and have mergeable dye lots. This concept launched what became Interface's i2™ category, with the benefit that one person can install more than two and a half times as much i2 tile in one day as they could of broadloom carpet. Besides this, i2 floors result in as little as 1.5% waste, compared to broadloom with as much as 14%.

Other product innovations have included the Cool Carpet (offsetting greenhouse gas emissions) and carpets using fly ash waste and poly-lactic acid (PLA) fibres, derived from non-food grade corn. Perhaps most famously, in 2006, Interface invented the world's first totally glue-free, free-lay carpet tile (TacTile®), inspired by gecko-foot 'tech-nology'. The result is less mess, less waste and greater savings, not to mention an environmental footprint that is over 90% lower than car-pets using traditional glue adhesives.

In 2007, another technological breakthrough, dubbed ReEntry 2.0™, means that Interface can now recycle – or 'reinyarnate' – reclaimed and separated type 6 and 6,6 nylon, as well as separated GlasBac® and similar competitor backings into new non-virgin PVC carpet tile backing. This has been somewhat controversial, as there are some (including the authors of *Cradle to Cradle*) who argue that PVC should be phased out completely. Anderson's response is that the world is awash with PVC and high performance natural alternatives are still in their developmental infancy. Hence, for now, it is essential to reclaim and reuse the PVC, rather than simply to burn or bury it.

Taking stock in 2010, Anderson's EcoMetrics™ tell him that they are about 60% of the way towards what Interface now calls its Mis-sion Zero™ goal to have no negative environmental impacts by 2020. Translated into numbers, the results are impressive. Of the 400 million pounds of raw materials purchased in 2009, only 3.4 million pounds of waste went to landfills, 6.9 million pounds of raw material was recycled to be used again, and 9.6 mil-lion pounds of waste was sent to energy recovery as a use of last resort. Continued savings from Interface's QUEST programme have netted $433 million in cumulative avoided costs since 1995. And ReEntry 2.0, Interface's reclamation and recycling initiative, diverted 25 million pounds of reclaimed carpet and post-industrial scrap from the landfill in 2009.

It has been a long and painful – but ultimately rewarding – journey. Anderson reflects on the transformational challenge that Interface faced, and we all still face, saying:

> The status quo is a very powerful opiate and when you have a system that seems to be working and producing profits by the conventional way of accounting for profits, it's very hard to make yourself change. But we all know that change is an inevitable part of business. Once you have ridden a wave just so far, you have to get another wave. We all know that. For us, becoming restorative has been that new wave and it's been incredibly good for business.

Admittedly, Interface had a tough time through the financial crisis (who didn't?), losing as much as 85% of its pre-crisis value in early March 2009, but it has since rebounded strongly. In fact, Anderson regards their Zero Mission as one of the reasons they survived and ultimately thrived through the recession. It's hard to bet against what has become a billion-dollar corporation, named by *Fortune* as one of the 'Most Admired Companies in America' and the '100 Best Companies to Work For', with sales in 110 countries and manufacturing facilities on four continents.

Anderson can't help but see the opportunities, saying: 'I believe there are new fortunes to be made as we define this, the next industrial revolution.' He is quick to add, however, that it's not all about the money. 'There's a lot of psychic income with people who feel they are associated with something bigger than themselves, something that's important.' But Anderson is also under no illusions about the scale of the challenge that we face. 'Part of what needs to change', he says, 'is our focus on short time horizons, i.e., the focus on the next quarter, for both companies and for their investors. Sustainability by its very nature requires a long view on the future, as we consider the impact of our decisions today on future generations.'

A long-term view necessitates that we 'eventually cut the fossil fuel umbilical cord'. And this is where Anderson believes the government has a critical role to play in creating what he calls an 'honest bottom line'. By contrast, 'today that bottom line is vastly subsidized. If any one of us were paying the full cost of oil, our bottom lines would be very different. If you internalize the cost of oil, look at the cost of the war in the Middle East or the cost of global warming for future generations, if you internalize those external costs, that bottom line would look very different, whatever business you are in.' And it's not just about carbon. 'If we somehow put a value on species extinction and factor that into our costs, that bottom line would look very different. If we put any resource depletion into costs, our bottom line would change. So what we have is a dishonest market that does not take into account all the costs when it establishes its prices. We need an honest marketplace before we can let the market work for sustainability rather than against it as it works today.'

It is clear that 16 years after creating his 'round-the-bend' vision of Interface becoming a truly sustainable and responsible company, Anderson is older and wiser. And despite all the success and accolades that Interface has enjoyed – both financial and in terms of its sustainability achievements – the piercing pain of the 'spear in the chest' has not dulled for Anderson. He remains profoundly concerned – disturbed even – at the growing state of crisis in the world's ecosystems. Asked in 2010 whether he was optimistic about the future and our chances of reaching sustainability, he said: 'I am optimistic that *we* [Interface] will get there. I am *not* optimistic that the industrial system will change quickly enough to avoid catastrophe.'

To me, Anderson's answer is both a celebration of what is possible, based on Interface's experience, and a warning of what is probable if we don't act more urgently and dramatically as a society and as business.

Radical confessions

What makes Ray Anderson and Interface different from, say, BP or Cadbury, is the depth of their admission and the scale of their ambition. Anderson's latest book is called *Confessions of a Radical Industrialist*, in which he concedes not only that today's economic system is broken, but that he and his company are part of the problem. He is able to see himself as a plunderer – not through malicious intent, or even greed, but by failing to question the true impacts of business on society and the environment. As Alcoholics Anonymous will tell you, admission is the first step to recovery. Unfortunately, most companies stuck in the Ages of Greed, Philanthropy, Marketing and Management are all still in denial, thinking that either there is *no* problem, or it's not *their* problem, or that it's a problem to *benefit* from, or that it's only a *minor* problem.

The Age of Responsibility is not just about admission though; it's also about ambition. As far as I can tell, Interface was the first major company to set the BHAG (big hairy audacious goal) of zero negative impact, as well as going beyond 'no harm' to also become a restorative business – to genuinely make things better and leave this world with a net-positive balance. It is only such audacious goals that can lift the triple curses of incremental, peripheral and uneconomic CSR 1.0. As Robert Francis Kennedy reminds us: 'There are those who look at things the way they are, and ask why. I dream of things that never were, and ask why not?' We need more pragmatic dreamers, business leaders who practise what brain-mind researcher and author Marilyn Ferguson calls 'pragmagic'.

Anderson was not the first radical business leader, nor perhaps even the most radical. The late Anita Roddick, founder of Body Shop International, had a missionary zeal that few will ever rival. Famous for her business-led activism, which began as an alliance with WWF in 1986 to save the whale, she went on to tackle issues as far ranging as animal rights, women's self-esteem, human rights, fair trade and indigenous people's rights. In her autobiography *Business As Unusual*, she distilled her philosophy as follows:

Business is a renaissance concept, where the human spirit comes into play. It does not have to be drudgery; it does not have to be the science of making money. It can be something that people genuinely feel good about, but only if it remains a human enterprise.

Ben Cohen and Jerry Greenfield who 'hated running but loved food' and therefore founded Ben & Jerry's ice cream, became flag bearers for a more radical kind of responsibility as well. Their mission 'to make the best possible ice cream in the nicest possible way' was not just sweet talk. They put it into action in various ways, from going free range and supporting fairtrade to setting up a Climate Change College and sponsoring research into eco-friendly refrigeration. Their biography, *The Inside Scoop: How Two Real Guys Built a Business with a Social Conscience and a Sense of Humor*, tells the story. 'If you open up the mind', they concluded, 'the opportunity to address both profits and social conditions are limitless. It's a process of innovation.'

Ricardo Semler, CEO of the Brazilian manufacturing company Semco, is another self-confessed maverick who turned many assumptions about 'good management' on their head.[31] For example, at Semco he allowed workers to set their own salaries and working hours, he taught everyone in the company (including shop floor workers) how to read a balance sheet and he made everyone's salary public. 'If you're embarrassed about the size of your salary', he said, 'you're probably not earning it.' His radical philosophy was this: 'Most companies hire adults and then treat them like children. All that Semco does is give people the responsibility and trust that they deserve.'

Web 2.0: seeds of a revolution

Throughout my 20-year career in corporate sustainability and responsibility, these are the kinds of pioneers I have looked to for hope and

---

[31]These have been written up in several articles published in the *Harvard Business Review*, as well as his two books, *Maverick* and *The Seven Day Weekend*.

inspiration. The frustration has been that these 'radical industrialists' have always remained the exception, rather than the rule. They are the outliers, which is okay if – in line with Everett Rogers' Diffusion of Innovation model – they are the innovators that make up 2.5% of the population. The problem is that most of their ideas and practices haven't diffused to the early adopters and the early majority, let alone the late majority and laggards.

So what will it take to get the kind of transformation we need to move beyond innovation towards mass change? I find an analogy is always helpful and in early 2008, I discovered the perfect metaphor: Web 2.0. The term, of course, had been around for a while – coined in 1999 by IT consultant Darcy DiNucci in an article called 'Fragmented Future' and popularized in 2004 by the landmark O'Reilly Media Web 2.0 conference. Tim O'Reilly's 2005 article 'What is Web 2.0?' had already become an Early Adopters' touchstone for a rapidly evolving new lexicon, and remains a classic piece. People like me, part of the technosphere's Early Majority, were a bit slower in waking up, and it took Dan Tapscott and Anthony Williams' 2006 book *Wikinomics* to switch me on to the revolution in progress.

Before coming to why Web 2.0 is a good metaphor for the transformation of CSR, let me try to bed down the concept. Today, Wikipedia defines Web 2.0 as 'web applications that facilitate interactive information sharing, inter-operability, user-centered design and collaboration'. Fair enough, but let's dig a little deeper, drawing on the term's evolution. In 1999, DiNucci was writing for programmers, challenging them to adapt to the increasing use of portable Web-ready devices. This was just a small part of what Web 2.0 would come to mean. In 2005, O'Reilly brainstormed a far more wide ranging list of examples and contrasts between Web 1.0 and Web 2.0. Examples included DoubleClick versus Google AdSense, Britannica Online versus Wikipedia, personal websites versus blogging, publishing versus participation, directories (taxonomy) versus tagging (folksonomy) and stickiness versus syndication, to mention but a few. His article concluded with seven core competencies of Web 2.0 companies:

❑ services, not packaged software, with cost-effective scalability;

❑ control over unique, hard-to-recreate data sources that get richer as more people use them;

❑ trusting users as co-developers;

❑ harnessing collective intelligence;

❑ leveraging the long tail through customer self-service;

❑ software above the level of a single device; and

❑ lightweight user interfaces, development models and business models.

In 2006, Tapscott and Williams gave an applied view on Web 2.0 in the form of *wikinomics*, which they defined as 'the effects of extensive collaboration and user-participation on the marketplace and corporate world'. Wikinomics, they said, is based on four principles:

❑ *Openness*, which includes not only open standards and content but also financial transparency and an open attitude towards external ideas and resources.

❑ *Peering*, which replaces hierarchical models with a more collaborative forum, for which the Linux operating system is a quintessential example.

❑ *Sharing*, which is a less proprietary approach to (among other things) products, intellectual property, bandwidth and scientific knowledge.

❑ *Acting globally*, which involves embracing globalization and ignoring physical and geographical boundaries at both the corporate and individual level.

The birth of CSR 2.0

By May 2008, it was clear to me that this evolutionary concept of Web 2.0 held many lessons for CSR. I published my initial thoughts in a short article online entitled 'CSR 2.0: The New Era of Corporate Sustainability and Responsibility', in which I said:

> The field of what is variously known as CSR, sustainability, corporate citizenship and business ethics is ushering in a new era in the relationship between business and society. Simply put, we are shifting from the old concept of CSR – the classic notion of 'Corporate Social Responsibility', which I call CSR 1.0 – to a new, integrated conception – CSR 2.0, which can be more accurately labelled 'Corporate Sustainability and Responsibility'. The allusion to Web 1.0 and Web 2.0 is no coincidence. The transformation of the internet through the emergence of social media networks, user-generated content and open source approaches is a fitting metaphor for the changes business is experiencing as it begins to redefine its role in society.

Table 3 Similarities between Web 1.0 and CSR 1.0

Web 1.0	CSR 1.0
A flat world just beginning to connect itself and finding a new medium to push out information and plug advertising.	A vehicle for companies to establish relationships with communities, channel philanthropic contributions and manage their image.
Saw the rise to prominence of innovators like Netscape, but these were quickly out-muscled by giants like Microsoft with its Internet Explorer.	Included many start-up pioneers like Traidcraft, but has ultimately turned into a product for large multinationals like Wal-Mart.
Focused largely on the standardized hardware and software of the PC as its delivery platform, rather than multi-level applications.	Travelled down the road of 'one size fits all' standardization, through codes, standards and guidelines to shape its offering.

Table 4 Similarities between Web 2.0 and CSR 2.0

Web 2.0	CSR 2.0
Being defined by watchwords like 'collective intelligence', 'collaborative networks' and 'user participation'. Tools include social media, knowledge syndication and beta testing.	Being defined by 'global commons', 'innovative partnerships' and 'stakeholder involvement'. Mechanisms include diverse stakeholder panels, real-time reporting and social entrepreneurship.
Is as much a state of being as a technical advance – it is a new philosophy or way of seeing the world differently.	Is recognizing a shift in power from centralized to decentralized; a change in scale from marginal to mainstream and a change in application from single and exclusive to multiple and shared.

As our world becomes more connected and global challenges like climate change and poverty loom ever larger, businesses that still practise CSR 1.0 will (like their Web 1.0 counterparts) be rapidly left behind. Highly conscientized and networked stakeholders will expose them and gradually withdraw their social licence to operate. By contrast, companies that embrace the CSR 2.0 era will be those that collaboratively find innovative ways to tackle our global challenges and be rewarded in the marketplace as a result.

The principles of CSR 2.0

Initial responses to my framing of CSR 2.0 were largely positive and confirmed that I was onto something – perhaps a new language or conceptualization of responsibility, or at the very least a nexus for talking about the radical changes needed in CSR. However, I felt it needed an institutional vehicle if it was going to have any chance of success, and so CSR

International was born, with the express mission to be an incubator for CSR 2.0. The think tank was launched in March 2010 in London, complete with the ritualistic burial of the old CSR and its rebirth as CSR 2.0.[32]

It quickly became clear, however, that a metaphor can only take you so far. What was needed was a set of principles against which we could test CSR. These went through a few iterations, but I eventually settled on five, which form a kind of mnemonic for CSR 2.0: Creativity (C), Scalability (S), Responsiveness (R), Glocality (2) and Circularity (0). These principles, which will be explored in detail in the next chapters, can be described briefly as follows:

Creativity (C) – The problem with the current obsession with CSR codes and standards (including the new ISO 26000 standard) is that it encourages a tick-box approach to CSR. But our social and environmental problems are complex and intractable. They need creative solutions, like Freeplay's wind-up technology or Vodafone's M-Pesa money transfer scheme.

Scalability (S) – The CSR literature is sprinkled liberally with charming case studies of truly responsible and sustainable projects. The problem is that so few of them ever go to scale. We need more examples like Wal-Mart's 'choice editing' by converting to organic cotton, or Tata creating the affordable eco-efficient Nano car, or Muhammad Yunus's Grameen Bank microfinance model.

Responsiveness (R) – More cross-sector partnerships and stakeholder-driven approaches are needed at every level, as well as more uncomfortable, transformative responsiveness, which questions whether particular industries, or the business model itself, are part of the solution or part of the problem. A good example of responsiveness is the Corporate Leaders Group on Climate Change.

---

[32]Videos of the 'Death and Rebirth of CSR' ceremony are on YouTube and the CSR International website.

Glocality (2) – This means 'think global, act local'. In a complex, intercon-nected, globalizing world, companies (and their critics) will have to become far more sophisticated in combining international norms with local contexts by finding local solutions that are culturally appropriate, without forsaking universal principles. We are moving from an 'either-or' one-size-fits-all world to a 'both-and' strength-in-diversity world.

Circularity (0) – Our global economic and commercial system is based on a fundamentally flawed design, which acts as if there are no limits on resource consumption or waste disposal. Instead, we need a cradle-to-cradle approach, closing the loop on production and designing products and processes to be 'inherently good', rather than 'less bad', as Shaw Carpets does.

Shifting from CSR 1.0 to CSR 2.0

These principles are the acid test for future CSR practices. If they are applied, what kind of shifts will we see? In my view, the shifts will happen at two levels. At a meta-level, there will be a change in CSR's ontological assumptions or ways of seeing the world. At a micro-level, there will be a change in CSR's methodological practices or ways of being in the world.

The meta-level changes can be described as follows: Paternalistic relation-ships between companies and the community based on philanthropy will give way to more equal partnerships. Defensive, minimalist responses to social and environmental issues will be replaced by proactive strategies and investment in growing responsibility markets, such as clean technology. Reputation-conscious public-relations approaches to CSR will no longer be credible and so companies will be judged on actual social, environmental and ethical performance, i.e. are things getting better on the ground in absolute, cumulative terms?

Although CSR specialists still have a role to play, each dimension of CSR 2.0 performance will be embedded and integrated into the core operations of companies. Standardized approaches will remain useful as guides to

Table 5 CSR 1.0 to CSR 2.0 – macro shifts

CSR 1.0	CSR 2.0
Philanthropic	Collaborative
Risk-based	Reward-based
Image-driven	Performance-driven
Specialized	Integrated
Standardized	Diversified
Marginal	Scalable
Western	Global

consensus, but CSR will find diversified expression and implementation at very local levels. CSR solutions, including responsible products and services, will go from niche 'nice-to-haves' to mass-market 'must-haves'. And the whole concept of CSR will give way to a more culturally diverse and internationally applied concept.

How might these shifting principles manifest as CSR practices? Supporting these meta-level changes, the anticipated micro-level changes can be described as follows: CSR will no longer manifest as luxury products and services (as with current green and fairtrade options), but as affordable solutions for those who most need quality of life improvements. Investment in self-sustaining social enterprises will be favoured over chequebook charity. CSR indexes, which rank the same large companies over and over (often revealing contradictions between indexes) will make way for CSR rating systems, which turn social, environmental, ethical and economic performance into corporate scores (A+, B−, etc., not dissimilar to credit ratings) and which analysts and others can usefully employ in their decision making.

Reliance on CSR departments will disappear or disperse, as performance across responsibility and sustainability dimensions are built increasingly into corporate performance appraisal and market incentive systems. Self-selecting ethical consumers will become irrelevant, as CSR 2.0 companies begin to choice-edit, i.e. cease offering implicitly 'less ethical' product

Table 6 CSR 1.0 to CSR 2.0 – micro shifts

CSR 1.0	CSR 2.0
CSR premium	Base of the pyramid
Charity projects	Social enterprise
CSR indexes	CSR ratings
CSR departments	CSR incentives
Product liability	Choice editing
Ethical consumerism	Service agreements
CSR reporting cycles	CSR data streams
Stakeholder groups	Social networks
Process standards	Performance standards

ranges, thus allowing guilt-free shopping. Post-use liability for products will become obsolete, as the service-lease and take-back economy goes mainstream. Annual CSR reporting will be replaced by online, real-time CSR performance data flows. Feeding into these live communications will be Web 2.0 connected social networks that allow 'crowdsourcing', instead of periodic meetings with rather cumbersome stakeholder panels. And typical CSR 1.0 management systems standards like ISO 14001 will be less credible than new performance standards, such as those emerging in climate change that set absolute limits and thresholds.

The DNA model of CSR 2.0

Pulling it all together, I believe that CSR 2.0 – or Systemic CSR (I also sometimes call it Radical CSR or Holistic CSR, so use whichever you prefer) – represents a new model of CSR. In one sense, it is not so different from other models we have seen before. We can recognize echoes of Archie Carroll's CSR pyramid, Ed Freeman's stakeholder theory, Donna Wood's corporate social performance (CSP), John Elkington's triple bottom line, Stuart Hart and C.K. Prahalad's bottom of the pyramid (BoP), Michael Porter's strategic CSR and the ESG approach of socially responsible investment

Table 7 DNA model of CSR 2.0

DNA code	Strategic goals	Key indicators
Value creation	Economic development	Capital investment
		Beneficial products
		Inclusive business
Good governance	Institutional effectiveness	Leadership
		Transparency
		Ethical practices
Societal contribution	Stakeholder orientation	Philanthropy
		Fair labour practices
		Supply chain integrity
Environmental integrity	Sustainable ecoystems	Ecosystem protection
		Renewable resources
		Zero waste production

(SRI), to mention but a few. But that is really the point – it integrates what we have learned to date. It presents a holistic model of CSR.

The essence of the CSR 2.0 DNA model are the four DNA Responsibility Bases, which are like the four nitrogenous bases of biological DNA (adenine, cytosine, guanine and thymine), sometimes abbreviated to the four letters GCTA (which was the inspiration for the 1997 science fiction film-*GATTACA*). In the case of CSR 2.0, the DNA Responsibility Bases are Value creation, Good governance, Societal contribution and Environmental integrity, or VEGS if you like. Each DNA Base has a primary goal and each goal has key indicators, which begin to show the qualitative and quantitative differences between other models of CSR and the CSR 2.0 DNA model.

Hence, if we look at *Value Creation*, it is clear we are talking about more than financial profitability. The goal is economic development, which means not only contributing to the enrichment of shareholders and executives, but also improving the economic context in which a company operates, including investing in infrastructure, creating jobs, providing skills development and so on. There can be any number of KPIs, but I want to highlight two that I believe are essential: beneficial products and inclusive business. Do the company's products and services really improve our quality of life, or do they cause harm or add to the low-quality junk of what Charles Handy calls the *'chindogu society'*. And how are the economic benefits shared? Does wealth trickle up or down? are employees, SMEs in the supply chain and poor communities genuinely empowered?

Good Governance is another area that is not new, but in my view has failed to be recognized or integrated properly in CSR practices. The goal of institutional effectiveness is as important as more lofty social and environmental ideals. After all, if the institution fails, or is not transparent and fair, this undermines everything else that CSR is trying to accomplish. Trends in reporting, but also other forms of transparency like social media and brand- or product-linked public databases of CSR performance, will be increasingly important indicators of success, alongside embedding ethical conduct in the culture of companies. Tools like Goodguide's product rating, OpenEye's sustainability expert exchange platform and Covalence's EthicalQuote ranking will become more prevalent.

Societal Contribution is an area that CSR is traditionally more used to addressing, with its goal of stakeholder orientation. This gives philanthropy its rightful place in CSR – as one tile in a larger mosaic – while also providing a spotlight for the importance of fair labour practices. It is simply unacceptable that there are more people in slavery today than there were before it was officially abolished in the 1800s, just as regular exposures of high-brand companies for the use of child labour are despicable. This area of stakeholder engagement, community participation and supply chain integrity remains one of the most vexing and critical elements of CSR.

Finally, *Environmental Integrity* sets the bar way higher than minimizing damage and rather aims at maintaining and improving ecosystem sustainability. The KPIs give some sense of the ambition required here – 100% renewable energy and zero waste. We cannot continue the same practices that have, according to WWF's Living Planet Index, caused us to lose a third of the biodiversity on the planet since 1970. Nor can we continue to gamble with prospect of dangerous – and perhaps catastrophic and irreversible – climate change.

CSR 2.0 – standing for corporate sustainability and responsibility – also proposes a new interpretation for these terms. Like two intertwined strands of DNA, sustainability and responsibility can be thought of as different, yet complementary elements of CSR. Hence, sustainability can be conceived as the destination – the challenges, vision, strategy and goals, i.e. what we are aiming for, while responsibility is more about the journey – our solutions, responses, management and actions, i.e. how we get there. The next part of the book explores the five principles of CSR 2.0 and will look at some of the pioneers that are beginning to show us the way to integrate these two strands, through their sustainable visions and responsible actions.

The principles of CSR 2.0

CHAPTER 7

The principle of creativity

When patterns are broken, new worlds emerge.

—Tuli Kupferberg

Creativity represents a miraculous coming together of the uninhibited energy of the child with its apparent opposite and enemy, the sense of order imposed on the disciplined adult intelligence.

—Norman Podhoretz

Discovery consists of seeing what everybody has seen and thinking what nobody has thought.

—Albert Szent-Györgyi

Sometimes I've believed as many as six impossible things before breakfast.

—Lewis Carroll

Box 6: The principle of creativity – in a nutshell

Iconic leaders	A Little World
	Ashoka
	Freeplay
	FUNDES
	Google
Period	Rising from 1980, when Ashoka was founded
Key ideas	Complex problems require creative solutions
	Don't expect dinosaurs to change
	Diversity and cross-discipline thinking breeds creativity
	Investment in innovators and early adopters is key
	Social and environmental entrepreneurship must be unleashed
Commentators	David Bornstein and Susan Davis (authors)
	John Elkington and Pamela Hartigan (authors)
	Tania Ellis (author)
	Kevin Lynch and Julius Walls (authors)
	Muhammad Yunus (author & social entrepreneur)
References	*Banker to the Poor* (Muhammad Yunus, 2003)
	The Power of Unreasonable People: How Social Entrepreneurs Create Markets that Change the World (John Elkington & Pamela Hartigan, 2008)
	Mission Inc.: A Practitioner's Guide to Social Enterprise (Kevin Lynch & Julius Walls, 2009)
	Social Entrepreneurship: What Everyone Needs to Know (David Bornstein, 2010)
	The New Pioneers: Sustainable Business Success Through Social Innovation and Social Entrepreneurship (Tania Ellis, 2010)

Case 6: Anurag Gupta and A Little World[33]

It is 2006 in the Seiling village of Aizawl District in Mizoram, India. A woman in her 40s – let's call her Niroshini – wearing a beautiful purple sari, is standing in a short queue. Despite her elegance, Niroshini is, by virtually any definition, poor. She earns $912 a year. In her village, she is one of the fortunate few to have a steady job, sewing clothes. Even so, she has no property, no car, no official identity papers, no proof of address and – at least until today, 6 November – no bank account. She reaches the front of the queue, which is in the living room of her friend and neighbour, Indira. She is excited, but nervous, as she exchanges greetings and takes a seat at the simple desk.

Indira smiles reassuringly, picks up a mobile phone, and asks Niroshini to speak her name clearly into the receiver, thereby creating a voice imprint. Then she asks Niroshini to look into the lens of the phone and takes a head-and-shoulders photograph. Next, Niroshini is asked to place each of her fingers in turn on the glass lens of a small, hand-held device, which is a biometric scanner that records her fingerprints. Finally, as she doesn't read or write very well, Indira helps her to fill in a one-page form, attesting to her name and address, which Niroshini has to sign. The whole process takes about ten minutes. 'Congratulations!' says Indira, 'you have just opened your first bank account.' Niroshini shakes her head, incredulous. She doesn't know whether to laugh or cry, so she hugs Indira. 'Thank you, sister! Thank you!'[34]

---

[33]This story is based primarily on two sources: (1) an interview I conducted with ALW founder Anurag Gupta in April 2010; and (2) the UNDP Growing Inclusive Markets publication entitled 'A Little World: Safe and Efficient M-Banking in Rural India', prepared by Bimal Arora and Ashley Metz Cummings in 2010.

[34]The people in this little vignette are fictitious, used for illustrative purposes. The facts are that ALW began their pilot micro-banking on 6 November 2006 in Seiling. The process described for opening a bank account is also accurate.

What just happened was the result of a six-year entrepreneurial journey by Anurag Gupta to create a viable method for banking and payments in the villages of India – a technology-enabled microbank that brings basic financial services to the some of the country's remotest and poorest communities. This is no trivial challenge. According to Duvvuri Subbarao, Governor of the Reserve Bank of India, only 40% of the Indian population have a bank account, 10% have life insurance coverage and less than 1% have non-life insurance. Furthermore, a mere 5.2% of Indian villages have a bank branch.

Gupta – like Grameen Bank founder, Muhammad Yunus – is not a banker. He qualified as an architect in the 1980s and started working in the remote villages of India as a 'barefoot architect'. Then, on 30 September 1993, the most devastating Stable Continental Region (SCR) earthquake in the world hit Latur in the state of Maharashtra, killing over 10,000 people. Gupta was deeply moved and spent the next few years working in the region, designing earthquake-resistant village houses. Indeed, if his story ended there, it would be a remarkable and inspiring tale. But Gupta is a true entrepreneur, always curious, always challenged, always innovating.

Towards the end of the 1990s, the dotcom boom was sweeping the world and Gupta wanted in on the action. But being a social entrepreneur, he wondered how he could use the burgeoning ICT revolution to make a difference in the villages of India. The breakthrough idea came in 2000, when Gupta was on a visit to Belgium. Being self-employed, he had struggled to obtain a credit card from the banks in India. However, in Belgium, he discovered he could use a smart card-based electronic purse (e-purse) to manage his expenses during the week-long trip. Gupta immediately saw the potential of this offline micro-payment technology for carrying out small transactions in Indian villages. On his return, he registered a company called A Little World (ALW) to see if he could adapt and introduce the e-purse system to India.

Over the next few years, Gupta worked hard on bringing all the necessary players together in a partnership called the Zero-Mass Consortium, including companies such as Proton of Belgium, Gemplus International of France, Giesecke, Devrient and Infineon Technologies of Germany, and ERG Group of Australia. Meanwhile, the rapid rise of mobile phone technology changed their initial focus on smart cards and instead they developed a P2P (person-to-person) payment product called mCHQ (later renamed mChek) as an application on mobile SIMs, in collaboration with Escotel and later with Airtel. Major Indian banks like ICICI Bank and SBI signed up for mCHQ in 2005, as did VISA.

Despite its success, Gupta was not convinced that mCHQ did enough to tackle financial inclusion. Then fortuitously, in 2006, the confluence of an important change in Indian banking legislation and a breakthrough in mobile phone technology gave him the means to realize his mission. As a result, he spun off mCHQ's technology and business assets into a separate company, and refocused ALW on his original vision of financial inclusion. The legislative change was the introduction by the Reserve Bank of India of so-called 'Business Correspondent (BC) Guidelines', whereby non-profit-making entities are allowed to function as intermediaries (BCs) of mainstream banks in rural areas. So Gupta set up a non-profit organization called ZMF (Zero Microfinance and Savings Support Foundation) to act as a BC, supported by ALW as the technology partner.

Gupta was already focused on the mobile phone as the key enabler for his vision of micro-banking. By 2006, the new generation of mobile phones included NFC (Near Field Communication) capabilities that allowed easy, wireless connection to peripheral devices like printers and biometric scanners. This eliminated the need for prohibitively expensive, skills-dependent, battery-hungry laptops. However, they faced another problem. With the banks initially insisting that all transactions take place 'live' (in real time) online – and as connectivity is rather haphazard in the villages – transactions were extremely time consuming. 'All 600 people from a village would line up at once, losing a day's wage to wait in line', recalls Gupta.

This problem was solved by the launch of Nokia's 6131 handsets. Gupta explains the significance of this breakthrough:

> Conventional devices can never meet an unconventional set of challenges. The offline transaction service was possible because the new Nokia 6131 phone that succeeded the earlier Nokia 3220 NFC had 2GB of available local storage on a micro-SD card. The new phone also had bluetooth. This encouraged us to combine the printer and fingerprint scanners (which were separate devices initially), and attach a serial bluetooth interface to the combination device to enable communications with the NFC phone.

> We were struggling to find an affordable smart card. The new Nokia 6131 handsets gave us the most important breakthrough so far: the ability to eliminate smart cards altogether. Instead of the villager's biometric and account data being stored on expensive smart cards, which could be lost or damaged and were costly to replace, we started issuing plain plastic cards that were only used for photo and ID number verification and the mobile phone's memory held the villager's transactional and identification data. We could now hold up to 50,000 customers' data on a single mobile, in a securely encrypted database, thanks to the PKI level of security provided by NFC. The mobile had finally become a core banking branch in every sense.

With all the pieces of the puzzle in place, the story of Niroshini (the formerly unbanked person) and Indira (the one-person village microbank) became possible. Working with and on behalf of the State Bank of India, ALW ran pilot projects in the unbanked rural areas of Aizwal (Mizoram), Medak (Andhra Pradesh) and Pithoragarh (Uttarakhand). Each pilot enrolled about 5,000 villagers for no-frills bank accounts, which allowed them to deposit, withdraw and transfer small amounts, as well as to take out microloans.[35] Less than six months later, in April 2007, ALW also piloted the disbursement of government benefits (Electronic Benefit Transfer, or EBT) through the microbanks and on behalf of six major Indian commercial banks.

The EBT innovation had profound effects. In one village, a woman said: 'I used to get my payment from the post office with a delay of several weeks, sometimes months, after repeated trips. Now I get it here, much earlier, in my village.' And because it is an automated, electronic transfer that can only be paid to a fingerprint-authenticated individual, ALW is also cutting out corruption. After switching to the microbanking method, 10–15% of social security pensions remained unclaimed, suggesting the extent of 'phantom beneficiaries' that were defrauding the government before. The microbanks have other benefits too. Because ALW develops a credit history for rural villagers, they will eventually have access to credit at rates 2–3 times cheaper than what they would normally get from informal moneylenders and microfinance institutions. There is also huge potential for what a 2010 Allianz report calls 'microinsurance'.

Four years after its launch, in 2010, ALW is on the tipping point of serious scalability, with 11,000 microbank branches operating in all states of India and serving 5.5 million customers. Part of the reason for its success has been Gupta's relentless pursuit of efficiency and low-cost options, so that today each microbank branch costs less than $85 a month to run and customers are only charged around 5 rupees (10 cents) a month to use the bank's services. At the time when I interviewed him, in April 2010, Gupta expected ALW to become the largest micro-banking system in the world

---

[35]Deposits are limited to Rs50,000 ($1,000), transactions must be less than Rs10,000 ($200) and turnover less than Rs200,000 ($4,000) a year.

within six months and – pending capital injection of around $60 million – to have set up in 150,000 locations in India over the next two to three years.

Impressed yet? Believe it or not, Gupta is just getting started. He sees the branch network as an enabler to deliver all kinds of other essential services to India's rural poor. Already, he has innovated rechargeable LED light boxes to replace polluting and hazardous kerosene lamps, as well as enhancements to wood- or cow-dung burning stoves, using a fan that halves cooking time, halves fuel requirements and almost eliminates the poisonous smoke. Future innovations include water filters, bicycles, televisions, spectacles, radios, medicines and textbooks.

To make all these products affordable, Gupta plans to use a lease-purchase model, whereby costs are divided into weekly instalments for six, 12, 18 or 24 months, depending on the product. So, for example, a rural villager pays just a few rupees for one-week's use of a rechargeable LED lamp. At the end of the week, they return it and pay the next week's instalment for an already recharged LED light-box replacement. Using a similar approach, villages will also be able to buy communal toilets, with monthly instalments of just 20 rupees (40 cents) for a period of five or ten years.

ALW's vision remains ambitious: To touch a billion people through innovative technologies and alliances at the bottom of the pyramid for delivering multiple financial (and other) services at the lowest cost through mainstream financial (and other) institutions. Having spent a little time with Gupta, I would not bet against his inspiring vision becoming a reality. ALW is a testimony to Gupta's creativity and to the power of innovation – not only in technology, but also in partnerships and business models – to tackle some of society's most intractable social challenges.

Stagnation through standardization

In contrast to the story of Anurag Gupta and A Little World, one of the great dangers of the Age of Management – especially its focus on standardization – is that it does not foster the kind of creativity that is needed to solve the complex social, environmental and ethical problems that we face. The reasons are fairly obvious. An incremental approach, in which companies set their own CSR-related objectives voluntarily, does not tend to create the kind of stretch targets that incubate innovation. Also, standardization is by its very nature a compliance-based approach, with systems, procedures, measures and audits. As a result, those running on the standards treadmill develop a tick-box mentality, rather than thinking outside the box.

Here is an example of how it happens in practice, which is based on a true story. A colleague of mine works in CSR at one of the production plants of a multinational pharmaceutical company. When I interviewed him a few years ago, he was deeply disappointed by the conservative, compliance-driven approach of their international head of environment, health and safety (EHS):

> There was quite a level of frustration for me when we had the top EHS guy come out from America and visit the site. We were actually training The Natural Step to shop floor guys, and we were quite excited that he would take this thing on, and he had the power to change the whole way the corporation thinks. . . . Well, he obviously had a very different take on it and the approach that has been taken in the company has very much on the surface been the legal type ISO approach.

Sometimes the standards themselves are (perhaps unwittingly) to blame. For instance, when the Global Reporting Initiative (GRI) launched its G3 Sustainability Reporting Guidelines, they included Application Levels. According to the GRI:

> They are intended to communicate to the readers of your report to what extent the G3 Guidelines have been utilized in your sustainability report

[and] to provide GRI reporters with a pathway in which they can continuously improve their reporting.

There are 3 Application Levels: A, B and C. These levels can be self-declared, third-party-checked and/or GRI-checked and each with the option of recognising external assurance, by adding a '+' to the rating. So far, so good. The problem is that, because the levels are directly related to the number of indicators reported (more indicators equal a higher rating), many companies have slavishly reported on many irrelevant or marginal issues, despite GRI's request that they use the levels 'with due regard to the Materiality Principle'.

In such compliance-driven environments, incentivized by CSR standardization, two things typically happen. Most managers will go strictly by the book – whatever the letter of the standard dictates – without experimentation, without pushing the envelope and hence with less likelihood of making mistakes. After all, measurement, auditing and reporting are widely perceived as a strategy to eliminate mistakes. The other thing that happens is that managers become creative about how to trick the system. If the standard calls for continuous improvement on pollution reduction and pollution has gone up, then why not report against units of production so that it appears to have gone down? If a multinational supply chain auditor requires SA 8000 compliance, why not run two factories: one 'model site' for the international auditors to check, and one without labour controls to supply the mass market? What the Age of Management does, therefore, is at best stifle creativity and at worst foster perverse creativity, causing companies to regress into the Age of Marketing.

This was somewhat evident in a 2010 McKinsey survey, which showed that while more than 50% of executives considered sustainability 'very' or 'extremely' important in a wide range of areas – including new-product development, reputation building, and overall corporate strategy – only around 30% said their companies actively seek opportunities to invest in sustainability or embed it in their business practices. Not that corporate sustainability and responsibility lacks the potential for innovation. Back in 1997, leading academic Stuart Hart was already saying that 'greening has been framed in terms of risk reduction, reengineering, or cost cutting. Rarely is greening linked to strategy or technology development, and as a result, most companies fail to recognize opportunities of potentially staggering proportions.'

More than ten years later, these sentiments were echoed in the *Harvard Business Review* (September 2009) which observed that 'companies won't innovate successfully – and as a result won't grow – unless they throw themselves whole hog into green initiatives'. The authors, Ram Nidumolu, C.K. Prahalad and M.R. Rangaswami, concluded that 'smart companies now treat sustainability as innovation's new frontier'. Similarly, Jeffrey Hollender and Bill Green declare in *The Responsibility Revolution* that 'green marketing campaigns don't cut it anymore; insurgent good companies focus on innovation rather than reputation'.

When creativity is a bad thing

Of course, there has never been a shortage of creativity in business. In fact, one of the strongest drivers of creativity today is the market. However, the market has by and large only tracked and rewarded economic measures of progress. It is hardly surprisingly, therefore, that a great deal of the creativity in business has gone towards making more money, not towards minimizing the negative impacts of business on society. The derivatives boom since the 1980s is a classic case in point. This has been creativity on a grand scale by 'the smartest guys in the room', but with the sole objective of making unprecedented amounts of money from speculation. The result is that, in extreme cases like Enron and Lehman Brothers, innovation literally manifests as creative accounting.

The lesson from these cases – and more generally from the Age of Greed – is that it is not just financial incentives but also the cultural context that drives our behaviour. Sometimes that culture is about pure, unbridled greed, but more often it is an insidious culture of materialism and consumerism. Chilean 'barefoot economist' Manfred Max-Neef believes this prevailing culture is due to a fundamental misunderstanding (or misdirection) of how we satisfy our fundamental human needs. The belief that buying a product can give us more status or acceptance or intimacy, for example, is simply a misnomer. Max-Neef calls these pseudo-satisfiers. They will never make us truly content or happy.

But that hasn't stopped us trying. Since 1980, the global economy has tripled in size and is expected to expand by a factor of five in the next 50 years. World energy consumption rose from 207 quadrillion British thermal units (btus) in 1970 to 375 quadrillion btus in 1996 and is projected to reach 612 quadrillion btus in 2020. Average annual anthropogenetic carbon emissions, which were less than two billion tons between 1850 and 1950, rocketed to 7.1 billion tons during the 1980s and will soar further to an expected 9.8 billion tons by 2020. Speaking to me in 2008, L. Hunter Lovins observed that 'we are using resources so inefficiently that our economy digs up, puts through various resource crunching activities and then throws away, half a trillion tonnes of stuff a year. Out of all this stuff, less than 1% of it ever gets in a product, and is still there 6 months after sale. All the rest is waste.'

And what, more than anything else, is pushing our consumerist lifestyle? In a word, advertising. The $450 billion advertising industry – which is surely the very epitome of business creativity – has a very dubious ethical foundation. How often are advertisements about providing useful product information and how often are they about manipulating the psyche of prospective 'consumers'? Advertising today is all about associating a brand with an emotion – usually triggered by images of aspirational lifestyles or popularity, irrespective of their relevance to the product. 'Pseudo-satisfiers', Max-Neef reminded me in 2008, 'have justified the emergence and the development of one of the most colossal industries that have ever existed which is advertising. The purpose of advertising is to generate pseudo-satisfiers.'

And so, while the Age of Management acts in many ways as the antidote to creativity, the Age of Marketing acts as a disease of maliferous creativity. BP's 'Beyond Petroleum' campaign was creative, but towards what end? Lehman Brothers' NINJA mortgages were creative, but for whose benefit? Creativity is necessary for ushering in the Age of Responsibility, but like technology, it depends how that creativity is directed.

Creative destruction

One of the most popular theories on innovation is creative destruction. The concept is most associated with Joseph Schumpeter, following his 1942 book *Capitalism, Socialism and Democracy*, in which he described creative destruction as 'the process of industrial mutation that incessantly revolutionizes the economic structure from within, incessantly destroying the old one, incessantly creating a new one . . . [The process] must be seen in its role in the perennial gale of creative destruction; it cannot be understood on the hypothesis that there is a perennial lull.'

The idea, of course, is much older. In Hinduism, the goddess Shiva is simultaneously the creator and destroyer of worlds. In modern times, the German sociologist Werner Sombart described the process in 1913, saying 'from destruction a new spirit of creation arises; the scarcity of wood and the needs of everyday life . . . forced the discovery or invention of substitutes for wood, forced the use of coal for heating, forced the invention of coke for the production of iron'. Even Marx and Engels had an attempt at describing the process in their *Communist Manifesto*, stating that 'constant revolutionizing of production, uninterrupted disturbance of all social conditions, everlasting uncertainty and agitation distinguish the bourgeois epoch from all earlier ones. . . . All that is solid melts into air.'

The idea of melting solids is very similar to the metaphor used by sustainability and social enterprise thought-leader John Elkington to explain the disruptive changes going on in the world. When I interviewed him in 2008, he said:

What happens in an earthquake? The land becomes thixotropic; what was solid suddenly becomes almost semi-liquid. I think we are headed towards a period where the global economy goes into a sort of thixotropic state. Key parts of our economies and societies are on a doomed path really, and I think that's unavoidable. I think we're heading into a period of creative destruction on a scale that really we haven't seen for a very long time, and there are all sorts of factors that feed into it – the entry of the Chinese and Indians into the global market, quite apart from things like climate change and new technology. All of these pressures are going to mobilize a set of dynamics which are unpredictable and profoundly disruptive to incumbent companies, so some companies will disappear.

As to what this means for business, Elkington says:

I think most companies that we currently know will not be around in fifteen to twenty years, which is almost an inconceivable statement. But periodically this happens and there's a radical bleeding of the landscape. We'll find this sort of reassembly going on. Over a period of time we're going to have some fairly different products, technologies and business models coming back into the West, and I think it's going to be quite exciting, but very disruptive.

We see all kinds of examples of creative destruction in corporate sustainability and responsibility. For virtually the whole of the 20th century, the biggest companies in the world were the oil and motor giants – companies like Exxon, BP, General Motors and Toyota. But the 21st century, with growing concerns over energy security and climate change on the one hand and the rising geo-political and economic power of the East on the other, are ushering in a new era. Already in 2006, the richest man in China was reported to be Shi Shengrong, CEO of the solar company Suntech, and the richest women, Zhang Yin, made her fortune from recycling. By 2009, it was Wang Chuanfu, founder of BYD, which manufactures batteries and electric cars. A 2010 report published by the Pew Environmental Center found that in 2009, China invested $34.6 billion in the clean energy economy, while the US invested only $18.6 billion. In June 2010, China also launched its own Clean Tech Index. The US is fighting back. Venture capital (VC) investment in renewable energy, electric cars, energy efficiency, and other green technology jumped to $1.5 billion in the US in the second quarter of 2010, a near 64% spike over the same period in 2009. Green tech investment in the US has now returned to the record levels of the third quarter of 2008, before the global economic collapse.

This explosive growth was brought home to me, at an event of Women In Sustainability Action (WISA) in Shanghai where I was speaking in June 2010. I got talking to a supplier of wind turbines to Europe simply put, he cannot keep up with the demand. He is turning customers away because there is already a 12-month lead time of orders in the pipeline. Even Germany, an early leader in the clean-technology space, can no longer compete with China in this sunrise industry. It is no coincidence that while Obama's energy reform bill was scuppered by the US Congress, Malaysia created an Energy, Green Technology and Water Ministry. And while the British company BP was virtually on its knees in May 2010, the Korean company Samsung unveiled an eye-watering investment plan to 'future-proof' the company by sinking $21 billion into its green technology and healthcare businesses. It claimed that the investment would generate $44 billion in annual sales and 45,000 new jobs by 2020.

Making money mobile

It is clear from these examples that creativity comes from a mixture of risk and opportunity. One of the megatrends I see, however, is that so many of the greatest risks (be they terrorism, financial instability or obesity) are shifting to the industrialized world, while many of the greatest opportunities (like economic growth, clean technology and social enterprise) are shifting to the developing world. Emerging markets are on the rise and developed countries are in danger of saturation or stagnation. There is a simple driver behind this shift: risk is fed by satisfaction and complacency, while opportunity is driven by hunger and need. And of course, in developing countries, the scale of social needs and the hunger for improving their lot in life are still massive. Necessity is the mother of invention and desire is the father of effort.

One place where these dynamics are playing out is in the telecommunications sector. In a Vodafone sponsored study of 92 countries over the period 1996 to 2003, it was concluded that a developing country with an average increase of 10% mobile penetration showed 0.59% higher growth in GDP than an otherwise identical country. This study was replicated by Deloitte in 2007 using more recent data, which found that a 10% increase in mobile penetration would produce an additional 1.2% increase in annual GDP growth rate.

Today, two thirds of the world's mobile phone subscriptions are in developing nations, with the highest growth rate in Africa. It took just six years – from 1994 to 2000 – for mobile phones to overtake fixed lines on the continent, with an average 1000% annual growth rate. And the rapid take-up continues: while just one in 50 Africans had a mobile in the year 2000, now 28% have a cellular subscription. There are many reasons for this phenomenal growth, including shorter payback periods on investment, the relatively low skill levels needed to operate a mobile phone (as compared, say, with a computer), low barriers to entry (especially in terms of infrastructure) and business model innovations (such as prepaid systems, Grameen-style micro-entrepreneurship and mobiles as public telephones or telecentres).

Beyond simply expanding traditional mobile services to Africa, however, companies like Vodafone have also used the continent as an incubator for innovation. In Kenya in 2005, for example, 80% of the population did not have a bank account. Also, more money was coming into the country through remittances from family members living abroad than through oversees development assistance. However, these transfers were expensive, with Western Union typically taking a big slice in commission. Hence, Vodafone developed and piloted a new service called M-PESA, whereby customers could use their mobile phones to perform basic financial services, including depositing, withdrawing and transferring money using SMS texts.

The project was jointly funded by the UK Department for International Development (DFID) Financial Deepening Challenge Fund and the pilot ran for over six months in Kenya from October 2005, in partnership with Faulu Kenya, a local Microfinance Institution. Since rolling out through its national partner, Safaricom, the service has been wildly successful. For many, the service has been life-changing, giving access to financial services from which they were excluded and allowing them to receive remittance payments from the UK directly. Besides employing and empowering thousands of M-PESA agents, the scheme has also cut out a lot of corruption, as all transactions are electronic. When Vodafone extended the M-PESA service to Tanzania in April 2008, they signed up more than 3 million customers in less than a year. In 2009, Safaricom also launched the continent's first commercial solar powered mobile phone, the Coral-200. Building on their success in Kenya, Tanzania and Roshan in Afghanistan (branded M-Paisa), they announced in February 2010 that they would bring M-PESA to South Africa as well, which is Africa's biggest economy. Given its efforts, it is not surprising that Vodafone was placed first as a sustainable business in the Tomorrow's Value Rating of the ICT and Telecoms sector. Building on the success of Vodafone and others, a 2010 study by Arthur D. Little estimates that global transaction volume in mobile financial services will reach approximately $280 billion by 2015.

Self-sufficient electronics

Another innovation coming out of Africa started with music – or to be more precise, radios. It was whilst watching a BBC documentary in April 1994 that Chris Staines first realized the potential of an innovative idea from the British inventor Trevor Baylis. 'The Clockwork Radio', as the device was first known, was proposed as a means of halting the spread of AIDS in Africa through better education. Traditional radio, although widespread, relied on an electrical supply or the availability of disposable batteries – both of which were in short supply across the continent (in sub-Saharan Africa only 29% of the population has access to electricity). By contrast, the wind-up radio was powered by a spring-charge mechanism that only required human power.

Staines and his business partner Rory Stear realized immediately the potential for self-sufficient electronics and so the Freeplay Energy Group (the company formed to develop the idea) was born. The growth of Freeplay, like so much innovation, was only possible through the support of many partners. Starting with a grant from the British government, subsequent investors have included, among others, the co-founders of the Body Shop, Gordon and Anita Roddick. On one of their community trade trips to South America, Gordon Roddick came across a Brazilian native who had obtained one of the Freeplay radios and was making a living selling people chances to listen to the radio in the jungle.

With a core purpose 'to make energy available to everybody all of the time', the company innovated to expand the product range to include wind-up torches, lanterns, portable 'power-sticks' and mobile device chargers. Most recently, they have also ventured into primary healthcare. 'Freeplay itself is the first company in the world intended to make electronic products for deep-rural environments', explained John Hutchinson, Chief Technology Officer of Freeplay Energy in Cape Town, South Africa. 'A number of people came to us and said, "Why don't you think of medical products because hospitals in Africa are littered with derelict Western-derived equipment. They require disposable or replaceable elements, and they're just not right for the job." Africa, you know, is a very harsh user environment. Things break in Africa.'

The opportunity came when Hutchinson met a doctor, John Wyatt, a professor of neonatology at University College of London Hospital. 'He works in a very up-tech environment', explained Hutchinson, 'and he had a bit of a crisis where he thought, "I spend so much money on saving one kid's life in this high-tech environment, whereas there are children dying elsewhere for lack of appropriate care".' Wyatt was painfully aware that 95% of infant mortality happens in developing countries, but they only have 5% of the world's technology available to them. So Wyatt managed to get some seed money from the Halley Stewart Trust and worked with Hutchinson to look at three potential devices – a pulse oxymeter (which measures oxygen saturation in the blood of children), a syringe driver (which assists in giving newborns intravenous nourishment safely) and a jaundice pigment measurer (to determine degrees of jaundice in infants).

In the end, these turned out to be beyond the capacity of Freeplay, but they came up with an alternative product that they felt they could support: an off-grid foetal heart rate monitor. *The Washington Post* reports that half a million women die annually in childbirth, often from causes that could be prevented with basic care. Getting an aid like this into the hands of midwives in the developing world could mean the difference between life and death, both for mothers and infants. Together with Philip Goodwin and Stefan Zwahlen, Hutchinson completed the design, which won a 'Design to Improve Life' Innovator's Award. Reflecting on why he continues to innovate for Freeplay, Hutchinson said: 'I've been with this company since the beginning in 1995, and it's still about providing the benefits of modern technology to people who otherwise would be completely excluded.'

Entrepreneurs on a mission

People like Chris Staines and Rory Stear are a special breed of individual, people who have become popularly known as social entrepreneurs and form part of the social enterprise movement. There are examples throughout history of companies that have worked for social benefits – think for example of the credit unions started in the 1850s in Germany by Franz Hermann Schulze-Delitzsch – but the movement really only gained formal recognition in the 1980s. This was the decade in which Bill Drayton founded Ashoka in Washington, DC, Muhammad Yunus registered Grameen Bank as an independent bank, and former Archbishop of Panama Marcos McGrath and Swiss businessman Stephen Schmidheiny set up FUNDES in Panama, all with a mission to support social entrepreneurs.

Since 1981, Ashoka has elected over 2,000 leading social entrepreneurs as Fellows, providing them with living stipends, professional support, and access to a global network of peers in more than 60 countries. Ashoka defines social entrepreneurs as those 'who have innovative solutions to social problems and the potential to change patterns across society. They demonstrate unrivalled commitment to bold new ideas and prove that compassion, creativity, and collaboration are tremendous forces for change.' Put more simply, 'the life purpose of the true social entrepreneur', says Bill Drayton, 'is to change the world'.

And many have done just that. Ashoka evaluates the impact of its Fellows five years after their election and start up. In 2010, the Corporate Executive Board Company reported the results of a survey of Ashoka's impact, which they conducted in 12 languages across the globe. They found that 52% of the Ashoka Fellows had changed national policy within five years and 76% had changed the pattern in their field nationally (on average 3.2 times) within the same five years. 'These results are especially striking', reflects Drayton, 'since five years is early in the lifecycle of the social entrepreneur.'

The social enterprise movement was given a boost in the 1990s with the establishment of the Schwab Foundation for Social Entrepreneurship (started by the World Economic Forum's founder, Klaus Schwab), which supports 'pragmatic visionaries who achieve large scale, systemic and sustainable social change through new invention, a different approach or a more rigorous application of known technologies or strategies'. Jeff Skoll, first president of eBay, also set up a fund – the Skoll Foundation – to support social entrepreneurs. 'I like to support causes where a lot of good comes from a little bit of good', says Skoll. 'In other words, where the positive social returns vastly exceed the amount of time and money invested.'

One of the projects supported by the Skoll Foundation was a series of studies by SustainAbility on social entrepreneurship. The first report, *Growing Opportunity*, concluded that three different mindsets have characterized business thinking in relation to social and environmental issues. 'If 1.0 was about compliance and 2.0 about citizenship, 3.0 is about creative

destruction and creative reconstruction.' They identified five main components to this Mindset 3.0: (1) systems thinking and design, like cradle-to-
cradle; (2) consumer engagement, like at Villagereach; (3) new business
models, like Aravind Eye Hospitals; (4) 360° accountability, as promoted
by Transparency International; and (5) base-of-the-pyramid markets, like
the Danone & Grameen Bank partnership.

One of the leading think-tank organizations focused on the social enterprise space today is Volans Ventures, co-founded by John Elkington which,
among its other activities, produces a roll call of 'The Phoenix 50' pioneers
in the business of social innovation, nominated by entrepreneurs and other
stakeholders.

Kickstarting development

What many of these institutions like Skoll and Volans realize is that the
creative entrepreneurs often already exist, but lack capital, management
expertise and access to markets. This is precisely the sort of gap that Martin
Fisher and Nick Moon were trying to address when they founded Appro-
TEC in 1991, which in 2005 became KickStart. Their early efforts were
focused on building and food processing technologies and applying them
to Africa, where 80% of the poor are small-scale farmers who depend on
unreliable rain to grow their crops and have, at most, two harvests per year.

KickStart understood that irrigation would allow people to move from subsistence farming to commercial agriculture. Therefore, they developed a
line of manually operated MoneyMaker Irrigation Pumps that allow farmers
to easily pull water from a river, pond or shallow well, pressurize it through
a hose pipe (even up a hill) and irrigate up to two acres of land. The pumps
are easy to transport, install and operate and retail between $35 and $95.
It is a very efficient use of water, and unlike flood irrigation, does not lead
to the build-up of salts in the soil.

KickStart continued to expand their range of irrigation and other products,
including for example a Stabilized Soil Block Press, which makes strong

building blocks from soil and cement, and the Mafuta Mali oilseed press for sunflower and sesame seeds in the East and Central African region. Using this experience, Fisher and Moon developed a five-step process to develop, launch and promote these simple money-making tools that social entrepreneurs could use to create their own profitable businesses.

As a result, since 1991, 97,500 successful new businesses have been started all over Africa, with more than 800 being created each month. Since each of these enterprises supports a family, KickStart conservatively estimate that these businesses have already lifted 488,000 people out of poverty. Each year these businesses generate over $98.6 million in new profits and wages and have created 147,300 new waged jobs. In Kenya alone, users are generating new revenues equivalent to 0.6% of GDP. Today, people from around the world can make donations on the KickStart website, with the reassuring possibility that 'each dollar donated can turn into $15 in profits and wages'.

In a similar resource matching initiative, the Microfinance Information Exchange (MIX) acts as an intermediary that is catalysing the efforts of the microfinance industry. MIX supplies detailed financial and social performance information about microfinance institutions to potential investors, as well as to the institutions themselves. This data not only helps individuals and organizations make wise decisions, it also strengthens the microfinance sector as a whole. In a similar way, Local Initiatives Support Corporation (LISC) magnifies the efforts of community development organizations by connecting them to corporate, government, and philanthropic resources. LISC helps local organizations secure funding, change policy, and enlist technical and management assistance. As a result of its matchmaking, LISC has helped build 253,000 affordable homes, 38 million square feet of retail and community space, and 132 schools.

These so-called 'clicks-to-bricks' schemes help to scale up entrepreneurial solutions. For example, in its first ten years, KaBOOM! helped communities build nearly 750 playgrounds, but its reach was partly limited by the number of staff it could deploy to each site. When it shifted from hands-on management to a Web-based platform that helps communities organize their projects, approximately 4,000 more playgrounds were constructed in just three years. Sun Ovens International, founded by Paul Munsen, is a similar development-related entrepreneurial solution that is seeking to scale up around the world.

Africa's first free university

Another example of social innovation in Africa that has inspired me over the years is the story of the CIDA Campus in Johannesburg. When I was still working at KPMG, I met CIDA's co-founder and CEO, Taddy Blecher. He was a privileged white South African who qualified as an actuary and was earning a six-figure salary before he gave it all up to start a social enterprise. His motivation was seeing the extremity of need that surrounded him: 'South Africa today is a sea of youth, with no direction, no guidance. These kids roam around the townships, they grow up in shacks, in squatter camps. So it's actually a huge challenge in this country to try to pull the youth back.'

'Traditionally, people have always looked at Africa as a basket case and they've said Africans are not able to do it for themselves. So when they are sick, we send medicines and when people are starving to death, there's a food drop somewhere, and the food disappears or it goes rotten. As far as we're concerned that's a superficial way of thinking about development. Africans have genius; they have the ability to create for themselves.' It was really around that philosophy that Blecher decided to create the first free University in South Africa. 'We wanted to prove that it was possible to take a child off the streets who had come through a very disadvantaged education and turn them into a chartered accountant, turn them into a merchant banker, a stock broker, a Java programmer. Because if we could prove that it was possible, we could take the country forward into a new reality.'

CIDA Education Manager Sandra Musengi explains that 'CIDA is unique in that our students run the campus itself, and obviously that helps us to cut down a lot of costs. We've got our cleaning services; we've got our basic operations. By having our students run the campus, they start to understand basic principles of management, basic principles of operations. As a result, by the time they go out into the workplace, they have already acquired a certain level of skills.' In fact, they leave not only with these skills, but also with a social entrepreneurial mindset. 'When we come to CIDA, we are all from different backgrounds, but something makes us one', explains Musengi. 'We have this will, we have this drive, we have this passion of wanting to bring change.'

Beyond relying on the students to run the campus, CIDA relies on voluntary contributions from guest lecturers and business suppliers. 'We've had to find a way of getting materials, teachers, money, making it accessible so that we could reinvent this paradigm of university', says Blecher. Today, CIDA has thousands of graduates earning tens of millions in salaries every year. 'That's going back to families that had absolutely nothing', reflects Blecher. 'So we're creating a human chain, it's a human network. And I do believe we could change Africa and the developing world if we could create a human network where everybody's holding hands. It's only really selfishness that stops us from building stable, decent societies.'

'This is really what CIDA is trying to do is be a life raft that pulls people out of the majority of the population to the other side of the river where there is employment and opportunity. And as we pull them, they pull everybody else behind them and that's really what our model is.' And Blecher's vision for the future? 'If we get the support, and people adopt these ideas, we could open up universities, colleges, vocational schools and relevant high schools right across the whole of Africa for next to nothing and they could be fully self sufficient.'

EVOKE-ing a responsibility revolution

Another way of teaching tomorrow's leaders creatively is by using games. On 3 March 2010, the World Bank Institute (WBI) and InfoDev launched their alternate reality game EVOKE. Players who successfully completed ten game challenges in ten weeks were able to claim their honours, as Certified World Bank Institute Social Innovator – Class of 2010. The top players could also earn online mentorships with experienced social innovators and business leaders from around the world, and scholarships to share their vision for the future at the EVOKE Summit in Washington, DC.

EVOKE ended on 19 May 2010, far exceeding expectations for participation. Some 19,300 people from 150 countries registered to play. They submitted over 23,500 blog posts (about 335 each day), 4,700 photos and more than 1,500 videos highlighting challenges and solutions to the development issues featured each week. Players went into their communities to learn about challenges on the ground and shared potential solutions to what they saw and heard. One player collected all of these ideas into a single blog post. EVOKE has created a unique space for dialogue around important issues that may not be discussed in other social networking forums.

Another WBI educational initiative was an Innovation Fair held in Cape Town, South Africa, in February 2010. The Fair, with the theme 'Moving Beyond Conflict', brought together project teams, conflict and fragility experts, social entrepreneurs, local software developers and potential funders to discuss 32 finalist projects selected through a combination of crowd voting and expert juries. One finalist was Map Kibera, which is creating the first detailed and digitized map of the sprawling Nairobi slum where one million people live without water, sanitation, and other basic services. Other projects suggested using new technologies to improve the delivery of legal services in Ethiopia, connect rural communities electronically in Sri Lanka, support peacekeeping in Nepal and monitor elections in 24 African countries.

Of course, there are thousands more social entrepreneurial tales to tell. One social entrepreneur that made the headlines in 2008 was Wang Chuan-Fu, the owner of BYD, dubbed by *Fortune* magazine as 'an obscure Chinese battery, mobile phone, and electric car company', who attracted

$230 million from Warren Buffet for a 10% equity investment. Despite being relatively unknown in the West, by 2000, BYD had already become one of the world's largest manufacturers of cell phone batteries, and went on to design and manufacture mobile-phone handsets and parts for Motorola. It entered the electric car market in 2003 and began selling a plug-in electric car with a backup gasoline engine ahead of GM, Nissan and Toyota.

BYD's plug-in, called the F3DM, goes farther on a single charge than other electric vehicles and sells for about $22,000, less than the plug-in Prius and much-hyped and belated Chevy Volt. By 2009, BYD employed 130,000 people in 11 factories, eight in China and one each in India, Hungary, and Romania. Wang Chuan-Fu, at 43, topped the annual *Hurun* Rich List of the nation's wealthiest, with assets of $5.1 billion, jumping 102 places from the 2008 ranking. Interestingly, second place went to another environmental entrepreneur, 'Paper Queen' Zhang Yin, from Nine Dragons Paper. Her company imports recyclable paper and processes it into packaging and paper materials, primarily for export. She is worth $4.9 billion.

As these examples show, big companies can also be innovators. The classic example remains General Electric's clean technology investment initiative, which it dubbed 'Ecomagination'. GE has invested $5 billion in Ecomagination R&D since its inception in 2005 and committed to investing another $10 billion in the coming five years. Launched with 17 products, the Ecomagination portfolio now includes more than 90 and in the next 24 months, about 30 other products will be added. In a related project, in July 2010, GE announced a $200 million open innovation challenge that seeks breakthrough ideas to create a smarter, cleaner, more efficient electric grid, and to accelerate the adoption of more efficient grid technologies. The money will be invested globally into promising start-ups and ideas. 'Innovation is the engine of the global effort to transform the way we create, connect and use power', CEO Jeff Immelt said. 'This challenge is about collaboration and we are inviting others to help accelerate progress in creating a cleaner, more efficient and economically viable grid. We want to jump-start new ideas and deploy them on a scale that will modernize the electrical grid around the world.'

We are the champions

So what do Taddy Blecher, Anurag Gupta, Wang Chuan-Fu, Jeff Immelt and all of the other social entrepreneurs have in common? Is this a special breed of human being? Are social entrepreneurs born or can they be made? In the academic literature, there is an interesting thread of research centred around the concept of 'champions' in organizations, especially 'environmental champions'. The idea draws on prior conceptions of the human resources champion in the 1970s and 1980s, before HR became institutionalized.

Academics define environmental champions as people who can express attractively a personal vision about environmental protection that is in tune with both industry's needs and wider public concern and who convince and enable organization members to turn environmental issues into successful corporate programmes and innovations. Environmental champions have been shown to be imbued with a combination of characteristics, including being a catalyst, champion, sponsor, facilitator and demonstrator. Their skills include the ability to identify, package and sell environmental issues within their organizations. Their effectiveness in engaging others rests heavily on expertise, top management support and a strong appreciation for the problems that every business unit or operations manager faces.

Research on champions is not confined purely to the environmental dimension of sustainability. Others have written about socially responsible change-agents, as well as managers' individual discretion as a component of corporate social performance. British academic Christine Hemingway, for example, finds that CSR can be the result of championing by a few managers, based on their personal values and beliefs, despite the personal and professional risks this may entail. Individual managers are also often mediators in corporate philanthropy and stakeholder influence. Hence, the notion of CSR champions has emerged as an important concept, which I will return to this in the final chapter on individual change agents.

Bill Drayton, who has been involved in selecting and tracking the progress of the 2,700 Ashoka Fellows, believes social entrepreneurs 'focus everyday on the "how to" questions. How are they going to get from here to their ultimate goal? How are they going to deal with this opportunity or that barrier? How are the pieces going to fit together? They are engineers, not poets. . . . The entrepreneur's job is not to take an idea and then implement it. That is what franchisees do. The entrepreneur is building something that is entirely new – by constantly creating and testing and recreating and then testing and recreating again.'[36]

There are other characteristics as well, says Drayton:

> The true social entrepreneur also has an almost magical ability to move people, a power rooted in exceptional ethical fibre. He or she is always asking people to do things that are unreasonable – and people do them. . . . The entrepreneur has an inner confidence that most sense but do not understand. While others think entrepreneurs are taking risks, entrepreneurs don't see it that way because they have thought things through extremely well. They also believe in their ability continuously to adapt the idea as they drive toward a goal that they know is a huge win for everyone, and ultimately to reach that goal. They know, in other words, that they have the gift that brings the greatest happiness in the world, the gift of being able to give at the highest level. Once one grasps who the true social entrepreneur is, one would have to be crazed to bet against him or her ultimately changing the world at large scale.

Mapping the innovation territory

Examples of social entrepreneurs like Taddy Blecher of CIDA and many others suggest that sustainability and responsibility innovation is alive and well and, if anything, growing rapidly. Consider what Danone has done with food fortification. Working with Muhammad Yunus's Grameen group in Bangladesh, the company set out to put enough vitamin A, iron, zinc and

---

[36]Drayton, B. (2010) 'Tipping the world: The power of collaborative entrepreneurship'. Published on the *McKinsey What Matters* site, 8 April 2010.

iodine into a 60 g or 80 g cup of yogurt to meet 30% of a child's daily needs. That proportion was beyond anything Danone had ever attempted. It took a year and dozens of tries to figure out how to do it without the nutrients reacting with one another and souring the yogurt.

The question remains: Is such innovation a random and unpredictable phenomenon, or is there some underlying rationale or theory that we can use to better understand and advance social innovation? In 2007, a joint Nordic project was launched to focus on CSR as a key innovation driver. The ambition was to develop a systematic approach to CSR-driven innovation to make SMEs break new ground on, for example, low-income markets or strengthening competitiveness by linking innovative solutions to key social or environmental problems. Inspired by the concept, social entrepreneurship is now being supported in Denmark by the government-funded Center for Social Economy.

In 2008, I did a research project with my colleagues at Cambridge University on sustainability innovation.[37] In our attempt to 'map the territory', we created a model that looked at the Enablers, Processes and Agents of sustainability innovation. There were a number of interesting findings.

First, of the four *Enablers* of innovation that we identified – government, finance, technology and culture – most people are focused either on finance or technology. For example, in the SustainAbility survey of over 100 social entrepreneurs, 72% cited 'access to finance' as their primary challenge, and much of the report is dedicated to understanding this issue.[38] Furthermore, many typical cases held up as innovation success stories – whether they be GE's Ecomagination programme or Vodafone's M-Pesa service – are almost inevitably technology solutions. The corollary of this finding is that the role of government and culture is being neglected. Government, by setting clear, long-term policy targets on social and environmental issues like biodiversity, climate change

---

[37]Blowfield, M., Visser, W. & Livesey, F. (2007) *Sustainability Innovation: Mapping the Territory*, University Cambridge Programme for Industry Research Paper Series: No. 2.

[38]*Growing Opportunity: Entrepreneurial Solutions to Insoluble Problems* (2007).

or access to health and sanitation, can create an enabling environment that allows business to innovate. Likewise, fostering a corporate and national culture of innovation – of opportunity orientation rather than risk obsession – is a necessary precondition for innovation.

In the area of *Processes*, of which we identified three – individual actions, management systems and tailored approaches – most of the focus has been on individual actions. This mirrored our findings for *Agents*, where individuals were favoured over companies and non-business agents. Hence, the notion of a sustainability champion or a social entrepreneur trains our hopes on the creative, business-savvy individual. This overlooks the important role of innovation within large companies – what the second in the SustainAbility series of reports called 'intrapreneurship' – as well as the potential for NGOs like Water and Sanitation for the Urban Poor (WSUP) to be part of the innovative solution.

Volans Ventures has a different take on the process, which they see happening in five stages: (1) *Eureka!* in which the opportunity is revealed via the growing dysfunction of the existing order; (2) *Experiment*, a period of trial and error for innovators; (3) *Enterprise*, during which investors and managers build new business models, creating new forms of value; (4) *Ecosystem*, when critical mass and partnerships create new markets and institutional arrangements; and (5) *Economy*, when the economic system flips to a more sustainable state, supported by cultural change.

Another interesting finding from my Cambridge research was that most cited cases seem to be innovation processes specifically targeting sustainability issues, rather than efforts at embedding sustainability principles in core innovation processes. This is a fundamental distinction, because it means that most R&D going on in companies – and hence most innovation – is not systematically building in social and environmental criteria. As a result, much like CSR more generally, innovation is a peripheral, project/product-specific activity, which is exactly what is preventing scalable solutions from emerging in the mainstream economy. Until CSR is built into every organizational process – and especially into strategic functions like R&D or new product development – we will always be playing on the fringes of the Age of Responsibility.

The Googlemorph

I want to end this chapter with one more example – Google – because it tells us so much about the role of creativity in creating the Age of Responsibility. There was a time when we all believed that Google was a search-engine company. But that was before the 'Googlemorph' – that phenomenon that Google has perfected of not only changing its spots but almost magically shapeshifting before our very eyes into a completely different creature. Understanding how and why Google manages to do this leads to some great insights.

It all begins with the leadership – or in this case two audacious Stanford PhD students who decided in 1996 that if they 'made a copy' of the Internet and applied a complicated set of esoteric mathematical algorithms, they could make a search experience that was far superior to those offered by the highly respected, heavily funded and well entrenched Yahoo! and Microsoft Explorer search engines. From this, we can gather that Google founders Larry Page and Sergey Brin are both highly ambitious and creative. But what happened next? They quickly became the most popular search engine, and once they figured out a clever pay-per-click-based advertising revenue model that worked (note that this came *after* figuring out the superior product), the money started pouring in. By the end of 2009, they were a $23 billion company.

That 13-year growth story is remarkable in and of itself, but far more interesting for us is how Google has used its success in search and its gargantuan wealth to pursue a much larger mission: to organize the world's information and make it universally accessible and useful. In practice, we see this manifesting in innovations that have changed and continue to shape all our lives: Google Maps, Google Earth, Google Finance, Google Docs, Google Books, Google Scholar, Google Images, Google Translate,

Google Alerts – and so the list goes on and on. One of the latest is Google Health, which is in a Beta testing phase and allows you to organize your health information all in one place, gathering medical records from doctors, hospitals, and pharmacies and then allowing you to share the information securely with a family member, doctors or caregivers.

To get an idea of the scale of Google's ambition and creativity, let's look briefly at two specific examples. In 2002, Google was grappling with the question: How long would it take to digitally scan every book in the world? No one knows. As part of this fact-finding mission, Page reached out to the University of Michigan, his alma mater and a pioneer in library digitization. When he learned that the estimate for scanning the university library's seven million volumes was 1,000 years, he told University president Mary Sue Coleman that Google could help make it happen in six. After experimenting with various scanning technologies, Google announced in 2004 that its Print Library Project – in partnership with the New York Public Library and the Universities of Harvard, Michigan, Oxford and Stanford – would digitize 15 million volumes.

Then, in 2007, just when we'd got used to the idea that Google was not only about search, but also making the world's knowledge archive freely available, it Googlemorphed again. Through its Google.org fund, which it established with $1 billion in 2004, it announced a new strategic goal of RE<C, or renewable energy less than carbon. Translated, the goal is to produce one gigawatt of renewable energy capacity that is cheaper than coal (one gigawatt can power a city the size of San Francisco). 'We are optimistic this can be done in years, not decades', said Page. 'If we meet this goal and large-scale renewable deployments are cheaper than coal, the world will have the option to meet a substantial portion of electricity needs from renewable sources and significantly reduce carbon emissions. We expect this would be a good business for us as well.' Google's proposal – 'Clean Energy 2030' – provides a potential path to weaning the US off coal and oil for electricity generation by 2030 (with some remaining use of natural gas as well as nuclear), and cutting oil use for cars by 44%.

What is particularly relevant for the CSR 2.0 Principle of Creativity is how Google has managed to sustain such a culture of innovation. One crucial element is that all engineering staff are allowed to spend one day a week (i.e. 20% of their work time) on their own pet projects. People are given the time and space to be creative. And when you foster such an enabling environment, innovation flows naturally and copiously. At Google, an ideas mailing list is open to anyone at the organization who wants to post a proposal. Then Marissa Mayer has the task of making sure good ideas bubble to the surface and get the attention they need. What Mayer thinks will be essential for continued innovation is for Google to keep its sense of fearlessness. 'I like to launch [products] early and often. That has become my mantra', she says. 'Nobody remembers Madonna's Sex Book or the Apple Newton. Consumers remember your average over time. That philosophy frees you from fear.'

So what's next? In 2009, Google Ventures was launched to invest in, among other areas, clean tech, biotech, and health care, all critical focus points for the Age of Responsibility. So watch this Googlemorphing space.

The principle of scalability

If you can make a change in Walmart, even if it's a small change, it's really a big change, especially if it affects the supply chain.

—*Grist* magazine

Our economy and culture is shifting from mass markets to millions of niches.

—Chris Anderson

Green technology – going green – is bigger than the Internet. It could be the biggest economic opportunity of the 21st century.

—John Doerr

At some point, you can't lift this boulder with just your own strength. And if you find that you need to move bigger and bigger boulders up hills, you will need more and more help.

—Vinton Cerf

Box 7: The principle of scalability – in a nutshell

Iconic leaders	General Electric
	Grameen Group
	Suntech
	Tata Group
	Wal-Mart
Period	Rising from 2004, with the publication of *The Fortune at the Bottom of the Pyramid* and the start of Wal-Mart's reformation
Key ideas	Choice editing
	Democratizing or mainstreaming sustainability and responsibility
	Legislation as a game changer
	The long tail of CSR
	The race to the top
Commentators	Chris Anderson (journalist & author)
	Charles Fishman (author)
	C.K. Prahalad (academic & author)
	Jim Collins (author & consultant)
	Stuart Hart (academic & author)
References	*Good to Great: Why Some Companies Make the Leap . . . and Others Don't* (Jim Collins, 2001)
	The Fortune at the Bottom of the Pyramid: Eradicating Poverty Through Profits (C.K. Prahalad, 2004)
	The Long Tail: Why the Future of Business is Selling Less of More (Chris Anderson, 2006)
	The Wal-Mart Effect: How the World's Most Powerful Company Really Works – and How It's Transforming the American Economy (Charles Fishman, 2006)
	The Next 4 Billion: Market Size and Business Strategy at the Base of the Pyramid (Allen L. Hammond, William J. Kramer, Robert S. Katz, Julia T. Tran & Courtland Walker, 2007)

Case 7: Lee Scott and Wal-Mart

'Rapacious behemoth', 'aggressive', 'bully' and 'evil empire' are just some of the public epithets Wal-Mart had acquired by the time Harold Lee Scott Junior took over as President and CEO in 2000. *Fortune* magazine said 'the firm had what could be charitably described as an "us-versus-them" mentality, in which "us" was Wal-Mart and "them" was everybody else, from critics to the competition, the government, and yes, sometimes even its own employees. The company's public image as a rapacious behemoth reflected that.' *Business Week* reported a 'mounting socio-political backlash to Wal-Mart's size and aggressive business practices' and urged Wal-Mart to 'stop the bullying . . . stop squeezing employees and suppliers, and charge customers a little more'.

The source of all these jibes and accusations can be traced to two killer facts. One, ever since founder Sam Walton opened the company's first store in Arkansas in 1962, Wal-Mart has been all about discount operations – low cost and low price. And two, from its humble beginnings, Wal-Mart mushroomed into the largest company in the world – a $405 billion giant with over 2 million employees, serving customers more than 200 million times each week at more than 8,400 retail units under 55 different banners in 15 countries around the world. There is nothing about Wal-Mart that can be described as small, other than its prices.

'When it comes to price, it's hard to beat Wal-Mart', admits *Business Week*, 'but the "everyday low prices" come at a high cost to its employees.' The result has been dozens of lawsuits brought by employees claiming to be overworked and underpaid, including 'the mother of all sex discrimination class actions', which alleges the company discriminated against 1.6 million women. In fact, there are two union-funded activist organizations, Wakeup Wal-Mart and Wal-Mart

Watch, that exist for the sole purpose of criticizing Wal-Mart. And that's just on labour issues.

When it comes to green issues, 'the name "Wal-Mart" has always triggered a shudder', says *Grist* magazine. The company has been charged with 'exacerbating suburban sprawl, burning massive quantities of oil via its 10,000-mile supply chain, producing mountains of packaging waste, polluting waterways with runoff from its construction sites, and encouraging gratuitous consumption'. The litany of alleged sins doesn't end there either – putting small companies out of business, maltreating suppliers, offering inferior employee benefits, the list goes on and on.

The point is that when Scott took charge, and for at least the first five years of his reign, Wal-Mart was under siege, with a siege mentality to fit. 'We would put up the sandbags and get out the machine guns', Scott recalls. 'If somebody criticized us, my first thought was, "Why don't they like us?" Or, "What could we do to them?" versus now, when I think, "Could the criticism have some truth?".' *Fortune* later concluded that 'Scott had apparently learned that the best way to respond to an attacker was not with an attack of one's own, but to embrace them'. And embrace them he did, to the extent that his journey to openness – alongside that of Wal-Mart – is today one of the most remarkable leadership stories of our time. So what happened? And why, and how?

It seems some of the seminal credit must go to one of Sam Walton's sons and to the NGO, Conservation International (CI). Rob Walton, Chairman of Wal-Mart's Board of Directors since 1992, is a lover of the outdoors and found himself in February 2004 on a ten-day trip to Costa Rica, hosted by Peter Seligmann, co-founder and CEO of CI. After pointing out the destructive havoc that fleets of fishing boats were wreaking on the delicate Costa Rican marine habitat, legend has it that Seligmann looked the Wal-Mart chairman in the eye as said: 'We need to change the way industry works. And you can have an influence.' Rob was moved and promised to introduce Seligmann to Scott.

The timing was serendipitous, as Scott had just concluded a review of Wal-Mart's legal and public relations problems, and it wasn't a pretty picture. The discrimination lawsuit had been certified as a federal class action, new stores were blocked by activists in Los Angeles, San Francisco and Chicago, and the company had just forked out millions to regulators for air and water pollution infringements. The findings of two recent studies only made matters worse: one that showed that Wal-Mart's spending on health benefits for its employees was 30% less than the average of its retail peers, and another, by McKinsey, concluded that up to 8% of shoppers had stopped patronizing the store because of its increasingly tarnished reputation.

The watershed meeting took place without fanfare in June 2004, with Rob Walton, Scott, Seligmann, Glenn Prickett (also of CI) and Jib Ellison, a river-rafting guide turned management consultant. Whatever was said, it convinced Scott to dip Wal-Mart's toes into green waters. No doubt it helped that CI's board included former Intel chairman Gordon Moore, BP chief executive John Browne, and former Starbucks CEO Orin Smith, and that CI were already advising Starbucks on fairtrade issues and McDonald's on sustainable agriculture and fishing. Whatever the reasons, Scott commissioned Ellison's management consulting firm BluSkye to measure Wal-Mart's total environmental impact.

It was a bold move, but it quickly paid off. BluSkye found that, for example, by eliminating excessive packaging on its Kid Connection private-label line of toys, Wal-Mart could save $2.4 million a year in shipping costs, 3,800 trees and one million barrels of oil. And on its fleet of 7,200 trucks, rather than letting the truck engine idle during the drivers' mandatory ten-hour breaks, it could save $26 million a year in fuel costs by installing auxiliary power units to heat/cool the cabs. In short, Wal-Mart had belatedly discovered the win-win world of eco-efficiency, which WBCSD had been promoting since 1992. 'As we headed down this first path in our sustainability journey and started to see these results, we really got excited', recalls Scott.

If the truth be told, these initiatives were neither radical nor especially high impact in the context of Wal-Mart's global footprint. And Scott could easily have stopped there, having gained the PR-benefits and the easy-picking cost savings. Fortunately, however, fate intervened. On 29 August 2005, Hurricane Katrina hit the Louisiana coast and devastated New Orleans. 'Katrina was one of the worst disasters in the history of the United States', reflected Scott, 'but it also brought out the best in our company. . . . We responded by doing what we do best: We empowered our people and leveraged our presence and logistics to deliver the supplies that hurricane victims so desperately needed. Hurricane Katrina changed Wal-Mart forever. And it changed us for the better. We saw our full potential – with absolute clarity – to serve not just our customers, but our communities, our countries and even the world. We saw our opportunity and our responsibility. In the aftermath of the storm, we asked ourselves: How can we be that company – the Wal-Mart we were during Katrina – all the time? Sustainability became a big part of the answer.'[39]

And so began one of the most unexpected and remarkable stories of corporate transformation. Scott soon announced three radical goals: (1) to be supplied 100% by renewable energy; (2) to create zero waste; and (3) to sell products that sustain people and the environment. Admittedly, they are described as 'aspirational' with no timelines attached, but if they get anywhere close, or even half-way there, they will have been a major catalyst for the post-industrial revolution. Already, we see the Wal-Mart effect of

---

[39]From the 2007 London Lecture of HRH Prince of Wales's Business and the Environment Programme.

scalability in action in three areas: fish, cotton and light bulbs. Let's look at each in turn.

Wal-Mart plans to purchase *all* of its wild-caught fresh and frozen fish for the US market from Marine Stewardship Council (MSC) certified fisheries by 2011. They are also working with Global Aquaculture Alliance (GAA) and Aquaculture Certification Council (ACC) to certify that all foreign shrimp suppliers adhere to Best Aquaculture Practices standards in the US by 2011. By 2009, they were already halfway there. Speaking to the *Wall Street Journal*, George Chamberlain, president of the Aquaculture Alliance put the move in perspective: 'The endorsement drew attention; Wal-Mart buys more shrimp than any other US company, importing 20,000 tons annually – about 3.4% of US shrimp imports. With Wal-Mart's nod, we went from trying to convince individual facilities to become certified to having long waiting lines.'

Scott also made a commitment to phase out chemically-treated textile crops. By 2008, Wal-Mart was the largest buyer of organic cotton, with more than 10 million pounds purchased annually. They are also the world's largest purchaser of conversion cotton – cotton grown without chemicals, but waiting to be certified as organic. Scott is under no illusions about the ripple effects: 'Cotton farmers can now invest in organic farming because they have the certainty and stability of a major buyer. Through leadership and purchasing power, all of us can create new markets for sustainable products and services. We can drive innovation. We can build acceptance. All we need is the will to step out and make the difference.'

Another product Scott targeted for greening was lightbulbs. A compact fluorescent light bulb (CFL) has clear advantages over the widely used incandescent light – it uses 75% less electricity, lasts ten times longer, produces 450 pounds fewer greenhouse gases from power plants and saves consumers $30 over the life of each bulb. But it is eight times as expensive as a traditional bulb, gives off a harsher light and has a peculiar appearance. As a result, the CFL bulbs only ever achieved 6% penetration, B.W. (Before Wal-Mart). To tip the scales in favour of CFLs, Wal-Mart set the goal of selling 100 million energy-saving bulbs. Success would mean total sales of CFLs in the US would double, saving Americans $3 billion in electricity costs and avoiding the need to build additional power plants for the equivalent of 450,000 new homes.

To ram home the point about Wal-Mart's mighty sway, according to the *New York Times*, when they proposed this audacious goal, light-bulb manufacturers, who sell millions of incandescent lights at Wal-Mart, immediately expressed reservations. In a December 2005 meeting with executives from General Electric, Wal-Mart's largest bulb supplier, 'the message from GE was, "Don't go too fast. We have all these plants that produce traditional bulbs." The response from the Wal-Mart buyer was uncompromising: "We are going there. You decide if you are coming with us".' Unsurprisingly, GE decided to tool up and scale up to meet the demand.

Today, these and other initiatives are all part of Wal-Mart's Sustainability 360° programme. Compounding the scalability effect is the fact that Wal-Mart plans to take its more than 100,000 suppliers along with it on this sustainability journey. In 2009, it announced the creation of a 'worldwide sustainable product index'. Step 1 was providing each of its suppliers with a survey of 15 simple, but powerful, questions to evaluate their own company's sustainability in four areas: energy and climate; natural resources; material efficiency; and people and community. Step 2 is to develop a global database of information on the lifecycle of products, to be shared on a public platform. And step 3 will be to translate the findings into a simple, convenient, easy to understand rating, so customers can make choices and consume in a more sustainable way.

Wal-Mart is not second-guessing what these assessment, measurement and information systems will look like. However, it has said that by 2012, all direct import suppliers will be required to source 95% of their production from factories that receive one of Wal-Mart's two highest ratings in audits for environmental and social practices, including standards of product safety, quality and energy efficiency. In February 2010, it also committed to reducing 20 million metric tons of carbon pollution from its products' lifecycles and supply chains over the next five years. That's equivalent to eliminating the annual greenhouse gas emissions from 3.8 million cars by 2015.

To be sure, Wal-Mart still has plenty of critics – of its Sustainability Index, its labour practices, its supply chain performance and its Goliath tactics. But – to borrow from the Marvel comic-adapted movie *Transformers* – it is getting harder and harder to cast Wal-Mart as the evil Megatron (part of the Deceptacon race) and far more plausible to see it as Optimus Prime, an awesomely powerful yet ultimately well-intentioned Transformer. The moral of the Wal-Mart story is that it is making sustainability and responsibility scalable. Scott's take on it is that 'more than anything else, we see sustainability as mainstream. . . . We believe working families should not have to choose between a product they can afford and a sustainable product.' That is nothing short of the CSR holy grail, and the jury is still very much out – especially since Scott stepped down in 2009 – but if anyone can tip us into the Age of Responsibility, it's the new 'sustainability superpower' Wal-Mart.

The limits of ethical consumerism

What makes Wal-Mart such a good example of scalability is not just its size, but the principles underlying its actions, such as mainstreaming sustainability, measuring total impacts, empowering customers, working with suppliers and setting audacious goals. Indeed, it is now part of an industry that seems intent on transforming itself, with many of the largest players like Tesco and Marks & Spencer (M&S) trying to out-compete one other on the sustainability and responsibility stakes. This has come as a bit of a surprise to many, including so-called CSR experts. As the well respected CSR commentator Mallen Baker observed:

> British retailer Marks & Spencer used to be best known as a pillar of the establishment. No fiery wild-eyed radical, it would do a select number of good things for the community, and it would steadfastly refuse to beat its own drum about it. All that has changed, and the measure of just how much could be seen with the retailer's recent pronouncement that it is aiming to become the world's most sustainable retailer by 2015.

At the heart of this ambition is 'Plan A (Because There is No Plan B)', which sets out 100 sustainability targets and which they seem well on their way to achieving.

These are indeed encouraging signs for the future. However, in order that we don't repeat past mistakes, it is worth looking back and learning a key lesson of retail history, namely that the so-called 'ethical consumer' may unwittingly be hindering progress. That may seem like a crazy thing to say, but here is why I say it. Simply put, by creating a premium-priced, niche market for 'ethical consumption' (whether it be organic, fairtrade or eco-friendly), companies have been able to present a responsible front to the world, while leaving the vast majority of their products – which are, by implication, less than ethical – unquestioned and unchanged. At the same time, a small group of usually well-off Western consumers have been able to ease their conscience by feeling that they are making a positive difference.

Now let me be clear. I am not against organic or fairtrade or eco-friendly products per se. That *would* be insane. Clearly, there are groups of producers – usually poor farmers in the Third World – that have benefited enormously from these initiatives. What I *am* against is the voluntary nature and premium pricing of sustainable and responsible products. The combination of these two factors has ensured that, with one or two exceptions, these products have never gone to scale. Compared with the collective and ongoing impacts of mainstream shopping habits, ethical consumption, laudable as it is, has remained marginal at best and totally insignificant at worst.

Let's look at some of the facts. The UK Soil Association launched the world's first organic standard in 1967 and Germany launched its Blue Angel eco-label in 1978. The first fairtrade coffee, introduced by the Max Havelaar Foundation, was in 1988, and the Rainforest Alliance launched its SmartWood certification in 1989. Today, we even have oddities like carbon neutral 'climate change chocolate', launched by Bloomsberry & Co. So we have had more than 40 years of ethical consumption. And where has that left us? Well, certainly, it is a growing trend. In the UK, where the proportion of ethical consumers is among the highest in the world, a survey of 4,000 consumers by PwC found that shoppers buying fairtrade products rose from 20% in 2005 to 50% in 2008 and organic food purchasing increased from 22% to 43% over the same period.

However, this £300 billion sector accounted for just 4% of the UK retail market in 2008 and only 60% of basic grocery products had sustainable alternatives, falling to 40% for some subcategories, such as clothing and non-food items. According to the PwC survey, the high prices associated with fairtrade and organic products remained the main inhibitor to further growth. On average, the price premium for environmentally and ethically friendly products – taken across 75 items at the UK's top six grocers – was 45%. Almost 50% of those shoppers surveyed said they were unwilling or unable to pay this premium, claiming that on average they were not willing to pay a premium in excess of 20% for greener alternatives.

How then do we explain polls, like the one done in 2009 by the Fairtrade Labelling Organization among 14,500 people across 15 countries, which found that more than half said they were 'active ethical consumers'? Well, as all professional market researchers will tell you, these figures are horribly skewed due to what is called the 'socially acceptable response bias'. You are basically asking people if they are ethical, or if they care about poor farmers in the Third World, or if they are okay with trashing the planet. What would *you* answer? The UK's Sustainable Consumption Roundtable confesses that they know that there is a considerable gap – the so-called *value-action gap* – between people's attitudes, which are often pro-environmental, and their everyday behaviours'.

Fairtrade coffee for you, sir?

We know the 'value-action' gap is explained partly by price and availability of alternatives, but there is something else going on as well. Simply put, context matters. To illustrate this, Timothy Devinney, author of *The Myth of the Ethical Consumer*, reports on a very interesting experiment he conducted while researching his book. The experiment took place at a coffee shop in central Sydney, Australia, over a period of several weeks. This coffee shop displayed a large and prominent sign indicating the products available, their prices and active specials. To this was added, quite obtrusively, another special, indicating: 'We have Fairtrade coffee! No extra charge. Just ask.'

Here's what he found. Unprompted, with only the sign to notify them of the availability of the 'ethical' alternative, less than 1% of customers bothered to ask for fairtrade coffee, even though it was the same price as 'normal' coffee. However, when the barrister prompted customers with a reminder that the 'ethical' alternative was available, the number of customers opting for the fairtrade option rose to 30%. They then went a step further and took the customer's privacy away: each time the barrister prompted a customer with the fairtrade option, they ensured there was someone standing next to that person at the counter. In this situation, the number of 'ethical consumers' rose to 70%.

Throughout the experiment, Devinney's research team gave different coloured cups to customers who indicated that they wanted the fairtrade product. They then questioned those remaining in the coffee shop about the meaning of fairtrade and what they thought they were doing by purchasing, or not purchasing, fairtrade coffee. On the whole, they received informed and insightful answers: customers talked about fairtrade; they talked about the conditions of Guatemalan farmers; they could cite many reasons why they had opted for fairtrade coffee.

But – and it's a very big *but* (with one 't') – 'none of this meant anything', concluded Devinney. 'When a customer chose the fairtrade alternative, his or her decision was based entirely on the context we had created; it had nothing to do with that person's values or preferences.' This is a hugely important lesson: If we want to achieve scalability of sustainable and responsible products and services, we cannot leave it to the passive choices of customers. Context is critical, and a little bit of peer pressure goes a long way.

Choice editing for good

But do we really want to resort to public embarrassment to achieve scalability? The UK's Sustainable Consumption Roundtable, which was jointly hosted by the National Consumer Council (NCC) and the Sustainable Development Commission (SDC), did some research on this question and concluded that 'the focus needs to be on creating a supportive framework for collective progress, rather than exhorting individuals to go against the grain. This is the approach that we heard time and again in our engagement with consumers and business – encapsulated in the notion of *I will if you will*. It is possible to make sustainable habits and choices easier to take up, by drawing on insights about consumer behaviour and using people's preferences for purchasing shortcuts, and what we call the trend towards *choice editing*.'[40]

The idea of choice editing is likely to get free-market fundamentalists all in a huff, but the fact is that manufacturers and retailers choice edit all the

---

[40]*I Will If You Will* (2006) Report of the UK's Sustainable Consumption Roundtable.

time – on quality, price, aesthetics and brand offering. The only difference is that now we are asking them to add sustainability and responsibility to their list of criteria. Wal-Mart certainly wasn't the first to wake up to this possibility. In 1997, the UK retail chain Iceland (now The Big Food Group) announced that it would ban all ingredients derived from genetically modified (GM) crops from its Own Label products. Then-chairman and chief executive Malcolm Walker said: 'The proposal [by other manufacturers and retailers] to only label products which contain protein from GM soya or maize . . . would result in probably less than 5% of processed foods being labelled, whereas if all GM derivatives are included as much as 60% of processed foods could be labelled accordingly.'

Iceland's gamble paid off and the response of customers was overwhelmingly supportive. As a result, Iceland continued its trailblazing 'race to the top' by banning all artificial colours and flavours from its products and investing heavily in organic food. In fact, in June 2000, Iceland bought up 40% of the world's organic vegetable crop to become an organic-only supermarket. And herein lies a cautionary tale, because this time, customers did not back the store's choice to stock only the more expensive organic products. Sales slumped and the company went into a financial crisis that resulted in Walker leaving under a cloud. Subsequently, Iceland brought back non-organic products and its sales and profitability were restored.

There are two lessons from this case. First and most obviously, Iceland went too far ahead of its customers. Perhaps their shoppers were not conscious or committed enough. Perhaps the ethical case had not been made strongly enough by the company and by the UK's media, or at least not in the same way that the anti-GMO case had been made. But there is another way to read this. Perhaps it was not the moral ineptitude of customers, but rather the premium price tag that put the nail in the coffin of Iceland's pioneering pro-organics move. Perhaps you have to be the size of Wal-Mart to achieve sufficient economies of scale to justify 'everyday low prices' for sustainable and responsible products. And since there is only one Wal-Mart, how can all the rest of the world's companies achieve scalability of ethical consumerism without hitting the price premium wall?

Government's visible hand

There is a very simple answer: regulation. Once again, as with choice editing, this is likely to bring Friedmanite free marketeers out in a rash. However, we need to remember that Adam Smith never assumed that the 'free market' was unregulated. He was a moral philosopher and assumed the existence of societal controls in which competition could flourish. He also probably never anticipated that his 'invisible hand' of the market would spend quite so much time engaged in the act of self-pleasuring. Today, we know that free market capitalism is a myth, an idealized fantasy that never has existed and never will exist. Rather, what we have seen in practice, even in the world's largest free market capitalist country, is that the visible hand of state intervention is very active.

For example, the reason that America (like most countries of the world) has such cheap oil and gas can be summed up in one word: subsidies. According to a 2009 Environmental Law Institute report, the US government paid roughly $72 billion to subsidize fossil fuels between 2002 and 2008. More than $54 billion of that was in the form of 23 different tax credits for oil, coal and natural gas producers, including those overseas, most of which are permanent provisions of the US Tax Code. By contrast, renewables such as wind, solar and hydropower received merely $29 billion, much of it also in the form of tax credits although, in this case, credits that expire after set durations. And more than half of the renewable subsidy – $16.8 billion – went to the controversial biofuels production of ethanol from corn.

Similarly, Europe subsidizes its agricultural and fishing industries to the tune of €48 billion, making up more than 40% of the EU budget. Leaving aside the ethics of both of these categories of subsidies – on fossil fuels and agriculture – what it tells us is that we know how to lower prices on things that we want. We do it by letting governments create incentives for scaling up. The problem is that, until now, governments haven't been bold enough to intervene at a scale that would make sustainable and responsible production consumption happen in a big way.

Let's consider for a moment the way in which governments finally intervened in most countries in order to ban smoking in public places. What can we learn from this? First, we know that it took decades of scientific research to make the health case irrefutable. Second, the reforms were helped along by a major exposé of the lies and manipulation by Big Tobacco to undermine progressive legislation. Third, it took the weight of a major public body like the United Nations – in this case the World Health Organization – to legitimize the findings of the scientists. And lastly, it took courage by the politicians to take strong action that was so clearly in the public's best interest, but would inevitably attract big-bully lobbying from the tobacco, restaurant and pub industries.

The interesting thing is that we have all but the forth ingredient already in place for the broader sustainability and responsibility agenda: the science and research is mounting and calling for urgent action; numerous companies have been exposed for wanton self-aggrandization; and the UN and other major bodies are putting their weight behind reforms. All that is still lacking is political courage, and even there, we see some signs of movement. For example, the UK's climate change targets, enshrined in the Climate Change Act, are highly ambitious, committing the country to reduce its carbon emissions by 80% by 2050, with an interim target of 34% cuts by 2030.

The simple fact is that – beyond a few products like iPods that create their own mass market driven first by innovation and then by clever marketing and latent customer demand – most sustainable and responsible products and services need bold government intervention to make them competitive and scalable. There are at least two good reasons for this. First, as we have already seen, many of the less sustainable and responsible markets are being subsidized, so there is no level playing field on which to compete. And second, most of the more sustainable and responsible products and services that need scaling stray into the territory of being public goods, where the market fails. Speaking to me in 2008, sustainability guru Amory Lovins claimed that there are 'sixty to eighty well-known market failures to buying energy and resources efficiency'. Put another way, if we want CSR to be scalable, smart government regulation is absolutely essential.

A flotilla of little boats

Of course, the Wal-Mart effect and government intervention are all very well in countries where there are massive, branded companies and the state is in firm control of a relatively stable and effective political landscape. But what about in the countries where governments are weak, failing or corrupt? Are there other ways to achieve scalability? And more to the point, what do we mean by scalability? Is bigger always better or can we still cling to the notion of *Small Is Beautiful*, as the pioneering economist E.F. Schumacher argued in 1973? Certainly, the 'muesli-eating, sandal-wearing' New Age approach to small-is-beautiful has been rather more of an advertisement for 'small is groovy, but ultimately ineffectual'. But what if we could do both big and small at the same time?

I discussed the issue of scalability with Simon Zadek, a widely respected thought leader on the civil corporation and accountability. Reflecting on climate change as an example he set out the challenge as follows:

> How do we move from an increasingly discredited CDM [Clean Development Mechanism] approach – where the evidence is increasingly of huge abuse of funds, huge misrepresentation of claims and altogether rather a waste of time and a lot of money – to a mechanism that can mobilize and move fifty, a hundred, two hundred billion dollars a year trans-border? That can mobilize, assess, invest, monitor and communicate credibly in the area of mitigation or adaptation? It seems to me we need the equivalent of a Global Fund for HIV, AIDS and Malaria on steroids.

'So that's one version of a collaborative mode', continued Zadek, 'that will in any case spring up at a micro-level. But can we go to scale, and indeed is scale large institutional functionality, or is it a flotilla of little boats?' This is where Chris Anderson's Web 2.0 concept of 'the long tail' is very useful. *The Long Tail* – named after the extended tail of a statistical distribution curve – is the idea that selling less to more people is big business. It's the business model that has spawned the most successful companies of the Web 2.0 age. The Long Tail questions the conventional wisdom that says success is about generating 'blockbusters' and 'superstars' – those rare few products and services that become runaway bestsellers.

Anderson sums up his message by saying that: (1) the tail of available variety is longer than we think; (2) it's now within reach economically; and (3) all those niches, when aggregated, can make up a significant market. He also notes that this Long Tail revolution has been made possible by the digital age, which has dramatically reduced the costs of customized production and niche distribution. There are three enablers of successful long tail businesses, according to Anderson: (1) democratizing the tools of production (e.g. digi-cams, content editing software, blogging tools); (2) democratizing the tools of distribution (e.g. Amazon, eBay, iTunes, Netflix); and (3) connecting supply and demand (e.g. Google, blogs, Rotten Tomatoes).

The long tail of CSR

Back in 2008, having read Anderson's book, I set to wondering: Is there a Long Tail of CSR?[41] And if so, what does it look like? To me, the Long Tail of CSR is all about extending the reach of CSR, and improving its ability to satisfy specific social and environmental needs. Let's use Anderson's enablers as a framework for thinking about this.

Democratizing the tools of CSR production – This is about breaking CSR silos and extending CSR beyond multinationals. At the early stages of CSR

---

[41]I published my thoughts on this in December 2008 as 'The Long Tail of CSR', CSR Inspiration Series No. 5.

adoption, it is often confined to public relations, corporate affairs or marketing departments. As CSR implementation matures, responsibility tends to migrate to specialized CSR departments of various descriptions (environment, health and safety, accountability, corporate citizenship, etc.). However, these versions of CSR are like the Hollywood model of blockbuster films. They suggest that CSR is about a few, high visibility programmes that are designed by CSR experts and delivered by big companies.

By contrast, democratizing CSR production would mean firstly embedding CSR across the organization – making it the responsibility of operations managers, financial managers, shop floor workers, basically everyone. This is only possible if CSR becomes part of the culture and incentive systems of an organization. CSR would also need to be extended beyond the usual suspects (i.e. the high profile, branded multinationals) to the less visible B2B (business to business) and national (rather than multinational) organizations, as well as to SMEs (small and medium sized enterprises) and down the supply chain.

Democratizing the tools of CSR distribution – To date, CSR has mainly be 'distributed' via a few select projects – typically philanthropic or charitable activities – in which the company offers its help to the 'less fortunate masses'. Usually, the nature and scope of CSR activities is determined top-down and offered as a fairly undifferentiated 'service', e.g. Nike might decide to focus on sponsoring sports teams, events and celebrities and Coca-Cola might choose water as its key CSR issue. The most common delivery mechanisms are money (sponsorship and other forms of charity), or for the more advanced companies, adhering to generic CSR codes and standards.

By contrast, democratizing the tools of CSR distribution should include allowing staff to participate in CSR delivery through volunteer programmes, and developing more geographically tailored and sector-specific CSR codes and standards, such as the Roundtable on Sustainable Palm Oil, or the Global Reporting Initiative guidelines for HIV/AIDS reporting. Beyond this, embracing Bottom of the Pyramid (BoP) markets and supporting social entrepreneurs will allow the reach of CSR to be extended so that the needs of formerly unserved or underserved people can be met.

Connecting CSR supply and demand – Traditionally, CSR has been offered in the form of grants by multinational head offices, which control the budget and set the criteria by which prospective philanthropic projects should be selected. For the more advanced companies, this has been extended to adherence by their operations to corporate codes of CSR practice and communicating this through CSR reports. Demand has typically come from community groups applying to corporate foundations for funding, or NGOs taking an activist approach to demanding improved CSR practices.

By contrast, connecting the Long Tail of CSR supply and demand will rely increasingly on cross-sector partnerships and multi-stakeholder groups. For example, Rio Tinto works with the World Conservation Union to identify biodiversity needs and satisfy them through appropriate CSR activities. Companies may also use extended stakeholder networks of community groups, social entrepreneurs and microcredit enterprises to better match their capacity to make a positive impact among those who can most benefit, as BP is doing with smokeless stoves in India and SC Johnson is doing with cleaning products in Kenya.

Hence, applying the Long Tail concept to CSR requires a different way of thinking about how CSR is generated, delivered and managed. It means making CSR a more inclusive and embedded process within the company, and a more diverse and far-reaching set of activities outside the company. It also means creating meaningful stakeholder partnerships to ensure that the right kinds of CSR benefit the right groups of people, where and when they need it. The Long Tail in a nutshell, according to Anderson, is: 'culture unfiltered by scarcity'. By extension, the Long Tail of CSR in a nutshell is: 'responsibility liberated by collaboration'.

Bottom of the pyramid (BoP)

One of the most popular visions of scalability is C.K. Prahalad and Stuart Hart's concept of doing business at the 'bottom of the pyramid' (BoP), the roughly 4 billion people living on less than PPP$1,500 a year. The concept was popularized in several academic papers in 2002 and subsequently by Prahalad's book *The Fortune at the Bottom of the Pyramid* (2004). Prahalad argues that the poor, defined as people living on less than $2 per day, at purchasing power parity (PPP) rates, represent a market size of $13 trillion. Allen Hammond, vice president of World Resource Institute (WRI), believes it may be as much as $15 trillion a year. Estimates in *The Next 4 Billion*, drawing on income data from 110 countries and standardized expenditure data from 36 countries across the globe, are lower at $5 trillion, but still by no means trivial.

Much of this colossal market will remain untapped, however, unless business learns to do business differently. In order to access the BoP, argue Prahalad and Hart, several myths need to be busted. For example, contrary to popular belief, BoP markets are brand-conscious and connected and BoP consumers accept new technology. However, in order to conduct business in these markets, companies have to create the capacity to consume, by making products affordable, accessible and available. The provision by Hindustan Lever of single-serve sachets of shampoo in India is now a classic – and much debated – case in point.

Building trust is also a prerequisite. I remember asking Muhammad Yunus why the Grameen Bank had succeeded where so many other commercial banks had failed in doing business with the poor. His answer was that he began the bank in an area that he had lived and worked in for many years. He had built up social capital and earned their trust. As a result, he was able to grow a $2.5 billion banking enterprise with over 7 million active clients, affecting 35 million family members. Most remarkably, Grameen's loan repayment rate is over 98%, and borrowers of the bank owning 90% of its shares. By 2007, the microcredit model had scaled to over 50 countries, with 3,316 microcredit institutions reaching over 133 million clients. Of these, 93 million (up from 7.6 million in 1997) were among the poorest when they took their first loan. And of these poorest clients, 85%, or 79 million, were women.

The BoP model has been hotly debated and criticized. Speaking to me in 2008, Hart conceded two main problems: One is that 'companies will take existing, unsustainable polluting or toxic products or product systems or manufacturing processes, strip some cost out of them and take it out into these under-served markets, and then just do a lot more environmental damage'. The second, captured by Aneel Karnani in 'The misfortune at the bottom of the pyramid', is that companies are entering rural villages and urban slums and shanty towns and just 'selling stuff to poor people that they really don't need, extractive products that are just going to take what little cash they have in their pockets, extract wealth, not create it, and at the end of the day do more harm than good from the standpoint of poverty alleviation'. On this point, Yunus told me, 'Our primary responsibility is to lift [the poor at the bottom of the pyramid], rather than see it as an opportunity to make money. So we should not look at them as consumers of our product. We should see them as potential producers; potential creative people who can take charge of their own life and transform it.'

Taking these concerns into account, Hart, with Erik Simanis and others at Cornell University, has been leading an initiative to create a BoP Protocol, or BoP 2.0 model. Hart describes it as 'a new business process for actually engaging in those communities, building trust and then co-creating businesses'. There is an attitude difference that embodies humility. 'It's a co-creation methodology, rather than a talk-down imposition where the presumption is rich people are smarter, poor people are dumb and are victims. You have to change your mindset and think: we could be partners and colleagues and we could actually work together to develop a business that combines the best of both. We could bring incredible next generation, clean technology, but there's a lot of local knowledge, that if we combine those together, imagine what sort of interesting business we could create that could make a better way to live.' And as an example of scalability in this approach, he cites a BoP Protocol initiative in the US with Ascension Health, which is the third largest hospital corporation in the United States, focused on the 50 million people in the US with no health insurance.

Another example of BoP scalability is the Tata Nano, the $2,500 car launched in 2008 in India. The mission began back in 2003, when Ratan Tata, chairman of Tata Motors and the $50 billion Tata conglomerate, set a challenge to build a 'people's car'. Tata gave an engineering team, led by 32-year-old star engineer Girish Wagh, three requirements for the new vehicle: It should be low-cost, adhere to regulatory requirements, and achieve performance targets such as fuel efficiency and acceleration capacity. By design, it is small and eco-efficient and while many wring their hands over the environmental impacts of a billion Indians driving a car, no one has an ethical right to deny the same access to individual mobility that virtually the whole population of the developed world enjoys.

Other big companies have also got involved. For example, Philips is actively targeting rural India with two products: the smokeless *chulha*, or stove, and lighting products in the Philips Sustainable Model in Lighting Everywhere (SMILE) range. 'At Philips, we have a strategy in place to address the needs of consumers at the bottom of the pyramid', said Philips India CEO Murali Sivaraman. 'We look at this section of society as a viable market and have developed products catering to their needs.' Similarly, Envirofit, a spinout from the University of Colorado, claims that its $20 stoves cut smoke and toxic emissions by 80%, and halve the amount of fuel that is needed. Its goal is to sell 10 million in the developing world over the next five years. According to Simon Bishop, head of policy at the Shell Foundation, which seed funded the Envirofit venture, 'everything we do is about applying business thinking to poverty and environmental issues. There is never going to be enough aid to go around, so what you need to do is to focus our limited resources on self-financing mechanisms that can make a big impact.'

Blessed unrest

Another way to think about scalability is as a much more grassroots movement. Indeed, Paul Hawken, in his book *Blessed Unrest: How the Largest Movement in the World Came into Being and Why No One Saw It Coming*, suggests that they have already gone to scale on sustainability and responsibility in one sense. The title comes from a quote of Martha Graham to Agnes de Mille in *Dance to the Piper*:

> There is vitality, a life force, an energy, a quickening that is translated through you into action, and because there is only one of you in all time, this expression is unique . . . You have to keep open and aware directly to the urges that motivate you. Keep the channel open . . . [There is] no satisfaction whatever at any time. There is only a queer, divine satisfaction, a blessed unrest that keeps us marching and makes us more alive than the other.

Drawing inspiration from this idea, Hawken believes that in this movement without a centre, there are over one – or maybe even two – million organizations working towards ecological sustainability and social justice. The scale of this movement for change has gone largely undetected, he believes, because it is not formalized; it is a movement without central control or appointed leaders:

> The movement can't be divided because it is so atomized – a collection of small pieces, loosely joined. It forms, dissipates, and then re-gathers quickly, without central leadership, command, or control. Rather than seeking dominance, this unnamed movement strives to disperse concentrations of power. It has been capable of bringing down governments, companies, and leaders through witnessing, informing, and massing. The quickening of the movement in recent years has come about through information technologies becoming increasingly accessible and affordable to people everywhere. Its clout resides in its ideas, not in force.

Andres Edwards argues that we have gone from a sustainability movement to a sustainability revolution. He bases this on three distinct phases: genesis, critical mass, and diffusion. He notes that '(w)hereas movements tend to have narrower objectives and are led by a charismatic leader, such as Mahatma Gandhi . . . , social revolutions have wider objectives and are led by a large and diverse number of individuals.' Hawken sees this disaggregated collective acting in defence of the earth and society, saying that 'the shared activity of hundreds of thousands of non profit organizations can be seen as humanity's immune response to toxins like political corruption, economic disease, and ecological degradation'. A key insight from the metaphor is that, when we are sick, we feel the disease, but we seldom feel the immune system working away in the background to restore health. In the same way, the mass movement for sustainability and responsibility has been operating under the political and economic radar, focused on damage control and restoration of vitality to our societies and ecosystems.

In an audacious attempt to collate and categorize the multifarious organizations working to bring about positive change, Hawken set up WISER – The World Index of Social and Environmental Responsibility – as a collaborative platform for the movement. The first step was WiserEarth.org – the world's largest free and editable international directory of NGOs and socially responsible organizations, numbering over 110,000 in 243 countries, territories, and sovereign islands in 2010. There are also parallel sites planned for WiserBusiness and WiserGovernment.

Collaborative social entrepreneurship

A related movement that I have already introduced is the social enterprise movement. At the heart of the social entrepreneurial ethic is the achievement of scale. Catalyst Bill Drayton believes this is not only possible, but is happening already: 'To question whether social entrepreneurs can achieve large-scale change is to doubt the existence of Florence Nightingale, Maria Montessori, William Wilberforce, Fazle Abed, Jimmy Wales, or the 2,700 Ashoka Fellows!' he declares. But how does this happen? What do social entrepreneurs know about scalability that we could learn from?

According to Drayton, part of the answer lies in their ability to mobilize other change agents:

> Every social entrepreneur is a mass recruiter of local changemakers. Here is one of the few significant structural differences between the social and the business entrepreneur. The social entrepreneur has no interest in

capturing a market and digging a moat. Instead, the goal is, indeed, to change the world.

The way social entrepreneurs do this almost always is to make their idea as understandable, attractive, safe, and as supported as necessary precisely so that local people in community after community after community will recognize that the idea would be hugely valuable to their community and also judge that they could make that idea fly. The moment one or several local people make that decision, stand up, and champion the idea, they have become local changemakers. They will disrupt local patterns; they will recruit others to be changemakers; and a few will later become large-scale social entrepreneurs in their own right.[42]

A second way social entrepreneurs achieve scale is by collaborating with one another or their business peers. We have already seen how Freeplay collaborated with innovators in the medical industry to come up with the Foetal Heart Rate Monitor, and how A Little World collaborated with numerous technology and banking partners to develop and deliver its microbanking services. Similarly, we saw how the Grameen Bank has been collaborating with French food company Danone since 2006 to fight malnutrition in Bangladesh by producing a yoghurt enriched with crucial nutrients at a price of 6 BDT (0.06 EUR) which even the poorest can afford.

Social media sites like Amazee are also allowing social entrepreneurs to collaborate. Amazee calls itself 'the global action network' and cites successful groups that have engaged its members in building an IT learning centre in Sri Lanka, planning meetings of Internet entrepreneurs in Zurich or ensuring the complete supply of running water in a small South African village. Similarly, the Mayflower Foundation in Lagos, Nigeria, aims to work as a 'coordinated, synergistic and cooperative body' for pooling and integrating social development and CSR efforts to directly impact up to 100,000 Ebute-Metta citizens and as many as 300,000 more citizens indirectly. Drayton

---

[42]Drayton, B. *Tipping the World: The Power of Collaborative Entrepreneurship*. Published on the McKinsey What Matters site, 8 April 2010.

concludes that 'once there are several hundred leading social entrepreneurs in a field across the continents, one can be confident that a jump to the next paradigm in the field is near'.

Crowdsourcing CSR solutions

In today's world, they way social entrepreneurs increasingly achieve collaboration is through technology. Indeed, one of McKinsey's top 10 high tech-supported business innovation trends is 'collaboration at scale'. This is where the Web 2.0 concept of *crowdsourcing* comes into its own. The term was coined by Jeff Howe in a June 2006 *Wired* magazine article 'The Rise of Crowdsourcing', in which he argued that technology has shrunk the gap between professionals and amateurs. Howe saw crowdsourcing as an alternative to outsourcing.

Crowdsourcing is closely linked to the *Wisdom of Crowds* idea, popularized by a 2004 book by James Surowiecki of the same title. Surowiecki's opening anecdote captures the book's central tenant of 'Why the Many are Smarter Than the Few'. He recounts how Victorian English polymath (and half-cousin of Charles Darwin) Francis Galton discovered that it was the crowd at a county fair that accurately guessed the weight of an ox when their individual guesses were averaged, whereas individual guesses were invariably inaccurate.

Today, there are numerous examples, the most famous of which is Wikipedia, the free, online collaborative encyclopedia launched in 2001 that has more than 16 million entries today. Founder Jimmy Wales is quick to point out that 'Wikipedia is a social innovation, not a technical innovation. All the tools necessary to create Wikipedia existed in 1995 when Ward Cunningham invented the wiki editing concept.' Wikipedia was in fact Wales's second attempt: 'Before Wikipedia', he explains, 'we had a previous project called Nupedia. The goal was the same: a free encyclopedia for everyone, but the method was different. Very top down, very academic. The problem was, it was just too slow.'

What has all this to do with CSR? Well, when it comes to CSR challenges, sometimes speed (not to mention wisdom) is also of the essence. Like when Hurricane Katrina hit and some social entrepreneurs responded by developing PeopleFinder, a kind of crowdsourcing software that was developed to locate missing victims. Or what happened when the Haiti earthquake struck on 12 January 2010. Let's look at this one in a bit more detail. In the weeks after the tragedy, text messages to the dedicated Haiti emergency short code 4636 increased about 10% each day – with about one text a second coming through. With the scale of requests flooding in, how were the emergency response units to make sense of all the desperate messages, let alone respond? Faced with this conundrum, 'Mission 4636' was born – a joint project by FrontlineSMS, Ushahidi, Samasource and CrowdFlower to deploy a critical emergency communications system. This massive effort crowdsourced across multiple non-profit and for-profit companies and individual volunteers from around the country and globe.

In an interview with envisionGood.tv's Katrina Heppler, web developer for Ushahidi, Brian Herbert, explained how it worked:

> Someone on the ground in Haiti will send in a text message of their location and their needs to '4636' that populates a queue that is mostly all Creole messages that we can't read because we speak English. The [thousands of] volunteers [from 14 countries] will take the messages, they'll translate them, add any additional notes and categorize [and geo-tag] them. And when it goes to Ushahidi, they do a little bit more in-depth research into each message and we pass it on to the Coast Guard or Southern Command, and they'll do emergency response.

The power of crowdsourcing is that it can respond to diversity. Robert Munro, Translation Volunteer Coordinator at FrontlineSMS explained that they were 'looking at ways to automate the processing of messages but this is not easy when you get a lot of variation, as you do in Creole between spellings. So we had to make the decision very early on to crowdsource rather than automate the process.' Leila Janah, Founder of Samasource, adds that 'this whole project is not just an example of the power of crowdsourcing to be manifested in new ways like in disaster response, but also the power of social media and the new technology we have. Between Skype and Twitter and Google Documents, we've been able to collaborate with people that I've never met in person. And that would never have been possible even just a couple of years ago.'

Smart vs. dumb growth

All of these examples of growing, scalable responses to sustainability and responsibility crises are unknowingly questioning, if not entirely under-mining, the centuries old rallying cry for a steady-state economy, put for-ward by a long line of philosophers and economists – people like John Stuart Mill, John Maynard Keynes, Robert Solow, Nicholas Georgescu-Roegen and Herman Daly. The steady-state or zero-growth proposition begins with the presupposition that growth is bad. It draws on a wealth of evidence, which on the face of it, is rather convincing. Clearly, economic growth has scaled up our negative impacts – from resource depletion and environmental destruction to community disintegration and cultural impe-rialism. Furthermore, the much touted benefits of growth have not been equitably distributed between countries or even within countries, nor has wealth 'trickled down' as promised by the neoclassical economists.

Besides this, many of the benefits of growth are mere phantoms. For example, happiness in the US has remained fairly constant over the past 50 years, despite continuous economic growth and huge increases in per-sonal disposable income. The Index for Sustainable Economic Welfare (ISEW), designed by former World Bank economist Herman Daly, reaches similar conclusions: while GDP has gone up since the 1950s in the US, UK and many other countries where the study has been repli-cated, quality of life (as measured by the ISEW, which subtracts negative externalities like the costs of disease, war and pollution from GDP) has either levelled off or declined since the 1970s. Today, the Genuine Prog-ress Indicator continues to refine, test, and largely confirm, the ISEW hypothesis.

'There comes a point', Daly explained to me in 2008, 'where the benefits of expansion of the economy, which are real, may be outweighed by the cost inflicted on the rest of the system by the expanded economy'. This results in what Daly famously called uneconomic growth, of which there are five variations: (1) jobless growth, where the economy grows, but does not expand opportunities for employment; (2) ruthless growth, where the proceeds of economic growth mostly benefit the rich; (3) voiceless growth, where economic growth is not accompanied by extension of democracy or empowerment; (4) rootless growth, where economic growth squashes people's cultural identity; and (5) futureless growth, where the present generation squanders resources needed by future generations.

The consequent call for zero growth was especially strong following the emergence of the ecological economics and new economics movements in the 1980s and 1990s. But more and more, this approach is being questioned. Jonathon Porritt confesses that – despite having co-founded the Green Party in the UK in the 1970s – he's had reservations about the anti-growth thinking for a long time. There are two reasons for this, which Porritt explained to me as follows:

> I'm endlessly referring to the importance of massive growth in solar technology, massive growth in sustainable and organic agricultural systems, massive growth in better waste management practices. So a lot of the up-beat side of the sustainability agenda these days is actually growthest. If we don't get these huge transformations in these different sectors of the economy, which entails the creation of enormous amounts of new economic value, we're not going to get to the point we need to get to.

The second reason for Porritt's scepticism is that the concept of zero growth seems to imply a static, no-progress view of human nature and humankind:

> It sort of implies that sustainability is a fixed point, and once you've got there, you can relax. And that seems to me such a fallacious concept of human nature and what it is that makes humanity so special, that it doesn't have any psychological authority. If zero growth means getting to

a point and then nothing moving or changing dynamically, then I've got no real interest in it.

In his book *Capitalism as if the World Matters*, Porritt proposes that we change the debate from being about unlimited versus zero growth to being about smart versus dumb growth. Dumb growth is virtually everything we have been doing for the past century. Smart growth is something more difficult but still, Porritt believes, ultimately possible.

> If you can do the de-coupling of [economic growth] and the environmental footprint and the re-coupling on the social outcomes, the improvement in wellbeing, then you can theoretically see how you'd get to a point where growth makes sense. . . . Of course, it is so different from what we have now that some people would say, 'That's not really growth as we know it. That's a completely different measure of progress.' Well yes, that's precisely the point. It has to be a completely different measure of progress.

The era of 'leading big' on CSR dawns

One of the new leaders in this quest for smart growth is Unilever. CEO, Paul Polman said in a 2009 interview with McKinsey, "This world has tremendous challenges. The challenges of poverty, of water, of global warming, climate change. And businesses like ours have a role to play in that. And frankly, to me, that's very appealing." He went on to say, "We have every day, in our business, about two billion consumers that use our brands, and so [there is] a tremendous opportunity. And if we do the right thing, we can actually make major progress in society."

This drive to make a major difference seems, if anything, to have got bigger over the past year. At least, that's the impression you get from Unilever's new Sustainable Living Plan, which it launched last week. In it, they committed to double the size of the company, while halving the environmental footprint of their products, sourcing 100% of their agricultural ingredients sustainably by 2015 and helping 1 billion people out of poverty.

Commitments like that are what Sandy Ogg, Chief HR Officer for Unilever, calls 'leading big'. Speaking to Polly Courtice, Director of the Cambridge Programme for Sustainability Leadership earlier this year, he said, "There's so much going on now in the world that if you don't have amplification and time compression, then it doesn't rumble. So I call that leading big. You can't let it drool or dribble out into an organisation like ours and expect to have any impact."

The fact of the matter is that without 'leading big' on sustainability and responsibility, CSR efforts no longer have any real credibility. 'Leading big' is absolutely essential if we are break the pattern of dumb growth and CSR ineffectiveness. I mentioned before that the dual 'acid test' of CSR 2.0 is admission and ambition. Companies have to show their willingness to set bold, audacious targets that will reverse the negative social and environmental trends.

In today's world of low-trust and information overload, only bold leadership on CSR will inspire action and build credibility. Unilever and others are pointing the way and deserve our congratulations and support. They also require our unrelenting scrutiny, to ensure that 'leading big' is not simply 'talking big', but rather 'acting big' – making real change happen at scale and at pace.

CHAPTER 9

The principle of responsiveness

It is easy to ignore responsibility when one is only an intermediate link in a chain of action.

—Stanley Milgram

One cannot be deeply responsive to the world without being saddened very often.

—Erich Fromm

Power has to be insecure to be responsive.

—Ralph Nader

As our planet's life-support system begins to fail and our very survival as a species is brought into question, remember that our children and grandchildren will ask not what our generation said, but what it did.

—HRH The Prince of Wales

Box 8: The principle of responsiveness – in a nutshell

Iconic leaders	Hydro Tasmania
	Rio Tinto
	The Body Shop
	The Prince's Charities
	JustMeans
Period	Rising from 1984, with the publication of Ed Freeman's *Strategic Management* book on stakeholder theory
Key ideas	Positive and constructive lobbying
	Proactive (not defensive) engagement
	Serving Bottom of the Pyramid (BoP) markets
	Social media interactivity
	Stakeholder participation
Commentators	Robert Boutilier (author and consultant)
	Paul Collier (academic & author)
	R. Edward Freeman (academic & author)
	Maria Sillanpää and David Wheeler (consultant, academic & authors)
	William B. Werther and David B. Chandler (authors)
References	*Strategic Management: A Stakeholder Approach* (R. Edward Freeman, 1984)
	The Stakeholder Corporation: The Body Shop Blueprint for Maximizing Stakeholder Value (Sillanpää & Wheeler, 1997)
	The Bottom Billion: Why the Poorest Countries are Failing and What Can Be Done About It (Paul Collier, 2007)
	Stakeholder Politics: Social Capital, Sustainable Development, and The Corporation (Robert Boutilier, 2009)
	Strategic Corporate Social Responsibility: Stakeholders in a Global Environment (William B. Werther & David B. Chandler, 2010)

Case 8: HRH The Prince of Wales and the Corporate Leaders Group on Climate Change[43]

'We have begun to see – or I hope we have begun to see! – that the particular model of industrialization we have adopted needs a bit of reviewing and reforming – along with the current paradigm of economics – in light of the huge and growing threats to our existence, let alone to the successful functioning of Nature's delicate balance. In other words, we must put Nature back at the centre of what needs to be a virtuous circle. To be genuinely sustainable, we need a fresh approach.'

These words were spoken in July 2010 by His Royal Highness The Prince of Wales at the 25th anniversary of one of his oldest and most successful charities, Business in the Community (BITC). It is a fitting place to begin this chapter on responsiveness, because it demonstrates how Prince Charles – as an influential (and sometimes controversial) opinion leader and as a convener of business through his charities – has been promoting the CSR Principle of Responsiveness for most of his very public life. As former CEO of Wal-Mart Lee Scott put it, 'The Prince of Wales was a leader in sustainability long before sustainability was "cool". He has been making the business case for sustainability for decades.'

That being said, in his early public life, Prince Charles was better known for his outspoken and sometimes unpopular views on architecture, especially for saying things like, 'What is proposed is like a monstrous carbuncle on the face of a much-loved and elegant friend'

---

[43]This case is written up in more detail in a paper I wrote with Margaret Adey, called *A New Model of Business-Government Policy Dialogue on Sustainability: The Case of the Corporate Leaders Group on Climate Change*, University Cambridge Programme for Sustainability Leadership Research Paper Series: No. 3, 2007.

(in reference to an extension to the facade of the National Gallery). His critical stance on the agrochemical industry and his support for organic farming – long before these views became more mainstream – also earned him a bit of a reputation as a Luddite. Fully aware that his ideas were 'sometimes portrayed as old-fashioned', Prince Charles was clear in his rebuttal: 'Well, they may be. But what I am concerned about are the things that are timeless regardless of the age that we live in. Also I have been around long enough to see what were at the time thought of as old-fashioned ideas now come into vogue.'

What Prince Charles understands – and business leaders can learn from – is that to be responsive to the long-term needs of society and the planet is not necessarily a recipe for popularity. It requires that you take sides with the voiceless and vulnerable, and endure the barbed attacks of those in power that have a vested interest in the status quo. In Prince Charles' case, responsiveness has meant using his convening power to focus attention and action on the most pressing needs of our day. Most often, this is through 'The Prince's Charities', a group of 20 not-for-profit organizations, addressing areas as diverse as opportunity and enterprise, education, health, the built environment, responsible business and the natural environment. Today, this group is the largest multi-cause charitable enterprise in the UK, raising over £130 million annually.

As a case study in responsiveness, this story could just as easily focus on any one of these causes or the numerous projects that the Prince has championed over the years, whether it be The Prince's Trust (which has helped 550,000 vulnerable young people since it was founded in 1976), Youth Business International (which supports disadvantaged young people to become entrepreneurs), Duchy Originals (the organic food company he set up in 1992), Accounting for Sustainability (which launched in 2006 'to help organizations measure more effectively the wider environmental and social costs of their actions'), the Prince's Rainforest Project (established in 2007 as 'the biggest single and immediate opportunity to combat climate change'), or his START Programme (launched in 2010 to 'extol the virtues of a Sustainability Revolution').

I am choosing, however, to focus on one initiative in particular, the Prince of Wales's Corporate Leaders Group on Climate Change (CLG), which was set up in 2005 as part of his longstanding and pioneering Business and the Environment Programme that the University of Cambridge Programme for Sustainability Leadership has run on his behalf since 1994.[44] As will become clear, CLG is an inspiring example of responsiveness by business, set against the backdrop of a world in which negative, obstructive lobbying by companies to avoid greater regulation by government has become the disappointing norm. In 2005, SustainAbility and WWF released a report entitled *Influencing Power*, which ranked the world's top 100 companies on the transparency of their lobbying activities and contrasted this with their public statements on CSR. Their conclusion was that, even among those companies that ranked well in ethical terms on lobbying, 'their focus is generally on defending often controversial positions rather than on how corporate responsibility and related policy activities can support core business strategies'.

Given this reality then, how did a group of UK business leaders change lobbying from a dirty word and a defensive tactic into a force for genuinely progressive corporate sustainability and responsibility? It all began in September 2004 when British Prime Minister Tony Blair, in a speech at the Prince of Wales's Business and the Environment Programme's 10th Anniversary event, issued a challenge to business to do more on climate change. In response, a group of CEOs and senior executives – initially representing 13 companies, ranging

---

[44]This changed its name to the Business and Sustainability Programme in 2009.

from HSBC and Sun Microsystems to Shell and Johnson Matthey – formed the CLG under the leadership and patronage of Prince Charles.

Having set themselves a bold mission 'to trigger the step-change in policy and action needed both to meet the scale of the threat posed by climate change, and to grasp the business opportunities created by moving to a low climate risk economy', the CLG's first action was to deliver a bold and surprising message to the Prime Minister, in the form of an open letter issued in May 2005. First, they stated that investing in a low-carbon future should be 'a strategic business objective for UK plc as a whole'. However, to do this, a debilitating impasse needed to be resolved. They explained that 'the private sector and governments are in a "Catch 22" situation with regard to tackling climate change, in which governments feel limited in their ability to introduce new climate change policy because they fear business resistance, while companies are unable to scale up investment in low carbon solutions because of the absence of long-term policies'.

Citing the International Energy Agency's calculations that $16 trillion dollars of energy infrastructure investment will be needed worldwide over the next 25 years to satisfy the world's growing energy needs, the CLG suggested that this can 'set the stage for enormous commercial opportunities for the UK if it is coupled with a shift to a low carbon economy'. However, to grasp these opportunities, it argued, business needs *more*, not less, regulation. In particular, the CLG asked Blair to work to extend targets for emissions trading policies to 2025 and thereby to increase market confidence and reduce the risk of investing in low carbon technology.

This savvy strategy of creating 'permission' for politicians to act boldly paid off. In an article in the *International Chamber of Commerce International Energy Review*, Cambridge University's Aled Jones and Margaret Adey state that 'by developing a high-level political strategy with well-positioned messages, the CLG has "emboldened" senior politicians to make decisions on climate policy that go further than they would have done otherwise. Indeed, UK government insiders report that the CLG has had a direct impact on policy-making decisions relating to the UK's EU Emissions Trading Scheme National Allocation Plan Targets and the 2006 UK Energy Review.'

Encouraged by this success, the CLG continued to grow its corporate membership and issue ever more ambitious 'consensus statements', either in annual letters to the Prime Minister, or as communiqués at major international climate meetings. For example, in the 2006 Bali Communiqué, signed by the CEOs of 150 global companies, the CLG called for a comprehensive, legally binding United Nations framework to tackle climate change and concluded that 'as business leaders, it is our belief that the benefits of strong, early action on climate change outweigh the costs of not acting.'

Commenting further, Alain Grisay, CEO of F&C Asset Management, said: 'Business and investors can only play their part in tackling climate change if governments take decisive action to make this possible. This problem will not get solved through market forces alone in the time that we have left to act, because climate change presents a textbook example of market failure. This means that voluntary targets won't do; business needs a level playing field in order to take on the financial risks that adequate action on climate change requires.'

In 2008, the CLG wrote to UK political party leaders and warned that while the 'global economic slowdown may cause some to question whether the UK can afford to act so boldly . . . action cannot be delayed' and that 'decisive action will stimulate economic activity and job creation'. It went on to say that 'incremental change will not do', a message echoed in the Poznan Communiqué issued later that year. In particular, the CLG stated that 'we must deliver deep and rapid cuts in greenhouse gas emissions', adding that 'any credible comprehensive agreement must include mechanisms to reduce tropical deforestation'.

Meanwhile, the UK CLG had spun off an EU Group that was lobbying for bolder political leadership on climate change by Eurocrats. In the lead up to the UN climate negotiations in Copenhagen in 2009, the EU CLG sent an unequivocal message to sitting EU President José Manuel Barroso that a weak deal in Copenhagen would be 'bad for the climate and bad for the economy'. Furthermore, they expressed concern that the EU's 'leadership advantage' on the low carbon agenda was 'under threat' as other countries used their economic stimulus packages to promote investment in green technologies. The EU could 'see itself left behind in the clean technology race when China and other major emerging economies are already making large-scale investments in this area', it warned.

At the UN meeting itself, the CLG launched its Copenhagen Communiqué, endorsed by over 950 major companies from more than 60 countries, calling on world leaders to agree 'an ambitious, robust and equitable global deal on climate change that responds credibly to the scale and urgency of the crisis facing the world today'. It went on to say that 'it is critical that we exit this recession in a way that lays the foundation for low-carbon growth and avoids locking us into a high carbon future'.

Prince Charles was also in attendance at the Copenhagen meeting, urging the world's political leaders to take their responsibility seriously, saying:

> We live in times of great consequence and, therefore, of great opportunity. . . . Just as Mankind had the power to push the world to the brink so, too, do we have the power to bring it back into balance. You have been called to positions of responsibility at this critical time. The eyes of the world are upon you and it is no understatement to say that with your signatures, you can write our future.

Given all of this momentum and business support, the failure to broker a deal in Copenhagen was a bitter disappointment to so many people at so many levels. But this hasn't blunted the CLG's resolve. In 2010, the group was still pressing the EU to go further, faster; in particular, to revise its 20% greenhouse gas reduction target for 2020 upwards 'towards a more ambitious target'. Garrett A.G. Forde, CEO of Philips Lighting, said:

> Now is not the time for the EU to step on the brakes and give up its leadership position. . . . At Philips we have set the ambitious target to improve the energy efficiency of our entire portfolio by 50% by 2015. We believe we can set even more ambitious targets for beyond 2015 if the EU provides a clear, ambitious and long term commitment towards a low carbon economy.

The Prince has also not given up on setting a bold, responsive agenda. In a speech to the CLG in July 2010, he once again threw down the gauntlet:

> The challenge that I would like to lay before every single member of the Corporate Leaders Group on Climate Change is simple. Will you stand up and be counted? At every opportunity will you confront the sceptics and tell them they are wrong? Will you challenge your in house economists with the urgent need to define a new paradigm – in other words a macro economics for sustainability? Will you use the power of your brands and the power of your communications and, most of all, your marketing teams to support what the science tells us, and if necessary be prepared to take risks with your reputation to ensure you are on the right side of the debate? If you don't pick up this challenge and inspire many others, particularly those in your supply chains, then I fear the battle will be lost.

Prince Charles reminds us that responsiveness does not have to be all about doom and gloom or suffering and sacrifices. 'With issues of such magnitude', he says, 'it is easy to focus solely on the challenges;

the worst-case scenarios; the "what-if's" of failure. But take a moment to consider the opportunities if we succeed. Imagine a healthier, safer, and more sustainable, economically robust world. Because if we share in that vision, we can share the will to action that is now required.'

Pharmaceuticals on trial

Prince Charles and CLG are great examples of green responsiveness. But what about social issues? There are many inspiring cases. For example, Specialisterne is the world's first IT company with an affirmative business model built around the skills of people with Autistic Spectrum Disorder (ASD). And in the bio-tech industry – often criticized for its ethics – Merck announced plans in September 1994 to collaborate with Washington University to create a database (the Merck Gene Index) of the human gene sequence and to put this data into the public domain, to stimulate biogenetic medical advances.

Sadly, not all stories are so positive and inspiring. Let's take a look at one of the biggest crises the world still faces: HIV/AIDS. According to the November 2009 UNAIDS report, more than 25 million people have died of AIDS since 1981. The number of people living with HIV has risen from around 8 million in 1990 to 33 million today, and is still growing. Around 67% of people living with HIV are in sub-Saharan Africa and Africa has over 14 million AIDS orphans. At the end of 2008, women accounted for 50% of all adults living with HIV worldwide. In developing and transitional countries, 9.5 million people are in immediate need of life-saving AIDS drugs; of these, only 4 million (42%) are receiving the drugs.

The topic of drugs presents a good case study in responsiveness (and the lack thereof). In 2001, Oxfam launched a campaign called 'Cut the Cost', challenging the pharmaceutical industry to address responsible drug pricing. In the same year, the Indian pharmaceutical company Cipla cut the annual price of anti-retroviral AIDS drugs to Médecins Sans Frontières (MSF) to $350, as compared with the global industry standard of $1,000, and the Western market price of $10,400. Cipla also announced its intention to allow the South African government to sell eight of its generic AIDS drugs, the patents for which were held by other companies.

MSF put pressure on the five major pharmaceutical companies involved in the UNAIDS Accelerating Access Initiative to match Cipla's benchmark. And to some extent, they responded. Merck cut the price of its HIV/AIDS treatments for developing countries, including offering Crixivan at $600 and Stocrin at $500. Pfizer offered to supply antifungal medicine at no charge to HIV/AIDS patients in 50 AIDS stricken countries. Bristol-Myers Squibb announced that it would not prevent generic-drug makers from selling low-cost versions of one of its HIV drugs (Zerit) in Africa. And Glaxo-SmithKline granted a voluntary licence to South African generics producer Aspen, allowing them to share the rights to GSK's drugs (AZT, 3TC and Combivir) without charge.

So far so good. Apparently the drug companies are quite responsive. Why then, in 2001 (at the same time that they were doing all these good things), did 39 of the largest international pharmaceutical companies take the South African government to court over plans to introduce legislation aimed at easing access to AIDS drugs, arguing that it would infringe their patents and contravene the Trade Related Aspects of Intellectual Property Rights (TRIPS) agreement? Justin Forsyth, Oxfam Policy Director, said at the time, 'This court case demonstrates how powerful drug companies are bullying poor countries just so they can protect their patent rights on life-saving medicines.'

The pharmaceutical companies quickly realized that they had created a monster. Tens of thousands of people marched in protest all over the world, and 300,000 people from over 130 countries signed a petition against the action. Eventually, following public pressure, as well as pressure from the South African government and the European Parliament, Big Pharma dropped the case. Fanning the flames of public discontent, John le Carré's 2001 book

The Constant Gardener and the 2005 film adaptation depicted drug companies as corrupt profiteers. And so began the industry's PR damage control campaign. 'This is not about profits and patents', said John L. McGoldrick, Executive Vice President at Bristol-Myers Squibb, 'We seek no profits on AIDS drugs in Africa, and we will not let our patents be an obstacle.'

GSK's patent pool

It is nearly ten years later and the pharmaceutical companies are still trying to rebuild their reputations. As *Mail & Guardian* journalist Qudsiya Karrim reported for *Inside Story* in 2010:

> The past decade has been a public relations nightmare for big pharmaceutical companies – and deservedly so, their critics say. Activists and non-government organizations the world over have slated Big Pharma for putting profits ahead of people and vigorously enforcing their intellectual property rights, preventing many from gaining access to life-saving medication. It's an ugly story told repeatedly – in the media, over dinner, at AIDS conferences and during university seminars – and it has earned the pharmaceutical industry an unmatched notoriety.

But have they learned their lesson? The latest and possibly most responsive action has been from GlaxoSmithKline (GSK). Early in 2009, CEO Andrew Witty announced a major reform in their corporate policy on drug affordability and accessibility. In particular, he said GSK will cut its prices for all drugs in the 50 least developed countries to no more than 25% of the levels in the UK and US – and less if possible – and make drugs more affordable in middle-income countries such as Brazil and India. In addition, GSK will reinvest 20% of any profits it makes in the least developed countries in hospitals, clinics and staff and invite scientists from other companies, NGOs or governments to join the hunt for tropical disease treatments at its dedicated institute at Tres Cantos, Spain.

Many NGOs remain sceptical. Michelle Childs, director of policy and advocacy for Médecins Sans Frontières, says that in China, GSK charges over

$3,000 for the antiretroviral Lamivudine in the absence of generic competition, while in Thailand, by comparison, another pharmaceutical company, Abbott, offers the Lopinavir/Ritonavir co-formulation for $500. And as for reinvesting profits, Catherine Tomlinson of the Treatment Action Campaign says, 'Wouldn't it simply be better to slash profits and allow for countries themselves to invest in improving health infrastructure? The GSK argument is circular: We charge so much money so that we can give you some of your own money back!'

The most interesting and radical move, however, is that Witty committed GSK to put any chemicals or processes over which it has intellectual property rights that are relevant to finding drugs for neglected diseases into a 'patent pool', so they can be explored by other researchers. Explaining this move, Witty said, 'I think it's the first time anybody's really come out and said we're prepared to start talking to people about pooling our patents to try to facilitate innovation in areas where, so far, there hasn't been much progress.' He went on to say, 'Some people might be surprised it's coming from a pharma company. Obviously people see us as very defensive of intellectual property, quite rightly, and we will be, but in this area of neglected diseases we just think this is a place where we can carve out a space and see whether or not we can stimulate a different behaviour.'

On this score, some critics have been cautiously supportive. 'He is breaking the mould in validating the concept of patent pools', said the head of Oxfam's medicines campaign, Rohit Malpani. 'That has been out there as an idea and no company has done anything about it. It is a big step forward. It is welcome that he is inviting other companies to take this on and have a race to the top instead of a race to the bottom.'

Mining for a cure

It is not just the pharmaceutical companies that are part of the responsiveness story on HIV/AIDS. In South Africa, where someone dies of AIDS every two minutes and almost one-in-three women aged 25 to 29 – and more than a quarter of men aged 30 to 34 – are living with the HIV virus; on average 17% of employees are infected with the virus. In the face of such a crisis, one positive example of responsiveness is the multinational mining company Anglo American, which has been at the forefront of the war against the disease for nearly three decades. Their Group Medical Consultant, Dr Brian Brink, was there at the beginning – in 1980 he was set the task of discovering the first black South African that had contracted the disease – and he is still battling the scourge.

Their great leap of responsiveness came back in 2002 when Anglo American decided to go beyond simple AIDS awareness programmes and to offer their employees free access to the life-saving antiretroviral treatments (ARTs) that had become available. In a 2010 interview with the UK's *Telegraph*, Brink recalls: 'We decided to make the treatment available to all of our staff, despite the fact we didn't know what this would cost. Doing this was transformational and it solved a significant problem for the company – the fact that a lot of our staff were dying.'

Today, Anglo American has a much better handle on both the infection rates and the costs. The company estimates that approximately 12,000 of its 71,000 workforce are currently HIV positive. That is still a chronic situation, but compared with where they started – essentially training up two men for each job in the hope that one of them will survive – they have come a long way. Anglo American spends 3.4% of its payroll of the HIV/AIDS programme, a figure that will probably go up as HIV positive employees survive longer. The only way to reverse the upward trend is by stopping the new HIV infections.

When Anglo American first committed to offer the ARTs, it was a time when no other company in South Africa was doing so and when the 'business case' had yet to be quantified. Nevertheless, Brink made the persuasive argument to top management that 'purchasing anti-retroviral drugs isn't a cost that's going to kill the company; it's a cost that's going to protect the company'. They were convinced – as much by the moral case as the intuitively sound economic rationale – and today the evidence proves that Brink was right.

At Anglo American, the fully-accounted for cost of treatment is $126 per HIV positive employee. However, people on ART are more able to work. Therefore, absenteeism declines 1.9 days per employee per month, which saves $96 a month. The use of healthcare services also declines, saving $87. Added to this is the fact that staff turnover and benefits payments are reduced, which saves a further $36 a month. At the individual level, the total savings of $219 per patient per month amount to approximately 174% of the cost of providing treatment.

So, in the end, giving out ART free of charge makes economic sense. But it required Anglo American to take that leap of faith and to place responsiveness before short-term costs. The financial merits of the decision are retrospective. The commitment to free ARTs was proactive. The story is far from over, as this is literally a lifelong pledge by Anglo American. What's more, the company is now dealing with the added burden and complexity of an escalating drug-resistant tuberculosis epidemic. At least it has the experience of tackling the AIDS crisis to draw on, but it just goes to show that responsiveness is not a once-off CSR tactic; it is a continuous and dynamic commitment to living the company's values.

Cabbages and condoms

Sticking with the HIV/AIDS theme, one of the most remarkable stories of responsiveness comes out of Thailand; it makes the point that business responsiveness is not only the purview of large multinationals. This story is about the Population and Community Development Association (PDA) and its Founder and Chairman, Mechai Viravaidya. PDA is one of Thailand's largest and most successful private, non-profit development organizations. Among the many programmes and projects it runs is the quirkily-named Cabbages & Condoms restaurant in Bangkok, a social enterprise dedicated to raising awareness on family planning and HIV/AIDS. One of the more creative and colourful ways they do this is by making all the decor for the restaurant (including lampshades, etc.) from condoms and contraceptive pills.

Through PDA and his other activities, including serving as a Senator in the Thai government and Chairman of some of Thailand's biggest companies, Viravaidya has played a pivotal role in Thailand's immensely successful family planning programme, which saw one of the most rapid fertility declines in the modern era. The rate of annual population growth in Thailand declined from over 3% in 1974 to 0.6% in 2005, and the average number of children per family fell from seven to under two.

Viravaidya was also chief architect in building Thailand's comprehensive national HIV/AIDS prevention policy and programme. This initiative is widely regarded as one of the most outstanding national efforts by any country in combating HIV/AIDS. By 2004, Thailand had experienced a 90% reduction in new HIV infections. In 2005, the World Bank reported that these preventative efforts helped save 7.7 million lives throughout the country and saved the government over $18 billion in treatment costs alone. As a result of his outstanding work, in 1999 Viravaidya was appointed the UNAIDS Ambassador.

In 2010, as part of my CSR Quest world tour, I conducted an interview with Viravaidya and was most intrigued by his answers. I started by asking him what demonstrable impact social enterprises can make to society's problems, using Cabbages & Condoms as an example, to which he replied:

> We originally referred to the Cabbages & Condoms Restaurant as a 'Business for Social Progress', which is commonly known as a social enterprise in the West. The profits from our restaurant directly benefit our NGO, the PDA. The impact has included: promotion of family planning in Thailand, HIV/AIDS prevention through condom usage, poverty alleviation, and education in North Eastern Thailand. The restaurant has been a successful social enterprise, and we always encourage civil society leaders in Asia to set one up to help maintain financial sustainability, including with youth groups.

So what then are the barriers to scaling up social enterprises like Cabbages & Condoms? 'The biggest hurdles to social enterprise', said Viravaidya, 'are good ideas and funds for large-scale endeavours. It is best for new organizations looking at establishing a social enterprise to seek advice from the business community and start small.' Conscious of his extensive involvement in politics, I was curious on his view of government's role in enabling social enterprises to succeed. He said this varies from country by country. Whereas in the UK, the government is quite active in its support, the Thai Government currently plays no role in incentivizing social enterprise. What's more, Viravaidya would like to keep it like that: 'The best thing they can do is to kindly stay out of the way.'

So why use business as the vehicle for responding to the needs of society? Why not just create a charity? 'We needed to ensure that our poverty eradication and education initiatives performed under our NGO had long-term sustainability', explained Viravaidya, 'and were not entirely dependent on outside donations. The social enterprises we have established have earned approximately $150 million over 25 years and fund approximately 70% of our development endeavours. We would not have been able to accomplish half as much as we have without our social enterprises.'

How not to McDo engagement

Of course, not every company is as responsive as GSK, Anglo American or Cabbages & Condoms, and we can learn as much from the mistakes of others as from those shining success stories. McDonald's, for example, is a classic case study in how damaging and costly it can be to learn the lesson of responsiveness the hard way. In 1986, a UK environmental campaign group called The London Greenpeace Group published a six-page leaflet called 'What's Wrong with McDonald's? Everything they don't want you to know'. The leaflet contained accusations of McDonald's complicity in starvation in the Third World, rainforest destruction, negative health impacts (including food poisoning, heart disease and cancer), exploitation of children through advertising, 'torture and murder' of animals, anti-union behaviour and poor employee working conditions.

In 1990, five members of the group were issued a writ by McDonald's for publishing and distributing the leaflet, of which two – Helen Steel and Dave Morris – went to trial in June 1994. The resulting 313 day trial (popularly labelled 'McLibel') became the longest ever in British legal history and ended in June 1997, having heard 180 witnesses and reviewed 40,000 pages of documents and witness statements. The verdict was mixed – some of the allegations about McDonald's business practices were upheld, but Steel and Morris were found guilty of having libelled the company and were ordered to pay £60,000 in damages.

Steel and Morris refused to pay the damages (reduced on appeal to £40,000 in 1999), and in 2000, took their case to the European Court of Justice in Strasbourg, alleging that the original trial breached their human rights to a fair trial and freedom of expression. In February 2005, the Strasbourg court judged in their favour and awarded compensation. According to Gerry McCusker, author of *Talespin: Public Relations Disasters*, the trial cost McDonald's more than £10 million in legal fees.

In 2003, McDonald's faced its next responsiveness challenge. In February of that year, Morgan Spurlock decided to make a documentary film following his 30-day experiment, during which he ate food and items purchased exclusively from McDonald's. Among his 'rules' was that if the customer service representative asked if he wanted something in a larger size, he had to agree. Hence, the title of the film became *Super Size Me*, which was nominated for an Academy Award in 2004. Over the 30 days, Spurlock consumed an average of 5,000 kcal (the equivalent of 9.26 Big Macs) per day. He gained 24.5 lb (11.1 kg), a 13% body mass increase, and his Body Mass Index rose from 23.2 (within the 'healthy' range of 19–25) to 27 ('overweight'). He also experienced mood swings, sexual dysfunction, and liver damage. It took Spurlock 14 months to lose the weight he gained.

Although McDonald's may never admit to the film's direct impact on their reputation or sales, they seemed to have learned their lesson in responsiveness. Instead of suing the pants off of Spurlock, in 2005, McDonald's announced a Balanced Lifestyles initiative which involves offering healthier menu options, promoting physical activity and providing more nutritional information to customers about its products. Without a doubt, they have gotten savvier about playing the Strategic CSR game and making continuous improvements in an Age of Management mode. However, it remains an open question whether McDonald's – and indeed the entire fast food industry, as detailed in Eric Schlosser's *Fast Food Nation* – can make the transition to Systemic CSR in an Age of Responsibility.

Cross-sector partnerships

If McDonald's historical reactions to stakeholders are an example of how *not* to do engagement, then cross-sector partnerships are increasingly being seen as the more progressive and constructive alternative. They were given a strong boost at the World Summit of Sustainable Development in Johannesburg in 2002, and today, 78% of CEOs believe that companies should engage in collaboration with a variety of stakeholders to address sustainability issues, according to a 2010 survey by the UN Global Compact and Accenture. But we should acknowledge that partnerships are not a straightforward option. There can be issues of accountability and power imbalance, when unelected corporations and NGOs have influence in states where governments are weak or failing. And even where they are the best solution, there can be real obstacles in both the development and management of partnerships which are too easily ignored.

In 2007, I collaborated in some research with the University of Cambridge Programme for Sustainability Leadership, which analysed the experiences of participants in their Postgraduate Certificate in Cross-sector Partnership (PCCP) course over a period of seven years.[45] We found that the critical success factors for partnerships included mutual commitment by the partners, adequate resources and a clear partnership agreement. Conversely,

---

[45]This was written up in the following paper: Findlay-Brooks, Visser & Wright *Cross-Sector Partnership as an Approach to Inclusive Development*, University Cambridge Programme for Sustainability Leadership Research Paper Series: No. 4, 2007.

the greatest barriers were differences in expectations between the partners, power imbalances and communication problems.

One of the findings that stunned us was the lack of consultation with the intended beneficiaries of the partnerships. For example, engagement of beneficiaries and stakeholders only ranked joint fifth in the questionnaire results out of eight success factors. Also, although 22 out of the 25 partnerships that responded to this question had carried out a consultation exercise, at least 11 of these had not included the intended beneficiaries. This has serious implications for responsiveness. Companies, governments and civil society organizations that purport to be acting on behalf of certain vulnerable groups or causes cannot claim to be responsive if they are not even asking those they are trying to help what their real needs are.

After exploring the experiences of these partnership practitioners, we concluded that, if we are relying on partnerships to bring about structural change and long-term development impacts, then they need to be firmly tied into genuinely inclusive consultation processes, operate within accountability frameworks, be properly supported and evaluated, and where appropriate lead ultimately to policy change.

Despite these challenges of cross-sector partnerships, they are undoubtedly a key CSR 2.0 responsiveness strategy, and there are many successful and inspiring examples. Take Unilever's partnership with the FDI World Dental Federation, for instance. In a world where 50% of the global population don't brush their teeth, there are huge opportunities to promote good oral health. The partnership supports more than 40 oral health improvement programmes in 37 countries around the world. Unilever's Oral Care category also supports dental research through its partnership with the International Association of Dental Research (IADR) that has spanned 25 years.

Another example is the CSR business coalition AED (Asociacion Empresarial para el Desarrollo) in Costa Rica, which is partnering with the government and the national teachers syndicate on education. Specifically, they have developed an information system for public schools that has reduced the administrative burden of teachers by between 30 and 50 hours per month, giving the teachers more time to spend with the children. According to Olga Sauma, Director of Business Development for AED, the project is also 'allowing the school system to get more information and cross-variables to figure out exactly what the problems within the education system are and how we can develop public policy in order to address these issues'.

Cross-sector partnerships can also be a strategy for scalability. For example, in 2009 HSBC launched their Eco-Schools Climate Initiative in partnership with the Foundation for Environmental Education (FEE). This is a three-year project involving 1,000 HSBC staff volunteers in ten countries and reaching an estimated 1.2 million young people aged five to 18. The aim of the programme is to inspire action on climate change by improving schools' environmental efficiency. Similarly, Seventh Generation has partnered with Kaplan EduNeering to set up the Sustainability Institute, an online learning programme designed to teach the strategic integration of sustainability to thousands of businesses and their millions of employees.

The ten future faces of CSOs

Some of the most important players in cross-sector partnerships – and in the responsiveness game more generally – are civil society organizations (CSOs, which I prefer as a term to NGOs). Reflecting on how this sector is changing in the face of increased calls for responsiveness, I have distinguished ten 'Paths to the Future' for CSOs.

Drawing on examples from around the world, I believe CSOs will increasingly become:

Platforms for transparency – The role of CSOs as agitators for, and agents of, greater transparency seems set to continue. For example, in Senegal, Benin, and Guinea, CSO intervention has been critical in the development of a free press. And in India, Karmayog allows citizens to report specific instances of bribery and corruption on a live, public website, including through their mobiles using MPower. DespreFirme is a

Table 8 Ten paths of the future for CSOs

Emerging roles	Key features or activities
Platforms for transparency	Undertaking investigative exposés and hosting disclosure forums
Brokers of volunteerism	Providing project opportunities for employee volunteers
Champions of CSR	Raising awareness and increasing public pressure for CSR
Advisors of business	Offering consulting services to business on responsibility
Agents of government	Working with or on behalf of regulatory authorities
Reformers of policy	Pressuring for government policy reforms to incentivize CSR
Makers of standards	Developing voluntary standards and inviting business compliance
Channels for taxes	Receiving and deploying specially earmarked tax revenues
Partners in solutions	Partnering with business or government to tackle specific issues
Catalysts for creativity	Creating social enterprises and supporting social entrepreneurs

Romanian site where users reveal accurate information about labour conditions, rating companies publicly. Scorecard.org is a US pollution information site, which allows the public to compare pollution in communities across the country, and find out who the biggest polluters are.

Brokers of volunteerism – As companies increasingly see the benefits of volunteerism (greater job satisfaction, productivity, commitment and loyalty), CSOs are becoming people-brokers, as sources of projects for employee volunteers. For example, the Voluntary Workcamps Association of Ghana (VOLU) coordinates volunteers to help with the construction of schools, reforestation and AIDS campaigning.

Champions of CSR – While some CSOs remain sceptical about CSR, in many countries they are the main agents for promoting CSR. For example, in Iran, a group of CSOs have joined forces with the UNDP to promote CSR through targeted training for managers under the umbrella of the UN Millennium Development Goals. And in Senegal, CSR awareness has grown mainly due to a CSO called La Lumière in Kédougou.

Advisors of business – A combination of genuine expertise, valuable perspectives and a crunch on funding means that many CSOs are turning to consultancy, working with and advising companies not only on specific social and environmental issues, but also more generally on sustainability and responsibility. For example, in Hungary, as opposed to the traditional role of watchdog, many CSOs engage in consultancy on CSR. Internationally, Oxfam's Enterprise Development Programme offers enterprise driven solutions to poverty, providing finance, skills and advice to businesses in the developing world.

Agents of government – The phenomena of GONGOs (government organized NGOs), GINGOs (government-inspired NGOs), GRINGOs (government regulated/run and initiated NGOs) and PANGOs (party-affiliated NGOs) are becoming more widespread, no longer confined countries like China. Even where governments are not setting up or running the CSOs, they are increasingly supporting them as key catalysts. For example, Belgian CSOs receive €3 in government funding for every €1 they raise themselves.

Reformers of policy – Realizing that the 'rules of the game' need to change, CSOs are getting more involved in legal reform. For example, in Indonesia, it was largely due to rising pressure from CSOs that Law No. 40/2007 concerning Limited Liability Companies was introduced to make CSR mandatory.

Makers of standards – In an effort to raise the bar on voluntary action by companies, many CSOs are developing their own social and environmental codes and standards, and then inviting business to comply with them. For example, in Israel, the Public Trust Organisation established The Public Trust Code, covering advertising, transparency, disclosure, service and product guarantees, honesty in contracts and privacy of information.

Channels for taxes – In some countries, the effectiveness of CSOs has earned them the ability to source tax dollars directly. For example, in Mexico, FECHAC (The Federation of Chihuahuan Industry) is a CSO, set up after devastating floods in 1990, that is funded through a special annual tax on more than 38,000 industries. And in Romania, the 2% Law (in terms of the Fiscal Code) allows citizens to redirect 2% of personal income tax to a CSO.

Partners in solutions – Not only are CSOs collaborating with business more and more, but also with governments and multilateral agencies. For example, in South Korea, 'Cross Sector Alliances' is one of five approaches to CSR being promoted, while in Africa the New Nigeria Foundation provides a platform for mobilizing non-traditional resources through public/private partnerships. In Turkey, TUSEV promotes linkages between domestic and international CSOs and encourages CSR by putting foreign and domestic firms in contact with appropriate CSOs. And in 2008, 18 collaborative 'CSR Laboratory' projects coordinated by CSR Europe launched their outputs as a joint European Toolbox for CSR.

Catalysts for creativity – CSOs are increasingly expected to provide solutions, not just point out the problems, especially by launching or supporting social enterprises. For example, in Bangladesh, BRAC (formerly Bangladesh Rural Advancement Committee) has been crucial in the microcredit movement, and in Singapore, the National Trades Union Congress (NTUC) has 12 social enterprises and four related organizations that are owned by more than 500,000 workers. Cambia is an international CSO with a mission to democratize innovation, using open-source approaches to create a more equitable and inclusive capability to solve problems using science and technology.

However the future unfolds, it is clear that CSOs will be a significant player in the new landscape of responsible governance and accountability, as both a counter-balancing force and a partner with governments and business. In fact, I believe CSOs will be the responsive glue that holds society together in the turbulent years ahead.

Opening an eco-patent commons

Of course, responsiveness goes beyond traditional partnerships and CSO effectiveness; it is also about innovative ways to collaborate. There are now numerous Web 2.0 inspired experiments in responsiveness that are opening up sustainability and responsibility solutions to the public. One is a new platform called the Eco-Patent Commons, which allows companies to share their intellectual property for the common good. The Commons was launched by WBCSD in 2008 and covers issues like waste, pollution, global warming and energy. 'The premise of the Commons', says Björn Stigson, president of the WBCSD, 'is that the free sharing of these patents leads to new collaborations and innovation aimed at helping others become more eco-efficient and/or operate in a more sustainable way.'

The Eco-Patent Commons' publicly searchable database already contains over one hundred eco-friendly patents from companies like Bosch, Dow, DuPont, Fuji Xerox, HP, IBM, Nokia, Pitney Bowes, Ricoh, Sony, Taisei and Xerox. Dow, for example, has added a technology to enable more efficient production of olefins – the basic building blocks for many materials used in packaging, electronics, adhesives, and durable goods – by reducing energy and material consumption in the process. Xerox has 11 pledged patents that cover a process that cuts the time it takes to remove toxic waste from soil and water from years to months, as well as a patent that covers technology that makes magnetic refrigeration less harmful to the environment.

HP, one of the most recent joiners, has added three patents: a convenient self-contained battery recycling station that will encourage consumers to exchange their used batteries for new ones or for credit; a weld process monitoring system that will reduce the resource and energy consumption associated with bad welds on assembly lines; and a process that eliminates the need for anti-oxidant metal coatings (such as gold) during certain stages of microchip and circuit board assembly.

Dr John E. Kelly III, IBM Senior Vice President and Director of IBM Research, believes that 'innovation to address environmental issues will require both the application of technology as well as new models for

sharing intellectual property among companies in different industries. . . .
In addition to enabling new players to engage in protecting the environment, the free exchange of valuable intellectual property will accelerate work on the next level of environmental challenges.'

Similarly, Donal O'Connell, Director of Intellectual Property for Nokia, thinks that 'environmental issues have great potential to help us discover the next wave of innovation because they force us all to think differently about how we make, consume and recycle products'. Nokia have pledged a patent designed to help companies safely reuse old mobile phones by transforming them into new products like digital cameras, data monitoring devices or other electronic items. 'Recycling the computing power of mobile phones in this way could significantly increase the reuse of materials in the electronics industry', concludes O'Connell.

Even more significant than the individual patents that have been added is the shift in thinking that this signals among some of the largest companies in the world. It is true none of them are exactly 'giving away the family silver' – they are not opening all their patents – but they are demonstrating responsiveness on a scale never seen before. They are recognizing that the global problems we face are larger than whatever individual solutions can accomplish. If we are truly going to be effective in tackling our most intractable challenges, we will need the wisdom of crowds and the collective efforts of millions of entrepreneurs.

Making a GreenXchange

A similar, more recent initiative is GreenXchange, a collaborative platform initially launched by Creative Commons, Nike and Best Buy. Current partners include 2degrees, nGenera and Salesforce.com. The fact that Creative Commons – a non-profit organization that previously developed licensing programmes to help in sharing creative and scientific content – has branched into the environmental arena is good news, not least because it brings a sophisticated understanding of the legalities of proprietary content, yet combines this with a commitment to open-source sharing.

The main difference between the Eco-Patent Commons and GreenXchange is that companies that contribute patents to the GreenXchange will have the option of charging users a fixed annual licensing fee and can also restrict any licensing by rivals or for competitive use. In addition, even if no annual fee is charged, patent users must register so there is a record of who is using what technology. The structure is more complex than the Eco-Patent Commons, but John Wilbanks, GreenXchange coordinator and vice president for science at Creative Commons, believes it will yield greater numbers of high-quality inventions. 'We don't depend on altruism', says Wilbanks. 'This system helps the environment while enabling a firm to make money from patents in applications outside its core business.'

Wilbanks cites a fictional example for illustration purposes: 'Nike's air-bag patent for cushioning shoes is crucial to its core shoe business, but may have environmental benefits in other industries – perhaps in prolonging the useful life of tires. GreenXchange could enable Nike to license the air-bag technology selectively to noncompeting companies.' Although this example may be speculative, Nike's commitment to the concept is not. According to Kelly Lauber, a global director in Nike's Sustainable Business and Innovation Lab, by sharing its water-based adhesive technology and working with footwear makers, average levels of environmentally harmful solvents used by Nike's suppliers decreased to less than 15 grams per pair of shoes from 350 in 1997.

Nike has issued a GreenXchange booklet, in which it says: To find solutions, you need to understand the equation:

$$P \uparrow NR \downarrow C\$ \uparrow = C(R)$$

As population (P) increases, the availability of natural resources (NR) decreases, raising costs (C\$) and causing consumers to choose and regulators to act (C(R)).

The booklet lays out the challenge: Will the pursuit of sustainability create the new Google? The new Nike? The new disruptive view of business models, markets, profits and consumers? The answer is almost certainly yes.

The conclusion is that 'it's time to dust off the research, the assets, the knowledge, the innovation you've developed on sustainability. Imagine the impact it could have if we gifted it to the world.'

Whether it is the Eco-Patent Commons or GreenXchange or some other platform for open-sourcing sustainability and responsibility that eventually prospers and becomes the new collaborative standard, the genie is out of the bottle. The idea is out there that, when it comes to technologies, processes, products and services that have potentially life-saving impacts, there is a moral obligation to share these with humanity. No doubt these collaborative platforms have started in the environmental space because, as was the case with reporting, green issues are easier to quantify and design solutions for. But we can expect them to spread rapidly to the social space as well. And as they do, they will continue to challenge companies to demonstrate the CSR principle of Responsiveness.

10

The principle of glocality

'Blessed unrest' is the rise of a movement that is a shift between a world created by and for privilege to a world created by community.

—Paul Hawken

We must ensure that the global market is embedded in broadly shared values and practices that reflect global social needs, and that all the world's people share the benefits of globalization.

—Kofi Annan

I am local, rural, communal. And I find that the whole world is a community. We have made progress in asserting our local community rights globally. We shall continue to do so.

—Tewolde Egziabher

I want to work for a company that contributes to and is part of the community. I want something not just to invest in. I want something to believe in.

—Anita Roddick

Box 9: The principle of glocality – in a nutshell

Iconic leaders	Anglo American
	BHP-Billiton
	Cemex
	SC Johnson
	Sony
Period	Rising from 1992, with the publication of Local Agenda 21
Key ideas	Context matters
	Culture shapes content
	Global principles, local practices
	Think global, act local
	Unity of purpose, diversity of means
Commentators	Stuart Hart (academic & author)
	Paul Hawken (author)
	David Korten (author & activist)
	E.F. Schumacher (economist & author)
	Vandana Shiva (scientist, author & activist)
References	*Small is Beautiful: Economics as if People Mattered* (E.F. Schumacher, 1973)
	Capitalism at the Crossroads: The Unlimited Business Opportunities in Solving the World's Most Difficult Problems (Stuart Hart, 2005, 2007, 2010)
	Earth Democracy: Justice, Sustainability, and Peace (Vandana Shiva, 2005)
	The Great Turning: From Empire to Earth Community (David Korten, 2007)
	Blessed Unrest: How the Largest Movement in the World Came into Being and Why No One Saw It Coming (Paul Hawken, 2007)

Case 9: AIESEC and me

'So, are you still killing the blacks down in South Africa?' This was one of the first questions I was asked at an African Leadership Development Seminar I was attending in Nairobi, Kenya, in 1991. The seminar was organized by AIESEC, an international economics and commerce students' organization for which I, in my final year of business studies, was serving as President of the Cape Town chapter. Behind that simple, arresting question lay an entangled maze of socio-cultural history that included discrimination, injustice, disinformation, distrust and misunderstanding – a situation not so very different from what prevailed in Europe in the wake of World War II, when AIESEC was founded.

In fact, 'devastation, turmoil, anger and despair' is how AIESEC later described 'the world in which it all began'. Recognizing society's malaise, a small group of students came together in Liege in 1946 to plan a new organization, which could 'bridge the gap across people and cultures'. Two years later, AIESEC was officially launched in Stockholm with a mission to 'expand the understanding of a nation by expanding the understanding of the individuals, changing the world one person at a time'. The following year, the organization held its first International Congress, where it kicked off its flagship programme – an International Traineeship Exchange Programme.

The idea behind the exchange programme was simple: match students to traineeship opportunities in foreign countries, thereby improving management skills and cultural understanding at the same time. It was an idea ripe for its time, and the programme flourished, growing from 89 students in 1949 to over 2,400 annual exchanges by 1960 and 4,200 by 1970. Today, the figure stands at around 10,000 and AIESEC has become the largest student-run organization in the world, with over 50,000 members on 1,600 campuses in 107 countries. What makes it so unique, however – and such an excellent example of 'glocality' – is not just its inspiring origins, or its impressive scale, but more importantly its vision of business as a way to bring about 'positive social change' and 'peace and fulfilment of humankind's potential'.

These are lofty ideals, no doubt about it, and hard to live up to. At the time that I joined AIESEC, in 1988, the organization was emerging from a period of deep questioning of its mission and ongoing relevance. 'Just try to close your eyes and imagine what these countries would look like without AIESEC', said Athos M. Staub, President of AIESEC International in 1985/86. 'Unfortunately, it would not be different.' As a result of this existential midlife crisis (the organization was just reaching 40), the AIESEC Global Seminar Series was initiated in 1988, culminating in the first World Theme Conference, held in Tokyo in August 1990. The theme for the conference was sustainable development and it brought together 200 delegates from 50 countries, including yours truly from South Africa.

The impact on young management students like myself was profound. In preparation, we had to research local case studies to share with our international colleagues. I chose waste management and found myself meeting local recycling groups and attending a metropolitan recycling meeting chaired by the mayor of Cape Town, which included representatives from the plastics, paper and bottling industries. I discovered many interesting things. For instance, South Africa had the third highest aluminium can recycling rate in the world, largely due to the armies of poor people that collected them for a small fee. I also learned that there was a glut in the city recycling system – not enough people were buying products with recycled content, so supply constantly exceeded demand.

At the conference itself, the learning curve was also steep. We had presentations from people like J. Hugh Faulkner, who joined with

Swiss industrialist Stephan Schmidheiny that same year to form the Business Council for Sustainable Development, serving as Executive Director. The BCSD in turn was invited by Maurice Strong, chair of upcoming 1992 UN Conference on Environment and Development (UNCED), to provide a business perspective on sustainable development. It was no coincidence, therefore, that one of the key outcomes of our AIESEC conference was a publication called 'A Youth Action Guide on Sustainable Development', presented as a significant contribution to the Rio Earth Summit the following year.

Beyond the conference itself, we also had 'study tour' visits, most notably to the Toyota headquarters in Nagoya, where we met with the senior management team. Seeing their R&D display area – where they had numerous eco-efficient and alternative fuel technologies already in the mature stages of development – made a deep and lasting impression on me. And then there was the cultural element – waking up to the sound of '*ohayo gozaimas*' (good morning) in the home of my Japanese host family, and observing that, although we lived differently and spoke differently, we shared many of the same values and concerns about life and the state of the world. As I later wrote and published, 'this culture that I've grown to love will always be a part of me. This country with its charming mixture of ancient and modern I will take with me to share with others.'

Of course, AIESEC isn't all about travelling to exotic places for conferences. Most of the impact was – and continues to be – its local projects. Among the numerous initiatives that we organized in Cape Town was one that was similar to the international exchange programme, but instead matched previously disadvantaged individuals in South Africa to skills development traineeships in the country. As part of another project, we arranged a talk by Professor Francis Wilson, co-author of *Uprooting Poverty*. I remember him saying something to the effect that if our commitment – evidenced by us all voluntarily attending a poverty lecture on a Saturday morning when we could be at the beach – was any indication of the calibre and social responsibility of the next generation of leaders, then South Africa and the world may be in better hands than he previously had imagined.

Today, when I think of the path that my own career took as a direct result of my AIESEC exposure, and of all of the 800,000 other alumni, then I wonder if he may have been right. One only need glance at what some of the alumni are doing today to be convinced of the 'glo-cal' impact that AIESEC has had. For example, Rong-I Wu was an AIESEC pioneer in Taiwan in the 1960s and says that AIESEC influenced him to become globally minded. Later, he set up the Taiwan Institute of Economic Research and became the Chairman of the Taiwan Stock Exchange. Ricardo Obregon helped to organize a World Energy Conference in Colombia in the 1970s and today he is CEO of Juan Valdéz Coffee. Arjun Bhagat, active in AIESEC India in 1980s, believes that the organization gave him the opportunity to learn. Today, he is an investor and has been the Chairman and CEO of Calibrated Group.

Ante Stjepan Glavas, after his experiences with AIESEC in Croatia in the 1990s, built a career in helping people with human passion and values. He went on to become Executive Director of Business as an Agent of World Benefit at Case Weatherhead School of Management in the United States. Ehaab Abdou was another 1990s alumnus. AIESEC in Egypt was the first non-profit organization that he joined, after which he focused his career on social development. He helped establish and became the first president of Fat'het Kheir, an Egyptian youth-led voluntary organization offering an innovative model in community development. Today, he is the co-founder and current chairperson of Nahdet El Mahrousa, an Egyptian youth-led NGO, and he is also the elected president of the Egyptian Federation of Youth NGOs. And so the list could go on. In fact, I bump into former AIESECers all the time in my CSR work today.

In order to stay glocally relevant, however, AIESEC has had to constantly adapt. One of the latest innovations is inspired by the idea of T-Leadership – a person that has both the essential generic competencies to lead positive change and has a strong interest and knowledge in one of the key topics of the world that needs positive leadership. A T-Leader, therefore, can go wide on broad impacts and deep on selected challenges. The way that AIESEC develops T-Leaders is through Issue Based Experiences (IBXPs), across the themes of finance, education, HIV/AIDS, corporate responsibility and entrepreneurship. IBXPs are seen 'as a way to ensure that young people who have identified a passion for a particular issue have the chance to live an experience that not only enables them to gain general leadership skills but also expertise on a particular issue'.

On reflection, AIESEC gave me a T-Leadership grounding as well – although the programme had not been formalized then. In particular, it allowed me to specialize early on in environmental issues. Apart from the conference in Japan, I attended meetings on wildlife management in Zimbabwe and helped to organize a national conference on sustainability. It was hardly surprising that when I had to choose a thesis topic for my business science honours degree, I chose 'green marketing'. My work with AIESEC had given me direct access to the CEO of Pick n Pay, a national retailer that was pioneering green marketing, so I used them as a case study for my research.

Graduating was not the end of my AIESEC journey either. In 1992, I was matched to a traineeship with the Royal Bank of Canada in Kingston, Ontario, which kick-started my working career. It also launched my writing career, as I had an article published about the experience. In it, I recounted the many insights and lessons I had learned from Canada. 'Canada's gift to me has been the light of understanding', I mused. 'After all, I had come from a country locked into a tragic mindset: belief that it is the victim of a cruel fate, facing problems so unique and insurmountable that all hope is in vain; a belief that the rest of the world doesn't understand what we are going through; a perception that criticism is rife but help scarce. How encouraging it has been for me to discover that Canada and South Africa are in many ways alike, facing similar problems and similar challenges.'

I observed some parallels, for example, between the 'cruel and unjust' way in which Canada and South Africa had treated its indigenous people. Furthermore, I reflected, 'like South Africa, modern Canada is a land of diverse heritage and ethnic origin which faces the difficulty of establishing unity without forfeiting its diversity. And, like South Africa, Canada is a young people faced with the challenge of building a proud, new nation.' I was inspired by the way Canada seemed to have learned from its mistakes and was making a real effort to embrace and celebrate diversity. My article concluded with a classic glocal sentiment: 'Surely South Africa can learn something from this kind of approach – this constructive spirit which I have perceived in Canada? Surely these are lessons which I can carry home with me and share with my people?'

I had learned other lessons along the AIESEC journey as well. Looking back at an article I published about the AIESEC leadership development seminar that I attended in Kenya, it is clear that the whole experience was an enormous wake-up call for me. The article began by saying, 'The problem with South Africa is that it still considers itself as an exclusive First World island off the tip of Africa.' By contrast, my fresh observation was that 'we're not that different from many of our brother and sister countries. Kenya also has flashy skyscrapers, card telephones and CNN; they also have a culturally diverse population and all the problems which come with it (they have 42 tribal groups); they also face the challenges of poverty and income inequality; and most importantly they also have beautiful, intelligent, concerned people living within their borders.'

I concluded that 'it's time we put our preconceptions and our mis-conceptions behind us, and start to realize that we have things to learn and to gain from reintegrating into the African family. South Africa has an important role to play in this continent; not as a patronising grandparent, but as a child among the children of Africa, learning, growing, sometimes squabbling, but ever striving to be better.' I realize that these words may seem trivial (or even amusing) reading them now. However, at a time when South Africa was still in the grip of apartheid and walking a tightrope between civil war and a negotiated political settlement, these were profound experiences for a young, naive white business student from Cape Town.

Today, I confess that I find the starry-eyed idealism a bit cringe-worthy. But maybe a healthy dose of idealism is just what we need in the world today, as we needed it then. After all, wasn't it idealistic to imagine that South Africa could avoid a blood-bath in its transition to democracy? Maybe one of the AIESEC songs – yes, we had songs too – is not simply to be filed away under 'embarrassing recollections from the distant past'. Maybe its chorus serves as a good reminder about what it was (and is still) all about: 'We've come a long way to make our dreams come true/We've come a long way to make our friendships last/We've come a long way and there's still a longer way to go/To make this world a better place for all.'

Origins of glocality

The term 'glocal' – a portmanteau of *global* and *local* – is said to come from the Japanese word *dochakuka*, which simply means global localization. Orig-inally referring to a way of adapting farming techniques to local conditions, *dochakuka* evolved into a marketing strategy when Japanese businessmen adopted it in the 1980s. It is said that the English word 'glocal' was first coined by Akio Morita, founder of Sony Corporation.[46] In fact, in 2008, Sony Music Corporation even trademarked the phrase 'go glocal'. Glocality was subsequently introduced and popularized in the West in the 1990s by sociologists Manfred Lange, Roland Robertson, Keith Hampton, Barry Wellman and Zygmunt Bauman.

The underlying concept of 'think global, act local' claims somewhat more varied origins. In a broad, abstract sense, it is captured in the ancient Hermetic idea of 'as above, so below' – the macrocosm is reflected in the microcosm and vice versa. Or as Goethe put it: 'If (we) would seek comfort in the whole, (we) must learn to discover the whole in the smallest part.' More concretely and recently, the Scots town planner and social activist Patrick Geddes applied the concept in his 1915 book *Cities in Evolution*, saying:

> Local character is thus no mere accidental old-world quaintness, as its mimics think and say. It is attained only in course of adequate grasp and treatment of the whole environment, and in active sympathy with the essential and characteristic life of the place concerned.

Sometimes, glocality maintains its geographical rootedness. For example, Neighborhood Knowledge California is a project of the Advanced Policy Institute at the University of California, Los Angeles, which serves as a state-wide, interactive website that assembles and maps a variety of databases that can be used in neighbourhood research. Its aim is to promote greater equity in housing and banking policy. In addition, it functions as a geographic repository for users to map their own communities by uploading their own datasets.

When and by whom the phrase 'think global, act local' was first applied to environmental issues is a matter of some dispute. It may have been introduced by David Brower, founder of Friends of the Earth, in 1969, or

---

[46]Tunc Medeni, of the Japanese Advanced Institution of Science and Technology, has also suggested the concept of 'lobal', i.e. think local, act global.

by Rene Dubos as an advisor to the 1972 UN Conference on the Human Environment. Also, in 1979, Canadian futurist Frank Feather chaired a conference called 'Thinking Globally, Acting Locally'. Whatever its origins, the notion of glocality has entered into the popular consciousness. It was given its most visible and practical expression when the Rio Earth Summit issued Local Agenda 21 in 1992, which was a programme of action for applying the global principles of sustainable development in local contexts. Today, there is also a *Glocalist* magazine in Austria that offers a daily online newspaper, weekly digital magazine and monthly print magazine.

In a CSR context, the idea of 'think global, act local' recognizes that most CSR issues manifest as dilemmas, rather than easy choices. In a complex, interconnected CSR 2.0 world, companies (and their critics) will have to become far more sophisticated in understanding local contexts and finding the appropriate local solutions they demand, without forsaking universal principles. It is also a caution against applying global models and standards, without allowing for the flexibility of local adaptation and expression. This chapter explores some of the diverse ways that CSR is manifesting in different regions and countries of the world.

CSR around the world

The importance of glocality for CSR really struck home to me when, in 2008 and together with my co-editor, Dirk Matten, I launched *The A to Z of Corporate Social Responsibility* in several regions and countries around the world, from Guatemala and South Africa to China and the UK. What became blindingly obvious was that while CSR had some global principles that most countries agreed on, the local manifestations were distinctive in each case. This led me to undertake a two-year research project that culminated in *The World Guide to CSR*, published in 2010 and profiling CSR in five regions and 58 countries. In her review of the book, Israeli CSR expert Elaine Cohen captures some of the essence of the idea of glocality:

> The country profiles [offer] a local flavour and sometimes even a little local language – *tzedakah*, the Hebrew word for charity; *sanpo yoshi* – 'three-way good' in Japan; *choregia*, the ancient form of sponsorship in Greece; and *ubuntu* in Southern Africa, which relates to community culture, to name but a few examples.

International comparative CSR research bears out my personal experiences and the content of the *World Guide to CSR*. One of my favourite studies was done in 2006 by my Cambridge colleague Jeremy Baskin, and looked at the reported CSR behaviour of 127 leading companies from 21 emerging markets across Asia, Africa, Latin America, and Central and Eastern Europe. It also compared the findings with over 1,700 leading companies in high-income OECD countries. The first finding was that CSR varies by region and level of economic development: it is highest in Europe, followed by Japan and North America, all of which are ahead of emerging markets. However, this conclusion masks a greater diversity of performance. For example, on community, philanthropy and human resource aspects, emerging markets have better CSR disclosure than North America and Japan, while on environmental issues, Japan is roughly on par with Europe and ahead of emerging markets and North America. The study also showed that, among the BRICS countries, CSR is strongest in South Africa, followed by Brazil, India, Russia and China.

Two GlobeScan surveys (in 2005 and 2007) also illustrate the glocality of CSR. In the first, the public was asked: What is the most important thing a company can do to be seen as socially responsible? The results showed that in the US, Canada and Brazil, community involvement was perceived as most important, while in Australia, UK and much of Europe it was protecting the environment, and in Mexico and China, quality and safety of their products was the priority. In the second survey, the public was asked: How responsible should companies be held for their impact on society? The findings were that more than 80% of Brazilians hold business responsible for its performance across ten dimensions of CSR, as compared with only 59% of British, 57% of Americans, 53% of Indians and 46% of Chinese.

A study by the Reputation Index also shows considerable variance. Asked about the importance of various factors to corporate reputation, it was found that corporate governance was most critical in Chile, South Korea and Australia, while social and environmental issues were top priorities in Finland, Norway and the Netherlands, and workplace and employee issues were highest on the agenda of Portugal, Denmark and Canada. Another study, by EIRIS in 2007, found that the percentage of high impact companies with advanced environmental policies was 90% in Japan and Europe, as compared with 75% in Australia and New Zealand, 67% in the USA and 15% in Asia (excluding Japan). Furthermore, it was determined that 75% of European companies operating in high-risk countries had developed a basic human rights policy, as compared with only 40% of US companies.

All of these studies, and many more besides, provide evidence for glocality. CSR varies by country and by region – in terms of level of maturity, the issues prioritized and the approaches adopted. This variation is especially evident between developed and developing countries, which has been a particular fascination for me in my work in CSR.

Myths of CSR in developing countries

I first tackled this question of whether the conceptions and models of CSR developed in the West are appropriate for developing countries by setting out what I believe to be seven popular myths about CSR in developing countries.[47] Most of these myths exist as a result of the feeding frenzy that inevitably occurs every time the media has hunted down and sunk its teeth into one or other juicy story of corporate exploitation. The myths are also sustained by legions of largely well-intentioned people who have vested interests in promoting their particular brand of the truth about CSR. Let's look at these myths briefly.

---

[47]Visser, W. (2003) 'Corporate Responsibility in a Developing Country Context', *Ethical Corporation* 20 (Aug): 32–4.

Table 9 Myths about CSR in developing countries

Myth 1	Economic growth is not compatible with CSR
Myth 2	Multinationals are the biggest CSR sinners
Myth 3	Multinationals are the biggest CSR saviours
Myth 4	Developing countries are anti-multinational
Myth 5	Developed countries lead on CSR
Myth 6	Codes can ensure CSR in developing countries
Myth 7	CSR is the same the world over

Myth 1: Economic growth is not compatible with CSR. What the Index for Sustainable Economic Welfare and the Human Development Index both show is that GDP growth and quality of life move in parallel until social and environmental costs begin to outweigh economic benefits. Most developing countries have yet to reach this divergence threshold. For them, economic growth and the expansion of business activities is still one of the most effective ways to achieve improved social development, while environmental impacts are increasingly being tackled through leapfrog clean technologies.

Myth 2: Multinationals are the biggest CSR sinners. On the ground in most countries, multinationals are generally powerful forces for good, through their investment in local economies, creation of jobs, upgrading of infrastructure, provision of basic services and involvement in community development and environmental conservation. The cumulative social and environmental impacts of smaller companies, which operate below the radar of the media and out of reach of the arm of the law, are typically far larger than that of the high profile multinationals.

Myth 3: Multinationals are the biggest CSR saviours. Not only do large companies have limited influence over government policy, but most multinationals, despite large capital investments, provide only a minuscule proportion of the total employment in developing countries. The real potential saviours are small, medium and micro enterprises (SMMEs), including social enterprises, which are labour intensive and better placed to effect local economic development. If the social and environmental impacts of these SMMEs can be improved, the resulting benefits will be proportionally much greater than anything that multinationals could achieve on their own.

Myth 4: Developing countries are anti-multinational. Developing countries are often caught in a no-man's land of underdevelopment in a competitive, monetized, global economy, and the sooner they can modernize and integrate, the better for them. Most often, developing country communities welcome multinationals and their CSR initiatives. This is not the same as saying that the developing world should repeat the past mistakes of the developed countries, such as highly polluting industrialization, or that multinationals should not be responsible and held accountable.

Myth 5: Developed countries lead on CSR. There are countless examples of how developing countries are proving themselves highly adept at delivering the so-called triple bottom line of sustainability, namely balanced and integrated social, economic and environmental benefits. It is actually not surprising, since in developing countries these three spheres are seldom separable – economic development almost inevitably results in social upliftment and environmental improvement, and vice versa.

Myth 6: Codes can ensure CSR in developing countries. The past few years have seen a mushrooming of corporate responsibility codes, standards and guidelines, which developing countries are keen to adopt, if only to satisfy their Western partners. This standardization trend is both inevitable and necessary in a globalizing world which is desperately searching for an alternative to command-and-control style business regulation in order to satisfy the governance and accountability void which still exists. But it would be a big mistake, for either companies, civil society, or regulators to assume that this codification bears much relation to relevant and appropriate CSR practices at grassroots level.

Myth 7: CSR is the same the world over. One of the biggest fallacies is that, in a globalized world, CSR can somehow conform to a unitary model. Of course, we need universal principles, like the UN Global Compact, and process frameworks, like ISO 14001. But standardized performance metrics, like those of the Global Reporting Initiative and the numerous sustainability funds and indexes, start to tread on shaky ground. The tendency is for developed country priorities to receive emphasis and for northern NGO agendas to dominate.

An alternative CSR Pyramid

Having unmasked these myths, I decided to look at Archie Carroll's CSR Pyramid of economic, legal, ethical and philanthropic responsibilities (described in the Age of Management) and see how well it fitted the African context.[48] My conclusion was that 'the relative priorities of CSR in Africa are likely to be different from the classic, American ordering' and that 'Carroll's CSR Pyramid may not be the best model for understanding CSR in general, and CSR in Africa in particular'. I then broadened this to propose an alternative CSR Pyramid for developing countries, which I will describe briefly below.[49]

Of course, I was not the first to question Carroll's model and Caroll himself was never opposed to alternative orderings to suit the local context. Leading CSR academics Andrew Crane and Dirk Matten observed in 2007 that 'all levels of CSR [described in Carroll's pyramid] play a role in Europe, but they have different significance, and furthermore are interlinked in a somewhat different manner'. In the same way, my contention is that the order of the CSR layers in developing countries – if these is taken as an indicator of the relative emphasis assigned to various

---

[48]Visser, W. 'Revisiting Carroll's CSR Pyramid: An African Perspective'. In E.R. Pedersen & M. Huniche (eds), *Corporate Citizenship in Developing Countries* (2006), pp. 29–56.

[49]Visser, W. 'Corporate Social Responsibility in Developing Countries', In A. Crane, A. McWilliams, D. Matten, J. Moon & D. Siegel (eds), *The Oxford Handbook of Corporate Social Responsibility* (2008), pp. 473–9.

Figure 2   CSR Pyramid for Developing Countries

responsibilities – differs from Carroll's classic pyramid. Hence, in developing countries, economic responsibilities still get the most emphasis. However, philanthropy is given second highest priority, followed by legal and then ethical responsibilities.

Economic responsibility is the most obvious and important focus of CSR. It is well known that many developing countries suffer from a shortage of foreign direct investment, as well as from high unemployment and widespread poverty. Therefore the economic contribution of companies in developing countries is highly prized, by governments and communities alike. Hence, in developing countries, CSR tends to stress the importance of 'economic multipliers' and 'economic value added'.

Philanthropic responsibility is next-most important for several reasons. First, there are often strong indigenous and religious traditions of philanthropy. Second, the socio-economic needs of developing countries are so great that philanthropy is an expected norm – it is considered the right thing to do by business. Third, companies realize that they cannot succeed in societies that fail, and philanthropy is seen as the most direct way to improve the prospects of the communities in which their businesses operate. Fourth, over the past 50 years, many developing countries have become reliant on foreign aid or donor assistance. Hence, there is often an ingrained culture of philanthropy. And finally, developing countries are often still at an early stage of maturity in CSR, sometimes even equating CSR and philanthropy, rather than embracing the more embedded approaches.

Legal responsibility generally has a lower priority than in developed countries because the legal system does not function as well. This does not necessarily mean that companies flout the law, but there is far less pressure for good conduct. This is because, in many developing countries, the legal infrastructure is poorly developed, and often lacks independence, resources, and administrative efficiency. Corruption and government capacity for enforcement in particular remain serious limitations and reduce the effectiveness of legislation as a driver for CSR.

Ethical responsibility has an influence on the CSR agenda in developing countries, but it remains limited. Despite progress on issues of corporate governance in some countries, these are still the exception rather than the rule. For instance, in Transparency International's annual Corruption Perception Index and Global Corruption Barometer, developing countries usually make up the bulk of the most poorly ranked countries. Furthermore, survey respondents from these countries generally agree that corruption still affects business to a large extent. The World Bank's Investment Climate Survey paints a similar picture.

It is important to say that this CSR pyramid is an illustration of how CSR typically manifests in developing countries, rather than an aspirational view of what CSR in developing countries *should* look like. For example, I am not proposing that legal and ethical responsibilities *should* get such a low priority, but rather that they do in practice. In contrast, if we are to work towards an ideal CSR Pyramid for CSR in developing countries, I would argue that improved ethical responsibilities, incorporating good governance, should be assigned the highest CSR priority in developing countries. In my view, governance reform holds the key to improvements in all the other dimensions, including economic development, rule of law, and voluntary action. Hence, embracing more transparent, ethical governance practices should form the foundation of CSR practice in developing countries, which in turn will provide the enabling environment for more widespread responsible business.

Anglo American's CSR pyramid

Let's use the global mining company Anglo American as an example to illustrate this alternative CSR pyramid. On *economic responsibilities*, they state that 'our economic contribution extends far beyond the profits we generate'. They divide them into two categories: (1) value added in the course of production and the wider effects of these activities (e.g. through payments to suppliers and multiplier effects) and through investments in staff development, technology transfer and investment; and (2) the value to society of their products, which are used in the manufacture of goods that underpin the modern way of life and for which there are few ready substitutes. Hence, their Value Added Statement includes disclosures for employment, distribution of economic benefits to employees and suppliers, tax and related payments to government, capital expenditure, black economic empowerment and returns to shareholders. Seen this way, Anglo American's economic contribution in Africa exceeds the GDP of many individual African countries.

Demonstrating glocality, Anglo American is now subject to the South African Mining Charter, which is a legally binding commitment by the industry to increase the access of previously disadvantaged individuals to the mineral resources of the country and their associated economic benefits. They do this through prioritized development and promotion of previously disadvantaged employees, entering into financial partnerships with empowerment companies and procurement from black-owned firms. In addition, Anglo American established the Anglo Khula Mining Fund to promote the entry of black economic empowerment participants into junior mining companies.

In terms of *philanthropic responsibilities*, Anglo American declared in one of its CSR reports that 'in developing countries there is still a significant role for philanthropic programmes'. Their primary vehicle for charitable engagement in Africa is the Anglo American Chairman's Fund, which was established in 1975 and aims 'to enable people to take greater control over their daily lives'. One of the major focuses of this fund in Africa – demonstrating a glocal prioritization – is HIV/AIDS.

On *legal responsibilities*, not surprisingly, Anglo American claim legal compliance as one of their fundamental business principles, saying 'we respect the laws of host countries' and 'we will comply with all laws and regulations applicable to our businesses and to our relationships with our stakeholders'. In addition, each year they disclose legal actions against the company for breaches of safety legislation and environmental incidents, both resulting in fines. The point is not so much the company's commitment to legal compliance, but rather that it is given relatively less importance as a driver in the pursuit of CSR, as compared with economic and philanthropic pressures.

Finally, regarding *ethical responsibilities*, Anglo American notes its support for the Extractive Industries Transparency Initiative 'as a means of increasing stakeholder confidence, reducing opportunities for embezzlement and stimulating debate around how revenues are allocated most effectively in resource-dependent economies'. In their statement of business principles Anglo American also insist that 'we are implacably opposed to corruption. We will not offer, pay or accept bribes or condone anti-competitive practices in our dealings in the marketplace and will not tolerate any such activity by our employees.' To back up this commitment, in 2003, they launched a whistle-blowing facility in order to allow employees to anonymously report any violations of Anglo American's business principles or any legal or ethical concerns.

Local CSR drivers

One of the ways glocality is determined is that each region, country or community has a different combination of CSR drivers. The art of glocality, therefore, is to determine which CSR incentives and pressures are most applicable to the local context. Of the ten typical CSR drivers I have identified, five are local (or internal) drivers, namely pressures from within the country or community. These are briefly discussed below.

Cultural tradition – In many countries and regions, CSR draws strongly on deep-rooted indigenous cultural traditions of philanthropy, business ethics and community embeddedness. For example, in a survey of over 1,300 small and medium-sized enterprises in Latin America, Antonio Vives found that the region's religious beliefs are one of the major motivations for CSR. In Asia, a study by scholars Wendy Chapple and Jeremy Moon reached a similar conclusion, namely that 'CSR does vary considerably among Asian countries but that this variation is not explained by [levels of] development but by factors in the respective national business systems'. And in Africa, I have found that the values-based traditional philosophy of African humanism (*ubuntu*) is what underpins many of the modern, inclusive approaches to CSR on the continent.

Table 10 Local drivers of CSR

Cultural tradition	CSR often draws strongly on deep-rooted indigenous cultural traditions of philanthropy, business ethics and community embeddedness
Political reform	CSR cannot be divorced from the socio-political policy reform process, which often drives business behaviour towards integrating social and ethical issues
Socio-economic priorities	CSR is often most directly shaped by the socio-economic environment in which firms operate and the development priorities this creates
Governance gaps	CSR is a way to plug the 'governance gaps' left by weak, corrupt or under-resourced governments that fail to adequately provide various social services
Crisis response	CSR responses can be catalysed by economic, social, environmental, health-related or industrial crises

Political reform – CSR cannot be divorced from socio-political reform processes, which often drive business behaviour towards integrating social and ethical issues. For example, the political and associated social and economic changes in Latin America since the 1980s, including democratization, liberalization, and privatization, have shifted the role of business towards taking greater responsibility for social and environmental issues. In South Africa, the political changes towards democracy and redressing the injustices of the past were also a significant driver for CSR, through the practice of improved corporate governance, collective business action for social upliftment, black economic empowerment and business ethics. Likewise, more recently, the goal of accession to EU membership has acted as an incentive for many Central and Eastern European countries to focus on CSR.

Socio-economic priorities – CSR is typically shaped by local socio-economic priorities. For instance, while poverty alleviation, health-care provision, infrastructure development and education may be high on many developing country agendas, this stands in stark contrast to many Western CSR priorities such as consumer protection, fairtrade, green marketing, climate change concerns, or socially responsible investments. Stephen Schmidheiny questions the appropriateness of imported CSR approaches, citing examples from Latin America where pressing issues like poverty and tax avoidance are central to CSR, but are often absent from international CSR agendas.

Governance gaps – CSR is frequently seen as a way to plug the 'governance gaps' left by weak, corrupt, or under-resourced governments that fail to adequately provide various social services (housing, roads, electricity, health care, education, etc.). Academics Dirk Matten and Jeremy Moon see this as part of a wider trend in developing countries with weak institutions and poor governance, in which responsibility is often delegated to private actors, be they family, tribe, religion, or, increasingly, business. A survey by WBCSD illustrates this: when asked how CSR should be defined, Ghanaians stressed 'building local capacity' and 'filling in when government falls short'.

Crisis response – Crises often have the effect of catalyzing CSR responses, albeit mostly of the philanthropic kind. For example, the economic crisis in Argentina in 2001 marked a significant turning point in CSR, prompting debates about the role of business in poverty alleviation. Similarly, Hurricane Katrina in the USA and HIV/AIDS in South Africa had the effect of galvanizing CSR. The examples are endless, be they the industrial accidents of the 1970s and 1980s (Seveso, Bhopal, *Exxon Valdez*), the environmental and human rights fiascos of the 1990s (Shell, Nike, McDonald's) or the corporate governance and natural disasters of the 2000s (Enron, Katrina, Sichuan).

Global CSR drivers

Other sets of drivers are more global (or external) and tend to have an international origin. Remember, it is the varied combination of drivers that determines glocality.

Table 11 Global drivers of CSR

Market access	CSR may be seen as an enabler for companies in one country or region trying to access markets in other parts of the world
International standardization	CSR codes, guidelines and standards are a key driver for companies wishing to operate as global players
Investment incentives	CSR is given an incentive by the trend of socially responsible investment (SRI), where funds are screened on ethical, social and environmental criteria
Stakeholder activism	CSR is encouraged through the activism of stakeholders or pressure groups, acting to address the perceived failure of the market and government policy
Supply chain integrity	CSR activities among small and medium-sized companies are boosted by requirements imposed by multinationals on their supply chains

Market access – The flipside of the socio-economic priorities driver is to see these unfulfilled human needs as an untapped market. This notion underlies the now burgeoning field of 'bottom of the pyramid' (BoP) strategies already discussed. CSR may also be seen as an enabler for companies in developing countries trying to access markets in the developed world. For example, a survey of CSR reporting among the top 250 companies in Latin America found that businesses with an international sales orientation were almost five times more likely to report on CSR than companies that sold products regionally or locally.

International standardization – Codes are frequently a CSR response, especially in sectors where social and environmental issues are deemed critical, such as textiles, agriculture or mining. Often, CSR is driven by standardization imposed by multinationals striving to achieve global consistency among its subsidiaries and operations in developing countries. For example, a study by Wendy Chapple and Jeremy Moon in Asia found that 'multinational companies are more likely to adopt CSR than those operating solely in their home country, but that the profile of their CSR tends to reflect the profile of the country of operation rather than the country of origin'.

Investment incentives – The belief that multinational investment is inextricably linked with the social welfare of developing countries is not a new phenomenon. However, increasingly these investments are being screened for CSR performance. Hence, socially responsible investment (SRI) is becoming another driver for CSR in many countries. Often, this is as a result of global SRI funds and indexes, like the Dow Jones Sustainability Index and FTSE4Good, but the influence of regional and national SRI instruments is also on the rise, with Brazil and South Africa among the first to go glocal in this respect. In addition, there are sector-based indexes emerging, like the ICT Sustainability Index launched in 2008.

Stakeholder activism – In the absence of strong governmental controls over the social, ethical and environmental performance of companies in some countries, activism by stakeholder groups has become another critical driver for CSR. In developing countries, four stakeholder groups emerge as the most powerful activists for CSR, namely development agencies, trade unions, international NGOs and business associations. These four groups provide a platform of support for local NGOs, which are not always well developed or adequately resourced to provide strong advocacy for CSR. The media is also emerging as a key stakeholder for promoting CSR

Supply chain integrity – Another significant driver for CSR, especially among small and medium-sized companies, is the requirements that are being imposed by multinationals on their supply chains. This trend began with various ethical trading initiatives, which led to the growth of fairtrade auditing and labelling schemes for agricultural products. Later, poor labour conditions and human rights abuses resulted in the development of certifiable standards like SA 8000. Major change has also been achieved through sector-based initiatives such as the Forest Stewardship Council and more recently through the 'Wal-Mart effect' already discussed, involving choice editing to source only from sustainable and responsible suppliers.

Going native and becoming indigenous

Making these glocal drivers work in practice requires a special skill, which Stuart Hart, in his book *Capitalism at the Crossroads*, calls 'native capability'. He explained it to me like this:

> Where multinationals have engaged with Base of the Pyramid (BoP) communities, in rural areas or slums and shanty towns, it's almost always been through an NGO partner; they outsourced it to that partner. Very seldom would you see employees or staff from multinationals actually being in those places. That's beginning to change. People from the company actually have to be in those spaces and develop relationships on the ground. You can't just outsource the work to NGOs and expect any capability to develop.

'So it's really a new capability', says Hart, 'the idea of native capability or becoming indigenous, and it requires effort to develop it. But if you do it and do it well, it can yield new business opportunities based on trust and social capital that makes you virtually impossible to dislodge. So from the standpoint of sustainable competitive advantage, becoming embedded in the community, developing that sort of social capital and trust and relationship, is the highest form of sustainable competitive advantage.'

One of the companies that Hart is working with – through the BoP 2.0 Protocol initiative – is SC Johnson, particularly in Kenya. I remember hearing a story, told by one of the people working on this project, which provides a perfect example of what glocality and native capability is all about. He explained that SC Johnson saw great opportunities for selling their household cleaning products to poor communities in rural Kenya. However, after some consultation with the community, they quickly discovered that tackling hygiene and cleanliness issues of the communal toilets was their real top priority. SC Johnson was delighted, as they have a great range of toilet cleaning detergents and related products.

However, when they brought samples for testing, the community was extremely disappointed. 'They don't work!' said the community. 'But they must work', said SC Johnson, 'we have tested them extensively in America and customers are very happy with the results.' 'Well, they might work for the private toilets of America', said the community, 'but they don't work for the communal toilets of Kenya.' Slightly nonplussed, SC Johnson went 'indigenous' and sent a team to investigate on the ground. And indeed, 'on the ground' was the key, because the walls and floors of the communal toilets were all made from dried mud. And – surprise, surprise – SC Johnson's cleaning products weren't designed to work on mud surfaces. So they went back to the drawing board and designed something that would work. They had learned the lesson of developing native capabilities.

One of the ways of assessing glocality in terms of the UN Millennium Development Goals (MDGs) is a tool developed by Business in Development (NCDO) and Sustainalytics called the online MDG Scan. Companies can create an account on the website and insert key performance data related to the company's presence in developing countries. The MDG Scan then converts this data into numbers of beneficiaries in developing countries whose lives have been positively affected by the company's activities. The Scan measures this positive contribution to the MDGs through a company's economic value added, employment creation, products and services and community investments. It's by no means comprehensive, but for many companies, it will be a good start.

In March 2009, Ted London also reported in *Harvard Business Review* on a framework he has developed, which is aimed at helping BoP ventures assess the impact their initiatives are having locally, in the short term and over time. It measures how a venture affects the well-being of its critical constituencies in three important dimensions: their economic situation, their capabilities, and their relationships. Another initiative is the Impact Reporting and Investment Standards (IRIS) being developed by the Acumen Fund, The Rockefeller Foundation and B Lab, in conjunction with PwC and Deloitte, in an attempt to better assess social and environmental impacts.

Social media muddle

One of the new Web 2.0 ways of demonstrating glocality is using social media platforms like Facebook, Twitter and others. At one level, it seems a match made in heaven. As Jonathan Ballantine reported for *Ethical Corporation* in 2009:

> Social media and sustainability share similar histories and future paths: both started out as bottom-up movements, both go against mainstream beliefs and both present the same sets of issues when integrating into a company's core values. What unites social media and sustainability is their focus on people as individuals. They also put a premium on cultivating long-term relationships based on value

and trust as well as on building networks and communities. Everyone has a voice and every voice counts. Every voice is its own; every voice is unique.

In the CSR world, two of the most successful social media platforms are Justmeans and Development Crossing. Justmeans claims to be 'the world's leading source of information and connections for people doing business better' and that, through their site, companies are able to reach over 250,000 thought leaders. Among the interesting features of their site is that individuals can declare themselves as stakeholders of companies that are registered on the site by 'following' their posts, in a similar way to Twitter. This is a convenient way for companies to spread their CSR gospel – be it their latest CSR report or press release – but they also have to accept the unfiltered, public feedback from these self-selected stakeholders. In other Web 2.0 sites, like Kiva.org, Globalgiving, Donorschoose and Facebook Causes, glocality is promoted by the fact that small online donors have the chance to see how their money is being used.

The truth is that social media is still a double-edged sword as a glocality tool for companies. This was demonstrated dramatically by the Greenpeace campaign against Nestlé in March 2010. I happened to be in Kuala Lumpur on my CSR Quest world tour at the time when the Greenpeace anti-Kit-Kat campaign video was going viral on the internet. Together with Indonesia, Malaysia supplies most of the world's palm oil, an ingredient found in about one in every ten products we buy. Greenpeace accused Nestlé of endangering orang-utans through deforestation caused by its irresponsible palm oil supply chain in Indonesia. The concern is a real one. Between 1967 and 2000 the area under cultivation in Indonesia expanded from less than 2,000 square kilometres (770 square miles) to more than 30,000 square kilometres. Deforestation in Indonesia for palm oil and illegal logging is so rapid that a report in 2007 by the United Nations Environment Programme (UNEP) said most of the country's forest might be destroyed by 2022.

The 60 second Greenpeace video, which was at the heart of their campaign, shows a bored office worker biting into a Kit-Kat, and as he does so, it turns into the finger of an orang-utan and 'crunch!' the blood spills down his chin and over his clean white shirt. One estimate by Scott Douglas on Prezi calculated that within four days the Greenpeace report and shock video may have reached half a million people through social media like Twitter and Facebook. This viral effect was seemingly boosted by Nestlé's attempt on its Facebook page to censor comments made by its critics (including activists who had changed their Facebook profile pictures to a defamed logo of Nestlé, which said 'Killer' instead).

The fact that Nestlé took swift action by dropping the accused Indonesian supplier and that their hands are effectively tied by a lack of available sustainable palm oil did little to quell the angry reactions of online activists. Greenpeace later called off the campaign, which Nestlé Executive Vice President for Operations Jose Lopez says was achieved 'by putting on the table a very technical view of the issues we are talking about. We've demonstrated that we have a logic, a path and a process that drives continuous improvement into topics of high concern, which in this case is deforestation.'[50] Nestlé's successful resolution of the matter does not take away the fact that social media is a tricky area for companies to master. For this very reason, we may see new emerging platforms like OpenEyeWorld coming to the fore, where companies have a bit more control over their interactive spaces.[51]

A new way of SEEing

OpenEyeWorld has designed a technological platform – which they call their Sustainability Expert Exchange Network (SEEN) – to help companies to engage with stakeholders and CSR experts. Leveraging the power of crowdsourcing, OpenEyeWorld's aim is to provide a trusted online exchange capability that allows businesses to engage with experts to

---

[50]Interview with Polly Courtice, Director of the Cambridge Programme for Sustainability Leadership, 17 June 2010.

[51]Disclosure: I am an advisor to OpenEyeWorld and have shares in their company.

design, improve, validate and communicate their CSR practice. For example, companies can share a CSR report, a press release, a challenge they are facing, a campaign they are considering, or anything else they seek to gain deeper insight on.

Whatever the type of content, the companies invite individuals and CSR organizations that were involved as validators (e.g. auditors or certifiers) to add their endorsement. Once the content is posted and supported, companies can then search the thousands of OpenEyeWorld experts to build the crowd they want to engage with, sorted and selected by issue, practice, industry, geography of impact or other parameters. Whether the crowd in the tens, or in the thousands, the scalable platform allows the company to define the type of insight they are seeking by employing a variety of feedback mechanisms, including ratings, surveys or general comments.

In the end, a company's brand equity is as unique as a thumbprint. Some that are already excelling in CSR may choose to leverage a glocal expert crowd as a way to maintain and credibly communicate their leading position. Others that are just beginning the journey might use it as a sandbox to play in, learning more about the CSR issues for their industry or particular practices. Either way, what's clear is that the power of Web 2.0 is on a confluence course with CSR through crowdsourcing solutions like this.

Glocality in practice

I want to end this chapter with a few examples of glocality from my own experience. The first is something that occurred when I was working for KPMG. We had been brought in by the global mining and metals company BHP-Billiton to review their performance on Business in the Community's Corporate Responsibility Index. More specifically, they wanted to understand why they had performed so poorly, when they felt their CSR practices were strong. After digging into BITC's assessment questionnaire, we put our finger on something that was quite interesting. At the time, it should be explained, the BITC Index was a UK initiative, with the scorecard reflecting regional concerns accordingly. In particular, there were many questions on the emerging agenda of energy and climate change. As a result energy efficiency programmes scored lots of points in the Index.

So, what was the problem? Well, BHP-Billiton was certainly not unconcerned about energy issues. After all, its new aluminium smelter in Mozambique was an energy-hungry beast. But it also happened to be located next to South Africa, which has some of the cheapest electricity in the world. As a result, energy efficiency was not their foremost priority in the region. Rather, it was the epidemic of malaria in Mozambique that was killing many of their workers and devastating their local communities. The company responded by developing a malaria control and treatment programme, which was highly effective. In fact, it was one of their great CSR success stories. The problem was that the BITC Index had not prioritized public health, so BHP-Billiton – despite their laudable glocal approach – didn't get much credit for their CSR efforts on malaria. I hasten to add that BITC's revised Corporate Responsibility Index is today far more comprehensive and sensitive to glocality.

A second example is from a trip to Guatemala in 2007, where I had an opportunity to visit one of the local sugar plantations. They had kindly prepared a presentation on their approach to CSR and imagine my delight when I saw that they also have a CSR pyramid! The interesting thing, however, was that it was not Carroll's CSR Pyramid. Economic responsibility was still at the base of the pyramid, but the next most important responsibility was to the families of their employees. The third tier was community responsibility and, rather intriguingly, the apex of the pyramid was engagement in responsible national policy development. Was theirs right and Carroll's wrong? Of course, they were both right. That is the beauty of glocality. It is not an 'either-or' mentality, but a 'both-and' approach. The other interesting observation is that they had formed a cooperative of farms. Individually, they were too small to justify a CSR programme, but collectively, it made sense.

This brings me to my final example, which has to do with glocality through empowering SMEs to incorporate CSR. On a 2009 trip to Mexico, I became aware of some excellent work being done on CSR and SMEs by the IDEARSE Centre at Anahuac University. In response to a government sponsored programme aimed at SME Growth Acceleration, IDEARSE put together an approach for supporting the businesses' growth through the implementation of a CSR business administration model that would develop competitive advantages for the companies. Built into their business training programme, therefore, were six elements for SME development: self-regulation, stakeholders, human rights, environment, labour and social/community impact. Working with the supply chains of big brands like Sony, Coca-Cola and Cemex, IDEARSE have taken more than 70 SMEs through the programme, with stunning results. On average across the six CSR dimensions, the SMEs improved from a score of 23% to 43%, while simultaneously showing average annual sales growth of 30%.

All of these examples show that it is not only imperative, but entirely possible, to adopt the CSR Principle of Glocality. Without it, companies risk being branded as cultural imperialists. But more tragically, they risk failing in their CSR efforts, because they have not struck the magic balance between global principles and local application.

The principle of circularity

We're talking not so much of technologies as of design methods or design mentality. It's optimising a whole system for multiple benefits, not isolated components for single benefits.

—Amory Lovins

Right now, the world runs on consuming and discarding. We're saying that we're taking responsibility for our products from birth 'til birth.

—Yvon Chouinard

It is really about the management of the biosphere and of the techno-sphere as technical nutrients and biological nutrients. So there is no waste.

—Michael Braungart

In economics, they talk about 'end of life' as if something has just lost its value and it's just fallen off a cliff somewhere. We don't talk about end of life, so that's a fundamental difference.

—William McDonough

Box 10: The principle of circularity – in a nutshell

Iconic leaders	Coca-Cola
	Fuji Xerox
	Nike
	Patagonia
	Tesco
Period	Rising from 2002, with the publication of *Cradle to Cradle*
Key ideas	All waste equals 'food' for future production
	Beyond cradle-to-grave, towards cradle-to-cradle
	Closed loop manufacturing and services
	Technical and biological nutrients
	Zero waste is possible
Commentators	Amory Lovins and L. Hunter Lovins (authors & consultants)
	Ernst von Weizsäcker (author)
	Paul Hawken (author)
	Paul Palmer (author & journalist)
	William McDonough and Michael Braungart (authors & consultants)
References	*The Ecology of Commerce: A Declaration of Sustainability* (Paul Hawken, 1993)
	Natural Capitalism: Creating the Next Industrial Revolution (Paul Hawken, Amory Lovins & L. Hunter Lovins, 1999)
	Cradle to Cradle: Remaking the Way We Make Things (William McDonough & Michael Braungart, 2002)
	Getting to Zero Waste (Paul Palmer, 2005)
	Factor Five (Ernst Von Weizsäcker, Karlson C. Hargroves, Michael H. Smith, Cheryl Desha & Peter Stasinopoulos, 2009)

Case 10: Yvon Chouinard and Patagonia[52]

'It was back in 1990 or so', recalled Yvon Chouinard, founder and CEO of the $300 million Patagonia clothing company. 'We were growing the company by 40% to 50% a year and we were doing it by all the textbook business ways – adding more dealers, adding more products, building stores, growing it like the American dream, you know – grow, grow, grow. And one year we predicted 40% to 50% growth and there was a recession and all the sudden we only grew 20%. And at the same time, our bank was going belly-up and we had cash-flow problems and it went to absolute hell. And I realized that I was on the same track as society was – endless growth for the sake of growth.'

This was the turning point, the Damascus experience, on a journey that would lead Patagonia, founded in 1957 by Chouinard selling mountain-climbing pitons out of the boot of his car, to become one of the true business pioneers in sustainability and responsibility. Chouinard always had an affinity for nature and was a somewhat reluctant entrepreneur; he would rather have been out fishing or mountain climbing. So it was entirely natural that he would commit the company, since 1985, to giving at least 1% of its annual sales to environmental charities; or that, in 1988, he initiated a national environmental campaign to deurbanize the Yosemite Valley. But the real wake-up call, the U-bend in the pipe, was that 1990s recession.

Chouinard's first step was to kick the company's growth habit. He put the brakes on and reverted to what he called 'natural growth'.

---

[52]The Chouinard quotes in this story are taken from his book *Let My People Go Surfing*, as well as interviews conducted by Grist (2004), Treehugger Radio (2008), Fast Company (1 July 2009), and Jeffrey Hollender & Bill Breen in *The Responsibility Revolution* (2010).

What that means is that 'only when our customers want something do we make more, but we don't prime the pump'. Taking this stance was a radical departure from 'business as usual' in an industry that runs on the steroids of aggressive advertising and celebrity endorsements. His competitors were dumbfounded, but Chouinard's mind was made up: 'I basically want to make clothing for people who need it rather than for people who want it.' The next step was to begin assessing the environmental impacts of Patagonia's products. This time, it was Chouinard's turn to be shocked.

The big surprise came from the results on industrially grown cotton. 'The "natural" fibre used in most of our sportswear proved to be by far the greatest environmental evildoer of the fibres studied. We learned that 25% of all the toxic pesticides used in agriculture was (and is) used in the cultivation of cotton, that the resulting pollution of soil and water was (and is) horrific, and that evidence of damage to the health of fieldworkers is strong, though difficult to prove. Cotton was the biggest villain – and it didn't have to be. Farmers had grown cotton organically, without pesticides, for thousands of years. Only after World War II did the chemicals originally developed as nerve gases become available for commercial use and start being applied to eliminate weeding fields by hand.'

Chouinard has developed a philosophy over the years, namely that 'a company has a responsibility to not wait for the government to tell them what to do, or wait for the consumer to tell them what to do; that as soon as you find out you're doing something wrong, stop doing it'. And that's exactly what he did. In 1994, he gave Patagonia 18 months to wean itself off industrially grown cotton. And that was no mean feat. 'We had to revolutionize the industry', Chouinard explains. 'We had to co-sign loans for farmers because if they went organic they couldn't get a loan from the bank because the bank's tied in with the chemical companies. We had to convince gins to clean their cotton gins and then process our stuff. We had to find the right mills.

It was a really big process. But we've never made a single product using industrially grown cotton since then [1996] and it's working out fantastic. It put us on a whole other level from our competitors.'

By the early 2000s, the Age of Management was already in full swing around the world and Chouinard started coming under pressure to produce a GRI-compliant sustainability report. So, in 2004, Patagonia audited itself against the GRI and produced a draft report. Chouinard concluded that it was 'absolute bullshit'. It was boring, it didn't challenge the company and, perhaps most importantly, he felt it was misleading. Chouinard wanted total transparency – warts and all – and he wanted it presented in an engaging way. 'We're very self critical and we're very idealistic', Chouinard explains. 'I think only by being honest can we show the full extent of the problem. Right now there's a lot of green glossing going on, green marketing. There's a lot of misinformation out there, especially with all these companies claiming to be green. So we want to be absolutely dead honest with how difficult it is.'

As a result, and as part of Chouinard's commitment to 'lead an examined life', Patagonia launched its Footprint Chronicles® in 2007. The Chronicles are a remarkable experiment in transparency, telling the story of products from design through fibre creation to construction and shipment. To date, it has assessed the social and environmental impacts of over 150 of its products, the findings of which are available for all to see on its website. Let me take one recent addition – organic cotton jeans – to give you a flavour of how it works. The first thing I see when I click on a picture of the jeans is a map of the world, with pins in key locations and dotted lines joining them. As I hover my mouse over each pin, I get a quick snapshot of the supply chain: design in Ventura, California; fibre and fabric in Acola District, India; sewing in Tehuacan, Mexico; and distribution in Reno, Nevada. I can click on any one of these to get more information of that particular micro-process.

So let's look at what happens in India. I am taken to a slide show with a colourful and insightful 19 page presentation on Patagonia's supplier, the Arvind Worldwide Inc.'s Fairtrade Organic Cotton Project. It describes how Arvind helped to organize struggling farmers into self-help groups consisting of 20 or so individuals who joined together to improve their yields and incomes, through the adoption of organic practices. Each step in the planting, growing, harvesting, packaging and shipping process is explained, with photographs and video clips that bring it all to life. And I can do the same for the other staging posts in the manufacturing process. The result is that I am left with a much greater understanding of the supply chain and some sense of the people and processes involved. But what about the impacts?

Returning to the main Chronicles page for the organic cotton jeans, I see five symbols, each of which reveals information when I hover my mouse over the icon. I find out that a single pair of jeans takes 187 megajoules (52 kWh) of energy, which I am helpfully told is equivalent to burning an 18 W energy saving bulb for 120 days, 24 hours a day. The jeans have travelled 14,300 miles (23,014 kms) to get to me, equivalent to a roundtrip from Annecy, France, to Mar del Plata, Argentina. They have also produced 62 pounds (28 kgs) of CO_2 emissions and 82 oz (2.3 kgs) of waste, equivalent to 47 times and four times the weight of one pair of jeans respectively. Finally, 174 litres of water were used, enough to provide 58 people with drinking water for one day. I now have a much better handle on the impacts I am having by buying these jeans.

But there is more information: the Good, the Bad and What We Think. *The Good* states that 'we use organic cotton, working with contract farmers in India, teaching them about organic farming and fairtrade. The cotton is mainly rain-fed. During dry periods, it is irrigated with water previously captured in ponds. Fields are mulched to slow evaporation. We make them to last and when they wear out they can be recycled.' *The Bad* confesses that 'while the use of organically grown cotton is environmentally preferred to conventionally grown cotton, recycled cotton would be even better'. And *What We Think* provides some thought-provoking insights, saying, 'Many customers want jeans that look worn and faded. Distressing denim requires the use of chemicals, energy, water and manual labour, with some environmental downside. We continue to research new developments in denim processing, hoping to further reduce water use and employ even cleaner chemistry. Arvind makes denim with recycled content, but the cotton is not organic, so we do not use it. We hope to develop a recycled organic cotton blend.'

The Footprint Chronicles clearly have benefits for the customer, but what about for Patagonia? Elissa Loughman, Environmental Strategy Analyst, explains what they have learned from the process:

> Some of the earliest data that we found showed us that the transportation energy use is actually quite small in comparison to the total energy use to make a product. So this has allowed us to shift our focus from worrying about the distance that our products are travelling – as long as they are being shipped by boat, that's the most efficient way – to instead focusing on the energy use in the manufacturing process. Another thing we learned was that the treatment we were using on our wool to de-scale it, to make it shrink resistant and itch free, was using a lot of energy. It was a chlorine-free process so it was good in terms of not using chlorine, but it was using more energy than we'd like. So we're currently looking for a less energy intensive solution that also avoids using toxins.

The Chronicles have not only had environmental benefits. 'Changes have occurred with our partner suppliers as well', says Loughman. 'One specific example is Everest, one of our fabric vendors. We had a group of Patagonia employees go to visit them and on their tour they noticed that there was a smell coming from the laminating area. They also noticed that the workers in that area weren't wearing masks, so they enquired about why the masks weren't being worn and they learned that the employees, during the monsoon season, found them unbearable to wear and refused to wear them.' In an effort to resolve this issue and as part of their process to become Blue-sign certified, Everest invested $1.3 million in a system to recover the solvent fumes on their coating line. 'The coolest thing about the Footprint Chronicles', concludes Loughman, 'is that it has given us a venue to have an open and honest conversation with our customers and our [website] viewers, and it's allowed us to be transparent about our business and talk about the good things and the bad things. And the more we've learned about how we make our products, the more we want to know.'

Behind the Footprint Chronicles and many of Patagonia's other sustainability and responsibility initiatives is the key concept of cradle-to-cradle production and consumption. They have teamed up with some Japanese companies with the goal of making all of their clothing out of recycled and recyclable fibres. In particular, they are switching all their nylon to Nylon 6, which can be recycled infinitely. They're also recycling cotton and recycling wool. 'Of course, the best thing to do is make clothing so it never wears out, right?' says Chouinard. And failing that, he says, 'we're going to accept the responsibility. We're going to accept ownership for our products from birth 'til birth. So as much as we can, we're going to make all of our products so that if you buy a jacket, a shirt, a pair of pants or whatever, when you're done with it, you can give it back to us and we'll make more shirts and pants out of that, which is a different idea about consuming.'

Reflecting on the company's journey, Chouinard concludes that the key is curiosity. 'We had to ask a million questions. But then once you educate yourself, then you're left with choices. This company exists to ask the questions and make the choices and then to prove that it's good business to other companies so that they can do it.' As far as sustainability goes, Chouinard says that he is 'trying to run this company as if it's going to be here 100 years from now', but believes that 'there's no such thing as sustainability. There are just levels of it. It's a process, not a real goal. All you can do is work toward it.' In the meantime, he admonishes that 'every business should say, "We're polluters, we're using nonrenewable resources, and therefore we should tax ourselves".' One way to do that is to join One Percent for the Planet, co-founded by Chouinard in 2001 as an alliance of mostly small companies that pledge to give 1% of their profits to environmental causes. One Percent recently notched its 1,000th member and in total, its members have given $42 million to more than 1,700 groups.

Chouinard, despite his company being hailed as 'The Coolest Company on the Planet' by *Fortune* magazine, believes that we're a long way from having a sustainable society. To change that, he says we have to stop focusing on the symptoms and start focusing on the causes, which are growth, over-consumption and poorly designed manufacturing processes. 'I believe the accepted model of capitalism that demands endless growth deserves the blame for the destruction of nature, and it should be displaced. Failing that, I try to work with companies and help them change the way they think about resources.' And the reward for that? 'Leading an examined life is a real pain in the ass', Chouinard says wryly. 'It adds an element of complexity to business that most businessmen just don't want to hear about.' So why has he done it? He sums it up in his business biography, *Let My People Go Surfing*: 'Not to do so would have been unconscionable.'

Holistic science

The Principle of Circularity is certainly not new. Its origins lie in the development of holistic science over the past half-millennium. Systems scientist and author Fritjof Capra told me that 'these ideas of holism have been around for a long time. I think Leonardo da Vinci was the first in the

15th century.[53] Leonardo had developed a science which is absolutely holistic, systemic and ecological, and he talked about things like the metabolism of a city. He said in a healthy city there is an unimpeded flow of people, of objects, of material goods and of waste. And he designed cities at several levels where you had several kinds of these flows. So he was the first to use the term healthy city.'

In the 20th century, one of the pioneers to take da Vinci's ideas forward was South African statesmen Jan Smuts. In his 1926 book *Holism and Evolution*, he proposed the theory of holism (from the Greek *holos*, meaning 'whole'), which he described as a synthesis between Darwin's theory of evolution (1856), Einstein's theory of relativity (1905) and his own reflections on the evolution of matter, life and mind. The result was a revolutionary concept with far-reaching implications. What Smuts claimed to have identified was nothing less than 'the ultimate synthetic, ordering, organizing, regulative activity in the universe, which accounts for all the structural groupings and syntheses in it'.[54]

Smuts's theory of holism was the precursor to what came to be known as systems thinking, which was emerging in Europe in the 1930s and 1940s and was ultimately formalized by the Austrian Ludwig Von Bertalanffy in his 1968 book *General Systems Theory*. By the early 1980s, these ideas had begun to influence various disciplines from physics and biology to healthcare and economics. This was eloquently synthesized in Capra's 1982 book *The Turning Point*, which had its origins in a course that he taught at the University of California Berkeley which was called 'Beyond the Mechanistic World View'. The theory – which Capra now calls Living Systems Theory – has continued to evolve, and is presented in his subsequent books, like *The Web of Life* (1996) and *The Hidden Connections* (2002).

---

[53]This is the subject of Capra's new book, *The Science of Leonardo* (2008).

[54]In 1995, I published an article 'Holism: A New Framework for Thinking about Business' (*New Perspectives*, No. 7, 1995), which described how Smuts' theory could be applied to business.

'What has happened in the last 25 or 30 years', Capra told me, 'is that science has developed the language and the tools to really build theories that embody this holistic philosophy. What has happened with the help of computers is that mathematicians and scientists have developed complexity theory, known technically as non-linear dynamics, where they can actually map this non-linear interconnectedness and set up equations and solve them. And so there's a whole new language, the language of chaos theory and of complexity theory, with concepts like attractors and bifurcation diagrams and fractal geometry and things like that. These concepts did not exist 30 years ago. So now when we study non-linear systems we know which questions to ask. We know how to go about it.'

Spaceship earth

At the same time as these ideas were gaining traction in science and mathematics in the 1960s, there was a parallel movement that began applying similar thinking to the field of ecology, resulting in the popular metaphor of 'Spaceship Earth'. In a 1965 speech to the UN, the American politician Adlai Stevenson said: 'We travel together, passengers on a little space ship, dependent on its vulnerable reserves of air and soil.' The following year, economist Barbara Ward published a book called *Spaceship Earth*, declaring that 'our planet is not much more than the capsule within which we have to live as human beings. . . . We depend upon a little envelope of soil and a rather larger envelope of atmosphere for life itself. And both can be contaminated and destroyed.'

The theme was echoed by fellow economist Kenneth E. Boulding, who published an essay in 1966 called 'The Economics of the Coming Spaceship Earth.' He contrasted the 'cowboy economy' – an open economy with seemingly boundless frontiers and limitless resources – with the 'spaceman economy' – a closed economy of the future 'in which the earth has become a single spaceship, without unlimited reservoirs of anything, either for extraction or for pollution, and in which, therefore, man must find his place in a cyclical ecological system'. Two years later, the polymath

R. Buckminster Fuller furthered these ideas in his book *Operating Manual for Spaceship Earth*.

In *The Top 50 Sustainability Books*, I observed that Fuller's ideas are as remarkable for their overall message as for their elaboration of concepts that were ahead of their time. For example, he introduced terms like 'synergy' ('behaviour of wholes unpredicted by behaviour of their parts') and 'topology', which began to build a theory of systems thinking for ecology. Even the concept of externalities was in evidence, when he said: 'I feel that one of the reasons why we are struggling inadequately today is that we reckon our costs on too shortsighted a basis and are later overwhelmed with the unexpected costs brought about by our shortsightedness.' Today, former CEO of Seventh Generation Jeffrey Hollender agrees, saying 'the deck has been stacked against those companies who are attempting to apply the principles of full-cost accounting to their operations, and it would be disingenuous to shy away from discussing the large challenges we must overcome in order to transition to a more just and sustainable society'.

According to Fuller, 'it is obvious that the real wealth of life aboard our planet is a forwardly-operative metabolic and intellectual regenerating system'. And yet 'we have been misusing, abusing, and polluting this extraordinary chemical energy-interchanging system for successfully regenerating all life aboard our planetary spaceship'. He concludes (somewhat verbosely) that 'this all brings us to a realization of the enormous educational task which must be successfully accomplished right now in order to convert man's spin-dive toward oblivion into an intellectually mastered power pull-out into a safe and level flight of physical and metaphysical success, whereafter he may turn his Spaceship Earth's occupancy into a universe exploring advantage'.

Taking the concept of Spaceship Earth even further is the British scientist James Lovelock, who first published his Gaia hypothesis in 1979, and has continually updated the theory since, with books like *The Revenge of Gaia* (2006) and most recently *The Vanishing Face of Gaia* (2009). Lovelock explained the Gaia hypothesis to me as follows: 'I did produce a theory of the earth which is a holistic one . . . and it does seem to answer a lot of questions about the earth and suggests that it is a self-regulating system, that is to say the climate and the atmospheric composition, the ocean composition, the surface soils, all stay more or less at a state which favours the biosphere.' Despite its controversy, Lovelock says that the Gaia theory has now had over ten tests and they all either come out positive or there's no falsification.

Life cycle assessment

At a more pragmatic level, there was also a movement since the 1960s that led to the modern practice of Life Cycle Assessment (LCA). In an illuminating review of the history of LCA, the US Environmental Protection Agency claims that its origins can be traced to a publication launched at the World Energy Conference in 1963 by Harold Smith, which contained his calculation of cumulative energy requirements for the production of chemical intermediates and products. Then, in 1969, a study by Coca-Cola laid the foundation for the current methods of life cycle inventory analysis. Their research assessed different beverage containers to determine which had the lowest releases to the environment and least affected the supply of natural resources. In a process now familiar to LCA practitioners, the Coca-Cola study quantified the raw materials and fuels used and the environmental loadings from the manufacturing processes for each container.

This emergent methodology became known as a Resource and Environmental Profile Analysis (REPA) in the US and as an Ecobalance in Europe. The EPA estimates that approximately 15 REPAs were performed between 1970 and 1975 and although this dropped off once the OPEC oil crises were over, the technique continued to develop quietly. During this time, Europe took the lead, with the establishment of an Environment Directorate (DG X1) by the European Commission. In addition to standardizing pollution regulations throughout Europe, DG X1 issued the Liquid Food Container Directive in 1985, which required member companies to monitor the energy and raw materials consumption and solid waste generation of liquid food containers.

Toward the end of the 1980s, especially with growing concerns around waste management, LCA was revived and refined as a tool for analyzing environmental problems. In fact, it became so popular that, in 1991, 11 State Attorney Generals in the USA expressed concerns that LCAs were being used to make misleading green claims. They therefore urged that companies desist from using LCA until a clear methodology could be standardized and agreed. This action, together with pressure from elsewhere in the world, led to the development of two LCA standards as part of the International Standards Organization (ISO) 14000 series: ISO 14041:1998 on Life cycle assessment (goal and scope definition and inventory analysis), and ISO 14043:2000 on Life cycle interpretation. These have subsequently been replaced by ISO 14040:2006 and ISO 14044:2006.

Besides these efforts by ISO, in 2002, the United Nations Environment Programme (UNEP) joined forces with the Society of Environmental Toxicology and Chemistry (SETAC) to launch the Life Cycle Initiative, an international partnership. The Initiative comprises three programmes: on Life Cycle Management (LCM), which mainly focuses on skills development; Life Cycle Inventory (LCI), which focuses on open access life cycle data; and Life Cycle Impact Assessment (LCIA), which focuses on expert exchange of best practices. The result of all of these developments is that today LCA is widely understood and employed – often using software like SIMAPRO – as 'the assessment of the environmental impact of a product in a cradle-to-grave approach', whereby 'all the pollution from the stage of digging or harvesting raw materials to the waste that remains after using a product is taken into account'.[55] The aim is to minimize the environmental burden throughout the complete production chain rather than optimizing individual production processes within that chain.

---

[55]As defined by Theo de Bruijn in *The A to Z of Corporate Social Responsibility*, edited by Visser, Matten, Pohl & Tolhurst (2010).

Sustainable production and consumption

Towards the end of the 1980s, a related concept called 'industrial ecology' emerged. It was popularized in 1989 in a *Scientific American* article by Robert Frosch and Nicholas E. Gallopoulos, in which they declared: 'Why would not our industrial system behave like an ecosystem, where the wastes of a species may be resources to another species? Why would not the outputs of an industry be the inputs of another, thus reducing use of raw materials, pollution, and saving on waste treatment?' Hence, the idea of industrial ecology is that businesses should not only look at the life cycle impacts of individual products of individual companies, but rather look for ways in which to link up with other businesses to minimize their impacts. For example, there is a Danish industrial park in the city of Kalundborg where a power plant, oil refinery, pharmaceutical plant, plasterboard factory, enzyme manufacturer, waste management company and the city itself all link together to share and utilize resources, by-products, energy and waste heat.

Another concept that was gaining popularity around the same time was 'cleaner production', which resulted in the UNEP Declaration on Cleaner Production in 1998. Later, this evolved into the concept of 'sustainable consumption and production', which was defined at the UN's 2002 World Summit on Sustainable Development as an approach 'to promote social and economic development within the carrying capacity of ecosystems by addressing and, where appropriate, de-linking economic growth and environmental degradation through improving efficiency and sustainability in the use of resources and production processes and reducing resource degradation, pollution and waste'.

The University of Cambridge *Business Primer on Sustainable Consumption and Production* (2007) gives an example to underscore the importance of creating more sustainable industrial processes. On average, the report says, a gold wedding ring weighs 6,000 kilograms. The enormous discrepancy between the actual retail product and the remaining weight is explained by accounting for all the materials used and the waste created during the production life cycle of the ring. The gap between a gold ring's actual, physical weight and its 'resource weight' highlights the scale of physical and financial impacts that are associated with the creation of apparently simple, everyday products. The report concludes that 'the increased cost that results from the difference between sustainable and unsustainable production is not good for anyone. It is not sustainable financially – such low resource efficiency is wasteful and inefficient. And it is not sustainable socially or environmentally – hazardous or damaging waste products are produced systematically, and resources are increasingly depleted.'

Recognizing this challenge, the EU government began working with business to create 'product roadmapping' as a way of systematizing what might otherwise be a more haphazard approach to developing products and the policies that support them. 'Integrated Product Policy' (IPP) is how the government describes conducting life cycle assessments with a view to potential policy interventions. The IPP of the EU, adopted in 2003, aims at reducing the environmental impact of products, instead of specific industries or processes. Two familiar products with diverse impacts were chosen by the EU to demonstrate IPP. One was a mobile phone, put forward by Nokia; the second, a teak garden chair proposed by Europe's largest retailer, Carrefour. The result of the exercise showed that, for Nokia, energy consumption is the greatest impact, both during manufacture of components and during use – when chargers left on 'no-load' consume electricity constantly. It was estimated that, if 10% of worldwide subscribers unplug their chargers once their phone is fully charged, enough energy would be saved to supply 60,000 European homes for one year.

Cradle to cradle[56]

One of the most integrated and powerful methodologies to emerge from all of these trends toward circularity is 'cradle to cradle'. While the phrase

---

[56]Quotes are from the *Cradle to Cradle* book, as well as the interviews I did with William McDonough and Michael Braungart in 2008, as part of the University of Cambridge Top 50 Sustainability Books Project.

was coined by Walter R. Stahel in the 1970s, its modern interpretation grew out of a system of 'life cycle development' initiated by Michael Braungart and colleagues at the Environmental Protection Encouragement Agency (EPEA) in the 1990s and explored through the publication 'A Technical Framework for Life-Cycle Assessment'. Braungart told me how it all got started: 'I was looking at complex household products and I identified in the TV set 4,360 different chemicals, and I thought it doesn't help just to take any toxic stuff out of it.' The concept was popularized when Braungart teamed up with US architect William McDonough and produced the book *Cradle to Cradle: Remaking the Way We Make Things* in 2002.

Cradle to cradle goes beyond 'cradle to grave' thinking. As McDonough explained to me, 'What's typically done with life cycle assessments is a cradle to grave assessment and so you end up with these limits. With cradle to cradle you go past these limits. So you don't say "there's only so much lithium", or "there's only so much copper", you say "the deployment of this material on a global basis could be optimized in a cycle that looks like this". It becomes an optimization process rather than a minimization process.'

Hence, rather than simply considering impacts across the life cycle of a product and trying to minimize waste, the authors argue for closed-loop production, where waste is only acceptable if it is entirely reused by the system. Hence, all waste becomes 'food' input to the cycles of nature and the cycles of industry, i.e. either as a biological nutrient or a technical nutrient. McDonough elaborates:

> The idea is that you would design something as a biological nutrient, so that it can go back to the soil to refresh the soil and rebuild the soil, rather than be wasted or toxify the soil through the air and the water. And then other things we see as technical nutrients that are designed to be in infinite closed cycles in technology and manufacturing.

Cradle to cradle is essentially about designing for sustainability and being ambitious about it. As McDonough and Braungart say in the book, 'As long as human beings are regarded as "bad", zero is a good goal. But to be less bad is to accept things are they are, to believe that poorly designed, dishonourable, destructive systems are the best humans can do. This is the ultimate failure of the "be less bad" approach: a failure of the imagination. From our perspective, this is a depressing vision of our species' role in the world. What about an entirely different model? What would it mean to be 100% good?' In some senses, cradle to cradle even goes beyond common conceptions of sustainability. 'Sustainability is boring', Braungart told me. 'What would you say if I would ask you about your relationship with your wife? How would you characterize it? As sustainable? If this is the bigger goal, sustainability, then I feel really sorry because it doesn't celebrate human creativity and human nature.'

To take forward the idea, the two authors have formed a company, McDonough Braungart Design Chemistry (MBDC), through which they offer cradle to cradle certification of products. As to which companies are leading, McDonough points to Shaw carpets in the USA, which 'takes its old carpet back and all the new carpet is designed around the Cradle to Cradle protocol. So you have this closed cycle of intelligent, safe material chipping away at a four and a half billion pound a year waste issue. That's a huge shift.' The US Postal Service is another example. 'If you get an envelope from the postal service in the United States that's express mail it's cradle to cradle certified. So there are 700 million of them, all with the cradle to cradle stamp on them.' Braungart meanwhile believes 'you will see the Netherlands become a complete cradle to cradle country'. In addition, he sees rapid progress in Israel, New Zealand and Wales, concluding that 'it's amazing because it frees people from feeling guilty for being here, giving them the opportunity to become native, and to celebrate human genius on this planet'.

Nike's considered design

Towards the end of the 1990s, the Nike Environmental Action Team (NEAT), led by Sarah Severn, then Nike's Director of Corporate Sustainable Development, began shaping what would become Nike's cradle to cradle approach. Working closely with Heidi McCloskey, Global Sustainability

Director for Apparel, and Anne Peirson-Hills, Senior Manager of Environmental Affairs, Severn encouraged Nike's designers to go back to first principles, questioning basic design traditions in order to get to a new and better product outcome which addresses the environmental footprint required to source, manufacture, and recycle shoes.

Severn liked the innovative and ambitious approach of cradle to cradle. 'So much of the environmental debate had addressed end-of-pipe problems and end-of-pipe solutions', she recalled. 'And here was a strategy that was turning that on its head. It was not about restriction or reaction. It created positive solutions at the front of the design process. That meshes very well with the culture in Nike. And it's an exciting message. If you talk about environmental management systems and eco-efficiency, people just roll their eyes. But if you talk about innovation and abundance, it's inspirational. People get very, very excited.'

The first manifestation of all that excitement was a new brand, 'Considered', which Nike launched with its Considered Boot in 2005, using a single shoe lace woven between the leather parts of the upper and stitching that secured the upper to the sole, thereby eliminating adhesives and allowing for easier disassembly. Design insights gained from this work helped inform subsequent innovations like the Pinnacle Air Jordan XXIII, launched in January 2008, and the Nike Trash Talk, made from post-manufacturing waste.

Today, Considered design for shoes includes a number of modifications. Leather pieces are stitched in an overlapping fashion so as to produce smooth internal seams, obviating the need for comfort liners and reducing the shoes' material mass. The leather pieces are tanned using a vegetable-based process and metal eyelets aren't used. The two-piece outsole is designed to snap together, eliminating harmful adhesives and simplifying recyclability, and there is no use of PVC. Where possible, materials are also sourced locally to reduce transportation energy use. The result is that Considered shoes generate 63% less waste in manufacturing than a typical Nike design. The use of solvents has also been cut by 80% and 37% less energy is required to create a pair of shoes.

Considered is not just about shoes. In order to measure progress of all of its products and designs against its cradle to cradle principles, Nike developed a Considered Index, which is a tool for evaluating the predicted environmental footprint of a product prior to commercialization. This system examines solvent use, waste, materials and innovation for footwear. Apparel products are evaluated on waste, materials, garment treatments and innovation. Nike claims that 'by continually raising that standard, we envision a future where the shoes you wear today become the shoes, shirts or equipment you use tomorrow. This closed loop manufacturing process, where nothing is wasted and everything is kept in play, is not just wishful thinking, it's the future.'

In order to create this future, Nike has committed to having all newly developed Nike footwear coming out of its US headquarters meet or exceed Considered Design baseline standards by 2011. This will be extended to apparel and European and Hong Kong offices by 2015, and sports equipment by 2020. One of the reasons Nike may very well succeed in meeting these targets is that Considered is bold and inspiring. As Ed Thomas, Director of Advanced Materials Research, put it, 'You've got to take the stake and you've got to plant it somewhere big and you've got to say that's what we're driving for. It's not just going more slowly. It's not just going to zero. It's actually turning around and picking a new direction.'

Other companies in the textiles industry are also evaluating their cradle to cradle impacts. In 2010, Levi's released the results of its total product life cycle (TPLC) analysis of a pair of 501 jeans. As CSR Asia reported, the data collected showed that a typical pair of 501s had CO_2 emissions of 32.3 kg (equivalent to driving 78 miles or 125 km in a typical car), a water footprint of nearly 3,500 litres (that's the same as 53 seven-minute showers) and the total life cycle consumed 400 MJ of energy (equal to the amount of energy required to watch a plasma screen TV for 318 hours). What was even more surprising was how these footprints were accounted for by the different phases in the life of a pair of jeans: the usage (or consumer ownership phase) was by far the most intensive phase due largely to the regular washing of a pair of jeans, with 45% of the water, 57% of the energy, and 58% of the overall contribution to climate change being consumed at this stage.

Timberland's eco-confession

One of Nike's biggest competitors is Timberland, which has been learning the lessons of sustainability for as long as, if not longer than, Nike. In spring 2007, Timberland introduced the 'Green Index' – a measure of the environmental impact of their products. 'Our goal', they declared, 'is to provide consumers with visibility into the footprint our business creates.' The Index programme was expanded in 2008 to include a full range of outdoor products from boots to sandals.

CEO Jeffrey Swartz says he got the idea for the design of the Green Index labels from the signage at Whole Foods. 'The signs were very simple in their assertions: Here's where this produce comes from. Here's why it's organic. I thought, why can't we put some kind of signage or label on our products, as a way to show their environmental impact? All the regulatory folks at Timberland told me my idea was dumber than dirt. We'd be admitting that we pollute, that we aren't good at what we do. They argued that we don't have a legal requirement to disclose, so why do it? But I believe naively that if you tell the truth, most people will applaud.'

Here's how the Green Index works. Using a shoe as an example, the following three factors are measured: Climate Impact (the greenhouse gas emissions created through production), Chemicals (the presence of hazardous substances like PVC and Solvent Adhesives) and Resources (the percentage by weight of recycled, organic and renewable materials). The three scores are normalized to a scale of 1 to 10, added together and divided by three. The score with the least environmental impact is 0, while 10 has the highest impact.

The Green Index is certainly a clear and insightful way to provide customers with information. However, Swartz admits that it's not all about the customer:

When we say that 5% of our energy is renewable, we're also admitting that 95% of our energy isn't. So I asked our team, how does that 5% compare to Nike? Their answer: There's no way to know. My reply: There's one way to know. Let's put the number on a label, and if consumers decide that that's important, Nike will have to tell them. Now, Nike is competitive, and they won't want to disclose their energy from renewables unless it's at least 1% higher than ours.

Putting the label on our products is not about the consumer, because honestly, the amount of pushback from the consumer has been minimal. But as an action-forcing mechanism inside our industry, it's been dramatic. If Nike gets to 6% renewable, we won't have a problem as long as we get to 7%. In other words, transparency can force all of us to try to get from 5% to 15% to 50% renewable energy. That's a conversation that couldn't have been forced until the motivation was market-based. At the end of the day, if the consumer doesn't care about this, it won't work. But the consumer is really a proxy to spur the industry to push the envelope on sustainability.

Beyond Timberland, others like GoodGuide, founded in 2007 by Dara O'Rourke, a professor of environmental and labour policy at the University of California at Berkeley, are taking this idea of transparency and labelling to a whole other level. Using publicly available data, GoodGuide offers health, environment and society scores, based on its own database, for 65,000 products. It is even accessible with a bar-code-scanning iPhone app. Similarly, at ProjectLabel.org, you can type in the name of a company and receive numerical scores on matters like worker treatment and waste management, based on a combination of published reports and user votes.

Seventh Generation cleans up

Nike and Timberland's efforts are laudable and I hope they succeed. Likewise, for other mega-companies like Unilever that are being forward thinking and ambitious. After all, every day around 160 million people in

150 countries buy a Unilever brand. It is encouraging to know, therefore, that in 2005, Unilever set out to understand how these brands impact on people and the environment in the areas where they are sourced, produced, distributed and used. Today, this is called their Brand Imprint programme, the results of which include the development of social missions for its Lifebuoy, Signal, Pepsodent and Close Up brands, and an ambitious environmental plan for the company's laundry category. This so-called 'Cleaner Planet Plan' aims to reduce the environmental footprint of the company's laundry brands, design products that help its consumers to reduce their environmental impacts, and motivate people to adopt laundry habits that reduce their environmental impacts. Most critically, all this takes place within the frame of a bigger, more audacious vision: to double the size of Unilever's business in a way that halves their absolute environmental footprint.

For these companies, getting to sustainability is like turning around an oil tanker. However, there are also smaller, more nimble companies, like Seventh Generation, that are able to go much further, much faster. Seventh Generation, an American household cleaning products business started more than 20 years ago by Jeffrey Hollender, took inspiration for its name and philosophy from the Iroquois Confederacy (a council of Native American Indian tribes), which included the admonition that 'in our every deliberation, we must consider the impact of our decisions on the next seven generations'.

From the beginning, this meant thinking in a circular way about the impact of their products. To begin with, this was like swimming upstream. 'When Seventh Generation told executives at the old Fort Howard Paper Company that we wanted to market bathroom tissue made from unbleached recycled fibre, they laughed', recalls Hollender. Despite such early resistance, however, Seventh Generation has remained steadfast in its commitment to 'becoming the world's most trusted brand of authentic, safe, and environmentally-responsible products for a healthy home'. And indeed, it now has an impressive catalogue of cradle to cradle designed products, and has been doing extremely well, showing strong growth even through the recession.

Of course, ensuring that Seventh Generation lives up to their promise of authenticity is something that requires constant vigilance. For example, in March 2008, the company was 'exposed' by the Organic Consumers Association for having detectable levels of the contaminate 1,4-dioxane in their dish liquid. In fact, Seventh Generation's product was declared the safest of those available and they had been working with suppliers for more than five years to remove it. But, as Hollender later declared, 'Our effort was simply not good enough. Our real mistake was to exclude consumers and key stakeholders from our ongoing dialogue about dioxane. In short, we flunked the transparency test.'

The very foundation of transparency is information and the most basic kind is a full list of product ingredients, which, unbelievably, is not required by US law for household products. Consequently, Seventh Generation launched a 'Show What's Inside' initiative, which included an educational website and an online Label Reading Guide, downloadable to shoppers' cell phones, which helped them interpret labels at the point of purchase, especially any associated risks. As Hollender and Bill Breen report in their book *The Responsibility Revolution* (2010), not long after, SC Johnson launched a cloned version called 'What's Inside'. 'That's just what we had hoped for', declared Hollender and Breen. 'When a $7.5 billion giant like SC Johnson puts its brawn behind ingredient disclosure, it's likely that the rest of the industry will follow, regardless of what the regulators do.'

Despite its green image, Seventh Generation also knows that it needs to create virtuous cycles for its social as well as its environmental impacts. As a result, in 2009, the company partnered with Women's Action to Gain Economic Security (WAGES) – an organization committed to building worker-owned, cooperatively-structured, eco-friendly, residential cleaning businesses in San Francisco. Together, they launched Home Green Home, WAGES' 4th worker-owned cooperative. This unique social enterprise serves the city of San Francisco and is creating healthy, dignified jobs for women in an industry known for long hours and low pay. The women who own and work in the business earn wages that average 50% more than their non-coop counterparts, and receive health care and paid vacation benefits. In future, Seventh Generation and WAGES hope to expand the innovative practice beyond San Francisco.

Water neutral Coca-Cola

Coca-Cola received its wake-up call to the Principle of Circularity in 2002, when residents of Plachimada, a village in India's southern state of Kerala, accused the company's bottling plant there of depleting and polluting groundwater. Two years later, the local government forced Coke to shut down the plant. In 2006, their situation got worse when a New Delhi research group found high levels of pesticides in Coca-Cola and PepsiCo's locally produced soft drinks, resulting in several Indian states banning their products. Coke denied any wrongdoing, claiming that bore-hole water-fed farming was mainly responsible for lowering the water table and that the pollution claims were unsubstantiated. However, the public perceptions battle had already been lost.

Speaking to *Time* magazine in 2008, Jeff Seabright, the company's Vice President of Environment and Water Resources, admitted that Coke had mishandled the controversy. 'If people are perceiving that we're using water at their expense, that's not a sustainable operation', he said. This realization resulted in a serious shift in Coke's strategic positioning of its CSR towards tackling water as priority number one. 'It's great that companies used to hand out checks for scholarships or to clean up litter', said Seabright, 'but increasingly the real relevance is using the company's core competence to address issues that are of societal concern.' And for Coke and the communities in which it operates, the concern is water.

About 2.4 billion people live in water-stressed countries, according to a 2009 report by the Pacific Institute. Water demand in the next two decades will double in India to 1.5 trillion cubic metres and rise 32% in China to 818 billion cubic metres, according to the 2030 Water Resources Group. China – where Coke's sales have been in double-digit figures – is home to roughly 20% of the world's population, but only about 7% of the world's water. That means there are around 300 million people living in water-scarce areas. According to a 2007 World Bank report, water scarcity and pollution reduce China's gross domestic product by about 2.3%. Meanwhile, Coca-Cola sells 1.5 billion beverages a day in over 200 countries, using about 2.5 litres of water to produce just one litre of its products.

Coke realized that it needs to be seen as part of the solution, not part of the problem. As a result, it has put resources into water at an unprecedented scale. In 2007, the company announced it would spend $20 million over five years to help the WWF preserve seven of the world's major rivers. It also set up the $10 million Coca-Cola India Foundation, which began installing over 4,000 rainwater harvesting programmes and providing clean drinking water to 1,000 schools across the country. More significantly, in June of the same year, CEO Neville Isdell flew to Beijing and pledged that his company would become 'water neutral'.

Coke uses the term 'water neutral' to describe the ratio of ground water usage by any user against the quantity put back into nature. It is a contentious topic and not everyone believes it is possible. But the scale of Coke's ambition – and indeed the progress it is making towards its targets – is going a long way to advancing the circularity agenda. Speaking in 2009, Coca-Cola India's Director of Quality and Environment Navneet Mehta said, 'Our target is to neutralize all ground water usage by the company in India by the end of the current calendar year and become water neutral for all products and processes by 2012.' Mehta reported that the company had already achieved a replenishment level of 82% on its annual ground water usage in India and that their ground water usage ratio had improved over 42% between 1998 and 2008.

Having learned the lesson of circularity, CEO Neville Isdell makes it clear that this is not about charity: 'Water is the main ingredient in nearly every beverage that we make. Without access to safe water supply, our business simply cannot exist.' To which Seabright adds, 'We sell a brand. For us, having goodwill in the community is an important thing.'

The second largest beer manufacturer in the world, SABMiller, has also been working hard on understanding their water footprint, and launched a joint report with WWF-UK in 2009 called 'Water Footprinting: Identifying & Addressing Water Risks in the Value Chain'. The report reveals that in South Africa, their total water footprint is equivalent to 155 litres of water for every 1 litre of beer, while in SABMiller's Czech operation the overall water footprint is significantly smaller at 45 litres of water to every 1 litre of beer. In both cases, the vast majority of this (over 90%) comes from the cultivation of crops, both local and imported. Efforts like these by SAB-Miller are being supported by the Water Footprint Network, which launched its Water Footprint Manual in 2010, covering a comprehensive set of methods for water footprint accounting. It shows how water footprints can be calculated for individual processes and products, as well as for consumers, nations and businesses, and includes methods for water footprint sustainability assessment and a library of water footprint response options.

Carbon neutral at Tesco

Another illustration of circularity is the trend towards carbon neutrality, which has been embraced by, among others, multinationals like Dell, HSBC and Tesco. Let's look at Tesco, the third largest retailer in the world and a member of the Prince of Wales's Corporate Leaders Group on Climate Change. CEO Sir Terry Leahy believes the company is uniquely positioned to 'make sustainability a significant, mainstream driver of consumption' because 17 million consumers visit its 1,900 stores every week. The challenge is significant, as Tesco emits 4 million tonnes of carbon a year, according to *The Guardian*.

One of Leahy's first steps was a pledge in 2007 to plough £500 million (around $770 million) over five years to turn the fringe green lobby into a mass consumer movement, starting with a donation of £5 million ($7.7 million) a year to help fund academic research into greener consumption. With this money, the Sustainable Consumption Institute was established, in partnership with Oxford University, to develop an accepted measure of the carbon footprint of every one of the roughly 70,000 products Tesco sells. Leahy thinks of this as establishing a 'carbon calories' system. Speaking to *The Independent*, he said, 'There aren't many things that keep me awake at night but this is one'.

Next, in 2008, Tesco launched a plan to reduce the carbon emissions from each of its stores by 50% by 2050, using a 2006 baseline, and to be carbon neutral as a company by 2050. Explaining this target in an interview with MeetTheBossTV, Tesco's Global Technology and Architect Director Mike Yorwerth said: 'We see our customers, consumers of the world, as playing a huge role in moving us towards a more sustainable economy and more sustainable consumption in a world where in 30 or 40 years' time, people will need to live on possibly a fifth of the carbon they use today.'

In 2009, Tesco extended the pressure to its suppliers, requiring that they achieve a 30% reduction in the carbon footprint of their products by 2030. By then, the company had already published the carbon footprints of 114 of the products it sells with special labels and was hoping to expand that to 500 products by the end of the year. This was not just about public relations. According to Leahy, 'a low-carbon strategy is vital if we are to minimize the risk to our business [which includes] the physical threat of climate damage to our supply chains, the resulting economic damage, and the serious effects of rushed and inefficient regulation if we fail to act in time and governments are forced to take draconian action'.

Most recently, in 2010, Tesco launched its first carbon neutral store in Ramsey, Cambridgeshire, in the UK. The sustainable design is timber rather than steel-framed, and uses skylights and sun pipes to cut lighting costs. It also has a combined heat and power plant powered by renewable bio-fuels, exporting extra electricity back to the national grid. In addition the refrigerators have doors to save energy and harmful HFC refrigerant gases have been replaced. The store cost 30% more to build, but it uses 50% less energy, which Leahy believes 'is a business case in itself'. To coincide with the store opening, Tesco also announced that it intended to spend more than £100m ($154m) with green technology companies. What's more, with sales up 10% in 2010, it does not appear that its bold carbon strategy is harming business. Ultimately, the Principle of Circularity is a path to profitability.

Encouragingly, the idea of carbon labelling is spreading beyond the big retailers like Tesco. Palsystem Consumers' Co-operative Union, a Japanese home delivery service provider that primarily serves local farms, started to show food mileage using the 'poco' unit on some of the products in its May 2010 catalogue. The co-op aims to improve Japan's food self-sufficiency and to reduce carbon dioxide emissions caused by food transportation from overseas.

Waste not, want not

Besides water and carbon, another critical aspect of circularity is waste. Zero waste strategies have their origin in the thinking of Walter Stahel of the Product Life Institute in Switzerland. So let us look finally at a few examples of pioneers in this field. Zero waste is a goal that several companies, including Fuji Xerox, Sony and Hewlett-Packard, are committed to. Many of these organizations are supported by associations like the Zero Waste International Alliance, which declare their mission as being 'to promote positive alternatives to landfill and incineration and to raise community awareness of the social and economic benefits to be gained when waste is regarded as a resource base upon which can be built both employment and business opportunity'. There are also books, like Paul Palmer's *Getting to Zero Waste*, which give inspiration to aspiring zero wasters.

Since Fuji Xerox was the first company in the industry to introduce products containing recycled parts to the Japanese market in 1995, let's look at their accomplishments. As a result of implementing an Integrated Recycling System, Xerox realized savings of $45 million in 1999. In August 2000, the company became the first in Japan to achieve Zero Landfill from collected used products. Based on this success, and recognizing its global responsibility, Fuji Xerox extended its efforts to its sales and service territories in the Asia-Pacific region and China. In particular, the company introduced recycling systems in Thailand in December 2004 and then in Suzhou, China, in January 2008.

The Thai operation, called Fuji Xerox Eco-Manufacturing, has been especially successful, collecting used Fuji Xerox products such as copiers, printers and cartridges from nine countries and regions in the Asia-Pacific, and disassembling and sorting them into 74 categories including steel, aluminium, lenses, glass and copper for recycling. Over the period from the operation launch to March 2010, the company collected approximately 131,000 units of used products and generated 21,200 tons of recycled resources. By 2010, Fuji Xerox Eco-Manufacturing was able to announce that it had effectively accomplished the Zero Landfill goal by recycling 99.8% of used products and consumables in the 2009 financial year.

And on a larger scale, in 2009, at the annual National People's Congress in Beijing, Chinese Prime Minister Wu Jintao signed into law a rule on e-waste that's been characterized as China's version of the European WEEE (waste electrical and electronic equipment) law. Around the same time, the first electronic products recycling supermarket in China was opened in Wuhan, Hubei. According to CSR Asia, the supermarket will target electronic products like waste or old telephones, washing machines, refrigerators, TV parts, and so on. The supermarket was set up by the district government and a battery recycling company.

Circular urban design

It is important to note that Zero Waste is not only a corporate goal. For example, Brazil is the world's leader in aluminium can recycling, with a rate of 96.5%. Communities can take up the cause as well, and indeed many have. A 2010 report by *The Christian Science Monitor* gives one recent example: 'Tucked almost imperceptibly into cedar-blanketed mountains an hour's winding drive from the nearest metropolis, Kamikatsu seems an unlikely spot for a revolution', the article begins. 'But try to throw even a candy wrapper away here, and it's quickly apparent that residents are radically reshaping their relationship to the environment.' This is a town in Japan that is singularly focused on banishing waste – all waste – by 2020. The 2,000 people of Kamikatsu have dispensed with public trash bins. They set up a Zero Waste Academy to act as a monitor. 'The town dump has become a sort of outdoor filing cabinet', accepting 34 categories of trash – from batteries to fluorescent lights to bottle caps. The town now has an 80% recycling rate, up from 55% ten years ago, as compared with the US national recycling rate average of about 34%.

Japan is not only innovating on solid waste, but also on air emissions. In 2009, a city-wide environmental accounting service, Eco-Hana, was launched for businesses in Naha City of Okinawa. Eco-Hana is an online service based on data input through personal computers and mobile phones. This is the nation's first service to enable bookkeeping of both finances and CO_2 emissions for households. The data from shoppers are processed automatically based on CO_2 emissions per unit sales according to the 2000 consumer price basis of the embodied energy and emission intensity data, calculated by the National Institute for Environmental Studies.

In the Middle East, we have Masdar City in Abu Dhabi, which is positioning itself as a global clean technology hub, powered by renewable energy and demonstrating the world's most sustainable, low carbon urban developments. Masdar City plans to house around 1,500 clean tech companies with 40,000 residents and 50,000 commuters, providing a research and test base for renewable energy technologies. The fact that it is being funded by oil wealth may be considered as one of the great 'swords into ploughshares' turns of history. In a separate development, in July 2009, 12 European companies launched a €400 billion ($560 billion) initiative to plant huge solar farms in Africa and the Middle East to produce energy for Europe.

To give these and other initiatives momentum, the World Bank launched an Innovative Cities dialogue series in 2010 to help mayors and policymakers share innovations to improve urban life across the globe. One best practice case that emerged was Marikina in the Philippines. With a vision of making a town with only one paved road into a 'little Singapore', Marikina's leaders set out to clean the rivers, eliminate graffiti, and build thoroughfares and waterfront parks where families could gather and feel secure.

It is examples like these and many others that show that the Principle of Circularity is not wishful thinking, but a practical strategy for achieving sustainability and responsibility, economically, socially and environmentally. And together with the other principles of CSR 2.0 – creativity, scalability, responsiveness and glocality – these inspiring innovations and bold actions are ushering in the new Age of Responsibility and with it, a new kind of 'susponsible' capitalism (sustainable and responsible). Without a doubt, however, achieving this vision requires change on a scale and with an urgency that has seldom been witnessed in human history. So the question remains, how do we make change happen?

PART IV

Our ability to change

12

The matrix of change

It is not necessary to change. Survival is not mandatory.

—W. Edwards Deming

You can avoid having ulcers by adapting to the situation: If you fall in the mud puddle, check your pockets for fish.

—Author Unknown

Neither a wise man nor a brave man lies down on the tracks of history to wait for the train of the future to run over him.

—Dwight D. Eisenhower

If you don't like something, change it; if you can't change it, change the way you think about it.

—Mary Engelbreit

Box 11: The matrix of change – in a nutshell

Iconic leaders	Google
	Johnson Matthey
	McDonald's
	Nokia
	Shell
Period	Rising from 2003, with the publication of *Leading Change Towards Sustainability*
Key ideas	Change requires systems thinking
	Collective change can be evolutionary or revolutionary
	Individual change can be inventive or intentional
	Scenarios are useful as stories of the future
	Watch out for tipping points and butterfly effects
Commentators	Bob Doppelt (author & consultant)
	Malcolm Gladwell (author & journalist)
	Otto Scharmer (author & consultant)
	Peter Senge (author & academic)
	Penny Walker (consultant)
References	*The Tipping Point: How Little Things Can Make a Big Difference* (Malcolm Gladwell, 2002)
	Leading Change Toward Sustainability: A Change-Management Guide for Business, Government and Civil Society (Bob Doppelt, 2003, 2010)
	Change Management for Sustainable Development (Walker, 2006)
	Learning for Sustainability (Senge, Laur, Schley & Smith, 2006)
	Theory U: Leading from the Future as It Emerges (Otto Scharmer, 2007)

Oases in the Desert and Plains of the Serengeti[57]

Imagine a future where greed-driven companies continue on their path of ascendancy towards global domination. The result is pockets of plenty existing in the midst of a desert of deprivation. It is almost as if the excesses of water and lush greenery in the oasis have been sucked from the rest of the landscape and accumulated in just a few spots. This is the net result of unrestrained companies' tendency to accumulate power and concentrate wealth in fewer and fewer hands. As a consequence, the majority of the world's population is pushed into a marginal existence and the natural environment is systematically degraded. Only the 'fat cats' get fatter. Like black holes in astronomy, wealth becomes so condensed that it creates its own 'singularity of greed'. All the money that flows into the corporate treasure chest never gets shared.

Those that are familiar with Frank Herbert's bestselling science fiction series *Dune* will have no difficulty imagining the scene. The story is set on the desert planet of Arakas, the sole source of 'spice', which is a mineral on which the galactic population is dependent. The mercenary tycoons that control the spice control the universe, and they're not about to share their accrued power, wealth and water with anybody else.

Back to our story of the future: At first, the tyrants – individuals, businesses and politicians that have exploited the current global situation relentlessly for their own selfish gain – revel in their opulence without concern. They think that they are simply collecting their just reward for being superior players in the modern game of materialism. After all, their mesmerized fans worship them as heroes. The super-players

---

[57]Adapted from my book, *Beyond Reasonable Greed*, co-authored with Clem Sunter (2002).

form exclusive clubs where only their own kind is welcome, so that they can show off their treasures to one another, strategize about how they can shape the destiny of the world and reassure one another that they deserve everything they've got. Occasionally, they fall out with one another and have trade wars, but they never allow these differences to jeopardize their overall control.

Their self-indulgent lives lack only one thing – peace of mind. Because, as everyone knows (to continue the *Dune* metaphor), water is a priceless commodity in the desert. And if you own and control the water supply, all those billions that are dying of thirst in the desert will do desperate things to gain access to the fountain, or just to vent their pent-up hatred – they may even commit murder. Therefore, security becomes a primary and constant concern for corporations and their leaders. High walls, alarm systems, bodyguards, hidden vaults, police investigators, secret escape tunnels, private armies, you name it: they install and employ them. But they never feel completely safe. Lingering in the background is the constant fear of the next crazed suicide bomber or undetected anthrax delivery.

Of course, these tycoons own what is left of the living environment – all the most pristine ecological reserves are their exclusive playground. Their homes, their offices and their vehicles are fitted with all the latest technological wizardry to insulate them from the pervasive pollution and saturation of toxins that incessantly plague the masses. And yet there are still some things that they just can't buy or own or control. The unpredictable weather patterns continue to be an expensive source of irritation, as are the collapse of shares in their portfolio when the company or the industry in which they are invested is implicated in the latest health scare, fatal accident or environmental disaster.

The era of the corporate kings does not last forever and it most likely ends with a bang or a squelch. As the vast majority of the world's population sees the gap ever widening between their own poverty-ridden and environmentally-degraded existence and the insular wealth of rich executives, large multinationals and First World countries, a global mass protest movement gathers momentum and becomes increasingly volatile and violent, eventually making the 'kingdom of commerce' ungovernable. This popular discontent is exacerbated as ecosystems continue to topple like dominoes, and the most vulnerable populations begin to suffer the ravages of pollution-induced disease. Terror strikes against unbridled capitalist countries and their rapacious companies become more common, fuelled by cultural and religious tensions. Ultimately, this leads to a chain reaction that descends into full-scale nuclear and biochemical warfare. Many corporate oases meet their end ahead of schedule. This is the future world of *Oases in the Desert*.

Now imagine another, rather different future. Global corporations have realized that their game of domination has a no-win conclusion and, voluntarily or begrudgingly, begin shapeshifting into something more benign, caring even. It's almost like the marketplace is a montage of breathtaking images from the fertile plains of East Africa, where the Great Rift Valley teems with wildlife, all living in a state of dynamic harmony with each other and the natural environment. A rich state of biodiversity exists, and even the predators find their rightful place within the larger animal kingdom. Competition is alive and well, but it is tempered by the more pervasive cooperative tendency in nature, which ensures that a healthy balance is maintained. The smaller, more entrepreneurial creatures flourish in this setting.

Such a future was only made possible because – at various levels of society, from the individual through to the community, from business through to the economy, from politics through to global governance – a consensus emerged regarding new rules of the game that were in everyone's collective interest, in terms of ecological sustainability and social justice. As a consequence of these new governance principles, the sixth mass species extinction and the poisoning of the environment has been halted and reversed, and the formerly marginalized and disempowered sections of the world's population have been given a fair stake in global society and the economy.

Much of the success of the transition to this more sustainable world had to do with restructuring of the economy. The incentive mechanisms were redesigned in such a way that excessive accumulation of wealth and concentration of power were strongly discouraged. Negative environmental impacts were made prohibitively expensive and meeting community needs became the social licence to operate at all levels in the economy. Money still exists, but following the Transition Towns movement it has shapeshifted into a multi-tiered commodity with community currencies being created as and when required as a means of facilitating local exchange of goods. Modifications to the interest and discount rate mechanisms are devised, and speculation is heavily taxed. The main difference from the previous *Oases* future is that now the economy is made to serve people and the environment, not the other way round.

Business still plays a critical role in the world, meeting people's needs with its products and services; but the power and influence that it previously had over global affairs is now subject to numerous social, environmental and ethical checks and balances. While an important purpose of companies remains profit making and shareholder returns, their overall objective is widened to making a permanent contribution in the communities in which they operate. Work itself is seen as a means to an end, a 'space' in which people can develop their potential, express their talents and make a positive contribution to society. Survival is no longer dependent on having a formal job. Most places of work and living are digitally connected, with an emphasis on decentralizing as much authority as possible to employees and providing them with congenial surroundings.

Among the fundamental principles that are embedded in society are creative diversity, freedom with accountability and the philosophy of holism. Although the technological revolution has continued apace and has greatly assisted with meeting human needs and ensuring ecological sustainability, this has been matched by a revolution in the outlook of business towards the planet. A new wave of discovery is focused on understanding the physiology and psychology of healthy living systems (including all levels of human interaction) and developing the personal and social skills to build these systems effectively. The highly competitive companies operating like predatory lions still exist, but with a crucial difference: the rules of the jungle don't automatically favour them at the expense of others anymore. This is the future world of *Plains of the Serengeti*.

Stories of the future

Oases in the Desert and *Plains of the Serengeti* are scenarios – stories of possible futures – taken from my first book *Beyond Reasonable Greed*. They help us to imagine divergent paths of change and they can be extremely helpful, because as corporate sustainability and responsibility enthusiasts, we are all implicitly or explicitly trying to make change happen. But, as Margaret Mead said, 'The only person who likes change is a wet baby', to which Hunter Lovins added 'and the baby squalls all the way through the process'. So change is never easy. And yet, we have been engaged and affected by change since time began. In business, as first the industrial revolution and then the information revolution transformed the landscape, various strategies, tools and techniques have been employed to minimize the risks and maximize the opportunities that change inevitably brings. This is not the place to explore these in detail, but it is worth being aware of some of them.

For many years, strategic planning was in vogue, especially for large companies that borrowed heavily from military models of organization and conceptualization – strategy, tactics, targeting, firing, beating the opposition.

However, as the world became more complex – in the sense of more dynamic and interconnected – formal strategic planning lost some of its effectiveness and its appeal. Forecasting, the once popular technique of using historical trends to predict the future, also proved inadequate to the task in the 20th century, let alone the 21st. Scenario planning, however, another method borrowed from the military, proved more durable and insightful.

Scenarios are not predictions or forecasts, merely stories of what could happen in the future, given a particular set of circumstances. Sometimes, these stories are grounded in complex mathematical models, such as the 1972 *Limits to Growth* study and the more recent Intergovermental Panel on Climate Change (IPCC) scenarios. More often, however, they are based on informed imagination. This technique has been effectively used since the 1970s by companies like Shell, and later by Anglo American and others. For instance, Shell's 2025 Global Scenarios identifies three key drivers of world development: market incentives (efficiency), the force of community (social cohesion and justice) and coercion and regulation by the state (security).

Based on the interplay and trade-offs between these drivers, the report identifies three possible future worlds (the 'Trilemma Triangle'): (1) *Low trust globalization*, where there is more globalization and market liberalization but also more coercive states and regulators; notably, the trust problem is not resolved; (2) *Open doors*, where heightened globalization and more cohesive civil societies mean that the crisis of trust and security has been resolved; there is more use of the precautionary principle and of 'soft power'; and (3) *Flags*, where states rally around the flag, trust is fragmented, national societies split into diverse groups, and efficiency and the market take a backseat to security and solidarity, resulting in more protectionism.

Looking through a sustainability lens, WBCSD has developed global scenarios for 2000–2050, in which they outline three pathways, which they explain as follows:

Will we simply ignore our social and environmental problems, trusting in the dynamic of economic growth and the innovations of technology, as people do in the *FROG!* story? Or, when problems reach a crisis point, will we turn away from our ineffective institutions of government and business to seek new models of governance – a *GEOpolity* – that will take into account the religious and democratic values our narrow economic myth seems to ignore? Or will we try to embody our growing environmental and social values within the economic myth – and, like *Jazz* players, experiment with ad hoc alliances and innovative forms in a world where the way we 'play' and everything else we do is open for everyone to see and judge?

The matrix of change

What these and other scenarios – like those done for the Millennium Ecosystem Assessment – have in common is that they see the world as a complex system, an interconnected whole, in which change happens in a variety of ways, depending on who acts and responds and how. I often use a cartoon in my presentations to illustrate the point: Two people are sitting in a boat, one on either end. At the one end, the boat has sprung a leak and the person is bailing out water furiously to save them from sinking. At the other end of the boat, the person is smiling, thinking to himself, 'I'm sure glad the hole isn't at my end!'

I have been fortunate that my work has given me wide exposure to change in practice – first as a strategy analyst for Cap Gemini, which had its own model of 'business transformation', and then with KPMG, advising and auditing companies on various CSR-related change initiatives. I have also had the opportunity to study the theories of change, both as part of my PhD research on what motivates individuals to be CSR change agents, and in my research and teaching for the Cambridge Programme for Sustainability Leadership. In the process, while trying to make sense of what is admittedly a complex and bewildering field, I have distilled what I've learned into what my students sometimes call a 'monster matrix'. Bear with me as I talk you through it.

At one level, change can be understood quite simply as a two-by-two matrix, with time on one axis and agency on the other. Hence, change is either gradual or rapid, and either brought about by individuals or collectively. To distinguish between each type of change at this simplistic level, I have named the quadrants *Invention* (rapid, individual change), *Intention* (gradual, individual change), *Evolution* (gradual, collective change) and *Revolution* (rapid, collective change). If you are more of a visual thinker, then imagine that *Invention* is a lightbulb, *Intention* is a beaver, *Evolution* is a beehive and *Revolution* is bacteria.

However, to understand the subtleties of how change happens and what kind of agents bring it about, we need to delve into each of these four basic

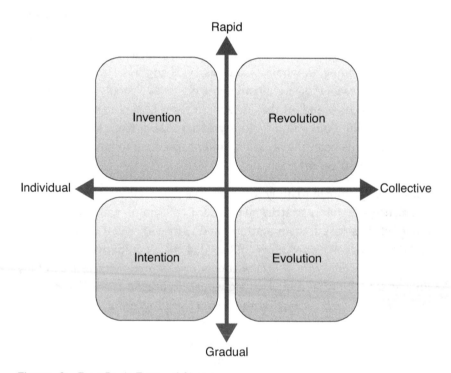

Figure 3 Four Basic Types of Change

types of change a little deeper. For each main type, there are three sub-texts, or stories, of how change happens.

The power of ideas

Starting with *Invention*, there are three kinds of individuals that act as agents of rapid change – the genius heretic, iconic leader and freedom fighter – which result in three different types of change: paradigmatic, charismatic and activist change. Let us look briefly at each in turn.

Paradigmatic change happens when an individual challenges assumptions and changes worldviews. They shift our pattern of thinking or our model of working and are often seen as heretical, or as an outcast (at least to begin with). They are more likely to 'invent' an idea than its practical applications. You might think of Copernicus or Einstein as prototypical genius heretics. In the CSR area, examples might include James Lovelock (with his Gaia theory), C.K. Prahalad (with his Bottom of the Pyramid, or BoP, model) and John Elkington (who coined the 'triple bottom line').

Charismatic change occurs when someone leads by the magnetism of his or her personality, embodying our aspirations or popularizing an ideal. They

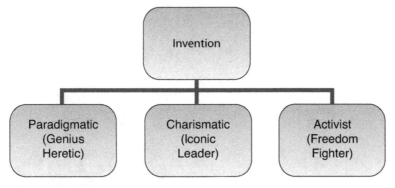

Figure 4 Types of Inventive Change

lead by example, commanding respect. While they may not have original ideas, they are great communicators. Here, we can think of Nelson Mandela or John F. Kennedy. In the CSR field, I would place Anita Roddick (founder of The Body Shop), Muhammad Yunus (founder of the Grameen Bank) and Al Gore (author of *An Inconvenient Truth*) in this category. Of course, some special individuals can fit into more than one category.

Activist change is the result of a leader that embodies the fight for human rights and justice in the world. They can generate mass support for a cause or movement and typically work at the grassroots level. They tend to be revolutionaries rather than institution builders. So we might think of Che Guevara or Malcolm X. In the CSR world, Ralph Nader (the US campaigner and consumer activist), Ken Saro-Wiwa (the Nigerian human rights advocate) and Chico Mendez (the Brazilian environmental activist) spring to mind for me.

Progress is slow but sure

With *Intention*, there are once again three kinds of individuals – the systematic scientist, structural engineer and personal exemplar – but the change they cause is gradual: Cartesian, Newtonian and Gandhian change respectively.

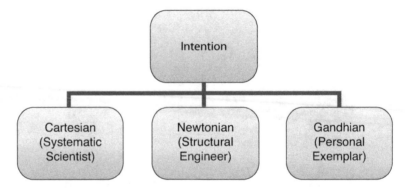

Figure 5 Types of Intentional Change

Cartesian change is based on the power of logic and evidence collected and presented by individuals who emphasize the testing of hypotheses or solutions. They work tirelessly on the details to build their case and are likely to be the expert that others turn to. As the name suggests, the iconic figure here is Rene Descartes, but perhaps Francis Bacon would also fit the profile. In CSR, I think of Rachel Caron (author of *Silent Spring*), Paul Crutzen (the Nobel Prize winner for his work on the ozone layer) and Nicholas Stern (author of *The Economics of Climate Change*). As you can see, they do not literally have to be scientists; rather it is their approach to change that matters.

Newtonian change is brought about by individuals who use the law of cause and effect. They work hard to identify and address the roots of an issue, and look for leverage points in the system to move the immovable. They see that people are often trapped in a system which limits their discretion. Hence, they try to change the incentives in the system. Sir Isaac Newton is the poster child, but I would argue Adam Smith also fits the bill. In CSR, people like Amory Lovins (founder of the Rocky Mountain Institute), Paul Ekins (a British environmental economist) and Karl-Henrik Robèrt (founder of The Natural Step) are examples.

Gandhian change is effected by people who believe – as Gandhi did – that you must 'be the change you want to see in the world'. Hence, they lead by example and practise what they preach. They are driven first and foremost by values and principles and become catalysts for change because they are revered. Apart from Mahatma Gandhi, Martin Luther King was such a person. In CSR-related circles, Vandana Shiva (the Indian scientist, activist and author), Wangari Maathai (a Kenyan green activist and Nobel Prize Winner) and Shanaka Fernando (founder of Lentil As Anything) tend to inspire change in this way.

When change gathers momentum

Evolution is a collective change process which manifests in three ways – as a tipping point, as people power or as a market dynamic – leading to gradual change that is Pivotal, Consensual or Incentivized.

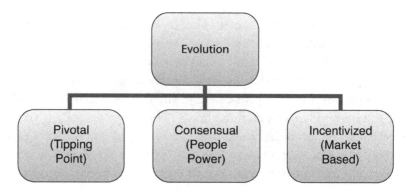

Figure 6 Types of Evolutionary Change

Pivotal change is characterized by small, gradual changes that scale up and speed up only after a tipping point is reached (which is much less than the majority). It is based on the idea of change as a virus or contagion and relies on the power of an influential minority. In terms of Malcolm Gladwell's book *The Tipping Point*, three types of individuals are critical in the process: connectors (people who know people who can make a difference), mavens (people who collect information and are keen to share what they know) and salespeople (people who can convince other people to do things). In the CSR sphere, I think that the fairtrade movement, ISO 14001 certification and low-energy (CFL) light bulbs may all be in this category.

Consensual change is driven by the popular vote and is based on the idea of governing by consensus. It believes in the power of an organized majority and therefore politics, institutions and dialogue are all essential. It makes me think of the anti-slavery movement, the World Social Forum and the Intergovernmental Panel on Climate Change, all of which use this approach to change.

Incentivized change is driven by many individual actions and incorporates the idea of an 'invisible hand'. It relies on the power of incentives in a system and therefore market structures and dynamics are critical to understand. Here, we might place companies like Johnson Matthey (makers of catalytic converters), General Electric (with their Ecomagination initiative) and Café Direct (producers of fairtrade coffee).

When the world changes forever

Revolution is a collective change dynamic that has three faces – emergency response, hockey-stick growth and the butterfly effect – leading to rapid change that is Cataclysmic, Exponential or Chaotic.

Cataclysmic change is something we are very familiar with. It is usually driven by an external, unforeseen event and based on the idea of dramatic shocks to a stable system. The importance of emergency aid is critical and emergency preparedness and voluntary action are key. Examples might include Shell's fiasco with the Brent Spar platform and the execution of Ken Saro-Wiwa in 1995, Enron's collapse in 2001, or the Sichuan earthquake in China in 2008.

Exponential change happens when there is a cumulative and self-reinforcing trend. It is based on logarithmic growth, which is often characterized as the 'hockey-stick' curve because of its shape as a plotted graph. This type of growth exists because of the power of reinforcing feedback loops, and makes it imperative to understand macro-system elements like culture, fashion, markets and norms. CSR-type examples could include the ban on CFCs after the adoption of the Montreal Protocol, the current explosive growth of the clean technology sector – with the *McKinsey Quarterly* estimating that $170 billion a year will be invested in energy efficiency alone

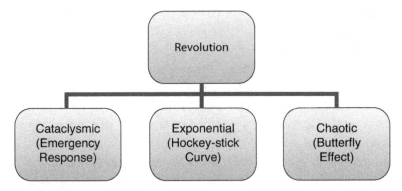

Figure 7   Types of Revolutionary Change

between now and 2020 – and the Wal-Mart effect on products like organic cotton and MSC-certified fish.

Finally, *Chaotic* change is about the unintended consequence of a seemingly unrelated action or event. It is based on ideas from chaos theory – especially the metaphor about a butterfly flapping its wings in one part of the world and causing a storm in another part. This change is not random, but rather due to the power of highly complex interconnectedness. Hence, understanding sensitivities in the system becomes critical. Butterfly effects in the CSR space might be the fact that Ray Anderson was reading Paul Hawken's *The Ecology of Commerce* at the very moment that he was asked to give a speech about the company's vision, the impact of Hurricane Katrina on former Wal-Mart CEO Lee Scott, or Google's unlikely venture into making RE < C (renewable energy cheaper than carbon).

Dynamics of the change matrix

So how might we apply the matrix? I like to think of it as a filter for understanding how change really happens in the world. The important insight is that it is almost never one type of change, but rather several acting together, simultaneously or sequentially, that result in the change we see.

An example will make it clearer. Let's take Shell's massive sustainability shake-up in 1995. Using the matrix, we can map out two intertwining threads of change happening. First, there was *Cartesian* change, as Shell did scientific studies that concluded it was best to dispose of the Brent Spar oil platform in the Atlantic Sea. Then there was a *Butterfly* effect in the form of Greenpeace's campaign against the proposal. In the same year, human rights critic Ken Saro-Wiwa's targeting of Shell and the Nigerian government was a form of *Activist* change that resulted in a *Cataclysmic* effect when he was executed. What followed was a *Chaotic* change dynamic in which Shell was implicated in the crisis.

These two events together resulted in *Pivotal* change through the gathering of anti-Shell protesters around the world that reached a tipping point, after which the *Market* (especially for young recruits) began typecasting Shell as an unethical company. The knock-on effect was that a *Charismatic* leader, in the form of Sir Mark Moody Stuart, changed Shell's strategy to embrace sustainable development, and started a 'Tell Shell' stakeholder engagement process that finally led to a *Consensus* that Shell was turning into a triple-bottom line pioneer. Hence, even though there were only two initial change events or triggers, there were at least eight change processes across all four of the quadrants of the matrix.

Disentangling the process of change can help us to understand change not only at the company level, but also at the industry sector level. For example (and keeping it simple for illustration), the chemical industry's Responsible Care initiative emerged from a series of explosions in the 1970s and 1980s (*Catastrophic* change) and is today the largest CSR standard in the world today (*Consensual* change, at least within the industry). The Marine Stewardship Council by contrast came about as the result of the personal beliefs and commitment of a few individuals within Unilever and WWF (*Gandhian* change) and now uses product labelling in the market to effect change (*Incentivized* change). Finally, McDonald's faced McLibel and Super Size Me (*Activist* change) which led to a tipping point in their attitudes on health and environmental impacts (*Pivotal* change).

The last thing to say about the matrix before I put it back in its box is that it can be useful when trying to plan or execute a change effort. The more types of change you can put in train, the greater your chance of success. So you might ask, for instance, who are the genius heretics, iconic leaders and freedom fighters in your company or sector or sphere of work? Are there systematic scientists, structural engineers or personal exemplars that you can get on board? Are you better off trying to build up to a tipping point, or to go for mass consensus, or maybe tweaking the incentives in the system? And what about crises, explosive growth areas and butterfly effects – are there any to be used to your advantage?

Change management

There are many different approaches and models for change management in organizations. Rather than trawl through them, here I want to focus on just three that I have found most useful. The first is Richard Beckhard and David Gleicher's Formula for Change: $D \times V \times F > R$. This means that three factors must be present for meaningful organizational change to take place. These factors are:

D = *Dissatisfaction* with how things are now;
V = *Vision* of what is possible; and
F = *First* concrete steps that can be taken towards the vision.

If the product of these three factors is greater than R (*Resistance*), then change is possible. I have seen CSR change efforts fail for all four reasons. Deep-seated resistance often exists because the benefits of the status quo to those in power are considerable. CSR initiatives, especially if they are integrated into the core business, are often seen as extra burden. For instance, an operations manager of a plant really doesn't want the extra hassle of collecting emissions data for a CSR report, or subjecting his staff and facilities to an audit.

Most often, I think, the dissatisfaction that we may feel with the state of the world or the company's actions really isn't widely shared enough. Jonathon Porritt, author of *Capitalism as if the World Matters*, after many years in the sustainability game (he started the UK's Green Party and chaired the government's Sustainable Development Commission, among other things), told me:

> Looking at people all over the world today, rich and poor, they are not remotely close to a state of mind that would call for anything revolutionary. There's no vast upheaval of people across the world saying, 'This system is completely and utterly flawed and must be overturned and we must move towards a different system.' There isn't even that, let alone an identification of what the other system would look like.

Likewise, on creating a compelling vision, Porritt concludes that 'we have not collectively articulated what this better world looks like – the areas in which it would offer such fantastic improvements in terms of people's quality of life, the opportunities they would have, a chance to live in totally different ways to the way we live now. We haven't done that. Collectively we've not made the alternative to this paradigm, this paradigm in progress, work emotionally and physically, in terms of economic excitement. We've just not done it.'

Taking first steps is something companies are generally much better at, especially picking the so-called 'low hanging fruit'. But the reason these steps so often don't get beyond the pilot or peripheral stage is because the other two factors – dissatisfaction and vision – are not strong enough.

A second model I find helpful was developed by a colleague from Cambridge University, Professor Charles Ainger, building on some work by McKinsey & Company. He created a matrix of organizational change, with

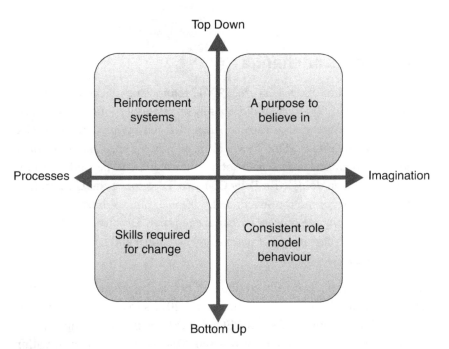

Figure 8 Ainger's Organizational Change Matrix

one axis showing a spectrum from top-down commitment to bottom-up passion, and the other plotting discipline and compliance processes through to creativity and innovation through imagination.

Hence, top-down compliance processes (reinforcement systems) may include objectives, goals, targets, track-records, measurements, rewards and penalties, while bottom-up compliance processes (skills for change) include manuals, standards, procedures, learning, skills, IT/knowledge management systems, protocols, quality management, audits and workshops. On the other hand, top-down imagination (a purpose to believe in) includes vision, mission, purpose, strategy and values, while bottom-up imagination includes culture, behaviour, inspiration, awareness, stories, meaning, understanding, demonstrations, pilots and trials. Hence, if you are engaging in a CSR change effort, you should ensure that you are working effectively in all four quadrants to raise the chances of success.

The process of change

Jim Collins, author of *Good to Great* (2001) reminds us that companies that went from being good to great did not rely on revolutions, dramatic change programmes or wrenching restructurings: 'Rather, the process resembled relentlessly pushing a giant flywheel in one direction, turn upon turn, building momentum until a point of breakthrough, and beyond.' In some research I've been doing with Polly Courtice, Director of the University of Cambridge Programme for Sustainability Leadership, we have identified a number of key change processes that are required for sustainability to be advanced. These happen at the macro, organizational and people levels and are described briefly below.

At the macro level, leaders need to foster or change the prevailing values, culture, incentives, rules and resources. In a 2010 survey by Accenture and the UN Global Compact, 54% of CEOs felt that a cultural tipping point on sustainability is only a decade away – and 80% believe it will occur within

15 years. At the organizational level, leaders can catalyse change for sustainability through various actions, including innovation, empowerment, accountability, closed-loop practices and collaboration. Let's look briefly at each element.

Sustainability leaders are good at promoting creativity in business models, technology, products and services that address social and environmental challenges. For example, The Ensus Group is tackling major concerns about the production of biofuels – in particular, food prices and food security – by co-producing animal feed in its production process in Europe's largest wheat refinery. The 350 thousand tonnes of high-protein animal feed produced by the plant will reduce European demand for soy meal imports, which contribute to high levels of deforestation in South America. To cite another example, Jorma Ollila, who became CEO of Nokia in 1992, is said to have built a culture – the Nokia Way – that is known for experimentation, continuous learning, and social responsibility.

Sustainability leaders also implement structures and processes for good governance, transparency and stakeholder engagement. Accountability does not have to be all about structures and controls, however. Collins believes great leaders foster a culture of discipline: 'When you have disciplined people, you don't need hierarchy. When you have disciplined thought, you don't need bureaucracy. When you have disciplined action, you don't need excessive controls.' According to Jeffrey Immelt, 'Enron and 9/11 marked the end of an era of individual freedom and the beginning of personal responsibility. You lead today by building teams and placing others first. It's not about you.'

Sustainability leaders adopt the principles of cradle-to-cradle production, internalizing externalities and extending these principles to the supply chain. For example, Motorola demonstrated life cycle thinking in mobile phones, with the launch of the world's first carbon neutral mobile phone – MOTO W233 Renew – early in 2009. Sustainability leaders build formal cross-sector partnerships, as well as innovative and inclusive collaborative processes such as social networking.

Flowers, co-author of *Presence*, poses the challenge as a question, saying, 'We know a lot about heroic action because that's in the past of leadership. But how do you have leadership in groups across boundaries, multi-nationally?'

At the people level, leaders catalyse change for sustainability through envisioning, inspiring, empowering and supporting. Sustainability leaders provide a compelling vision, encouraging long-term thinking, making strategic investments and promoting intergenerational equity. Immelt says that 'every leader needs to clearly explain the top three things the organization is working on. If you can't, then you're not leading well.' Ray Anderson sees this as a process of inclusion, saying, 'Today for Interface, sustainability is broader than before: sustainability reaches out to embrace people, processes, products, place, the planet and profits – we now know that none can long be afforded allegiance at the expense of the others.'

Sustainability leaders deepen knowledge and skills and provide opportunities and resources for appropriate action. Robert Greenleaf says: 'The servant-leader is servant first. It begins with the natural feeling that one wants to serve. Then conscious choice brings one to aspire to lead. The best test is: do those served grow as persons; do they, while being served, become healthier, wiser, freer, more autonomous, more likely themselves to become servants?' Collins endorses the importance of the people aspect of change. Good-to-great leaders 'first got the right people on the bus, the wrong people off the bus, and the right people in the right seats – and then they figured out where to drive it.'

Sustainability leaders also focus on creating a culture and structure that provides peer support and encouragement and recognizes achievement. The Centre for Effective Leadership claims that a sustainability leader 'builds a climate of support and accountability, rather than control'. Similarly, Immelt says, 'Today, it's employment at will. Nobody's here who doesn't want to be here. So it's critical to understand people, to always be fair, and to want the best in them.'

Wheels of change

Another way to think of change in a structured way is Bob Doppelt's Wheel of Change, taken from his book *Leading Change Towards Sustainability*. All organizational change, he argues, comprises seven steps: (1) change the dominant mindset; (2) rearrange the parts of the system; (3) alter the goals of the system; (4) restructure the rules of engagement; (5) shift the flows of information; (6) correct the feedback loops; and (7) adjust the parameters. Doppelt also reminds us that change is like an iceberg, where the most important parts are below the surface. What we usually see are events (crises, daily issues), whereas what don't see, and what makes change really effective, are patterns of behaviour (trends, recurrences), systemic structures (policies, relationships, norms), mental models (thinking, perspectives, assumptions) and visions (underlying values, beliefs).

Another 'wheel of change' is Peter Senge's concept of the learning organization, popularized in his book *The Fifth Discipline* (1994). He described the five interrelated disciplines as follows:

> Systems thinking [the fifth discipline] needs the disciplines of building shared vision, mental models, and personal mastery to realize its potential. Building shared vision fosters a commitment to the long term. Mental models focus on the openness needed to unearth shortcomings in our present ways of seeing the world. Team learning develops the skills of groups of people to look for the larger picture that lies beyond individual perspectives. And personal mastery fosters the personal motivation to continually learn how our actions affect our world.

In a follow-up book, *Learning for Sustainability*, Senge, together with co-authors from the Society for Organizational Learning, apply the fifth discipline model to sustainability. In particular, they emphasize connecting the inner and outer work that needs to be done:

> Connecting the inner changes in how we manage and lead with the outer effects our organizations have on larger systems; connecting the inner

changes in mental models and personal visions with the outer changes in management culture; and connecting the inner changes in who we are as human beings with how we act and interact.

In seeking to create change for sustainability, Senge and his colleagues once again emphasize the interconnected nature of all change processes, and the critical role of business:

> There has never before been a time when the social, ecological and economic conditions that challenge political leaders in any one part of the world have been so interwoven with what is occurring in so many other places. This phenomenon has arisen through the ever-growing web of interconnectedness spun by institutions, especially multinational corporations. Collectively, these organizations determine what technologies are created and how they are applied around the world: which markets develop and which are largely ignored. These institutions determine who benefits from the world economy and who does not.

Given this interconnectedness, Senge believes the key to change is collaboration. To illustrate his point at an MIT Sustainability Summit 2010, Senge asked the question: What would it take to get rid of disposable cups? Who would have to work together to eliminate disposable cups? The answers suggested include everyone from Starbucks and its competitors to paper manufacturers, food service providers, recyclers and municipal governments. Hence, to make real headway on tough sustainability issues is a 'massive undertaking in collaboration'. What's more, the parties that need to collaborate often aren't naturally inclined to do so.

Senge concludes that a good guy/bad guy mentality can be a barrier to collaboration: 'You've got to wake up and say "We're all part of the system." You know who is causing the destruction of species? You and me. You know who's causing the huge waste problems around the world? You and me.' Once you become more open-minded to this possibility, then you can look for collaborative solutions. 'Look for small steps of things you can do together with people with whom you traditionally would never have cooperated — and do something useful, no matter how small.'

Theory U

The theme of collaboration was echoed by Otto Scharmer in his book *Theory U*. Theory U was given a preview in *Presence* (a book that Scharmer did with Senge and others). It explores a new way of creating change through leadership. 'This time', says the Presencing Institute, 'calls for a new consciousness and a new collective leadership capacity to meet challenges in a more conscious, intentional, and strategic way. The development of such a capacity would allow us to create a future of greater possibilities. We know a great deal about what leaders do and how they do it. But we know very little about the inner place, the source from which they operate. And it is this source that "Theory U" attempts to explore.'

Theory U – or Presencing as it is also known – is depicted visually as moving down the one side of a 'U' and back up and out the other side. Essentially, it is a process of letting go of assumptions, listening to others, being open to something new and unexpected emerging, and then testing the new vision through pilots, before rolling out the solution. According to Scharmer, presencing is an antidote to a prevailing feeling of powerlessness in the world, of being a victim of forces beyond our control. He told me that 'it actually goes all the way up, including to the boardroom levels where you are chased by Wall Street. For those in leadership situations in business or government, the demands are so enormous that this deeper space of reflection becomes one of the anchor points that you use every day to be more effective.'

Scharmer sees this as part of a bigger story, where the way in which we can make change happen in the world is evolving:

If you look at the evolution of capitalism, we have three coordination mechanisms that have evolved over the past 200 years: regulation and hierarchy; market and competition; and dialogue and stakeholder negotiations. We have these three, and often the debate in sustainability is, is it regulation or is it markets and innovation or is it stakeholder dialogue and negotiation? But that's what we are already doing, and it's not getting us the results that we need. What we need is more of these three plus a fourth one. The fourth one is disruptive; it's the radical jump that we as a macro system are about to do. We can see it in the area of sustainability and climate change on a small scale. It has to do with seeing and operating from the whole. It means that the coordination is not some kind of market mechanism, it's not somebody's regulation, it is what spontaneously happens.

A new mythology

Scharmer's co-author of *Presence*, Betty Sue Flowers, believes this shift is part of a new mythology that is emerging. She told me:

> The economic myth – and by myth I don't mean something untrue, I mean a large story of reality that we swim in, the way the fish swim in the sea unconsciously – has, at its basis, growth, but it doesn't take into account quality. So growth itself, that upward line on the graph, is the endpoint of the economic myth. The strength of the economic myth is that economics is about interconnectedness and at its basis a kind of fundamental equality: that is, my dollar is as good as your dollar. But what I call the ecological myth could evolve from the economic myth, because it too is about interconnectedness, but interconnectedness of quality not of quantity.

I tend to agree. We need a new story. As I wrote in 2002, 'each time the world changes – when civilizations rise and fall, when new scientific theories challenge our understanding of the universe, when technological innovation reinvents our lifestyle, when political revolution breaks down the old structures of society, or when a global crisis threatens to destroy our planet – humanity is forced to let go of some of its most cherished beliefs in order to create a new mythology to guide its collective psyche'. We are at just such a fulcrum of change, and the beliefs we need to challenge and modify are many. Maybe it is our belief in the beneficence of the 'invisible hand' of the market? Or our belief that a global political deal is all we need to solve the climate crisis? Or that business has the power to act unilaterally in bringing about a more sustainable and responsible future?

If my experience of living through the political changes in South Africa taught me anything, it is that change is systemic. It happens because of millions of small actions by millions of people all over the world, some coordinated, some diffuse. Yes, change also happens because of bold leadership, but it always needs an enabling environment, a society or an organization that is ready to change. Change is something organic. It's worth remembering that the largest living thing in the world is a honey mushroom in Oregon – an interconnected fungus measuring 3.5 miles across. It is said to be 2,400 years old and takes up 2,200 acres (1,665 football fields), with the small mushrooms visible above ground only a tiny proportion of its real girth and substance. I think change is something like that too: spread out, interconnected, growing where the ground is most fertile ground, often invisible.

13

Making a difference

I never look at the masses as my responsibility; I look at the individual. I can only love one person at a time – just one, one, one. So you begin. I began – I picked up one person. Maybe if I didn't pick up that one person, I wouldn't have picked up forty-two thousand. The same thing goes for you, the same thing in your family, the same thing in your church, your community. Just begin – one, one, one.

—Mother Theresa

The greatest use for life is to spend it for something that will outlast it.

—William James

When we are no longer able to change a situation, we are challenged to change ourselves.

—Victor Frankl

If you would attain to what you are not yet, you must always be displeased by what you are. For where you are pleased with yourself there you have remained. Keep adding, keep walking, keep advancing.

—Saint Augustine

Cultivating radicals

Have you ever done something radical and felt really good about it?

Radicals are the root of all progress. Yet, in a world of convention, being unconventional takes courage. All our lives we are taught compliance. We learn to obey, we are careful not to rock the boat, and we lose our natural appetite for questioning – that childish insistence to know why. We are schooled in the ways of group-think, discouraged from challenging the status quo. And those who dare to question the ingrained assumptions, to challenge the established order, to reject popular opinion, are labelled radicals, outcasts, troublemakers, fringe lunatics.

Yet what does it mean to be radical? It means to get to the root of things, to tap a deeper source, to go below the surface of shallow consensus. Radicals are feared because they threaten those in power who rely on the unquestioning acquiescence of the masses. Radicals are persecuted because they are the harbingers of change in a society that clings to stability.

Yet radicals are the driving force behind human evolution. All the icons that history has judged to be great were radicals in their time. The Chinese philosopher Lao Tsu was radical when he proposed the way of flow in an era of rigid military imperialism. Gautama the Buddha was radical when he rejected his noble birth and founded the path of simple living. Moses was radical when he led the Israelites from slavery to freedom. Jesus was radical when he challenged the encrusted traditions of his own Jewish upbringing.

Other great reformers throughout the ages were similarly regarded as heretics by their peers: Newton for replacing Catholic cosmology with scientific theories, and Einstein for dismantling Newton's clockwork universe; da Vinci for imagining how people might fly, and the Wright brothers for turning his prophecy into reality; Darwin for confronting creationists with the evidence of evolution, and Rupert Sheldrake for suggesting that the laws of nature are more like habits of morphic resonance; Gandhi for taking on the colonial might of Britain, and Mandela for fighting the scourge of apartheid.

We greatly admire these giants of human civilization now, so what made them heretics in their day? The etymological root of the word heretic means 'able to choose'. Perhaps this gives us a clue as to why they were reviled then and are lauded now. Heretics are messengers of freedom. And freedom is an anathema to theocrats, bureaucrats and plutocrats alike. People who think for themselves are more likely to question the scripted beliefs of religious dogma; they are less likely to blindly follow the dictates of authority; and they are more difficult to control and manipulate with money.

Radicals are able to endure the ridicule of society because they have the power of conviction. Their ideas are rooted firmly in values, making their stand virtually unshakeable. But radicals never exist in isolation. If they stand out above a crowd, it is only because they are raised on the shoulders of a dedicated band of committed supporters. Radicals are always part of a wider groundswell of change, riding on the bow of a wave of reform.

Radicals are not agitators for the sake of contrariety. They shout in the deserts of the mainstream because they have a vision of a better way, a more honest way, a way which improves the lot of humankind. Radicals are the voice of the oppressed who cannot speak, and of the poor to whom no one listens. Radicals are the hands of the innovators whose minds are tied to contracts, and entrepreneurs whose souls are bought by commerce.

We are all radicals just waiting for our moment of destiny, straining for our calling to a higher purpose, wishing for the courage to do the right thing. The root of our actions, and indeed the route to action, lies within. As we reach deep down into the soil of our being, we tap into our radical core of inspiration.

So why not do something radical yourself today – for a change?

Are we happy?

In the face of unprecedented global challenges like financial market instability, persistent poverty and climate change, can we as individuals – radical or otherwise – really make a difference? And if we can, what motivates us to devote our time and energies to addressing social, environmental and ethical issues? Based on research for my PhD, which is written up in detail in my book *Making a Difference* (2008), I believe that corporate sustainability and responsibility provide a powerful way to address the 'existential gap' or lack of a deeper sense of personal meaning and job satisfaction felt by many people in business today.

A survey a few years ago by London PR firm Fish Can Sing hinted at the extent of the problem. It found that 66% all 18–35-year-olds were unhappy at work. The proportion rose to 83% among 30–35-year-olds. One in 15 respondents had already quit the rat race and 45% were seriously contemplating a career change. This last group was described as being made up of TIREDs, or Thirty-something Independent Radical Educated Dropouts. These otherwise highly successful and motivated professionals were found to be lacking something in their working lives. They wanted less work-related stress, shorter working hours, more job satisfaction, and higher quality of life – less demand, greater reward.

What's more, the existential crisis does not appear to be confined either to the thirty-something age group, or to the UK. According to the Worldwatch Institute, today the same number of Americans – about a third – report being 'very happy' as they did in 1957, even though they are as a group twice as wealthy as they were over 50 years ago. The New Economics

Foundation's 2009 Happy Planet Index (HPI), which measures the relative efficiency with which nations convert the planet's natural resources into long and happy lives for their citizens, is also revealing. High scores are only achievable by meeting all three targets embodied in the index – high life expectancy, high life satisfaction and a low ecological footprint.

The highest HPI score is that of Costa Rica (76.1 out of 100). Of the following ten countries, all but one is in Latin American. The highest ranking Group of 20 (G20) country in terms of HPI is Brazil, in 9th place out of 143. Together, Latin American and Caribbean nations have the highest mean HPI score for any region (59 out of 100). Rich developed nations fall somewhere in the middle. The highest-placed Western nation is the Netherlands – 43rd out of 143. The UK ranks midway down the table – 74th, behind Germany, Italy and France. It is just beaten by Georgia and Slovakia, but beats Japan and Ireland. The USA comes a long way back in 114th place.

So what is going on here? Victor Frankl, author of *Man's Search for Meaning* and a personal survivor of four Nazi concentration camps, suggests that the Western pursuit of economic growth may be to blame: 'Consider today's society', he says. 'It gratifies and satisfies virtually every need – except for one, the need for meaning. This spreading meaning vacuum is especially evident in affluent industrial countries. People have the *means* for living, but not the *meanings*.' Management thinker Charles Handy puts it another way: 'We seem to be saying that life is about economics, that money is the measure of things. My hunch is that most of us don't believe any of this, and that it won't work, but we are trapped in our own rhetoric and have, as yet, nothing else to offer, not even a different way to talk about it.'

Handy may be right. Then again, surely one 'different way to talk about it' is through the language of sustainability and responsibility? After all, these are matters which run deep. They are matters of values and beliefs, of higher aspirations and noble causes. And yet, even here, we find the prevailing rhetoric of CSR is mostly about the business case. Talk of the 'moral case' or the 'personal case' for CSR is taboo – as if stripping human emotion and personal motivation from the debate on how companies should behave somehow makes it more credible, more effective.

My research suggests that this corporatized, depersonalized approach to CSR is failing to tap the massive source of energy for constructive change that exists in companies and the world. The reason is that the 'CSR-zombie' view of the world – reflected in the mantra, 'I only do corporate sustainability and responsibility because it's good for business' – completely fails to appreciate why people choose to work in CSR, what satisfaction they derive from this work, and what motivates them to keep trying to make a positive difference, despite huge obstacles and frustrations. The simple fact of the matter is that CSR students, professionals and enthusiasts are change agents.

We are the champions

What do we know about the role of individuals as change agents? Intuitively, we resonate with adages such as Gandhi's 'be the change you want to see in the world', or Margaret Mead's famous quote: 'Never doubt that a small group of thoughtful, committed citizens can change the world; indeed, it's the only thing that ever does.' But beyond these clichés, what do we really know about change in the context of CSR?

The first rich vein of research to mine is the concept of 'champions' within organizations. This goes back to the emergence of human resource (HR) champions in the 1980s. In the 1990s, firms started to apply the idea to environmental management and corporate social performance as well. Hence, a CSR champion became someone who has the ability to translate a set of personal beliefs about creating a just and sustainable future into an attractive vision for their organization or sector. Or put another way, they are masters at identifying, packaging and selling social and environmental issues to those that have power and influence to address them.

CSR champions do not always have formal corporate sustainability and responsibility roles. They are often described as being action-oriented, enthusiasts, inspirers, experts, volunteers, communicators, networkers, sponsors, implementers and catalysts. They demonstrate that, contrary to popular belief, individuals have considerable discretion within organizations to pursue and promote agendas that they are passionate about. Crucially, however, they need a combination of knowledge and skills to be successful. For example, they need to be able to gather sufficient credible information to make a rational case for change. They need the ability to tell an emotionally compelling story about a more sustainable future. And they need enough political savvy and interpersonal skills to persuade others, especially leaders, to listen and take action.

CSR professionals are effective change agents, therefore, when they act as champions. One safety, health and environmental manager I spoke to talked about his role in convincing his organization (a large chemical company) to phase out the use of various harmful substances, such as CFCs, PCBs and asbestos: 'To me it was a major achievement to convince the 30,000 colleagues of mine in the company to move out of this business before legislation hits us.'

This still doesn't tell us what motivates us to engage with the agenda in the first place. Talking to CSR professionals – by which I mean managers, consultants, academics and NGO representatives working on corporate social, environmental and ethical issues – the desire to create change recurs as a consistent theme, but the way in which they make change happen, and the satisfaction they derive as a result, differs considerably.

For some, as one might have guessed, values play an important role. In particular, CSR is seen as a way to align work with personal values. For example, one manager I interviewed said: 'It's the inner drive, it's the way I am put together, my value system, my belief system, it's my Christian belief, my ethical approach.' Another explained that it is important to have 'inspirational leadership and people who align with your value sets'. For many CSR professionals, their motivation also derives from the fact that sustainability and responsibility are such dynamic, complex and challenging concepts. 'The satisfaction is huge', said one corporate responsibility manager. 'Because there is no day that is the same when you get into your office. It's always changing, it's always different.' Another reflected that CSR 'painted a much bigger picture' and is 'just as holistic as you want it to be. It requires a far broader vision.'

Types of CSR change agents

These two factors – values alignment and the CSR concept – were fairly cross-cutting motivators that I identified in my research. However, it was also possible to distinguish four fairly distinctive types of CSR professional, based on how they derive satisfaction from their work. In practice, every individual draws on all four types, but the centre of gravity rests with one, representing the mode of operating in which that individual feels most comfortable, fulfilled or satisfied.

The first type of CSR change agent is the *Expert*. Experts find their motivation though engaging with projects or systems, giving expert input, focusing on technical excellence, seeking uniqueness through specialization, and pride in problem solving abilities. To illustrate, one Expert-type CSR professional said: 'There were a couple of projects that I did find very exciting. . . . It was very exciting to get all the bits and pieces in place, then commission them and see them starting to work.' Another Expert said: 'I usually get that sense of meaning in work when I've finished a product, say like an Environmental Report and you see, you know, I've really put in a lot and here it is. Or you have had a series of community consultations and you now have the results.'

The second type of CSR change agent is the *Facilitator*. Common themes among Facilitators are deriving motivation from transferring knowledge and skills, focusing on people development, creating opportunities for staff, changing the attitudes or perceptions of individuals, and paying attention to team building. For example, one Facilitator-type CSR professional said: 'If you enjoy working with people, this is a sort of functional role that you have direct interaction, you can see people being empowered, having increased knowledge, and you can see what that eventually leads to.' Another Facilitator explained that 'the part of my work that I've enjoyed most is training, where I get the opportunity to work with a group of people – to interact with people at a very personal level. You can see how things start to get clear for them, in terms of understanding issues and how that applies to what they do.'

The third type of CSR change agent is the *Catalyst*. For Catalysts, motivation is associated with initiating change, giving strategic direction, influencing leadership, tracking organizational performance, and having a big picture perspective. One Catalyst-type CSR professional claimed: 'The type of work that I'm doing is . . . giving direction in terms of where the company is going. So it can become almost a life purpose to try and steer the company in a direction that you believe personally is right as well.' Another said: 'I like getting things changed. My time is spent trying to influence people. The real interesting thing is to try and get managing directors, plant managers, business leaders and sales guys to think differently and to change what they do.'

That is quite different from the fourth type of CSR change agent, the *Activist*. For Activists, motivation comes from being aware of broader social and environmental issues, feeling part of the community, making a contribution to poverty eradication, fighting for a just cause, and leaving a legacy of improved conditions in society. One Activist-type CSR professional said: 'It's also about the issue of being poor. It actually touches you. You see these people living in appalling conditions, the shacks, the drinking water is so dirty, or there's no running water at all, you see those kind of things, it hits you, and you think: What can you do?' Another confessed: 'I think my purpose here is to help others in some way and leave a legacy for my kids to follow. I could leave a legacy behind where I actually set up a school, a kids' school, or a campus for disadvantaged people, taking street kids out and doing something, building homes for single parents.'

Dynamics of CSR change agents

The different types of CSR change agents find some resonance in the broader management literature. The Catalyst type clearly draws on a strategic role and applies it to sustainability and responsibility, bringing in a lot of ideas from change management. Arguably, the Facilitator finds echoes in the 'servant leadership' concept, while Activists are probably best described in the work on social and environmental entrepreneurship. There are also glimpses of the Expert in much of the more technical scholarship on environmental and quality management.

It is important to note, however, that the CSR Change Agents typology is dynamic. In the same way that sources of meaning in life can vary over the life cycle or other changing circumstances, there is ample evidence to suggest that CSR professionals' default types can change as well. One CSR manager I interviewed seemed to have shifted from being an Activist to a Facilitator (moving from political campaigning when he was a business ethics lecturer to business training and lecturing in a large consultancy); another from Expert to Catalyst (doing laboratory work on eco-toxicity testing, then strategic policy advice in a safety, health and environmental centre); and yet another from Expert to Facilitator (a technical environmental manager for a chemical company who became the head of a team of sustainability consultants).

For some (but not all) CSR change agents, their formal job roles and their type are aligned, as in the examples cited above. Hence, there is a suggestion that either people are naturally attracted to roles that fit with their change agent types, or that their roles shape the meaning they derive, or perhaps both. One manager explained that 'in your career or in your work, the manager must be able to swing from the one type to the other'.

Another important influence is organizational context. For instance, one CSR professional observed that the 'organization dynamics of corporates require conformism to the organizational culture, which to a large degree requires maintenance of the status quo. . . . This makes it difficult for Activists.' Career stage or life cycle is another important factor. 'One of the

Table 12 Characteristics of CSR change agents

	Types of change agent			
	Expert	*Facilitator*	*Catalyst*	*Activist*
Primary source of meaning	Specialist input	People empowerment	Strategic input	Societal contribution
Level of concern	Individual	Group or team	Organization	Society
Source of work satisfaction	Personal development, quality input	Staff development, effective facilitation	Organizational development, strategic change	Community development, social change
Skills	Technical, process	Managerial, facilitation	Visionary, political	Collaborative, questioning
Knowledge	Specialist	Generalist	Key players, future trends	Community or macro needs
Legacy	Successful work projects	Staff or team's achievements	Organization or industry transformation	Sustainable environment and equitable society

things that you have to bear in mind is how much individual flexibility you get in working environments', said one CSR manager. 'I think at an earlier stage in someone's career, no matter what their typology might be, they don't necessarily yet have the luxury of finding themselves in the position that gives expression to their preference.'

Making a difference

Beyond simply improving our understanding of CSR change agents, there are several practical uses for the typology. The most obvious applications occur at an individual and team level, with benefits for CSR managers, managers of CSR teams and human resource managers. For CSR managers, the typology acts as a prompt for individuals to reflect on their most natural type, or mix of types. This allows them to think about what sorts of roles they derive the most satisfaction from, and to consciously compare this to their formal role. If there is not a natural fit between their type and their formal role, it may help to explain work frustrations or lack of motivation.

For managers of a CSR team, the typology helps to cast light on the mix of team members, from the perspective of their different sources of motivation. This can influence the way in which individuals are managed and allocated tasks, as well as the general management style adopted. For example, for a team full of Experts, incentives that recognize quality may be far more effective than for a Catalyst-heavy team, where tracking of strategic goals may be more motivational. The manager of a CSR team may decide that there is merit in having a balance of all four types represented, which will in turn affect recruitment decisions.

One of the underlying messages of my CSR change agency research is that companies stand to gain a lot by going beyond the business case for CSR, i.e. by justifying sustainability and responsibility efforts on the basis of values – what some call the 'moral case'. Taking this position – in addition to, rather than instead of, the business case – will enable companies to tap into a powerful source of motivation, namely the satisfaction that CSR managers (and in all likelihood many other employees) derive from the alignment of values with work.

Ultimately, the typology is a recognition that all of us working in CSR are motivated and satisfied by different things. At the same time, we are all trying to 'make a difference'. And being able to make a difference through our work is an immense privilege. As one of the CSR people I interviewed put it: 'I think people that are working in the area of sustainable development have a greater sense of purpose, in the sense of assisting people and making a difference, leaving a legacy and having strong values.'

To give a more practical example, someone working in the pharmaceutical industry told me about a massive programme where they were distributing 6 billion tablets to wipe out lymphatic fibrosis – a type of elephantitis disease in Africa. 'Definitely you feel like, wow, we're making a difference', he said. 'We're not just pumping out toothpaste.' Another, working in professional services, said 'there's making a difference in terms of what you suggest that a company does, but then there's the personal making a difference, which is very different. That's about putting your money where your mouth is, where you're personally committing your time, your own effort.'

And of course, most of the time, we are not contemplating our navel; we are out there fighting the good fight. One of my colleagues said, 'there's so much to do, I haven't got time much to think about the meaning of life. The alarm clock goes off and I'm out. . . . Just go, just go. I get home and I think, what the hell have I done today? But I've been incredibly busy, phoning, talking and making presentations. . . . It's just when you stand back that you see that perhaps you are making a difference. But most of the time you just do it.'

To scare or to inspire?

But how do we 'just do it'? What is the most effective strategy? And in particular, how do you get the balance between sharing the bad news (the state of the world) and the good news (the innovative solutions)? Betty Sue

Flowers, co-author of *Presence*, told me that 'if you attempt to scare people with the enormity of the problems, the tendency is simply to give up. When you dispirit people, when you remove the spirit, you also remove the capacity to change.' This is a common refrain – and indeed a dilemma. We can't deny the severity of the crises that we face, and yet we can't paralyse people with fear. 'I'm impaled on this every day of my life at the moment', Jonathon Porritt told me. 'What do you do? I think we still owe it to reality and to integrity in any communications process to share the empirical reality. But how do you come out of that without leaving people spread eagled with despair and just utterly disempowered?' Porritt went on to say:

> We're trying to create these upbeat, opportunity driven wish lists about what would happen if businesses seized hold of this set of opportunities here, and started to do things completely differently over there, and if politicians started to construct societal and economic responses based on a world not on growth hormones. But then you look at the scale of their responses and you set it against the scale of the analysis, and of course it looks frail. It looks insubstantial in terms of where we need to be. So I think the mechanisms we're using are the only ones available to us, but we haven't got it right yet. Whether we can get there building, building, building gradually over a period of time or whether we need some shocks in the system to accelerate the emergence of that positive energy, that for me is still a hard one to call.

Jorgen Randers, co-author of *Limits to Growth*, is equally ambivalent:

> Are scare tactics better than carrots? There are groups pursuing both avenues. I think I've moved to thinking that having a positive view has a stronger motivational force than scare tactics. But then you can ask the question, Is it possible to come up with sufficient carrots to make society act? And it looks as if support from some scare tactics or some of the disasters would help.

The 21st Century Living project, undertaken by Acona in conjunction with Homebase and The Eden Project, may provide some answers. Based on an

18 month study of 100 households in the UK, the findings showed that most people will act, given the right tools and information specifically for their needs:

> The data say clearly that environmental values are not a good predictor of action. The message we got back was clear: we can get on with cutting our environmental footprint without having to win the battle for the long-term soul of the nation. Don't browbeat people, don't frighten them – just show them where they are wasting money and resources and they will change themselves. Frame the topic like this and everyone is interested – young and old, wealthy and poor, green or not.

Like all of us in the CSR field, I have also been grappling with the issue of whether it is best to scare or inspire. In my case, however, this was also critical in a post-apartheid South Africa. The country was in the grip of pessimism after the euphoria of its political miracle had evaporated and the massive challenges of social upliftment became clear. This was the subject of my book *South Africa: Reasons to Believe*, in which my co-author, Guy Lundy, and I concluded that there are two basic ingredients to being positive. The first is to recognize that our pessimistic views are generally skewed by unbalanced media reporting. We have to remember that our mental state is determined by what we focus on. It's not that the media is lying; it's just that they are painting a picture of the world that is highly selective. They are like manic-depressive artists patching together a collage, using bits and pieces of real events, most of which happen to be dark or disturbing. So, we need to start exposing ourselves to more of the positive news stories, in order to get a more balanced perspective of what is going on around us.

The second ingredient to being positive is to recognize that our attitude influences the world around us, for better or worse. The neutral scientist in the white coat is a myth – he/she does not exist. The observer and the observed are not separate; they are always inextricably linked. Everything we think, or believe, or value, changes the world around us. It even affects our physical health. Attitudes are like lenses that colour what we see. But they are also like yeast in bread – they have a very real, visible effect on the outcome of whatever we are trying to make work, whether it is a family, a business, a nation, or even a whole planet. This is not just a philosophical point. Optimism comes from actively engaging with life's challenges.

Reasons to be optimistic

Stuart Hart shares this attitude of optimism, especially on the potential role of business, saying:

> I'm a pragmatist, in the sense that I look around and try to assess where the leverage points are for change to occur most rapidly. I don't see government and I don't see civil society being able to lead that process *per se*, or to act on their own to make it happen. And so it leaves the world of commerce really as the most logical and maybe the only institution left to look at. And there I see both the potential for great harm – and obviously that's the path that we've been on; we're headed rapidly for the cliff – but also great potential to change quickly. What makes the world of commerce interesting in my mind is its ability to creatively destroy itself. When the conditions are right, capitalist institutions – companies and the competitive process – can generate change in a hurry. And that's what we desperately need. So I think if we're able to turn this ship to really re-frame what capitalism might look like in the twenty-first century, then we have a mechanism through which this change could unfold at the rate that it needs to, in order to move us towards a sustainable world before it's too late.

Likewise, Jeffrey Sachs, author of *The End of Poverty*, is optimistic. 'Every time I turn around', he told me, 'whether it's in India, whether it's in China and Malaysia, Tanzania, there's no shortage of reasons for optimism. In fact, the power of our technologies, the wonders of our information linkages now [creates] a world where isolation, which was the essence of poverty, has been broken; where a cell phone is within reach in just about any village, thereby making a link for people who were desperately outside of the chain of information and are now part of markets and global knowledge. There's all the reason for optimism.'

For William McDonough, being a designer requires that he is an optimist, 'because the nature of design is to make the world better'. He explained this perspective to me, saying, 'When I see the energy in people directed to help solve these problems and the resources and funding that are being put towards these questions, I think it's quite a different moment. I don't think of it as a bubble, I think of it as a boom. There are harbingers of hope all over the landscape. It may be too late for a lot of the things around toxification and climate change and things like that, but if we let that stop us from our creative intention, then we stop designing. And the day we stop designing we lose all hope.'

Amory Lovins, in his typically quirky and insightful way, told me that he is not on the optimist/pessimist axis at all. 'I don't view the glass as half empty or half full. I think a glass has a hundred percent design margin expandable by efficiency. My old mentor, David Brower', he reflected, 'taught that optimism and pessimism are different faces of the same simplistic and irresponsible surrender to fatalism – treating the future as fate, not choice, and not taking responsibility for creating a future we want.'

To hope is human

So what does give us hope? For Amory Lovins, three things stand out. First, the rapid rise of awareness and leadership in the private sector and the corresponding awakening of civil society empowered by the emerging global central nervous system. Second, 'the fact that brains are evenly distributed one per person, and, as far as we know, there's nothing in the universe so powerful as six billion minds wrapping around a problem'. And, third, the quality in the new generation of young people, who realize there is less time and they need to get on with it.

Elizabeth Economy, author of *The River Runs Black*, said to me that she takes all of her inspiration and hope for the future of China from China's environmental activists and from the Chinese people themselves. 'They're pioneers, and every day any one of them is challenging a system that in many ways is antithetical to strong and good environmental protection, and they're pushing it in terms of those issues of transparency and the rule of law and accountability and putting their lives on the line in some cases.'

Simon Zadek, author of *The Civil Corporation*, told me that his hope doesn't arise from a sense that amazing things are about to happen, that human nature is about to change, that global consciousness is about to be formed, that a revolution is about to take place, that technology will solve a problem, or even in a sort of Margaret Mead way, that there's always some fantastic person down the road doing something amazing. 'My hope', he said, 'comes from my very direct experience of trying to make change. I think it's through the habit every day of trying to make change that one maintains an ambition about the possibility.'

Vandana Shiva agrees. Hope, she said to me, comes through 'engaging in positive action, with communities and people – every seed we save, every new farmer who goes organic, every time a new food product is brought by a local community, a good nutritious healthy ecological product, every one of those things – and that happens daily'.

Hunter Lovins, on the other hand, puts her hope in distributed leadership. She told me: 'I rather like the line from *Lord of the Rings* on leadership, where Gandalf says, "The rule of no realm is mine. That all worthy things that are in peril as the world now stands, those are my care, and for my part I shall not wholly fail if anything passes through this night that can still grow fair and bear fruit and flower again in the days to come. For I too am a steward. Did you not know?"' Her conclusion is that 'it doesn't matter if you are a wizard or a king or the CEO of Wal-Mart, because remember in the end it was the little people. It was the two fun loving, unassuming Hobbits who had to take on their shoulders that awesome task. And they were scared and they didn't know where they were going. But in the end all the kings and warriors and wizards could just stand by as the little people saved the world. I think real leadership is extraordinary courage by ordinary people.'

Experiments in generosity

When I think of what gives me hope, it is the extraordinary people I meet and come across in my work on corporate sustainability and responsibility, especially those conducting 'experiments in generosity'. For example, Derek Sivers, whom I only became aware of while writing this book. I will let him tell his own story:

> When I decided to sell my company – CD Baby – in 2008, I already had enough. I live simply. I hate waste and excess. I have a good apartment, a good laptop, and a few other basics. But the less I own, the happier I am. The lack of possessions gives me the priceless freedom to live anywhere anytime. Having too much money can be harmful. It throws off perspective. It makes people do stupid things like buy 'extra' cars or houses they don't use – or upgrade to first class for 'only' $10,000 so they can be a little more comfortable for a few hours.
>
> So I didn't need or even want the money from the sale of the company. I just wanted to make sure I had enough for a simple comfortable life. The rest should go to music education, since that's what made such a difference in my life. So I found a great way to do this. I created a charitable trust called the Independent Musicians Charitable Remainder Unitrust. When I die, all of its assets will go to music education. But while I'm alive, it pays out 5% of its value per year to me. 5% is the minimum allowed by law. It's still too much. I would have preferred 1%, but oh well, I'm free to use it to start new businesses to help people, or whatever.
>
> A few months before the sale, I transferred the ownership of CD Baby and HostBaby, all the intellectual property like trademarks and software, into the trust. It was irreversibly and irrevocably gone. It was no longer mine. It all belonged to the charitable trust. Then, when Disc Makers bought it, they bought it not from me but from the trust, turning it into $22 million cash to benefit music education. So instead of me selling the company – getting taxed on the income, and giving what's left to charity – that move of giving away the company to charity, then having the charity sell it, saved about $5 million in taxes.

Amazing story, huh? Another 'experiment in generosity' that I encountered over the past year, while I was on my CSR Quest world tour, was Lentil As Anything. I had the good fortune to spend some time with Shanaka Fernando, the founder entrepreneur of this Melbourne-based restaurant chain. Fernando is one of those rare pioneers who are prepared to live by their convictions, flout social convention and challenge the status quo. After a 'failed' stint as a Buddhist monk in his home country of Sri Lanka (he fell in love with a nun, had a torrid affair and got kicked out), he came to Australia and dabbled in law studies. It wasn't fulfilling, so he gave it up to travel on a shoestring around the Third World for six years, learning about culture and community along the way. When he returned to Australia, Fernando started a business importing saris made from recycled fabrics, which made him enough money to start his current social experiment, Lentil As Anything.

I call it a social experiment, because the business goes beyond simply being a social enterprise. Like other social businesses, Lentil As Anything embraces the entrepreneurial spirit while it 'seeks to have a significant, positive influence on the development of the community'. But there is something more unique, more challenging, more sublime and more subversive, because it gets to the heart of human nature and the essence of Western capitalism. I am talking about generosity and money.

Through Lentil As Anything, Fernando is trying to foster a culture of generosity. What would happen, he wondered, if there were no prices? What if people only paid what they could afford, or what they thought the food was worth, or what they were inspired to pay? Is there enough generosity left in Western society to run a viable business on the principle of giving and sharing, rather than profit maximization? Would the 'free rider' problem kick in, with people taking advantage of the 'free' food?

According to Fernando, all kinds of interesting things happen when people are faced with 'the magic box' – the little wooden chest that people can place their donations in as they leave. A few (very, very few) take advantage. Some, who genuinely can't afford to pay, offer to chop vegetables or do dishes. Others make their own assessment of what is a fair price to pay. Some are quietly generous, while others make a theatrical gesture of placing their donation in the magic box. But it goes beyond the money. Other unexpected things happen too. As I looked around the restaurant, I noticed that this is not a 'people like me' experience, where you are surrounded by those from your own socio-economic or ethno-cultural strata. Lentil has succeeded in mixing it up, cutting across traditional divides. And because of the philosophy of the place, you may find a wealthy businessman striking up a conversation with a subsistence artist.

When you create these kinds of creative connections, it is a potent recipe for innovation, for rediscovering what it means to be human. Fernando insists that Lentil is first and foremost about good food (interestingly, vegetarian food, because that is the most inclusive, making concerns about halal or kosher or meat-based preparation less tricky). But it is clearly more than that. It is an invitation to restore our faith in the essential goodness of humanity and the wholesome nature of community.

And what, you may ask, has all this to do with CSR? Well, I believe it is pioneers like Fernando and the others discussed in this book that are at the forefront of the CSR 2.0 wave. If we subject Lentil to the five tests of CSR 2.0, it scores well: (1) Is Lentil creative? (yes), (2) is it scalable? (not sure), (3) is it responsive? (extremely), (4) is it glocal? (yes, it thinks globally but acts locally), and (5) is it circular? (mostly, yes, local production and recycling are part of the philosophy and practice). Even on scalability, Lentil gave me pause to think about what I mean by that. If we accept Chris Anderson's 'Long Tail' approach to scalability, Lentil doesn't have to go from 4 to 40,000 restaurants to be scalable. It could be that 10,000 independent restaurants – inspired by a similar philosophy – pop up all around the world and turn the generosity experiment into a global movement.

As the world recovers from the Age of Greed that culminated in the global financial crisis, it is refreshing to be reminded of the rightful place of money in society. Money is always a means to an end; never the end in itself. Melbourne – and indeed the world – would be a poorer place if brave experiments like Lentil As Anything were allowed to fail. Let us make sure that, in the battle of generosity versus money, generosity wins hands down.

Answering the question 'why?'

And that seems a good note to end on. But I want to finish by telling one more story. It is a true story, with a message, told by Polish journalist Ryszard Kapuściński in his remarkable book *The Shadow of the Sun*. He was travelling to Onitsha, a small town in eastern Nigeria, which is legendary for having the biggest market in Africa, perhaps in the world. A few kilometres outside the town, he got stuck in a monumental traffic jam. After an hour of not moving, Kapuściński got out and walked into town, in an attempt to discover the source of the problem. I will let him tell the rest of the story:

> In one spot the street was crowded; there was a noisy, nervous commotion, engines were roaring, you could hear shouting and calling. Once I pushed myself through the throng, I saw an enormous gaping hole in the middle of the street: huge, wide, several metres deep. It had steep, sheer sides, and its bottom was an opaque, muddy pond. The street was so narrow here that you couldn't go around the hole, and everyone who wanted to drive into town had to descend first into this abyss, plunge into its swampy waters, and then hope that someone, somehow, would pull them out.

> I was immediately struck by how the area around the hole had become the epicentre of local life, how it drew people, engaged them, spurred them to initiative and action. In the normal sleepy, lifeless backwater on the outskirts of town, where the unemployed slumber in the streets and packs of dogs roam, there arose, suddenly and spontaneously, thanks solely to that unfortunate hole, a dynamic, humming, bustling neighbourhood. The hole created work for the unemployed, who formed teams of rescuers and made money hauling cars out of the pit. It brought new customers for the women operating sidewalk eateries. Because of the attendant traffic jam, shoppers appeared perforce in the previously empty local shops – the passengers and drivers of cars waiting to get through. Hawkers of cigarettes and cold drinks found buyers for their wares.

The curse of drivers travelling to Onitsha became the salvation of the residents of Oguta Road, and of this entire neighbourhood. It was further proof that every evil thing has its defenders, because everywhere there are those whom evil sustains, for whom it is an opportunity, life itself. For a long time, people did not allow this hole to be repaired. I know this because when years later I was telling someone in Lagos with great emotion about my adventure in Onitsha, he replied with an absolutely indifferent tone of voice: 'Onitsha? It's always like that in Onitsha.'

The moral of the story is that today, as a global society, we are facing that crater in the road – our social, environmental and ethical crises. It doesn't help to point fingers at who created the hole. It is the result of our collective actions; the erosion caused by the relentless drive of consumptive, inequitable capitalism. The sad fact of the matter is that many people still benefit from our gigantic pothole of unsustainability and irresponsibility – businesses, politicians, even NGOs. What's more, many of us working in CSR are like the street vendors: we help to make the inconvenience of the crisis a little more comfortable for the drivers; we sustain the rescue teams and we converse with the curious onlookers. But we're still not repairing the hole!

Of course, we all know – including the truck drivers of the global capitalist economy – that the situation is ultimately unsustainable and irresponsible. But we need the courage to challenge the status quo, to stand up to those who are entrenched in the system, to question the integrity and wisdom of the beneficiaries of inertia. The Age of Responsibility will only dawn when those of us working in corporate sustainability and responsibility – whether as business leaders, regulators, managers, consultants, activists, teachers or students – only when we focus our efforts not on those hauling the trucks out of the hole, but rather on filling in the hole. We are on the brink of the post-industrial revolution and we need to decide whether we will be accomplices in slowing that transition, or catalysts in speeding us towards a better future.

As Manfred Max-Neef, author of *Economics Unmasked* (2011), puts it: 'Let us imagine that economics becomes again the manner of managing the household in order to achieve the art of living and living well, respecting the right of all others to achieve the same, within the limits of the carrying capacity of our planet.'

There is a saying in Africa that there are two hungers – the lesser hunger and the greater hunger. The lesser hunger is for the things that sustain life – goods and services and the money to pay for them. The greater hunger is for an answer to the question 'Why?' For some understanding of what life is for. CSR change agents have a fantastic opportunity to feed the greater hunger, by making a constructive difference and leaving a positive legacy. As Victor Frankl said: 'Each person is questioned by life; and they can only answer to life by answering for their *own* life.'

This book has been an existential questioning for me: Is working in corporate sustainability and responsibility a good answer to my life's question? In the end, I am convinced that it *is*, but only if we can unmask the limitations of CSR 1.0 – the defensive, charitable, promotional and strategic versions of CSR – and embrace CSR 2.0 – systemic CSR: corporate sustainability and responsibility that judges its success by improvements in the overall socio-cultural, economic and ecological system. I hope you will join me on this quest and find your unique and invaluable way to make a difference through CSR.

You are invited to share your CSR 2.0 ideas and experiences with me at: wayne@waynevisser.com. If you want to stay up to date with the latest thinking and content on CSR 2.0, check out: http://ageofresponsibility.blogspot.com and www.csrinternational.org

Bibliography

Books

Andersen, R.C. (2009) *Confessions of a Radical Industrialist: Profits, People, Purpose – Doing Business by Respecting the Earth*. St Martin's Press.

Anderson, C. (2006) *The Long Tail: Why the Future of Business is Selling Less of More*. Hyperion.

Bakan, J. (2004) *The Corporation: The Pathological Pursuit of Profit and Power*. Free Press.

Barnard, C. (1938) *The Functions of the Executive*. Harvard University Press.

Bishop, M. and Green, M. (2008) *Philanthrocapitalism: How the Rich Can Save the World*. Bloomsbury.

Blowfield, M. and Murray, M. (2008) *Corporate Responsibility: A Critical Introduction*. Oxford University Press.

Bornstein, D. and Davis, S. (2010). *Social Entrepreneurship: What Everyone Needs to Know*. Oxford University Press.

Boutilier, R. (2009) *Stakeholder Politics: Social Capital, Sustainable Development and the Corporation*. Stanford Business Books.

Bowen, H. (1953) *Social Responsibilities of Business*. Harper.

Capra, F. (1984) *The Turning Point: Science, Society, and the Rising Culture*. Bantam.

Capra, F. (1996) *The Web of Life: A New Synthesis of Mind and Matter*. HarperCollins.

Capra, F. (2002) *The Hidden Connections: A Science for Sustainable Living*. HarperCollins.

Capra, F. (2008) *The Science of Leonardo: Inside the Mind of the Great Genius of the Renaissance*. Anchor.

Carnegie, A. (2008) *The Gospel of Wealth*. Dodo Press. [Originally published in 1889.]

Carroll, A. and Buchholtz, A.K. (2008) *Business and Society: Ethics and Stakeholder Management*. 7th ed. South-Western College Publishers.

Carson, R. (1962) *Silent Spring*. Houghton Mifflin.

Cheng, W. (2009) *Doing Good Well: What Does (and Does Not) Make Sense in the Nonprofit World*. John Wiley & Sons.

Clark, J.M. (1939) *Social Control of Business*. 2nd ed. University of Chicago Press.

Clinton, B. (2007) *Giving: How Each of Us Can Change the World*. Knopf.

Cohen, B. and Greenfield, J. (1994) *Ben & Jerry's: The Inside Scoop: How Two Real Guys Built a Business with a Social Conscience and a Sense of Humor*. Crown.

Collier, P. (2007) *The Bottom Billion: Why the Poorest Countries are Failing and What Can Be Done About It*. Oxford University Press.

Collins, J. (2001) *Good to Great: Why Some Companies Make the Leap... and Others Don't*. HarperBusiness.

Crane, A., McWilliams, A., Matten, D., Moon, J. and Siegel, D.S. (2009) *The Oxford Handbook of Corporate Social Responsibility*. Oxford University Press.

Crane, A. and Matten, D. (2010) *Business Ethics: Managing Corporate Citizenship and Sustainability in the Age of Globalization*. 2nd ed. Oxford University Press.

D'Agnes, T. (2001) *From Condoms to Cabbages: An Authorized Biography of Mechai Viravaidya*. Post Books.

Daly, H. (1996) *Beyond Growth: The Economics of Sustainable Development*. Beacon Press.

Devinney, T.M., Auger, P. and Eckhardt, G.M. (2010) *The Myth of the Ethical Consumer*. Cambridge University Press.

Doppelt, B. (2010) *Leading Change Toward Sustainability: A Change-Management Guide for Business, Government and Civil Society*. 2nd ed. Greenleaf.

Economy, E. (2010) *The River Runs Black: The Environmental Challenge to China's Future*. 2nd ed. Cornell University Press.

Elkington, J. (1997) *Cannibals With Forks: The Triple Bottom Line of 21st Century Business*. Capstone.

Elkington, J. and Hartigan, P. (1997) *The Power of Unreasonable People: How Social Entrepreneurs Create Markets That Change the World*. Harvard Business School Press.

Ellis, T. (2010) *The New Pioneers: Sustainable Business Success Through Social Innovation and Social Entrepreneurship*. John Wiley & Sons.

Esty, D.C. and Winston, A.S. (2009) *Green to Gold: How Smart Companies Use Environmental Strategy to Innovate*. 2nd ed. John Wiley & Sons.

Fishman, C. (2006) *The Wal-Mart Effect: How the World's Most Powerful Company Really Works – and How It's Transforming the American Economy*. Penguin.

Frankl, V.E. (2006) *Man's Search for Meaning*. Beacon Press. [Originally published in 1968.]

Freeman, R.E. (1984) *Strategic Management: A Stakeholder Approach*. Pitman.

Friedman, T.L. (2008) *Flat, Hot and Crowded: Why We Need a Green Revolution – and How It Can Renew America*. Farrar, Straus and Giroux.

Frumkin, P. (2006) *Strategic Giving: The Art and Science of Philanthropy*. University of Chicago Press.

Fuller, R.B. (1969) *Operating Manual for Spaceship Earth*. Simon and Schuster.

Gladwell, M. (2002) *The Tipping Point: How Little Things Can Make a Big Difference*. Back Bay Books.

Grayson, D. and Hobbs, A. (2004) *Corporate Social Opportunity: 7 Steps to Make Corporate Social Responsibility Work For Your Business*. Greenleaf.

Goldberg, S.H. (2009) *Billions of Drops in Millions of Buckets: Why Philanthropy Doesn't Advance Social Progress*. John Wiley & Sons.

Gore, A. (2006) *An Inconvenient Truth: The Planetary Emergency of Global Warming and What We Can Do About It*. Rodale Books.

Hammond, A.L., Kramer, W.J., Katz, R.S., Tran, J.T. and Walker, C. (2007) *The Next 4 Billion: Market Size and Business Strategy at the Base of the Pyramid*. WRI and IFC/World Bank Group.

Hart, S.L. (2010) *Capitalism at the Crossroads: The Unlimited Business Opportunities in Solving the World's Most Difficult Problems*. 3rd ed. Wharton School Publishing.

Hawken, P. (1994) *The Ecology of Commerce: A Declaration of Sustainability*. HarperBusiness.

Hawken, P. (2007) *Blessed Unrest: How the Largest Movement in the World Came into Being and Why No One Saw It Coming*. Viking.

Hawken, P., Lovins, A. and Lovins, L.H. (1999) *Natural Capitalism: Creating the Next Industrial Revolution*. Earthscan.

Hertz, N. (2001) *The Silent Takeover: Global Capitalism and the Death of Democracy*. Free Press.

Hollender, J. and Breen, B. (2010) *The Responsibility Revolution: How the Next Generation of Businesses Will Win*. Jossey-Bass.

Holliday, C.O., Schmidheiny, S., Watts, P. and WBCSD (2002) *Walking the Talk: The Business Case for Sustainable Development*. Berrett-Koehler Publishers.

Kapuściński, R. (2002) *The Shadow of the Sun*. Vintage.

Klein, N. (2000) *No Logo: No Space, No Choice, No Jobs*. Picador.

Klein, N. (2007) *The Shock Doctrine: The Rise of Disaster Capitalism*. Metropolitan Books.

Korten, D. (2005) *When Corporations Rule the World*. Berrett-Koehler Publishers.

Korten, D. (2007) *The Great Turning: From Empire to Earth Community*. Berrett-Koehler Publishers.

Krep, T. (1940) *Measurement of the Social Performance of Business*. US Government Printing Office.

Leipziger, D. (2010) *The Corporate Responsibility Codebook*. 2nd ed. Greenleaf.

Leopold, A. (2001) *A Sand County Almanac*. Oxford University Press. [originally published in 1949]

Lomborg, B. (2001) *The Skeptical Environmentalist: Measuring the Real State of the World*. Cambridge University Press.

Lovelock, J. (1979) *Gaia: A New Look At Life On Earth*. Oxford University Press.

Lovelock, J. (2006) *The Revenge of Gaia: Earth's Climate Crisis & The Fate of Humanity*. Basic Books.

Lovelock, J. (2009) *The Vanishing Face of Gaia: A Final Warning*. Basic Books.

Lydenberg, S. (2005) *Corporations and the Public Interest: Guiding the Invisible Hand*. Berrett-Koehler.

Lynch, K. and Walls, J. (2009) *Mission Inc.: A Practitioner's Guide to Social Enterprise*. Berrett-Koehler Publishers.

Macintosh, A. (2004) *Soil and Soul: People Versus Corporate Power*. Aurum Press.

Max-Neef, M. (1989) *Human Scale Development: Conception, Application and Further Reflections*. The Apex Press.

Max-Neef, M. and Smith, P.B. (2011) *Economics Unmasked*. Green Books.

McCusker, G. (2006) *Public Relations Disasters: Talespin – Inside Stories and Lessons Learnt*. Kogan Page.

McDonald, L. (2009) *A Colossal Failure of Common Sense: The Incredible Inside Story of the Collapse of Lehman Brothers*. Ebury Press.

McDonough, W. and Braungart, M. (2002) *Cradle to Cradle: Remaking the Way We Make Things*. North Point Press.

McLean, B. and Elkind, P. (2004) *The Smartest Guys in the Room: The Amazing Rise and Scandalous Fall of Enron*. Portfolio Trade.

Meadows, D., Randers, J. and Meadows, D. (2004) *Limits to Growth: The 30 Year Update*. Chelsea Green.

Nader, R. (1965) *Unsafe at Any Speed: The Designed-In Dangers of the American Automobile*. Grossman Publishers.

Palmer, P. (2005) *Getting To Zero Waste*. Purple Press.

Pedersen, E.R. and Huniche, M. (2006) *Corporate Citizenship in Developing Countries: New Partnership Perspectives*. Copenhagen Business School Press.

Porritt, J. (2005) *Capitalism as if the World Matters*. Earthscan.

Prahalad, C.K. (2004) *The Fortune at the Bottom of the Pyramid: Eradicating Poverty Through Profits*. Wharton School Publishing.

Roddick, A. (1991) *Body and Soul: The Amazing Success Story of Anita Roddick & The Body Shop*. Crown Publishers.

Roddick, A. (2001) *Business As Unusual*. Thorsons.

Sachs, J. (2006) *The End of Poverty: Economic Possibilities for Our Time*. Penguin.

Scharmer, O. (2007) *Theory U: Leading from the Future as It Emerges*. Berrett-Koehler Publishers.

Schlosser, E. (2005) *Fast Food Nation: The Dark Side of the All-American Meal*. Harper Perennial.

Schumacher, E.F. (1973) *Small is Beautiful: Economics as if People Mattered*. Harper & Row.

Schumpeter, J. (2008) *Capitalism, Socialism and Democracy*. Harper Perennial Modern Classics. [Original edition 1942.]

Semler, R. (1993) *Maverick: The Success Story Behind the World's Most Unusual Workplace*. Century.

Semler, R. (2004) *The Seven Day Weekend: A Better Way to Work in the 21st Century*. Century.

Senge, P.M., Laur, J., Schley, S. and Smith, B. (2006) *Learning for Sustainability*. SoL, the Society for Organizational Learning.

Senge, P.M., Scharmer, O.M., Jaworski, J. and Flowers, B.S. (2005) *Presence: An Exploration of Profound Change in People, Organizations, and Society*. Crown Business.

Senge, P.M., Smith, B., Schley, S., Laur, J. and Kruschwitz, N. (2008) *The Necessary Revolution: How Individuals and Organizations are Working Together to Create a Sustainable World*. Doubleday Publishing.

Shiva, V. (2005) *Earth Democracy: Justice, Sustainability and Peace*. South End Press.

Shiva, V. (2008) *Soil Not Oil: Environmental Justice in an Age of Climate Crisis*. South End Press.

Sillanpää, M. and Wheeler, D. (1997) *The Stakeholder Corporation: The Body Shop Blueprint for Maximizing Stakeholder Value*. Financial Times/Prentice Hall.

Smuts, J.C. (1999) *Holism and Evolution*. Sierra Sunrise Publishing. [Originally published in 1926.]

Soros, G. (1998) *The Crisis of Global Capitalism: Open Society Endangered*. PublicAffairs.

Stern, N. (2006) *The Economics of Climate Change: The Stern Review*. Cambridge University Press.

Surowiecki, J. (2004) *Wisdom of Crowds: Why the Many Are Smarter Than the Few and How Collective Wisdom Shapes Business, Economies, Societies and Nations*. Doublday.

Tapscott, D. and Williams, A.D. (2006) *Wikinomics: How Mass Collaboration Changes Everything*. Portfolio.

Tapscott, D. and Williams, A.D. (2006) *Macrowikinomics: Rebooting Business and the World*. Portfolio.

Visser, W. (2005) *Business Frontiers: Social Responsibility, Sustainable Development and Economic Justice*. ICFAI University Press.

Visser, W. (2008) *Making a Difference: Purpose-Inspired Leadership for Corporate Sustainability and Responsibility (CSR)*. VDM Verlag Dr. Müller.

Visser, W. and Cambridge Programme for Sustainability Leadership (2009) *Landmarks for Sustainability: Events and Initiatives that have Changed Our World*. Greenleaf Publishing.

Visser, W. and Cambridge Programme for Sustainability Leadership (2009) *The Top 50 Sustainability Books*. Greenleaf Publishing.

Visser, W. and Lundy, G. (2003) *South Africa: Reasons to Believe*. Aardvark Press.

Visser, W. and Sunter, C. (2002) *Beyond Reasonable Greed: Why Sustainable Business is a Much Better Idea!* Tafelberg Human and Rousseau.

Visser, W. and Tolhurst, N. (2010) *The World Guide to CSR: A Country-by-Country Analysis of Corporate Sustainability and Responsibility*. Greenleaf Publishing.

Visser, W., Matten, D., Pohl, M. and Tolhurst, N. (2010) *The A to Z of Corporate Social Responsibility*, 2nd ed. John Wiley & Sons.

Visser, W., McIntosh, M. and Middleton, C. (2006) *Corporate Citizenship in Africa: Lessons from the Past; Paths to the Future*. Greenleaf Publishing.

Vogel, D. (2005) *The Market for Virtue: The Potential and Limits of Corporate Social Responsibility*. Brookings Institution Press.

Von Weizsäcker, E., Hargroves, K.C., Smith, M.H., Desha, C. and Stasinopoulos, P. (2009) *Factor Five: Transforming the Global Economy Through 80% Improvements in Resource Productivity*. Earthscan.

Walker, P. (2006) *Change Management for Sustainable Development*. Institute of Environmental Management and Assessment.

Ward, B. (1966) *Spaceship Earth*. Columbia University Press.

Werther, W.B. and Chandler, D.B. (2010) *Strategic Corporate Social Responsibility: Stakeholders in a Global Environment*. 2nd ed. Sage Publications.

Yunus, M. (1999) *Banker to the Poor: Micro-Lending and the Battle Against World Poverty*. PublicAffairs.

Yunus, M. (2008) *Creating a World Without Poverty: Social Business and the Future of Capitalism*. PublicAffairs.

Yunus, M. (2010) *Building Social Business: The New Kind of Capitalism That Serves Humanity's Most Pressing Needs*. PublicAffairs.

Zadek, S. (2007) *The Civil Corporation*. 2nd ed. Earthscan.

Reports

Arora, B. and Metz Cummings, A. (2010) *A Little World: Safe and Efficient M-Banking in Rural India*. UNDP Growing Inclusive Markets publication.

Cambridge Programme for Sustainability Leadership (2007) *Business Primer on Sustainable Consumption and Production*. CPSL.

Christian Aid (2004) *Behind the Mask: The Real Face of CSR*.

Futerra Sustainability Communications (2007) *The Greenwash Guide*.

SustainAbility and UNEP (2001) *Buried Treasure: Uncovering the Business Case for Corporate Sustainability.*

SustainAbility, IRC and Ethos Institut (2002) *Developing Value: The Business Case for Sustainability in Emerging Markets.*

SustainAbility and Skoll Foundation (2007) *Growing Opportunity: Entrepreneurial Solutions to Insoluble Problems.*

Union of Concerned Scientists (2007) *Smoke, Mirrors & Hot Air: How ExxonMobil Uses Big Tobacco's Tactics to Manufacture Uncertainty on Climate Science.* January.

Chapters and articles

Ballantine, J. (2009) Social media and sustainability. *Ethical Corporation*, 16 October.

Blowfield, M., Visser, W. and Livesey, F. (2007) Sustainability innovation: Mapping the territory, *University Cambridge Programme for Sustainability Leadership Research Paper Series*, No. 2.

Boulding, K.E. (1966) The economics of the coming Spaceship Earth. Paper presented at the Sixth Resources for the Future Forum on Environmental Quality in a Growing Economy, Washington, D.C., 8 March.

Brenner, M. (1996) The man who knew too much. *Vanity Fair*, May.

Carroll, A.B. (1979) A three-dimensional model of corporate performance. *Academy of Management Review* 4(4): 497–505.

Carroll, A.B. (1991) The pyramid of corporate social responsibility: Toward the moral management of organizational stakeholders. *Business Horizons*, July–August.

Drayton, B. (2010) Tipping the world: The power of collaborative entrepreneurship. *McKinsey What Matters* website, 8 April.

Findlay-Brooks, R., Visser, W. and Wright, T. (2007) Cross-sector partnership as an approach to inclusive development. *University Cambridge Programme for Sustainability Leadership Research Paper Series*, No. 4.

Friedman, M. (1970) The social responsibility of business is to increase profits. *New York Times Magazine*, 13 September.

Frosch, R.A. and Gallopoulos, N.E. (1989) Strategies for manufacturing. *Scientific American*, September, p. 94.

Howe, J. (2006) The rise of crowdsourcing. *Wired magazine*, June.

Karnani, A. (2010) The case against corporate social responsibility. *Wall Street Journal*, 23 August.

Karrim, Q. (2010) Big promises from Big Pharma. *Inside Story*, 9 January.

Letts, C.W., Ryan, W. and Grossman, A. (1997) Virtuous capital: What foundations can learn from venture capitalists. *Harvard Business Review*, March–April.

London, T. (2009) Making better investments at the Base of the Pyramid. *Harvard Business Review*, May.

Mitchell, R., Agle, B. and Wood, D. (1997) Towards a theory of stakeholder identification: Defining the principle of who and what really counts. *Academy of Management Review* **22**(4), 853–86.

Newsweek (2007) The truth about denial. 13 August.

Nidumolu, R., Prahalad, C.K. and Rangaswami, M.R., (2009) Why sustainability is now the key driver of innovation. *Harvard Business Review*, September.

Porter, M.E. and Kramer, M.R. (2002) The competitive advantage of corporate philanthropy. *Harvard Business Review*, December.

Porter, M.E. and Kramer, M.R. (2006) Strategy and society: The link between competitive advantage and corporate social responsibility. *Harvard Business Review*, December.

Visser, W. (1995) Holism: a new framework for thinking about business. *New Perspectives*, No. 7.

Visser, W. (2003) Corporate responsibility in a developing country context. *Ethical Corporation*, 20 August, pp. 32–4.

Visser, W. (2006) Revisiting Carroll's CSR Pyramid: an African perspective. In Pedersen, E.R. and Huniche, M., *Corporate Citizenship in Developing Countries: New Partnership Perspectives*. Copenhagen: Copenhagen Business School Press, pp. 29–56.

Visser, W. (2008) Corporate social responsibility in developing countries. In Crane, A., McWilliams, A., Matten, D., Moon, J. and Siegel, D. (eds.), *The Oxford Handbook of Corporate Social Responsibility*. Oxford: Oxford University Press, pp. 473–9.

Visser, W. (2010) CSR 2.0: From the age of greed to the age of responsibility, In W. Sun, et al. (eds.) *Reframing Corporate Social Responsibility: Lessons from the Global Financial Crisis*, Bingley: Emerald.

Visser, W. (2010) The age of responsibility: CSR 2.0 and the new DNA of business, *Journal of Business Systems, Governance and Ethics* 5(3): 7–22. November, Special Issue on Responsibility for Social and Environmental Issues.

Visser, W. and McIntosh, M. (1998) An evaluation of the historical condemnation of usury. *Accounting, Business & Financial History*, **8**(2), July.

Films

Capitalism: A Love Story (2009) Directed by Michael Moore. USA: Michael Moore.

The Constant Gardener (2005) Directed by Fernando Meirelles. UK/Germany: Universal.

The Corporation (2003) Directed by Mark Achbar and Jennifer Abbott. Canada: Big Picture Media Corporation.

Enron: The Smartest Guys in the Room (2005) Directed by Alex Gibney. USA: PBS.

An Inconvenient Truth (2006) Directed by Davis Guggenheim. USA: United International Pictures.

The Insider (1999) Directed by Michael Mann. USA: Touchstone Pictures.

Thank You for Smoking (2005) Directed by Jason Reitman. USA: Room 9 Entertainment, TYFS Productions LLC and ContentFilm.

Index

Index compiled by Annette Musker

Other books by Wayne Visser
Non-fiction

Beyond Reasonable Greed: Why Sustainable Business is a Much Better Idea! (with Clem Sunter), Tafelberg Human and Rousseau, 2002.

South Africa: Reasons to Believe (with Guy Lundy), Aardvark Press, 2003.

Business Frontiers: Social Responsibility, Sustainable Development and Economic Justice, ICFAI Books, 2005.

Corporate Citizenship in Africa (with Malcolm McIntosh & Charlotte Middleton), Greenleaf Publishing, 2006.

The A to Z of Corporate Social Responsibility (with Dirk Matten, Manfred Pohl & Nick Tolhurst), John Wiley & Sons, 2007.

Making A Difference: Purpose-Inspired Leadership for Corporate Sustainability and Responsibility (CSR), VDM, 2008.

Landmarks for Sustainability: Events and Initiatives that have Changed Our World, Greenleaf Publishing, 2009.

The Top 50 Sustainability Books, Greenleaf Publishing, 2009.

The World Guide to CSR: A Country-by-Country Analysis of Corporate Sustainability and Responsibility (with Nick Tolhurst), Greenleaf Publishing, 2010.

Fiction

I Am An African: Favourite Africa Poems by Wayne Visser, 2nd ed. Yourpod, 2010.

Wishing Leaves: Favourite Nature Poems by Wayne Visser, Yourpod, 2010.